MADAME BLAVATSKY
Personal Memoirs

DISCOVERY PUBLISHER

2015, Discovery Publisher

No part of this book may be reproduced in any form or by any electronic or mechanical means including information storage and retrieval systems, without permission in writing from the publisher.

Author: Mary K. Neff
Introduction: Vera Petrovna de Zhelihovsky
Editor in Chief: Adriano Lucca

DISCOVERY PUBLISHER

616 Corporate Way
Valley Cottage, New York, 10989
www.discoverypublisher.com
books@discoverypublisher.com
facebook.com/DiscoveryPublisher
twitter.com/DiscoveryPB

New York • Tokyo • Paris • Hong Kong

TABLE OF CONTENTS

H. P. B.		2
Introduction		4
Helena Petrovna Blavatsky		6
Note		48
Editor's Note		52
CHAPTER I	Childhood And Heredity	56
CHAPTER II	The Child "Medium"	62
CHAPTER III	Life At Her Grandfather's	67
CHAPTER IV	Youth And Marriage	78
CHAPTER V	Disappearance	85
CHAPTER VI	Adventures In Egypt And Africa	88
CHAPTER VII	Explorations In The Americas	95
CHAPTER VIII	Her Master	103
CHAPTER IX	Seeking The Master	106
CHAPTER X	Adventures In Tibet	111
CHAPTER XI	With The Master In India	119
CHAPTER XII	"The Caves Of Bagh"	128
CHAPTER XIII	"An Isle Of Mystery"	137
CHAPTER XIV	Hatha Yogis And Raja Yogis	148
CHAPTER XV	Adventures In India, Burma, Siam And China	153
CHAPTER XVI	The Home-Coming At Pskoff	165
CHAPTER XVII	Rougodevo	169
CHAPTER XVIII	In The Caucasus	174
CHAPTER XIX	Psychic Development In Russia	183
CHAPTER XX	Third Attempt To Reach Tibet	189
CHAPTER XXI	Buddhist Lamaseries And Convents	197

CHAPTER XXII	In The Master's Ashrama At Last	207
CHAPTER XXIII	Flying Visit To Europe	218
CHAPTER XXIV	From The Master's Ashram A To The World	228
CHAPTER XXV	The Metrovitch Incident	237
CHAPTER XXVI	Count Witte's Version	247
CHAPTER XXVII	The Child	253
CHAPTER XXVIII	Poor And Penniless In New York	259
CHAPTER XXIX	Meeting Of The Founders Of The Theosophical Society	265
CHAPTER XXX	"The Philadelphia Fiasco" — H. P. B. Supports Spiritualism	279
CHAPTER XXXI	The "Spiritual Scientist"	293
CHAPTER XXXII	Marriage And The Shadow Of Death	303
CHAPTER XXXIII	The Great Psycho-Physiological Change	318
CHAPTER XXXIV	The Miracle Club	326
CHAPTER XXXV	The Founding Of The Theosophical Society	334
CHAPTER XXXVI	"Isis Unveiled"	342
CHAPTER XXXVII	Who Wrote "Isis Unveiled"?	353
CHAPTER XXXVIII	H. P. B. — American Citizen And Russian Patriot	364
CHAPTER XXXIX	Who Was H. P. B.	374

APPENDIX 386

ONE	Chronological Table	388
TWO	"A Modern Priestess Of Isis"	398
THREE	Bibliography	404
FOUR	References	406

Introduction

Helena Petrovna Blavatsky

—by Vera Petrovna de Zhelihovsky, H.P.B.'s sister
London, Nov. 15, 1894 — April 15, 1895.

y sister, Helena Petrovna Blavatsky, *née* de Hahn, better known in our country under the *nom de plume* of Radha-Bai, which she adopted for her writings in Russia, was a sufficiently remarkable person, even in these days, when striking personalities abound. Although her works are but little known to the general public, nevertheless they have given birth to a spiritual movement, to an organization founded on the theories therein contained which it pleases her disciples to allude to as "revelations" — I speak of the Theosophical Society, so well known and widely spread throughout America, England, India, and in a lesser degree throughout Europe.

This Society was planned and founded by Madame Blavatsky, in the year 1875, at New York, in which city she had established herself — why she herself hardly knew, except that thither she was drawn by an irresistible attraction, inexplicable at that time to her, as we shall see by her letters.

Without money, without any kind of influence or protection, with nothing to rely on but her indomitable courage and untiring energy, this truly extraordinary woman in less than four years succeeded in attaching to herself devoted proselytes, who were ready to follow her to India and to cheerfully expatriate themselves; and in less than fifteen years she had thousands of disciples, who not only professed her doctrines, but who also proclaimed her "the most eminent teacher of our times, the sphinx of the century," the only person in Europe initiated into the occult sciences of the east — they were, indeed, with few exceptions, ready to canonize her memory, had the philosophy she taught them permitted any such thing.

There was hardly a country in which the death of H. P. Blavatsky did not produce a most profound impression. All quarters of the globe responded, in one fashion or another, when the news reached them of the death of this poor Russian woman, whose only claim to such celebrity lay in her personal genius. For a time her name rang throughout the press of the entire world. Doubtless it is true that more bad than good was spoken of her, but none the less they spoke of her, some abusing her up hill and down dale and loudly complaining of the injuries wrought by her; and on the other side twenty or so theosophical journals proclaiming her "illuminated" prophetess and saviour of humanity — humanity which, without the revelations which she had given out in her works, above all in *The Secret Doctrine*, would — so they affirmed — be dragged to its doom by the materialistic spirit of the time.

It is not my business to decide as to whether the truth lay with her friends and enthusiastic disciples or with her bitter enemies. My intention is simply to offer to the public some impartial family reminiscences and to lay before them some letters of undoubted interest.

It would be easy for me to fill many volumes from the mass of materials which I have at my disposal; I will, however, merely select that which is most remarkable and weave it together with my personal recollections.

Our mother, Mdme Hélène de Hahn, *née* Fadeew, died when she was twenty-seven. Notwithstanding her premature death, however, such was the literary reputation she had already acquired, that she had earned for herself the name of the "Russian George Sand" — a name which was given her by Belinsky, the best of our critics. At sixteen years of age she was married to Pierre de Hahn, captain of artillery, and soon her time was fully occupied in superintending the education of her three children. Hélène, her eldest daughter, was a precocious child, and from her earliest youth attracted the attention of all with whom she came in contact. Her nature was quite intractable to the routine demanded by her instructors, she rebelled against all discipline, recognized no master but her own good will and her personal tastes. She was exclusive, original, and at times bold even to roughness.

When, at the death of our mother, we went to live with her relations, all our teachers had exhausted their patience with Hélène, who would never conform to fixed hours for lessons, but who, notwithstanding, astonished them by the brilliancy of her abilities, especially by the ease with which she mastered foreign languages and by her musical talent. She had the character and all the good and bad qualities of an energetic boy; she loved travels and adventures and despised dangers and cared little for remonstrances.

When her mother was dying, although her eldest daughter was only eleven years old, she was filled with well-founded apprehensions for her future, and said:

"Ah, well! perhaps it is best that I am dying, so at least I shall be spared seeing what befalls Hélène! Of one thing I am certain, her life will not be as that of other women, and that she will have much to suffer."

Truly a prophecy!

At the age of seventeen, H. P. Blavatsky married a man thrice her age, and some months later she left her husband in the same headstrong and impetuous manner in which she had married him. She left him under the pretext of going to live with her father, but before she got there she disappeared, and so successful was she in this that for years no one knew where she was, and we gave her up for dead. Her husband was the vice-governor of the province of Erivan, in Transcaucasia. He was in all respects an excellent man, with but one fault, namely, marrying a young girl who treated him without the least respect, and who told him quite openly beforehand that the only reason she had selected him from among the others who sought to marry her was that she would mind less making him miserable than anyone else.

"You make a great mistake in marrying me," she said to him before their marriage. "You know perfectly well that you are old enough to be my grandfather. You will make somebody unhappy, but it won't be me. As for me, I am not afraid of you, but I warn you that it is not you who will gain anything from our union."

He never could say that he did not get what he had bargained for.

H. P. Blavatsky passed the greater part of her youth, in fact almost her entire life, out of Europe. In later years she claimed to have lived many years in Tibet, in the Himalayas and extreme north of India, where she studied the Sanskrit language and literature together with the occult sciences, so well known by the adepts, wise men, or Mahatmas, for whom later she had to suffer so much. Such, at least, is the account of her doings that she gave to us, her relations, as also to her English biographer, Mr. Sinnett, the author of the work entitled, Incidents in the Life of Madame H. P. Blavatsky. For eight years we were without any news of her. It was only at the expiration of ten years, the period necessary to render legal the separation from her husband, that Madame Blavatsky returned to Russia.

After her return to Russia, she first came and settled herself in the Government of Pskoff, where at that time I was living with our father. We were not expecting her to arrive for some weeks to come, but, curiously enough, no sooner did I hear her ring at the door-bell than I jumped up, knowing that she had arrived. As it happened there was a party going on that evening in my father-in-law's house, in which I was living. His daughter was to be married that very evening, the guests were seated at table and the ringing of the door-bell was incessant. Nevertheless I was so sure it was she who had arrived that, to the astonishment of everyone, I hurriedly rose from the wedding feast and ran to open the door, not wishing the servants to do so.

We embraced each other, overcome with joy, forgetting for the moment the strangeness of the event. I took her at once to my room, and that very evening I was convinced that my sister had acquired strange powers. She was constantly surrounded, awake or asleep, with mysterious movements, strange sounds, little taps which came from all sides — from the furniture, from the windowpanes, from the ceiling, from the floor, and from the walls. They were very distinct and seemed intelligent into the bargain; they tapped once, and three times for "yes," twice for "no."

My sister asked me to ask them a mental question. This I did, selecting a question as to a fact only known to myself. I recited the alphabet, and the reply I received was so true and so precise that I was positively astounded. I had often heard talk of spirit-rappings, but never before had I had an opportunity of testing their knowledge.

Before long the whole town was talking of the "miracles" which surrounded Madame Blavatsky. The not only intelligent, but even clairvoyant answers given by these invisible forces, which operated night and day, without any apparent intervention on her part, all round her, struck more astonishment and wonder into the minds of the curious than even the movement of inanimate objects, which apparently gained or lost their weight, which phenomena she directly produced by merely fixing her eyes on the object selected.

All these phenomena were, at the time, fully described in the Russian newspapers. There was no longer any peace for us, even in the country, where we shortly went to live, on a property which belonged to me ; we were pursued by letters and visits. Matters became insupportable when, by the intervention of " messieurs les esprits," as our father laughingly called them, was discovered the perpetrator of a murder committed in the neighbourhood, and the officers of the law became convinced believers, clamouring for miracles. It was still worse when, one fine day, Hélène began describing " those whom she alone saw as having formerly occupied the house," and who were afterwards recognized from her descriptions by the old people and natives of the place as having been former lords of the manor and their servants, all long since dead, but of whom they still preserved the memory. I may as well remark that this property had only been mine for a few months. I had bought it in a district completely unknown to me, and none of us had ever before heard these people she described spoken of.

My father, a man of vast intellectual power, and most learned, had all his life been a sceptic, a " Voltairien," as we say in Russian. He was compelled by the force of circumstances to change his convictions, and before long passed days and nights writing, under the dictation of " messieurs les esprits," the genealogy of his ancestors the " gallant knights of Hahn-Hahn von Rotterhahn."

Ever since her return to Russian, H. P. Blavatsky was at a loss to explain her mediumistic condition, but at that time she by no means expressed the disdain and dislike for mediumship that she did later on. Ten or twelve years later she spoke of the mediumistic performances of her younger days with much repugnance — in those days the forces at work in the phenomena were unknown and almost independent of her will, when once she had succeeded in obtaining entire mastery over them she no longer cared to recall the memory. But at the age of twenty-eight she had not the power of controlling them.

With reference to this the following is of interest :

In the summer of 1860 we left the Government of Pskoff, for the Caucasus, to pay a visit to our grandparents the Fadeews and Madame Witte, our aunt, my mother's sister, who had not seen Hélène for more than eleven years. On our way there at the town of Zadonsk, in the Government of Voronege, we learnt that the Metropolitan of Kieff, the Venerable Isidore, whom we had known well when we were children at Tiflis, where he had been the head of the exarchate of St. George, happened to be in the town, passing through on his way to St. Petersburg, and was for the moment officiating in the monastery. We were most eager to see him; he remembered us, and sent us word to say that he would be very pleased to see us after mass. We made our way to the arch-episcopal church, but not without misgivings on my part. As we were on our way there, I said to my sister:

"Do please take care that your little devils keep themselves quiet while we are with the Metropolitan."

She began laughing and saying that she would like nothing better, but that she could not answer for them.

Alas! I knew it but too well. And so I was not astonished, but all the same suffered agonies when I heard the tapping begin as soon as ever the venerable old man began to question my sister about her travels.... One! two!... one! two! three! Surely he could not but notice these importunate individuals who seemed determined to join the party and take part in the conversation; in order to interrupt us they made the furniture, the looking-glasses, our cups of tea, even the rosary of amber beads, which the saintly old man was holding in his hand, move and vibrate.

He saw our dismay at once, and taking in the situation at a glance, enquired which of us was the medium. Like a true egotist, I hastened to fit the cap on my sister's head. He talked to us for more than an hour, asking my sister question after question out loud, and asking them mentally of her attendants, and seemed profoundly astonished and well pleased to have seen the phenomena.

On taking leave of us, he blessed my sister and myself and told us that we had no cause to fear the phenomena.

"There is no force," he said, "that both in its essence and in its manifestation does not proceed from the Creator. So long as you do not abuse the gifts given you, have no uneasiness. We are by no means forbidden to investigate the hidden forces of nature. One day they will be understood and utilized by man, though that is not yet. May the blessing of God rest on you, my child!"

He again blessed Hélène and made the sign of the cross.

How often must these kindly words of one of the chief heads of the Orthodox Greek Church have been recalled to the memory of H. P. Blavatsky in later years, and she ever felt gratefully towards him.

· · · · · · · ·

Helena Petrovna for the next four years continued to live in the Caucasus. Ever in search of occupation, always active and full of enterprise, she established herself for some time in Imeretia, then at Mingrelia, on the shores of the Black Sea, where she connected herself with the trade in the high-class woods with which that region abounds. Later on she moved southwards, to Odessa, where our aunts had gone to live after the death of our grandparent. There she placed herself at the head of an artificial flower factory, but soon left that for other enterprises, which in turn she quickly abandoned, notwithstanding the fact that they generally turned out well.

She was never troubled by any dread of doing anything derogatory to her position, all honest trades seemed to her equally good. It is curious to note, however, that she did not light on some occupation which would have better suited her talents than these commercial enterprises; that, for instance, she did not take instead to literature or to music, which would have better served to display her grand intellectual powers, especially as in her younger days she had never had anything to do with commerce.

Two years later she left again for foreign parts, first for Greece and then for Egypt. All her life was passed in restlessness and in travelling; she was ever, as it were, seeking some unknown goal, some task which it was her duty to discover and to fulfil. Her wandering life and unsettled ways did not end until she found herself face to face with the scientific, the humanitarian and spiritual problems presented by Theosophy; then she stopped short, like a ship which after years of wanderings finds itself safe in port, the sails are furled and for the last time the anchor is let go.

Mr. Sinnett, her biographer, alleges that for many years ere she left definitely for America, Madame Blavatsky had had spiritual relations with those strange beings, whom she later called her Masters, the Mahatmas of Ceylon and Tibet, and that it was only in direct obedience to their commands that she travelled from place to place, from one country to another. How that may be, I do not know. We, her nearest relations, for the first time heard her mention these enigmatic beings in 1873-4, when she was established in New York.

The fact is that her departure from Paris for America was as sudden as it was inexplicable, and she would never give us the explanation of what led her to do so until many years later ; she then told us that these same Masters had ordered her to do so, without at the time giving any reason. She gave as her reason for not having spoken of them to us that we should not have understood, that we should have refused to believe, and very naturally so.

From that moment all else was put on one side, and never from that moment forward did her thoughts for one moment deviate from the goal which had been suddenly revealed to her, namely, the publishing abroad in the world that most ancient of philosophies which bears witness to the supreme importance of things spiritual as compared with things material, to the psychic forces both of nature and of man, to the immortality of the human soul and spirit. Thus she writes to me :

"Humanity has lost its faith and its higher ideals ; materialism and pseudo-science have slain them. The children of this age have no longer faith ; they demand proof, proof founded on a scientific basis — and they shall have it. Theosophy, the source of all human religions, will give it to them."

Soon all her letters were full of arguments against the abuse of spiritism, that which she termed spiritual materialism, of indignation against mediumistic *seances*, where the dead were evoked — "the materializations of the dear departed," the dwellers in the land of eternal spring (the summerland) — who in her opinion were nothing more than shades, elves and lying elementaries, often dangerous, and, above all, evil in their effects on the health of the unfortunate mediums, their passive victims.

Her visit to the brothers Eddy, the well-known mediums of Vermont, was the last drop which made her cup run over. She became from thenceforward the deadly enemy of all demonstrative spiritualism.

It was at the Eddy homestead that Madame Blavatsky made the acquaintance of Col. H. S. Olcott, her first disciple, her devoted friend and future President of the Theosophical Society, the child of their creation, and on which all their thought was thenceforward centred. He had come there as a keen observer of spiritualistic phenomena, in order to investigate and write about the materializations caused through the agency of the two brothers, of which all America was talking. He wrote a book on this subject, a study called *People from the Other World* — that was the last service done by him for the cause of the propaganda of modern spiritualism. He accepted the views of Helena Petrovna Blavatsky, which the American papers readily published. Being both of them deadly enemies of materialism, they considered that spiritualism had rendered a great service to humanity, in demonstrating the errors of the materialistic creed; but that now that once spiritualism had proved the existence of invisible and immaterial forces in nature, its mission was fulfilled; it must not be permitted to drag society to the other error, namely, to superstition and black magic.

As we could not understand this sudden change of front in one whom we knew to be a powerful medium, and who quite recently had been the vice-president of the Spiritualistic Society of Cairo, she wrote to us beginning us to forget the past, her unhappy mediumship to which she had lent herself, as she explained, simply through ignorance of the truth.

"If I have attached myself to a certain group of Theosophists, a branch of the Indo-Aryan Brotherhood, which has been formed here," she wrote to us from New York, "it is precisely because they fight against all the excesses, the superstitions, the abuses of the false prophets of the dead letter — against the numberless Calchases of all the exoteric religions, as well as against the maunderings of spirits. We are spiritualists, if you choose so to call us, but not after the American manner, but after the ancient rites of Alexandria."

At the same time she sent us cuttings from the American newspapers publishing her articles, as well as the comments on what she had written, from which it was evident that her opinions met with much sympathy. Her brilliant powers as a critic revealed themselves, above all, in a number of articles treating of Professor Huxley's meetings at Boston and at New York — articles which attracted considerable attention. That which astonished us extremely was the profound learning, the deep knowledge, which became suddenly evident in all she wrote. Whence could she have gained this varied and abstruse learning, of which until that time she had given no sign? She herself did not know! Then it was that for the first time she spoke to us of her Masters, or rather of her Master, but in a most vague manner, speaking of him sometimes as "the voice," sometimes as Sahib (meaning Master), sometimes as "he who inspires me" — as if the source of these mental suggestions was unknown at that time; it did not assist us towards understanding her, and we began to fear for her reason.

"I am embarked on a great work treating of theology, ancient beliefs and the secrets of the occult sciences," thus she wrote to me in 1874: "but fear nothing for me; I am sure of my facts, more or less. I should not, perhaps, know well how to talk of these abstract things, but all essential matter is dictated to me.... All that I shall write will not be my own; I shall be nothing more than the pen, the head which will think for me will be that of one who knows all...."

Again Helena Petrovna writes to our aunt, N. A. Fadeew:

"Tell me, dearest friend, are you interested in the secrets of psychic physiology?... That which I am about to relate to you offers a sufficiently interesting problem for the students of physiology. We have, among the members of our small society, lately formed of those who desire to study the languages of the east, the abstract nature of things, as well as the spiritual powers of man, some who are well learned. As, for example, Professor Wilder, archaeological orientalist, and many others who come to me with scientific questions, and who assure me that I am better versed than they themselves are in abstract and positive sciences, and that I am better acquainted with the old languages. It is an inexplicable fact, but one none the less true!... Well! what do you make of it, old companion of my studies?... Explain to me, if you please, how it comes about that I, who, as you are well aware, was, up to the age of forty, in a state of crass ignorance, have suddenly become a *savant*, a model of learning in the opinions of real *savants*? It is an insoluble mystery. In truth I am a psychological enigma, a sphinx, and a problem for future generations as much as I am for myself.

"Imagine, dear friends, that poor '*me*,' who never would learn anything; who had no knowledge either of chemistry, of zoology, of physics, and very little of history and geography; this same 'me' holding my own in discussions on learned subjects with professors and doctors of sciences of the first rank, and not only criticizing them but even convincing them! I give you my word I am not joking when I tell you I am frightened. Yes, I am frightened, for I do not understand it!... Understand that all I now read seems to me as if I had known it long ago? I perceive errors in the articles by such masters of science as Tyndall, Herbert Spencer, Huxley and others. I speak with conviction concerning the views held by learned theologians and it is found that I am right.... Whence comes this learning?... I don't know, and sometimes I am tempted to think that my spirit, my own soul, no longer is mine...."

While her book, *Isis Unveiled*, was appearing in numbers, it was read and commented on in the newspapers. She sent us the criticisms; they were most flattering, and reassured us as to her literary reputation; but they contained, nevertheless, such strange revelations that we continued to feel anxiety. The statements of Olcott, of Judge (President of the American Section of the Theosophical Society), of numbers of reporters of the *Herald* and *Times* of New York, and other newspapers, spoke of remarkable phenomena. Of these we will speak later on. I will close this chapter by saying that, notwithstanding the poor opinion Madame Blavatsky herself had of her first great work, which she regarded as badly written, obscure and without definite sequence, she esteemed highly the truly exceptional triumphs and honours which it brought her. Leaving on one side the numberless articles which appeared dealing with this book, she had the honour to receive forthwith two diplomas and many letters from scientific men as eminent, for example, as Layman, John Draper and Alfred Russel Wallace. This latter, among others, wrote to her as follows: " I am truly struck, Madame, by your profound erudition. I have to thank you for opening my eyes to a world of things of which, previously, I had no idea from the point of view which you indicate to science, and which explains problems which seemed to be insoluble...."

The diplomas were sent by Masonic Lodges of England and Benares (Society of Svat-Bai), which recognized her rights to the superior grades of their brotherhoods. The first was accompanied by a cross of the rose in rubies, and the second with a most valuable and ancient copy of the *Bhagavad Gita*, the bible of India. But that which is more remarkable still is the fact that the Reverend Doctor of the Episcopal Church of the University of New York, took this book, *Isis Unveiled*, as a text for his sermons. For a series of Sundays he occupied his pulpit, and the Rev. McKerty, taking his themes from the third chapter of Vol. I., edified his parishioners by hurling thunderbolts and opprobrium on the materialist disciples of the Auguste Comte and such like.

H. P. Blavatsky, to the day of her death, remained Russian and a good patriot; the goodwill and approval of her compatriots were always the laurel she most coveted and most valued. Her works, prohibited in Russia by the censorship (notwithstanding their being incomprehensible to the majority of the people owing to the fact that they were in English, a language little known in Russia), had few readers. The honour, therefore, was the greater if those who had read them in speaking of them, quite independently, used terms almost similar to those of the Rev. Archbishop Aivasovsky (brother of our well-known painter), and the son of our celebrated historian Serge Solovioff, the well-known novelist Vsevolod Solovioff.

Aivasovsky asked me to lend him *Isis Unveiled*, also Olcott's *People from the Other World*. After reading the two, he wrote to me that in his opinion "there never had been and there never could be any phenomenon more wonderful than this writing of a book, such as *Isis*, by a woman in the space of a few months, when ten years would, in the ordinary course of things, hardly suffice a scientific man to complete such a work."

The following is the opinion of M. Vs. Solovioff, contained in a letter from him dated July 7th, 1884, after reading, in manuscript, the French translation of the same work.

"I have read the second part of *Isis Unveiled*, and am now entirely convinced that it is a true prodigy."

So they agreed! M. Solovioff and the Archbishop Aivasovsky have both often said to me, that it seemed to them to be unnecessary to speak of other of my sister's miracles, after that which she had accomplished in writing that book.

In regard to the phenomena, called natural, psychological tricks, as they were termed by H. P. Blavatsky, who always spoke of them with indifference and disdain, it would have been better both for her and for her Society if they had been less spoken about or not at all. Her too ardent friends, in publishing books like the *Occult World* of Mr. Sinnett, rendered her a bad service. Instead of adding to her renown, as they believed, the stories of the wonders worked by the Founders of the Theosophical Society did her a great deal of harm, making not only sceptics, but all sensible folks call it a falsehood and accuse her of charlatanism.

· · · · · · · ·

All these stories by Olcott, by Judge, by Sinnett and by many others, of objects created from nothing, of drawings which she caused to appear by merely placing her hands on a sheet of white paper, of apparitions of persons who were dead or absent, or of numbers of objects which had been lost for many years being found in flower-beds or in cushions, added nothing to the reputation of Madame Blavatsky and her Society; on the contrary, they gave a handle to her enemies, as proofs of bad faith and error. The world at large is alive with more or less convincing phenomena, but there will always be more people incredulous than believing, and more traitors than men of good faith. The number of ardent members of the Theosophical Society and zealous friends of Madame Blavatsky, who became her bitter enemies in consequence of the failure of their mercenary hopes, proves this once again....

Always indifferent as to incredulity regarding startling phenomena — material phenomena — H. P. Blavatsky profoundly resented want of confidence in her psychic faculties, in her powers of clairvoyance and in that quality of mental intuition which manifested in her when she either wrote or discussed serious matters. In 1875 she thus wrote to us, speaking of this invasion of her moral being by an outside force:

"It is evident that it is difficult for you to comprehend this psychic phenomenon, notwithstanding that there are precedents of which history speaks. If you will allow that the human soul, the vital soul, the pure spirit, is composed of a substance which is independent of the organism and that it is not inseparably linked with our interior organs; that this soul, which belongs to all that lives, to the infusoria as well as to the elephant and to each one of us, is not to be distinguished (from our shadow, which forms the almost always invisible base of its fleshly envelope) except in so far as it is more or less illumined by the divine essence of our Immortal Spirit, you will then admit that it is capable of acting independently of our body. Try and realize that — and many things hitherto incomprehensible will become clear. As a matter of fact, this was well recognized in antiquity. The human soul, the fifth principle of the being, recovers some portion of its independence in the body of one profane during the period of sleep; in the case of an initiated Adept it enjoys that state constantly. St. Paul, the only one of the apostles initiated into the esoteric mysteries of Greece — does he not say in speaking of his ascension to the third heaven 'in the body or out of the body' he cannot tell; 'God knoweth.' In the same sense the servant Rhoda says when she sees St. Peter, 'It is not him, it is his "angel,"' that is to say, his double, his shade. Again in the *Acts of the Apostles* (viii. 39), when the Spirit — the divine force — seizes and carries off St. Philip, is it in truth he himself bodily and living, that is transported to a distance? It was his soul and his double — his true 'ego.' Read Plutarch, Apuleius, Jamblichus.

You will find in them many allusions to these facts if not assertions which the initiated have not the right to make.... That which mediums produce unconsciously under the influence of outside forces evoked during their sleep, the Adepts do consciously, working by understood methods.... *Voilà tout*!

Thus it was that my sister explained to us the visits of her Master, who not only instructed and made suggestions to her by means of her intuition, from his own vast wisdom, but even came in his astral body to see them — her and Colonel Olcott and many others besides.

In the year 1885, for example, Mahatma Morya appeared to M. Vsevolod Solovioff, with whom he had a conversation, and who has described what took place to many people, with his usual eloquence. As for myself, however, I have never seen them, nevertheless I have no right to doubt their existence, testified to by persons whose truthfulness cannot be questioned. All the same these apparitions have always seemed to me to be very problematical, and this opinion I have never hesitated to express to my sister, on which she would reply:

"As you like, my dear.... I wish you a better understanding."

During the war between Russia and Turkey, Helena Petrovna had not a moment's peace. All her letters written during 1876-1877 are full of alarm for her compatriots, of fears for the safety of those members of her family who were actively engaged in it. She forgot her anti-materialist and anti-spiritualist articles in order to breathe forth fire and flame against the enemies of the Russian nation; not against our enemies themselves who were also to be pitied, but against the evil-minded hypocrites, against their simulated sympathies for Turkey, their jesuitical policy which was an offense to all Christian peoples. When she heard of the famous discourse of Pius IX, in which he taught the faithful that "the hand of God could direct the scimitar of the Bashi-bazouk towards the uprooting of schism," in which he gave his blessing to Mohammedan arms as used against the infidel Orthodox Greek Church, she fell ill. Then she exploded in a series of satires so envenomed and so clever that the whole American press and all the anti-popish journals called attention to them, and the Papal Nuncio at New York, the Scotch Cardinal MacKlosky, thought advisable to send a priest to parley with her. He gained little from that, however, for Madame Blavatsky made a point of relating the occurrence in her next article, saying that she had begged the prelate to be so good as to talk with her through the press and then she would most certainly reply to him.

We sent her a poem of Turgenyeff's, called "Croquet at Windsor," which represented Queen Victoria and her Court playing croquet with the bleeding heads of Slavs for balls. She quickly translated it, and it was in *The New York Herald*, if I mistake not, that it first saw publicity.

In October, 1876, H. P. Blavatsky gave fresh proof of her powers of clairvoyance. She had a vision of what was happening in the Caucasus, on the frontier of Turkey, where her cousin Alexander Witte, Major of the Nijni-Novgorod Dragoons, narrowly escaped death. She mentioned the fact in one of her letters to her relations; as, often before, she had described to us apparitions of persons who warned her of their death weeks before the news could be received by ordinary means, we were not greatly astonished.

All that she made in the way of money, during the war, from her articles in the Russian newspapers, together with the first payments she received from her publisher, were sent to Odessa and to Tiflis for the benefit of the wounded soldiers or their families or to the Red Cross Society.

In the spring of 1878 a strange thing happened to Madame Blavatsky. Having got up and set to work one morning as usual, she suddenly lost consciousness, and never regained it again until five days later. So deep was her state of lethargy that she would have been buried had not a telegram been received by Colonel Olcott and his sister, who were with her at the time, emanating from him she called her Master. The message ran, "Fear nothing, she is neither dead nor ill, but she has need of repose; she has overworked herself.… She will recover." As a matter of fact she recovered and found herself so well that she would not believe that she had slept for five days. Soon after this sleep, H. P. Blavatsky formed the project of going to India.

The Theosophical Society was thenceforth duly organized at New York. The three principal objects were then as they are to-day: (1) the organization of an universal brotherhood, without distinction of race, creed or social position, in which the members pledged themselves to strive for the moral improvement both of themselves and others; (2) for the common study of the oriental sciences, languages and literature; (3) the investigation into the hidden laws of nature and the psychological powers of man, as yet unknown to science — this last clause being optional; in fact, it is only the first which is considered binding on all the members of the Society, the other two are not insisted on.

The work of Madame Blavatsky and Colonel Olcott was, in America, confided to the care of the most zealous and devoted of their disciples, Mr. William Q. Judge, who is at the present time Vice-President of the Theosophical Society. As for the Founders, they left in the autumn of 1878 for India.

They were ordered, so they stated, by their Masters, the guides and protectors of the theosophical movement, to work on the spot and in concert with a certain Dayanand Sarasvati, a Hindu preacher who taught monotheism and who has been called the Luther of India.

• • • • • • • •

On the 17th of February, 1879, after a long stay in London, where they formed the first nucleus of their brotherhood, which for the time prospered, Madame Blavatsky and Colonel Olcott arrived at Bombay.

There the Arya Somaj Society, of which Swami Dyanand was the spiritual head, organized, in their honour, a welcome, which was reported in the Anglo-Indian newspapers, and which was described by H. P. Blavatsky herself in her book, *In the Caves and Jungles of Hindustan*, as well as in her letters written at the time; the following humorous extract is from one of the latter:

"Imagine the deputies of the Society coming out to greet us in boats, decorated with garlands of flowers, accompanied by an orchestra of musicians, blowing on trumpets and horns; no sooner had they got on board our vessel than we were surrounded. I raged and laughed at the same time, at the spectacle we presented to the eyes of all the loafers assembled on the bridge and on the quay. The Colonel appeared like a 'fatted ox' at an Italian carnival, and my ungraceful figure looked more like a balloon decked with roses and lilies than anything else. Thus adorned, we were conducted, band of music and all, towards the landing place. Then, behold, a new surprise! a ballet of native dancers, attired almost in the costume of the Queen Pomare, which is chiefly remarkable by its absence;... they at once commenced to dance around us, enveloping us in a circle of nudities and flowers which they threw beneath our feet, all the time leading us towards — carriages, think you?... Alas! towards a white elephant! Gods of Olympus! what it cost me to climb on to the back of this kneeling colossus, making use of the shoulders and naked backs of the coolies as a sort of living ladder. I clung to the columns of the howdah to save myself from falling out when the huge beast got on his legs. Our companions — more lucky than we — got into palanquins, and were carried by these same coolies, the human beasts of burden of the country; thus, accompanied by flourishes and drums, and a curious and laughing crowd, we were led, like 'learned monkeys,' or acrobats at a fair, towards the house prepared for our humble selves by the *too* hospitable members of the Arya Somaj."

Notwithstanding this grand demonstration on arrival, their life was a hard one at first. They worked eighteen hours a day; Olcott travelled the greater part of the year, forming branches of the Theosophical Society, which at once took root in the congenial soil of Oriental belief, and Madame Blavatsky hardly quitted her table, writing night and day, preparing material for their projected journal, *The Theosophist*, which was started that same year, and also in writing articles in the English, American and Russian newspapers to help their common resources. From their very first start they were harassed by the Anglo-Indian administration, which took a dislike to Theosophists and put them on their black books, treating them as spies and propagandists of the Russian Government.

It must be borne in mind that just at that time there was considerable excitement in England as to the fate of Afghanistan, on account of the success which had attended the Russian arms in the Transcaspian regions. The English had become more mistrustful and more full of Russophobia than ever. In vain the poor Theosophists protested and represented to the authorities that their mission was entirely concerned with philosophy and had nothing on earth to do with politics. They were put under police surveillance, their movements were watched and their correspondence opened.... So much the worse for the government of Queen Victoria, for H. P. Blavatsky added fuel to the flames, put no restraint upon her feelings in her letters, and doubtless the officials had often the pleasure of reading therein many home truths, which must have been somewhat trying to their vanity.... At last friends in London and the press took the matter up, and the police surveillance was removed — thanks, however, principally to a letter which Lord Lindsay, a Fellow of the Royal Society and President of the Astronomical Society in London, wrote to Lord Lytton, the Viceroy of

India, and which made him ashamed of any longer persecuting a woman and other persons engaged in abstract studies of a moral character.

Notwithstanding the prejudice against her among the members of Anglo-Indian society, Madame Blavatsky was able to make friends with some individuals amongst them, especially with those who were engaged in literary pursuits, and who were capable of being interested in the problems which occupied her. Soon she was in request in the highest social circles, especially after the *Pioneer* and *Indian Mirror* (the first-named being a Government organ) had made public the speech that the Viceroy, Lord Lytton, had made about her at a state dinner, after reading her works — it was as follows:

"I know but one person in the world who in the abstract sciences can compare with the author of *Zanoni* [Lord Lytton's own father], and that is Madame Blavatsky."

The visits, the dinners and the balls, and all the exigencies of society, were exceedingly irksome to Helena Petrovna, but she did her best to comply with them for the sake of her Society. She passed the hot weather in the hills, sometimes taking part in the Colonel's travels, but more often staying with friends, and always occupied, without intermission, on her writing.

She passed one summer at Simla, having accepted the invitation of one of her new friends, Mr. Sinnett, editor of the *Pioneer*, and his wife. Here it was that Madame Blavatsky made the great mistake of producing certain phenomena, in the presence of several persons who begged her to do so, and Mr. Sinnett had the imprudence to relate these phenomena in his newspaper, before publishing all those "facts," in which he most sincerely believed, in his well-known book, *The Occult World*. This led to endless debates. The clergy protested, not without reason, against "this anti-Christian propaganda, founded on jugglery." The calumnies against the founders of the Theosophical Society grew apace. They even went so far as to assert that not only was she a spy, but even an impostor — "a servant of the late Madame Blavatsky, who was dead and buried, whose papers she had seized and whose name she made use of."

All these slanders served to aggravate the maladies from which she suffered most terribly. She was obliged to have recourse to the authority of her relations and of her friends in Russia to prove her identity. Prince A. M. Dondoukoff-Korsakoff, at that time Commander-in-Chief of the

Caucasus, wrote her a most kind letter, describing himself as a friend who had known her from her youth, and enclosed a certificate of identity, which was published in nearly all the Anglo-Indian papers, to the great delight of her friends.

But, alas! she had more influential enemies than she had friends.

The Theosophical Society at that time numbered its recruits by the thousand among the natives, among those who held no official position, but had made very few converts among the leading classes in India. The English, bound by their official ties, or their social position, contented themselves for the most part with taking a general interest in the movement, and in the teachings in particular, but would have nothing to do with diplomas, and so forth, and, not being members of the Society, they lost no time in disowning it when it got into low water. Those who wish to acquaint themselves with the details of what occurred during the sojourn of H. P. Blavatsky in India can do so by reading the accounts written by Olcott and by Sinnett and by other eye-witnesses.

At length the adhesion of rich and influential natives, given to fraternity which reaffirmed the truth underlying their faiths, whether Hindu of Buddhist, irritated the missionaries to such an extent that they seemed to forget Christian charity. They saw already clearly enough that Madame Blavatsky, whether sincere or hypocrite, magician or conjurer, was the strength and the soul of the Theosophical Society, and they directed their attacks against her in consequence. She had not openly embraced Buddhism as had the President of the Society, but she proclaimed the equality and unity of all religious systems. For this very reason she was more dangerous than the Colonel, who was the author of a Buddhist catechism, approved by Sumangala, the High Priest of Ceylon. From thenceforward, therefore, she became the point of attack for the enemies of Theosophy and the scapegoat of the Society.

What with eighteen hours' work out of the twenty-four, the abuse and the constant worry, the mental strain added to her chronic bodily disease, which was aggravated by the bad climatic conditions, she at length came within an ace of death. During the five years H. P. Blavatsky passed in India she had no less than four attacks of illness of so serious a nature that the best doctors of Bombay and of Madras in each instance decided that she could not possibly live; but at the last moment some unlooked-for and at times unusual aid always came to her. On one occasion it was a native doctor, on another a Brahmin Yogi, or a poor "pariah," shrunken by fasting and austerities. They appeared unasked and offered their remedies, which proved to be efficacious. Then at the specified hour she fell into a deep sleep, from which, according to the European doctors, she should have passed into her last agony. Instead of which, she woke from this long sleep as if she had had nothing the matter with her. Twice, however, it fell out otherwise. Strange, unknown and unlooked-for visitors appeared, who took charge of her and carried her off no one knew whither.

Scores of witnesses testify to the fact, in addition to which her own letters prove it clearly. I have one before me, unluckily undated, as it was her habit in writing to us — her aunt and myself — not to trouble about the day of the month. In this letter she gives us news of a severe illness she was passing through; a "chela" (a disciple of the Masters and a student of the Occult sciences) had brought her an order from one of the Adepts for her to follow him, and she begged us not to be uneasy on account of her silence, which would necessarily be prolonged, as the place where she would be obliged to pass some time in order to recover was far removed from posts and telegraphs.

Here, again, is a letter addressed from Meerut, beyond Allahabad. This one was written in May, 1881, after a severe illness, of which those who were with H. P. Blavatsky had informed us, saying that we must be prepared for the worst. Her friends were taking Helena Petrovna into the country — she was convalescent, but still very weak — when she received the "order" to leave the main roads and to strike off into the mountains.

"There you will find certain individuals," thus it was said to her, "who will guide you from the jungles into the sacred forests of the Deobend." But, halfway, an accident befell her, which brought on another relapse. Here are a few lines from a letter which she wrote me three weeks later:

"I lost consciousness, and have no remembrance of the facts or the surroundings — all I do know was that I was carried in a palanquin, in which I lay at full length — to a great height. I only came to myself the following evening, so they told me, and then for a very short time only. I found myself lying in a large apartment, cut out of the solid rock and altogether empty, unless the statues of Buddha, which surrounded it, and the lighted braziers, which burnt around my bed, containing vases from which escaped sweet-smelling vapours, can be reckoned as furniture. An old man, quite white, bent over me, making magnetic passes, which steeped my body in a condition of indescribable well-being. I had barely time to recognize Delo-Durgai, the old Lama of Tibet, whom I had met *en route* a few days previously, and who had told me we should meet again soon."

This was an allusion to her previous letter, in which she had spoken of the fact of their meeting.

Having recognized the Tibetan Lama, my sister again relapsed into one of her strange sleeps and did not recover consciousness until she was again at the foot of the mountain, in the village where her European friends were waiting for her.

Never was it permitted, not only for the English but even for the natives themselves, to follow her on such secret expeditions, on which occasions it was presumed she went to see her Masters — notwithstanding this conviction, held by those who surrounded her, she never wrote to us of her visiting them; nevertheless, I have come across one of her first letters (written in 1879), in which she relates the participation of Mahatma Morya in one of her journeys with Colonel Olcott, amid the vaults and the ruins of ancient temples, which is of intense interest.

In the spring of 1881, H. P. Blavatsky fell seriously ill after receiving the fatal news of what had occurred in Russia on the 13th March in that year.

"Good God of mercy! what a bloody horror!" she wrote to us, "Are the last days of Russia come? ... Or is Satan himself incarnate in her children, in the miserable abortion of my poor country? After this unprecedented crime, what next? Where are the Russians of days gone by? Whither is my beloved Russia drifting? Yes, I am a renegade. Yes, I am a Buddhist, an atheist — according to you, a republican — but I am miserable, profoundly miserable, over this atrocious monstrosity! Oh! how I pity them all — our martyred Tsar, his unhappy family, and all Russia!

"Cursed be these monsters, these Nihilists, these reckless fools!

"How you will laugh at me — the republican citizen, the *esprit fort*, who has freed herself from the prejudices of her country; but in this moment of profound stupor I feel a shame so intense of my countrymen, a pity so deep for the victim of their cruel follies, a despair so true, that I defy the most faithful of the subjects of our Tsars, who have never left their native land, to suffer more than I do."

And she proved it by falling ill.

Her journal, *The Theosophist*, appeared in black borders. This was a most kind attention on the part of the President of the Theosophical Society; for she herself was far from being in a condition to think of such things. Hardly had she recovered from her first stupor, when she set to work to write a beautiful article for *The Pioneer*, in which she recounted all the acts of bravery, of humanity and kindliness done by Alexander II., and was delighted that all the Anglo-Indian press echoed what she said. As a reply to certain ill-disposed remarks in two clerical organs, alluding to "the American citizen and her journal dressed in mourning for the death of an autocrat," H.P. Blavatsky sent a collective reply to the *Bombay Gazette*, whence the other papers reproduced it.

"My kind friends make a mistake," so she wrote; "it is not as a subject of the 'Tsar of all the Russias' that I have put on mourning, but as a Russian by birth, as a unit among the thousands of my compatriots, whom this good and merciful man has covered with benefits, and who are all plunged in mourning. I desire, by so doing, to testify my sympathy, my respect, and my sincere grief for the death of the Tsar of my kindred, of my brothers and sisters in Russia, who will ever be dear to me, even to my last breath!"

In the winter of 1881-82 the Theosophical community transported its penates from Bombay to Adyar, a property in the neighbourhood of the city of Madras, bought by contributions from all the members of the Society, who desired to provide their founders and their staff with a permanent home. It is there that the President lives up to the present time, and it was here also that Madame Blavatsky passed the last two years of her life in India, and it was there that in that same year the seventh anniversary of the founding of the Society was celebrated with especial solemnity — I say "especial solemnity," as the number seven is an important one in theosophic beliefs, and as these anniversaries are numerous at Adyar, at New York and at London, those which contain this number are double marked.

During their frequent travels Colonel Olcott and Madame Blavatsky were always received with great pomp by the natives of the country they passed through; for all the Hindus were devoted to them, partly because by their translations of the Sanskrit books of the ancient Aryan literature they had done much to popularize them, partly on account of the efforts they had made to lessen the barriers between the castes, and also for what they had done in the way of modifying the unjust contempt with which the Anglo-Indians regarded the natives, even the learned Brahmius. In this work, according to the opinion of the natives, the Society had met with considerable success. Nowhere, however, were the Theosophists *feted* as they were in Ceylon. Each time they set foot there the Buddhist population were *en fete*, and led by their priests they organized a triumphal welcome.

It was in the interests of the Sinhalese that the President planned a journey to Europe and especially to London, in order to present a petition to Parliament in their favour.

It was towards the end of 1883 that H. P. Blavatsky found herself rather improved in health, thanks to a better climate and to the fact that she had a well-built house to live in. Nevertheless, her health left much to be desired, and all her doctors agreed that even a temporary change of climate would do her a great deal of good. It was therefore decided that she should accompany the President, and thenceforward Helena began to form projects of seeing once more her relatives. She immediately wrote to us; then in the month of December they left Bombay.

Before leaving the shore of India, however, my sister had three successive visions which indicated to her the death of her uncle, General Rostislav Fadeew, who died at that very time at Odessa.

As we knew she was about to leave, and were too upset ourselves by this heavy blow, her aunt and I neglected to send her news of what had happened. She was unaware of the illness of her uncle, when he himself came and told her that his trials were over.

The two or three letters of Madame Blavatsky dated early in January, 1884 — General Fadeew having died on the 29th December — proved conclusively by the truth of these visions, whilst the words from beyond the tomb, which she heard pronounced by this man, one who was esteemed and honoured by all who ever knew him, had for her a singular significance.

She had implicit belief in the truth and the importance of visions of this nature — not sought for but proceeding from the initiative of him who was dead. She had experienced them all her life, and nearly all the members of our family were privileged in the same manner.

· · · · · · · ·

Once in Europe, H. P. Blavatsky was besieged with invitations. All the Theosophists in London, in Paris, and her friends in all countries wanted to have her; but her idea was to see her own nearest relatives, and to this end, after resting at Nice at the house of the Duchesse de Pomar (Lady Caithness), President of the Eastern and Western Branch of the Theosophical Society in Paris, she settled down in Paris in a small flat, which she took in order to be able to receive my aunt and myself under her own roof, knowing that we should not care to accept any other hospitality. Harassed by the curious and by reporters, more than by friends or those seriously interested in her teachings, she went away and spent a fortnight in the country, accepting the invitation of M. and Mme. d'Adhemar, who owned a charming villa near Enghien. In *Lucifer* (the magazine since founded by H. P. Blavatsky in London) for July, 1891, I find a delightful letter from Countess d'Adhemar, giving her reminiscences of the musical phenomena produced by Madame Blavatsky during this visit, in the presence of several persons.

I regret that the limits of this article preclude my quoting at length this letter, and also many others, which would doubtless be more convincing to my readers than the depositions of a sister. I hope, however, to be able to do so at some future date, if only in order to undeceive the public regarding the lying accusations brought against Madame Blavatsky by evilly disposed persons, old pupils for the most part, who, finding their hopes of some immediate miraculous results disappointed, became her bitter enemies.

There were always enough and to spare of foolish people, who expected to receive occult gifts for the asking, and of mercenary folk who were ready to lend their aid and encouragement to H. P. Blavatsky in exchange for larger or smaller sums of money. As soon as these saw that she had neither the means nor the desire to pay them, either in ready cash or in occult powers conferred on them, they lost no time in becoming her deadly and too often unprincipled opponents.

I passed six weeks, in the spring of 1884, at Paris with my sister. She was all that time surrounded with crowds of people; not only those who had come from America, from England and from Germany, expressly to see her and to talk with her business connected with Theosophy, but also with numbers of Parisians interested in the teachings and particularly in the phenomena, who constantly assailed her.

The Theosophical Society in Europe was then in its infancy. Even in

London there were not more than a score of sincere and working members devoted to the cause; in Germany there was not even one branch duly organised; in Paris, there were indeed two Lodges, but they did not between them comprise a membership of more than twenty or thirty, while the " mother branches of New York and of Adyar" were constantly being split up by dissensions among their members, which did not promise well for their future prosperity. Amongst those, however, who were constant visitors at our house, 46, Rue Notre-Dame-des-Champs, were several of eminence. I remember seeing there many *savants*, doctors of medicine, and of other sciences, magnetisers and clairvoyants, and a number of women more or less acquainted with literature and the abstract sciences, among these many of our compatriots of both sexes. Among those whose names I remember, were C. Flammarion, Leymarie, de Baissac, Richet, Evette the magnetiser, the pupil and friend of Baron Dupotet, and M. Vsevolod Soloviofl, the Russian author, one of the most constant visitors and ever full of protestations of his devotion to the cause and person of Madame Blavatsky. Among the ladies were the Duchesse de Pomar, the Comtesse d'Adhemar, Madame de Barreau, Madame de Morsier, Mdlle. de Glinka and many others, French, Russian, English and American.

Colonel Olcott and Mr. Judge, the latter having arrived from New York, told us endless stories of the most wonderful phenomena of which they had been witnesses; we, however, saw none except such as had to do with psychology, with the exception of, on one or two occasions, hearing harmonious sounds, produced at will by Helena Petrovna; again, on one occasion not only was a sealed letter psychometrically read, but, having drawn in red pencil an arrow and a theosophical star on a sheet of paper, she caused the same marks to appear on an indicated place of the sealed letter, which was contained in an envelope and folded in four. This was vouched for by the signature of six or seven witnesses, amongst them M. Soloviofl, who described what happened in the Russian journal *Rebus*, under date of 1st July, 1884, and under the title of " Interesting Phenomena." There was also another, which I myself described at the time. It was the sudden appearance and equally sudden disappearance — without the least trace being left of it — of a Russian newspaper article, published at Odessa, three days before it appeared in the scrap-book of my sister, in which it was her custom to insert all that was published referring to her. That same morning we had all read this article with great astonishment (for the letters from Odessa to Paris took from four to five days to reach us) and that same evening not the smallest vestige of it remained in the book, which was a bound one and of which the pages were numbered. The disappearance of the article in question had not interrupted the series of consecutive numbers. With the exception of these two palpable facts, material phenomena, so to speak, I never — so far as my memory serves me — saw her produce any other than psychological phenomena, such as clairvoyance, psychometry and clairaudience. For my own part I never received any letters from the Adepts and I never perceived nor did I have the chance to see, as many others had, any apparition — neither lights nor letters falling from the skies. I do not contest their depositions — far from that! I am quite ready to believe them, for, so far as I see, no one has a right to contest the belief of others from the sole standpoint of ignorance or his want of perception; but I cannot put forward anything except what occurred in my own experience.

That, however, should not prevent my repeating the experiences of others, more fortunate or more endowed than myself, which they have related to me. It would be impossible, however, to relate all the stories told by the nearest disciples of my sister, and it is needless to do so, for all the Theosophical journals have told and retold those to which Messrs. Sinnett, Olcott, Judge, and many others bore witness; but I will quote the testimony of one who has not been hitherto reported in the English or French press. I allude to the remarkable phenomena which M. Vs. Solovioff has described in many letters.

After staying with my sister, in the month of September that same year, at Elberfeld, whither he went to see her, he wrote me a long letter about an interview which the Mahatma Morya had granted him, and also of the visions which he had experienced previous to the appearance of this great Adept. I will not describe what took place in detail, for he sent an account to the *Journal of the Society for Psychical Research* in London; this, however, is what he wrote to me in reply to my questions as to the authenticity of this apparition, on November 21st, 1885.

"Here again is a fact. I received (at Wurtzbourg) at the same time, to the great jealousy of all the Theosophists, an autograph letter from Mahatma Koot-Hoomi, written in Russian. I was not the least astonished when I found this letter lying precisely in the book I held in my hand. I had a presentiment it would be so. I knew it beforehand! What did astonish me, however, was that in it he spoke clearly and shortly of the very things we were discussing at the moment. In it I found a precise reply to my question of the moment before, although I was standing apart, and no one had approached me. Even if anyone had been able to insert the letter in the book, the individual who did so must have been able to control my thoughts, and cause me to pronounce the words I had spoken, for me to have found in it an exact reply. I have often observed the same phenomena in my own case and in that of others."

The occult powers of Madame Blavatsky were, without doubt, great. Nevertheless no one, so far as I know, has ever attributed her faculties to hypnotic suggestion, as M. Solovioff seems to imply. Besides which, his hypothesis will not stand criticism, for many times the letters from the Mahatmas and from Madame Blavatsky have been submitted to the inspection of experts, who have always pronounced the handwritings to be different. In addition to which, M. Solovioff has not been the only one to receive such letters under precisely similar conditions. Dr. Hubbe Schleiden, editor of *The Sphinx*, and many others who can prove it, have received their letters in the *absence* of Madame Blavatsky.

Returning to the testimony of M. Solovioff. He finishes his letter of 21st November with these words: "When her life ends, a life which, I am convinced, is only kept going by some magic power, I shall mourn all my life for this unhappy and remarkable woman." Indeed he might well say so, he who more than any other had had proof of her remarkable powers! Here are a few lines from another letter of his, written on December 22nd, 1884, at a time when my sister had been already in India for two months, and he was living in Paris.

"My dinner finished, I went to look for a cigar in my room. I went upstairs, opened my door, lit my candle... what did I see? Your sister, Helena Petrovna, in her black morning gown. She made me a bow, smiled and said, 'Here I am!' and disappeared. What is the meaning of it?"

As a matter of fact, it signified nothing at all serious. My sister merely wanted once for all to return, in her astral body, the frequent visits that M. Solovioff had at various times paid to her at Paris, Elberfeld, and at Wurtzbourg, in the flesh.

We left Paris on the same day in the month of June, I and my aunt N.

A. Fadeew for Odessa, Madame Blavatsky for London, whither she was urgently invited. She was there fully occupied in endeavouring to establish a permanent branch of the Society, under the presidency of Mr. Sinnett, and, although never out of pain, devoted much time to those who came to see her out of curiosity, and to social life. From the first she was feted and met with adulation. On her behalf they organised large meetings and conversaziones. At one of these, nearly one thousand persons were present at Princes' Hall, and more than three hundred persons were introduced to her. Among those who thus took notice of her were Professor Crookes, Lord Cross, Minister for India, and her friend and countrywoman Madame Olga Aleksevna Novikoff. Sinnett made a fine speech, in which he praised to the skies the energy and wisdom of Madame Blavatsky, the unceasing work of Colonel Olcott and the beautiful humanitarian and moral principles which formed the basis of their teachings. Unfortunately the health of H. P. Blavatsky was not equal to supporting the strain of her incessant work, together with the calls of society, coupled with the emotion caused by the receipt of bad news from Madras. I allude to the well-known conspiracy of her late servants, the carpenter Coulomb and his wife, who sold forged letters to the Journal of the Christian College of Madras, the sworn enemy of the T.S. and above all of its Foundress, and who, in the absence of the masters from Adyar, set to work to make, in Madame Blavatsky's room, hidden doors and cupboards with false backs, which she could never have ordered, for even if she had wished to deceive her visitors by such means, she would not have been so made as to have her secret arrangements carried out in her absence. All these made-up stories, well paid for by her adversaries, led to the sad history of the expose " of the frauds of Madame Blavatsky, the greatest impostor of the age," to quote the words of the report of the Psychical Society of London. This report has been over and over again shown to be false in its details, by many different individuals, who, being deeply versed in occultism and in the Theosophical teachings, went and diligently investigated the affair on the spot; but scandalous stories, especially those which are accusations, are very difficult to uproot. It is quite clear that the assertions of the Psychical Society — translated as they were into all languages — will serve, for a long time to come, as weapons in the hands of enemies of Madame Blavatsky, while the refutations of her devoted disciples, far better acquainted with all the details of the conspiracy, will remain in a great measure powerless owing to their want of publicity, appearing as they did in Theosophical journals, very little read by the outside public.

I have, in my portfolio, a whole series of articles written by friends of Madame Blavatsky in her favour, which no Russian journal would publish, for fear of polemics. In reply to an allusion in the *Novoic Vremia* to this very report of the Psychical Research Society — a score of members of the Theosophical Society in London, who had got to the bottom of the whole intrigue, sent a collective address to the editor, but this address never saw the light of day, and the defamatory article continued to appear in the paper, all founded on the calumnies of the Psychical Society.

The malevolence of the "Christian College" went so far as to affirm that "H. P. Blavatsky would never dare to return to India, for not only had she extorted money from her dupes, but had also stolen the cash-box of her own Theosophical Society." She! who had ruined her health in her efforts for the Society! She! who had given up all her fortune, her life, and her sole for it! This one statement alone from a so-called "Christian" journal proves the perfidy of her adversaries.

She hastened to leave for India, if only to give the lie to her persecutors. At Ceylon and even at Madras itself she met with a splendid reception. The students of the Madras Colleges presented her with a most flattering address, signed by eight hundred people. Certainly it was a most eloquent demonstration, and it consoled her not a little for her bitter vexations.

Still the storm grew. When Helena Petrovna took possession of her room at Adyar, she gave vent to cries of indignation, which caused her travelling companions, Mr. and Mrs. Cooper-Oakley, to hurry to the spot; it was the sight of the strange handiwork of the carpenter Coulomb which had struck her with stupefaction. (Mrs. Cooper-Oakley has described this scene and what followed, in her article, telling of their journey from London to Madras, in *LUCIFER*, of June, 1891). In a word, her enemies had done so much and so well that she fell ill and came near dying. This time her recovery was really miraculous, and all the witnesses have testified to it. In the evening her doctor left her dying, but when he returned in the morning, merely for the purpose of certifying to her death, he found her breakfasting on a cup of milk. The doctor could hardly believe his eyes. All she said to him was, "It is because you have no belief in the powers of our Masters."

The immediate danger had passed, but, nevertheless, she was so weak that they were obliged to carry her in an invalid chair and have her hoisted, almost unconscious, on board a steamer leaving for Italy, all the doctors being agreed that the approaching hot weather would be inevitably fatal to her.

· · · · · · · ·

The early months of the summer that Madame Blavatsky spent near Naples, at Torre del Greco, were months full of suffering. She felt ill, solitary, and deserted, and, what is more, she feared that the prosperity of the Theosophical Society was ruined by her unpopularity and by the calumnies at all times directed against her. But at the first suggestion of resignation she made, she raised a storm of unanimous protest from America, Europe, and above all, from India. The President was powerless to calm the malcontents, who urgently demanded the return of H. P. Blavatsky, and the resumption by her of the business of the Society and of Theosophical interests in general. In vain she tried to prove to them that she would really be of more use to the movement by devoting herself, in seclusion and uninterrupted by business affairs and troubles, to the writing of her new work, *The Secret Doctrine*. They replied with assurances of devotion to her and by asking her to come to London to Madras, and to New York; settle where she would, she would be welcomed, if only she would resume the leadership of the movement. As for leaving them, she must not for a moment think of it, for, according to the unanimous opinion, her leaving meant the dispersion of the Theosophical Society and its death!

As soon as it was known that one of the most foolish accusations against H. P. Blavatsky was that the Mahatmas did not exist, and that they were only the creation of her imagination, invented in order to deceive the credulous, hundreds of letters reached her from all parts of India, from persons who had knowledge of them before, they said, they had possessed the slightest acquaintance with Theosophy. Finally came a letter from Negapatam, the home of *pundits* bearing the signatures of seventy-seven of their learned men, emphatically affirming the existence of these superior beings, who were too well known and recognized in the history of the Aryan races for their descendants to be able to doubt their existence. (*Boston Courier*, July, 1886.)

Helena wrote to me from Wurzburg, where she had settled for the winter:

"I understand that the Psychical Research Society of London has suddenly perceived the possibility of making me pass for a charlatan. Above all things, they wish by any means to avoid differences with the orthodox science of Europe, and consequently it is impossible for them to recognize the occult phenomena as genuine and the result of forces unknown to the scientists. If they were to do this, they would at once have against them the whole clique of doctors of Science and Theology. Certainly their better plan is to trample on us Theosophists, who fear neither the clergy nor academic authorities, and who have the courage of our opinions. Well then! rather than excite the anger of the shepherds of all the European sheep of Panurge, is it not better to excuse my disciples (for there are many among the number who have to be taken care of!) and condole with them as being my poor dupes, and to place me upon the stool of repentance, and accuse me of frauds, of spying, of thefts, and what not? Ah! I recognize my usual fate; to have the reputation without having had the pleasure!... If only at least I could have been of real service to my beloved Russia! But no! The only service that I have had the chance of performing for her has been a very negative one; the editors of certain newspapers in India being my personal friends, and knowing that every line written against Russia gave me pain, abstained from attack oftener than they otherwise would have done.... Behold all that I have been able to do for my country now lost for ever!"

Her great consolation in this exile of hers was the letters and the visits of her friends, who knew where to find her in the depths of Germany, where she had taken refuge for the sake of quiet and to be able to write her book in peace. The letters all displayed confidence and friendship; of the visits, those of her Russian friends gave her the greatest pleasure. Amongst them were her aunt from Odessa and M. Solovioff from Paris. While there the latter had a letter from Mahatma Koot-Hoomi, and left again for Paris, enthusiastic over his visit and the extraordinary things which he had witnessed at Wurzburg, so much so that he wrote letter after letter, all in the style of the following extract:

"PARIS,
"*October 8th*, 1885.

"My Dearest Helena Petrovna,

"I am in correspondence with Madame Adam. I have spoken to her much of you; I have thoroughly interested her, and she tells me that her *Review* will be forthwith opened not only to Theosophical articles, but to your own justification, if needs be. I have praised Madame de Morsier to her (this lady formerly professed much devotion to Madame Blavatsky and her teachings); as it happens, at this very time she has staying with her a visitor who joins with me and speaks to the same effect. All is going as well as possible. I spent the morning with Dr. Richet, and again I spoke with him about you, with regard to Myers and the Psychical Research Society. I can say that I have convinced Richet as to the reality of your personal powers, and the phenomena taking place through your agency. He asked me three categorical questions — to the two first I replied in the affirmative; as to the third, I told him that without doubt I should be able to give him an affirmative answer within the space of two or three months. I have no doubt that my answer will be in the affirmative, and then — you will see — there will be a triumph which will crush all the 'psychists' (of London). Yes, so it must be, must it not? For assuredly you will not deceive me!... I leave to-morrow for Petersburg. — Yours,

"V. S. Solovioff."

All the winter, at Wurzburg, Madame Blavatsky was occupied in writing her *Secret Doctrine*. She wrote to Mr. Sinnett that never since the writing of *Isis Unveiled* had the psychometric visions appeared so clearly and plainly before her spiritual perception, and that she hoped that this work would revivify their cause. At the same time Countess Wachtmeister, who passed this winter with her (and thenceforward never wished to leave her) wrote letters full of admiration for the writings of Madame Blavatsky, and above all for " the surprising conditions under which H. P. Blavatsky worked at her great book."

"We are surrounded daily with phenomena" — thus she wrote to me — " but we are so used to them that they seem quite in the ordinary course of things."

Once again H. P. Blavatsky had a severe illness, from which she with difficulty recovered, thanks to the devotion of her friends, who never left her side for a moment. It was principally to Dr. Ashton Ellis, of London, Countess Wachtmeister, and the Gebhard family that she owed her recovery; but from this time forward her life was one of continuous suffering more or less acute.

In the month of April, 1887, her friends succeeded in removing her to England. The previous winter she had passed at Ostend, where she finished the first half of *The Secret Doctrine*, and here she was constantly surrounded with friends, especially with those who came to see her from London; amongst these was the President of the British Theosophical Society, Mr. Sinnett, who had just published his book, Incidents in the Life of Mme. H. P. Blavatsky.

The last four years of her life, which Madame Blavatsky passed in London, were years of physical suffering, of incessant labour, of mental over-excitement, which completely undermined her health; but these years were also years of success, of moral fruition, which fully compensated her for her sufferings, and gave her cause to hope that her book, the Theosophical Society, and her writings would remain as evidence in her favour after her death, and would serve to clear her name from the calumnies with which it had been covered.

Here is an extract from one of her letters, written in the autumn of 1887, excusing herself for her long silence.

"If you only knew, my friends, how busy I am! Just imagine the number of my daily duties; the editing of my new magazine, Lucifer, rests entirely with me, and besides that I have to write for it each month from ten to fifteen pages. Then there are the articles from the other Theosophical magazines — the *Lotus* at Paris, the *Theosophist* at Madras, the *Path* at New York — my *Secret Doctrine*, of which I have to continue the second volume and correct the proofs of the first two or three times over. And then the visits!.... Very often as many as thirty a day.... Impossible for me to get out of it!.... There ought to be a hundred and twenty-four hours in each day. Have no fear; no news is good news! You will be written to if I become more ill than usual..... Have you noticed on the cover of the *Lotus* the sensational announcement of the Editor? *Under the Inspiration of Madame Blavatsky*. Good Heavens, what 'inspiration'! when I have not had time to write one word for it. Does it reach you? I have taken three copies, two for you and one for Katkoff. I worship that man for his patriotism and the outspoken truth of his articles, which do honour to Russia...."

The activity of the Theosophical Society in London, its meetings, its monthly and weekly magazines, and, above all, the writings of its foundress, attracted the attention of the press and the reprisals of the clergy. But here their representatives never gave way to such unjust and calumnious excesses as did the Jesuits of Madras. Most assuredly there were many stirring meetings, at which H. P. Blavatsky, to use her own expression, was "treated like LUCIFER — not in its true sense, as *bearer of the heavenly light* — but in the popular sense, that which is ascribed to him in Milton's *Paradise Lost*. I was presented to the public as anti-Christ in petticoats." Nevertheless, her fine letter, entitled "LUCIFER to the Archbishop of Canterbury," made a great sensation at the time, and all but put an end to clerical hostilities.

In London there was no longer any question as to phenomena; Helena Petrovna took an aversion to them. Nevertheless, as Mr. Stead remarks with truth, in his article on Madame H.P. Blavatsky in *The Review of Reviews* for June, 1891, never before did she make so many distinguished converts or converts more devoted to her cause than during the last four years of her life. Her visions and her clairvoyance, however, never left her. In July, 1886, she told us of the death of her friend, Prof. Alexander Boutleroff, before it was mentioned in the Russian newspapers. In fact, she saw him at Ostend on the very day of his death. The same thing happened in the case of our celebrated politician, M. N. Katkoff, a patriot whom she cordially esteemed. She wrote to me (and the letter is fortunately still extant and precisely dated) one month before his end that he would be ill and would die. In July, 1888, when I was in London, she extricated me from serious perplexity, caused by a wrongly-interpreted telegram, and told me, after an instant's meditation, what had happened at Moscow on that very day. When in the spring of 1890, the Headquarters of the Society in London was moved into a new house, better adapted to accommodate her increased staff, H. P. Blavatsky said, "I shall never move again, they will take me from this house to the crematorium." When asked why she foretold this, she gave as a pretext that this house had not her lucky number; the number seven was lacking.

The health of Helena Petrovna continued to go from bad to worse with the increasing growth of her occupations. She formed around herself a group of ardent Theosophists who were anxious to study the occult sciences. With regard to this she wrote to me in 1889.

"You ask of me, what are my new occupations? None except the writing of fifty or so more pages each month, my *Esoteric Instructions*, which cannot be printed. Five or six unhappy voluntary martyrs, among my devoted esotericists, copy out 300 copies, so as to send them to the absent members of my Esoteric Section, but I have to revise and correct them myself into the bargain!.... And then our Thursday meetings, with the scientific questions of the *savants*, such as William Bennet or Kingsland, who writes on electricity; with stenographers in all the corners, and the assurance that my least word will be incorporated in our new journal of reports, *Transactions of the Blavatsky Lodge*, and that they will be read and commented on not only by my Theosophists, but by hundreds of the ill-disposed. My pupils in Occultism are overjoyed. They have sent out a circular through the Theosophical world, saying, ' H. P. B. is old and very ill; H. P. B. might die any day, and then from whom could we learn the things she can teach us. We must club together and record her teachings,' and so they pay for the stenographers and the printing, and it costs them much.... And their old H. P. B. *must* find time to teach them, although this cannot be done except at the cost of time which she formerly devoted to writing, in order to gain her daily bread, for foreign journals and newspapers. Well! H. P. B. will have her habits a little further upset — that is all! At the least word from me they would gladly indemnify me, but I won't accept one penny for such lessons. ' May thy money perish with thee, for thou hast thought to purchase the gifts of God for gold;' that is what I say to those who think they can buy the divine science of eternity for shillings and guineas."

Two years after she had settled in London, Madame Blavatsky made the acquaintance of a woman of extraordinary knowledge, merits, and talent.

I will let her speak herself.

"I fight more than ever with the materialists and atheists. The whole league of ' Freethinkers' is armed against me, because I have converted into a good Theosophist the best of their workers — Annie Besant — the famous woman author and orator, Bradlaugh's right hand and his tried friend.... Read her profession of faith, *Why I became a Theosophist* — a shorthand report of what she said in her public confession before a great meeting at the Hall of Science. The clergy are so well pleased with her conversion that at present they are full of praises of Theosophy.... What a noble and excellent woman she is! What a heart of gold! What sincerity, and how she speaks! A real Demosthenes. One never can tire of hearing her.... That is precisely what we have need of, for we have knowledge, but none of us — above all myself — know how to speak; whereas Annie Besant is a finished orator. Oh! this woman will never betray, not only our cause, but even my poor person!"

My sister had good grounds for what she said. With the support of Theosophists such as Mrs. Besant, Countess Wachtmeister, Bertram Keightley, and such like, she could have rested in peace and devoted herself quietly to her literary works, had her days not been already numbered.

The winter of 1890 was, as we all know, very severe in London, and, from the spring of 1891, the influenza, this new scourge of humanity which has the gentlest appearance and does not show its claws until later on, joined issue with the inclemencies of the season and carried off a larger proportion of the world than all the other diseases — our old friends — who do not deceive people by their airs of innocence. The whole community at 19, Avenue Road, was taken ill with it during the months of March and April. The younger members recovered, H. P. Blavatsky succumbed.

Mrs. Annie Besant was away; she had gone to the Congress of American Theosophists, to represent there the Foundress of the Society, and had been entrusted by her with an address to "her fellow citizens and brothers and sisters in Theosophy." The first successes of Helena Petrovna had their cradle in New York; the city of Boston had the privilege of giving her her last pleasure while on earth. The telegrams full of kind sentiments, of thanks and sincere good wishes for her, which reached her from America, after the reading of her letter, gave her real joy, at the very time she was confined to her bed and condemned.... Condemned? No. She who so often had been deceived herself and had so often proved false the sentence pronounced on her by the doctors, once again deceived them, but in another way. At eleven o'clock in the morning of May 8th, the doctors pronounced her out of danger, she got up and sat at her writing-table, without doubt wishing to die at her post, and at two o'clock she closed her eyes and — departed.

"She departed so quietly" — so wrote a witness of this unlooked-for death — "that we, who were near her, did not know even when she ceased to breathe. A supreme sensation of peace took possession of us, as we knelt there, knowing all was over." ("How she left us," by Miss L. Cooper, LUCIFER, June, 1891).

I had seen my sister for the last time in the summer of 1890. She had just been settling into her new house and was very busy and nearly always in pain. She was then forming a Home at the East End for working women.

"The Working Women's Club," founded at the cost of a wealthy Theosophist who wished to conceal his identity, prospered at this time under the protection of the lady patronesses belonging to the Theosophical Society. We passed the evenings talking of old days, of her beloved country; the injustice of the English Press and its calumnies against Russia seemed always to amount to injuries against herself. It is a great pity that her compatriots do not know all her articles on this subject. Many of them, those, above all, who formed their idea of her from the allegations of certain Russian newspapers, would have changed their opinions about her after reading, for instance, her article in L*UCIFER*, June, 1890, entitled, "The moat and the beam," written in reply to the false accusations against the Government of Russia, carried at indignation meetings held with regard to "Russian Atrocities in Siberia," which latter were, for the most part, invented by the too vivid imagination of George Kennan. And, curiously enough, the last words from her pen, which appeared on the same page of L*UCIFER* in which a hurried notice of her death was inserted, related to the Emperor of Russia. Therein she gave the Court of the Queen of England the good advice, that they should endeavour to follow the example offered by our Imperial family, in the practice of certain virtues, unknown to those devoid of "True Nobility," that being the title of this article.

On a fine May day, the remains of the Foundress of the Theosophical Society were taken in a coffin, completely covered with flowers, to the Crematorium at Woking. There was no elaborate ceremony, neither was mourning worn, she herself having expressly forbidden it.

It was in India and, above all, at Ceylon, that her death was commemorated with much pomp, but in Europe the ceremony was of the simplest, only a few words were spoken of her "who had created the Theosophic movement, who had been the apostle of universal charity, the apostle of a life of purity and labour for the sake of others and for the progress of the human spirit and, above all, of the eternal and divine soul." Then the body was committed to the flames and "three hours later, the ashes of her who had been Helena Petrovna Blavatsky, were brought back to her last home. Possibly some amongst her disciples were too fervent, but there were others who spoke nothing but the absolute truth concerning her. I quote, as a specimen, these words, which cannot fail to be approved by any impartial person.

"The friends of Madame Blavatsky merely ask that the rules of palpable common sense shall be admitted in any judgment of her, that testimony from those who know much shall be thought weightier than testimony from those who know nothing, that every well-established principle in the interpretation of human character shall not be reversed in her case, that the unsupported assertion of a daily newspaper shall not be conceded the authority of a Court or the infallibility of a Scripture. They do not even ask that the impartial shall read her books, but they *suggest*, not from hearsay, but from experience, that if any man wishes his aspirations heightened, his motive invigorated, his endeavour spurred, he should turn to the writing which express the thought and reflect the soul of Helena P. Blavatsky." — ("Test of Character," by A. Fullerton, *Path*, June, 1891).

"Amen," say we, her nearest relatives, to this tribute of a disciple.

As for myself, although I do not exactly hold with them, yet I may be allowed to say that the teachings of Theosophy should not be ignored by our contemporaries, even though the Society be dispersed and no trace remain of it as an organised body. These teachings will have their place in the history of the Nineteenth Century and — even if they do not materially influence the coming generations, as is the hope of her devoted followers — yet the name of a woman who was capable of calling forth a movement based on universal ideas, cannot be entirely lost in oblivion.

Vera P. Jelihovsky

[Our best thanks are due to the Editor of the *Nouvelle Revue* [1892], for permission to translate this biographical essay — Eds. [Editors of *Lucifer*.]]

SCHMIECHEN'S PORTRAIT

Madame Blavatsky
Personal Memoirs

Note

To this Autobiography of H. P. Blavatsky the compiler contributes nothing original except the idea of bringing together, for the information of those interested in Occultism and its greatest modern exponent, all the available events, experiences and relevant facts of that vigorous, brave, mysterious and wonderful life, and arranging them in their proper sequence.

This task has been somewhat similar to what H. P. B. describes as her method of writing *Isis Unveiled*: "When I think and watch my thoughts, they appear to me as though they were like those little bits of wood of various shapes and colours in the game known as *casse tête*: I pick them up one by one, and try to make them fit each other, first taking one, then putting it aside until I find its match, and finally there comes out in the end something geometrically correct." The difference lies in the fact that it was her thoughts which she was fitting together, while I have for my pieces of the game the facts of her life, gleaned from many sources.

This collecting and sifting has been carried on for seven years. It began when the compiler was called to Adyar in 1927 by Mr. C. Jinarajadasa at the order of the President, Dr. Annie Besant, to take up the work of arranging and cataloguing the Archives of the Theosophical Society. Such a task necessitated wide reading ; every book, pamphlet, magazine, newspaper, letter, etc., which had the least bearing on the events and subjects involved, must be considered.

It soon became evident that a great deal of matter relating to Mme Blavatsky was available, and that many of the gaps in her career might be filled, at least partially, by a thorough collection and careful assembling of the data so widely scattered. This idea took definite form when Dr. George Arundale urged me, as I was familiar with the Archives, to write articles on such topics as still had a current interest, and secured the permission of

Dr. Besant for such use of the Archives.

It is my hope that my own peculiar creation in this book is, first a portrait of H. P. B. which has never yet been painted in words and which could not have been accomplished without the wide, yet meticulous, collection of material, which produces not only a life-like general resemblance, but also correct details, all the little finishing touches which complete the picture. Second: a book which sheds new light on the Great Science, Occultism, by this exposition of the life of a great Occultist. H. P. B. asks : "Is it too much to believe that man should be developing new sensibilities and a closer relation with nature ?" And answers : "The logic of evolution must teach as much, if carried to its legitimate conclusion."

Thanks are due to Dr. Annie Besant and Dr. George Arundale for permission to use material from the Archives of the Theosophical Society. A considerable amount of hitherto unpublished matter is incorporated in this Autobiography from that source, as will be seen by a glance at the Table of References, where all such data are labelled "Archives" or "Scrap-books." Thanks are also due to Mr. Trevor Barker for permission to quote from *The Mahatma Letters* and from *The Letters of H. P. Blavatsky to A. P. Sinnett*, and to Dr. Eugene Rollin Corson for similar authorisation in regard to his book, *Some Unpublished Letters of Helena Petrovna Blavatsky*. Lastly, sincere appreciation is tendered to Miss Constance Rischbieth of Adelaide, who made possible the leisure required to assemble the book.

MARY K. NEFF

Advar, Madras, India,
February 27, 1935

Editor's Note

I n presenting to the public a book composed chiefly of extracts, written by various persons and at very different times, a dilemma inevitably arises. Either the quotations must be altered in regard to spelling, punctuation, etc., to make them conform to a common standard, or uniformity of presentation must be sacrificed to accurate quotation. We have preferred to adopt the latter policy. Madam Blavatsky herself was by no means consistent in her spelling and punctuation. She wrote *Kalmuck and Sarotow* at one time and *Calmuck and Saratoff* at another. But even when the sense of the quotation is difficult to understand it has been left unedited, as the object of the book is to let the original documents speak for themselves. Cross-references, clarifications, and annotations of actual misstatements have been supplied by the compiler in footnotes.

CHAPTER I
Childhood And Heredity

"My childhood? Spoilt and petted on one side, punished and hardened on the other. Sick and ever dying till seven or eight, sleep-walker, possessed by the devil. Governesses two — Mme Peigneux, a French woman, and Miss Augusta Sophia Jeffries, a Yorkshire spinster. Nurses — any number. No Kurd nurse. One was half Tartar. Born at Ekaterinoslow [1831]. Father's soldiers taking care of me. Mother died when I was a baby."[1]

It would be more correct to say "child" rather than "baby"; for she was eleven years old then. It seems that "Miss Augusta Sophia Jeffries... gave up her task in despair, and the child was again left to her nurses till about six years old, when she and her younger sister were sent to live with their father. For the next two or three years the little girls were chiefly taken care of by their father's orderlies; the elder, at all events, greatly preferring these to their female attendants. They were taken about with the troops to which their father was attached, and were petted on all sides as the *enfants du régiment*."[2]

Mme Blavatsky continues: "Travelled with father from place to place with his artillery regiment till eight or nine, taken occasionally to visit grandparents. When eleven, my grandmother took me to live with her altogether. Lived in Saratow when grandfather was Civil Governor, before that in Astrakhan, where he had many thousands (some 80,000 or 100,000) Kalmuck Buddhists under him."[3]

"I was quite familiar with the Lamaism of the Thibetan Buddhists. I passed months and years of my childhood among the Lamaist Calmucks of Astrakhan, and with their great priest.... I had visited Semipalatinsk and the Ural Mountains with an uncle of mine who had possessions in Siberia, on the very borderland of the Mongolian countries where the 'Terachan Lama' resides, and had numerous excursions beyond the frontiers, and knew all about Lamas and Thibetans before I was fifteen."[4]

Mme Pissareff, an old friend of the family, says: "The physical heredity of H.P.B. is rather interesting, as among her ancestors were representatives of France, Germany and Russia. By her father she was descended from the reigning Mecklenburg Princes, Hahn von Rottenstern-Hahn. Her mother was grand-daughter of Bandre du Plessy, an exiled Huguenot obliged to leave France on account of religious persecution, who, in 1787, married Prince Pavel Vasilievitch Dolgoruky; their daughter, Princess Helena Petrovna Dolgoruky, married Andrez Michailovitch Fadeef and was Helena Petrovna Blavatsky's grandmother, who herself brought up the early-orphaned children.

"She left the memory of a remarkable and highly cultured woman of unusual kindness, whose learning was quite exceptional in her age; she corresponded with many scholars, among them Mr. Murchison, the President of the London Geographical Society, with many noted botanists and mineralogists, one of whom named after her a fossil-shell discovered by him — Venus-Fadeef. She knew five foreign languages, painted beautifully, and was in every way a remarkable woman. She herself educated her daughter Helena Andreevna, mother of Helena Petrovna, and transferred to her gifted nature. Helena Andreevna wrote novels and stories, was well known under the *nom de plume* 'Zenaida R.' and was very popular in the forties. Her early death evoked universal grief and Brélomsky devoted to her several eulogistic pages, calling her 'the Russian Georges Sand.'

"I heard a good deal about the Fadeef family from Marie Griegorievna Ermoloff, who possessed a wonderful clear memory, and knew the family very well when the Fadeefs resided at Tiflis, while Madame Ermoloff's husband was the Governor of this Province in the forties. She remembered Helena Petrovna as a brilliant but very wilful young lady, who would not submit to anyone. The family enjoyed a high reputation, and Helena Petrovna's grandmother was so highly thought of that, notwithstanding her not visiting anybody, the whole town came 'to pay her homage.' Besides the daughter Helena Andreevna, who married an artillery officer Hahn, and another daughter (Witte by marriage) there were two more children:

Nadejda Andreevna,* and a son, Rostislav Andreevitch Fadeef....

"Left early an orphan, Helena Petrovna spent the greater part† of her childhood in the home of her grandfather Fadeef, first in Saratoff, later at Tiflis. In the summer, the whole family moved to the Governor's summer residence, a large and ancient mansion surrounded by a garden with many mysterious nooks, a pond, and a deep ravine, behind which ran a dark forest descending to the banks of the Volga.

"The ardent child saw in nature a mysterious life of its own; she often conversed with birds and animals, and during the winter her learned grandmother's study presented such an interesting world that it would have fired even a less brilliant imagination. The study contained many curious things: various stuffed animals, and grinning heads of bears and tigers; on one wall there were charming little humming-birds, glittering like so many bright flowers; on the other sat owls, falcons and vultures, and above them, under the very ceiling, a large eagle spread its majestic wings. But the most awful was a white flamingo, which stretched out its long neck, as if it were living. When the children came to their grandmother's study they sat astride on the black stuffed horse or on the white seal, and in the twilight they fancied all these animals began to move, and the little Helena Petrovna told many terrible and captivating stories, especially about the white flamingo, whose wings seemed to be sprinkled with blood.

"Besides the phenomena due to her near connection with nature and evident to all, there were others visible to her alone. From early childhood the clairvoyant child saw the majestic figure of a Hindu in a white turban, always one and the same. She knew him as well as she knew her own relatives, and called him her Protector, saying that it was He who saved her in dangers.

"One of those accidents happened when she was thirteen years old; a horse she rode became frightened and ran away; the child was unseated and, getting entangled in the stirrup, hung on to it; instead of being killed, however, she felt round her body somebody's arms, which supported her till the horse was stopped. Another accident happened much earlier, when she was quite a baby. She wished very much to examine a picture hanging high

---

* Who never married; Russian custom, however, gave her the title "Madame" in later life. She was H. P. B.'s greatly beloved aunt, only three years her senior, and educated with her.

† More correctly — a considerable part; namely, five years.

up on a wall and covered by a white curtain. She asked someone to uncover the picture, but her wish was not gratified. Once, being in the room alone, she pushed a table to the wall, put another small table over it, and a chair over this again, and succeeded in climbing to the top of it, holding with one hand to the dusty wall and with the other reaching out to the curtain. She lost her balance and remembered nothing else. Coming to, she found herself lying on the floor safe and sound, both tables and the chair standing in their usual places, the curtain drawn over the picture, and the only proof of all this having really happened was a little trace of the small hand, left on the dusty wall under the picture."[6]

Let Mme Blavatsky continue the story of her childhood: "Visit to London? I was in London with father in '44, not 1851?.... In 1845 father brought me to London, to take a few lessons of music. Took a few later also — from old Moscheles. Lived with him somewhere near Pimlico — but even this I would not swear."[6]

Mr. Sinnett relates this amusing incident of her first visit to London: " Her pride in her knowledge of the English language received a rude shock. She had been taught to speak English by her first governess, Miss Jeffries; but in Southern Russia people did not make the fine distinctions between different sort of English which more fastidious linguists are alive to. The English governess had been a Yorkshire woman and as soon as Mlle Hahn began to open her lips among friends to whom she was introduced in London, she found her remarks productive of much more amusement than their substance justified. The combination of accents she employed — Yorkshire grafted on Ekaterinoslow — must have had a comical effect, no doubt, but Mlle Hahn soon came to the conclusion that she had done enough for the entertainment of her friends, and would give forth her 'hollow o's and a's' no more."[7]

Mme Blavatsky continues her narrative thus: "Went to Bath with father, remained a whole week, heard nothing but bell-ringing in the churches all day. Wanted to go on horseback astride in my Cossack way; he would not let me, and I made a row, I remember, and got sick with a fit of hysterics. He blessed his stars when we went home; travelled two or three months through France, Germany and Russia. In Russia our own carriage and horses making twenty-five miles a day."[8]

"Writing in French, we Russians sign *de* before our names, if noblemen of the '*Velvet Book*' In Russian — unless the name is German, when they put *von* — the *de* is dropped. We were Mademoiselles *de* Hahn and *von* Hahn. I would not put the *de*, and never did to my Blavatsky name, though the old man was of a high noble family of the Ukraine — from the Hetmann Blavatko, becoming later Blavatsky in Russia, and in Poland Count Blavatsky.

"What more? Father was a Captain of Horse Artillery when he married my mother. Left service after her death, a Colonel. Was in the Sixth Brigade and came out a *Sous Capitaine* already from the *Corps des Pages Impériaux*. Uncle Ivan Alexievitch von Hahn was Director of the Ports of Russia in St. Petersburg. Married first to the *demoiselle d'honneur* — Countess Kontouzoff, and then *en secondes noces* another old maid of honour (a very stale one) — Mlle Chatoff. Uncle Gustav married first Countess Adlerberg — then the daughter of General Bronevsky, etc. etc. I need not be ashamed of my family, but *am* of being 'Mme Blavatsky' and if you can make me naturalised in Great Britain and become Mrs. Snookes or Tufmutton I will 'kiss hands' as they say here. I do not joke. Otherwise I cannot return to India."* [9]

"My own sister [Vera] is three years younger than I am. Sister Lisa is by father's second wife; he married in 1850, I believe, a Baroness von Lange, She died two years after. Lisa was born, I believe, in 1852 — am not sure, but think I am right. My mother died when my brother [Leonide] was born, six months after, in 1840 or 1839 — and this I can't tell." [10]

According to her sister, Vera (Mme Jelihovsky), who is more certain of dates, their mother died in 1842. Mme Jelihovsky says: "Our mother, Mme Helene de Hahn, *née* Fadeew, died when she was twenty-seven. Notwithstanding her premature death, such was the literary reputation she had already acquired, that she had earned herself the name of the 'Russian Georges Sand' — a name which was given her by Belinsky, the best of our critics. At sixteen years of age she was married to Pierre de Hahn, Captain of Artillery, and soon her time was fully occupied in superintending the education of her three children.

"Hélène, her eldest daughter, was a precocious child, and from her earliest youth attracted the attention of all with whom she came in contact. Her nature was quite intractable to the routine demanded by her instructors. She rebelled against all discipline, recognised no master but her own

* Written in Europe, in 1886.

good will and her personal tastes. She was exclusive, original, and at times bold even to roughness.

"When, at the death of our mother, we went to live with her relations, all our teachers had exhausted their patience with Helene, who would never conform to fixed hours for lessons, but who, notwithstanding, astonished them by the brilliancy of her abilities, especially by the ease with which she mastered foreign languages and by her musical talent. She had the character, and all the good and bad qualities of an energetic boy; she loved travels and adventures, and despised dangers, and cared little for remonstrances.

"When our mother was dying, although her eldest daughter was only eleven years old, she was filled with well-founded apprehensions for her future, and said: 'Ah well! perhaps it is best that I am dying, so at least I shall be spared seeing what befalls Helene! Of one thing I am certain, her life will not be as that of other women, and she will have much to suffer.'

"Truly a prophecy!"[11]

CHAPTER II

The Child "Medium"

he psychic powers of Helene von Hahn, which later caused such a stir in the world, manifested even in childhood. "I remember," she says, "a governess I had when I was a child. She had a passion for keeping fruit until it rotted away, and she had her bureau full of it. She was an elderly woman, and fell sick. While she lay abed, my aunt, in whose house I was, had the bureau cleaned out and the rotten fruit thrown away. Suddenly the sick woman, when at the point of death, asked for one of her nice *ripe* apples. They knew she meant a rotten one, and they were at their wit's end to know what to do, for there were none in the house.

"My aunt went herself to the servants' room to send for a rotten apple; and while she was there, they came running to say that the old woman was dead. My aunt ran upstairs, and I and some of the servants followed her. As we passed the door of the room where the bureau was, my aunt shrieked with horror. We looked in, and there was the old woman eating an apple. She disappeared at once, and we rushed into the bedroom. There she lay dead on the bed, and the nurse was with her (having never left her one minute for the last hour). It was her last thought made objective. A perfectly true story, a fact witnessed by myself in 1843."[1]

"For over six years, from the time I was eight or nine years old until I grew up to the age of fifteen, I had an old spirit (Mrs. T—— L——* she called herself) who came every night to write through me, in the presence of my father, aunts and many other people, residents of Tiflis and Saratoff. She gave a detailed account of her life, stated where she was born (at Revel, Baltic Provinces), how she married, and gave the history of all her children,

---

* H. P. B. supplied this name to Mr. Sinnett — Tekla Lebendorff.

including a long and thrilling romance about her eldest daughter Z——, and the suicide of her son F——, who also came at times and indulged in long rhapsodies about his sufferings as a suicide.

"The old lady mentioned that she saw God and the Virgin Mary, and a host of angels, two of which bodiless creatures she introduced to our family, to the great joy of the latter, and who promised (all this through my handwriting) that they would watch over me, etc., etc., *tout comme il faut*. She even described her own death, and gave the name and address of the Lutheran pastor who administered to her the last sacrament.

"She gave a detailed account of a petition she had presented to the Emperor Nicholas, and wrote it out *verbatim* in her own handwriting through my child's hand.

"Well, this lasted, as I said nearly six years — my writings — in her clear old-fashioned, peculiar handwriting and grammar, in German (a language I had never learnt to write and could not even speak well) and in Russian — accumulating in these six years to a heap of MSS. that would have filled ten volumes.

"In those days this was not called Spiritualism, but *possession*. But as our family priest was interested in the phenomena, he usually came and sat during our evening stance with holy water near him, and a *goupillon* (how do you call it in English?*) and so we were all safe.

"Meanwhile one of my uncles had gone to Revel, and had there ascertained that there had really been such an old lady, the rich Mrs. T—— L——, who, in consequence of her son's dissolute life, had been ruined and had gone away to some relations in Norway, where she had died. My uncle also heard that her son was said to have committed suicide at a small village on the Norway coast (all correct as given by 'the Spirit').

"In short, all that could be verified, every detail and circumstance, was verified, and found to be in accordance with my, or rather 'the Spirit's' account; her age, number and name of children, chronological details, in fact everything stated.

"When my uncle returned to St. Petersburg he desired to ascertain, as the last and crucial test, whether a petition, such as I had written, had ever been sent to the Emperor. Owing to his friendship with influential people in the *Ministère de l'Intérieur*, he obtained access to the Archives; and there, as he

---

* Aspergill.

had the correct date of the petition, and even the number under which it had been filed, he soon found it and comparing it with my version sent up to him by my aunt, he found the two to *be facsimiles*, even to a remark in pencil written by the late Emperor on the margin, which I had reproduced as exactly as any engraver or photographer could have done.

"Well, was it the genuine spirit of Mrs. L—— who had guided my medium hand? Was it really the spirit of her son F—— who had produced through me in *his* handwriting all those posthumous lamentations and wailings and gushing expressions of repentance? Of course, any Spiritualist would feel certain of the fact. What better identification, or proof of spirit identity; what better demonstration of the survival of man after death, and of his power to revisit the earth and communicate with the living, could be hoped for or even conceived?

"But it was nothing of the kind; and this experience of my own, which hundreds of persons in Russia can affirm — all my own relations to begin with — constitutes, as you will see, a most perfect answer to the Spiritualists.

"About one year after my uncle's visit to St. Petersburg, and when the excitement following this perfect verification had barely subsided, D——, an officer who had served in my father's regiment, came to Tiflis. He had known me as a child of hardly five years old, and had played with me, shown me his family portraits, had allowed me to ransack his drawers, scatter his letters, etc., and, amongst other things, had often shown me a miniature upon ivory of an old lady in cap and white curls and green shawl, saying it was his old aunty, and teasing me, when I said she was old and ugly, by declaring that one day I should be just as old and ugly.

"To go through the whole story would be tedious; to make matters short, let me say at once that D—— was Mrs. L——'s nephew, her sister's son.

"Well, he came to see us often (I was fourteen then), and one day asked for us children to be allowed to visit him in the camp. We went with our governess, and when there I saw upon his writing-table the old miniature of his aunt, *my spirit!* I had quite forgotten that I had ever seen it in my childhood. I only recognised her as the spirit who for nearly six years had almost nightly visited me and written through me, and I almost fainted.

"'It is, it is the spirit,' I screamed; 'it is Mrs. T—— L—'

"'Of course, it is my old aunt; but you don't mean to say that you have remembered all about your old plaything all these years?' said D——, who knew nothing of my spirit-writing.

"'I mean to say I see and have seen your dead aunt, if she is your aunt, every night for years; she comes and writes through me.'

"'Dead?' he laughed. 'But she is *not* dead. I have just received a letter from her from Norway,' and he proceeded to give full details as to where she was living, and all about her.

"That same day D—— was let into the secret by my aunts, and told of all that had transpired through my mediumship. Never was a man more astounded than was D——, and never were people more taken aback than were my venerable aunts, Spiritualists, *sans le savoir*.

"It then came out that not only was his aunt not dead, but that her son F——, the repentant suicide, *L'esprit souffrant*, had only attempted suicide, had been cured of his wound, and was at the time (and may be to this day) employed in a counting-house in Berlin.

"Well then, who or what, was 'the intelligence' writing through my hand, giving such accurate details, dictating correctly every word of her petition, etc., and yet romancing so readily about *her* death, *his* sufferings after death, etc. etc.? Clearly, despite the full proofs of identity, *not* the spirits of the worthy Mrs. T—— L, or her scapegrace son F——, since both these were still in the land of the living.

"'The evil one,' said my pious aunts; 'the Devil, of course,' bluntly said the priest. Elementaries, some would suppose; but according to what ——* has told me, it was all the work of my own mind. I was a delicate child. I had hereditary tendencies to extra-normal exercise of mental faculties, though, of course, perfectly unconscious then of anything of the kind.

"Whilst I was playing with the miniature, the old lady's letters and other things, my fifth principle (call it animal soul, physical intelligence, mind, or what you will) was reading and seeing all about them in the astral light, just as does the mind of a clairvoyant when in sleep. What it so saw and read, was faithfully recorded in my dormant memory, although, a mere babe as I was, I had no consciousness of this.

"Years after, some chance circumstance, some trifling association of ideas again put my mind in connexion with these long forgotten or rather I should say, never hitherto consciously recognised pictures; and it began one day to reproduce them. Little by little the mind, following these pictures into the

---

* One of the Brothers.

astral light, was dragged as it were into the current of Mrs. L——'s personal and individual associations and emanations; and then, the mediumistic impulse given, there was nothing to arrest it, and I became a medium, not for the transmission of messages from the dead, not for the amusement of elementaries, but for the objective reproduction of what my own mind read and saw in the astral light.

"It will be remembered that I was weak and sickly, and that I inherited capacities for such abnormal exercise of mind — capacities which subsequent training might develop, but which at that age would have been of no avail, had not feebleness of physique, a looseness of attachment, if I may so phrase it, between the matter and spirit of which we are all composed, abnormally for the time developed them. As it was, as I grew up, and gained health and strength, my mind became as closely prisoned in my physical frame as that of any other person, and all the phenomena ceased.

"How, while so accurate as to so many points, my mind should have led me into killing both mother and son, and producing such orthodox lamentations by the latter over his wicked act of self-destruction, may be more difficult to explain.

"But from the first, all around me were impressed with the belief that the spirit possessing me must be that of a dead person, and from this probably my mind took the impression. Who the Lutheran pastor was who had performed the last sad rite, I never knew — probably some name I had heard, or seen in some book, in connexion with some death-bed scene, picked out of memory by the mind to fill a gap in what it knew.

"Of the son's attempt at suicide, I must have heard in some of the mentally read letters, or have come across it or mention of it in the astral light, and must have concluded that death followed; and since, young as I was, I knew well how sinful suicide was deemed, it is not difficult to understand how the mind worked out the apparently inevitable corollary. Of course in a devout house like ours, God, the Virgin Mary and Angels were sure to play a part, as these had been ground into my mind from my cradle.

"Of all this perception and deception, however, I was utterly unconscious. The fifth principle worked as it listed; my sixth principle, or spiritual soul or consciousness, was still dormant, and therefore for me the seventh principle at that time may be said not to have existed."[2]

CHAPTER III

Life At Her Grandfather's

"The five years passed in safety with her grandparents seem to have had an important influence on Helena's future life. Miss Jeffries had left the family; the children had another English governess, a timid young girl to whom none of her pupils paid any attention, a Swiss preceptor, and a French governess.... Wild woods surrounded the large villa occupied by Mlle Hahn's grandparents during the summer months. It was only when roaming at leisure in the forests, or riding some unmanageable horse on a Cossack's saddle, that the girl felt perfectly happy."[1]

The dearly loved aunt, Mme Nadejda Fadeef who affectionately called the little Helena "Helinka," wrote of her in later years: "We who know Mme Blavatsky now in age can speak of her with authority, not merely from idle report. From her earliest childhood, she was unlike any other person. Very lively and highly gifted, full of humour, and of most remarkable daring; she struck everyone with astonishment by her self-willed and determined actions....

"Those who have known her from childhood would — had they been born thirty years later — have also known that it was a fatal mistake to regard and treat her as they would any other child. Her restless and very nervous temperament, one that led her into the most unheard-of, ungirlish mischief; her unaccountable (especially in those days) attraction to, and at the same time fear of, the dead; her passionate love and curiosity for everything unknown and mysterious, weird and fantastical; and, foremost of all, her craving for independence and freedom of action — a craving that nothing and nobody could control; all this, combined with an exuberance of imagination and a wonderful sensitiveness, ought to have warned her friends that she was an exceptional creature, to be dealt with and controlled by means as exceptional.

"The slightest contradiction brought on an outburst of passion, often a fit of convulsions. Left alone with no one near her to impede her liberty of action, no hand to chain her down or stop her natural impulses, and thus arouse to fury her inherent combativeness, she would spend hours and days quietly whispering, as people thought, to herself, and narrating, with no one near her, in some dark corner, marvellous tales of travels in bright stars and other worlds, which her governess described as 'profane gibberish'; but no sooner would the governess give her a distinct order to do this or the other thing, than her first impulse was to disobey.

"It was enough to forbid her doing a thing to make her do it, come what would. Her nurse, as indeed other members of the family, sincerely believed the child possessed by 'the seven spirits of rebellion.' Her governesses were martyrs to their task, and never succeeded in bending her resolute will, or influencing by anything but kindness her indomitable, obstinate, and fearless nature.

"Spoilt in her childhood by the adulation of dependants and the devoted affection of relatives, who forgave all to 'the poor, motherless child'—later on, in her girlhood, her self-willed temper made her rebel openly against the exigencies of society. She would submit to no sham respect for, or fear of public opinion. She *would* ride at fifteen, as she had at ten, any Cossack horse on a man's saddle! She would bow to no one as she would recede before no prejudice or established conventionality. She defied all and everyone.

"As in her childhood, all her sympathies and attractions went out towards people of the lower class. She had always preferred to play with her servants' children rather than with her equals, and as a child had to be constantly watched for fear she would escape from the house to make friends with ragged street boys. So, later on in life, she continued to be drawn in sympathy towards those who were in a humbler station of life than herself, and showed as pronounced indifference to the 'nobility' to which by birth she belonged."[2]

There was one, however, who could curb and guide this child with the "fiery temper of the Dolgoroukis" to some extent; namely, her grandmother, another Dolgorouki. Colonel Olcott relates an instance of it in

Old Diary Leaves: "I will now tell a story which I had from her own lips, and the incidents of which had a most lasting effect upon her through life. In childhood her temper was practically unrestrained, her noble father petting and idolizing her after the loss of his wife. When, in her eleventh year, the time came for her to leave his regiment and pass under the management of her maternal grandmother (the wife of General Fadeyef, born Princess Dolgorouki), she was warned that such unrestrained liberty would no longer be allowed her, and she was more or less awed by the dignified character of her relative.

"But on one occasion, in a fit of temper at her nurse, a faithful old serf who had been brought up in the family, she struck her a blow in the face. This coming to her grandmother's knowledge, the child was summoned, questioned, and confessed her fault. The grandmother at once had the castle bell rung to call all the servants of the household, of whom there were scores, and when they were assembled in the great hall, she told her grand-daughter that she had acted as no lady should, in unjustly striking a helpless serf who would not dare defend herself; and she ordered her to beg pardon and kiss her hand in token of sincerity.

"The child at first, crimson with shame, was disposed to rebel; but the old lady told her that if she did not instantly obey, she would send her from her house in disgrace. She added that no real noble lady would refuse to make amends for a wrong to a servant, especially one who by a lifetime of faithful service had earned the confidence and love of her superiors. Naturally generous and kind-hearted towards the people of the lower classes, the impetuous child burst into tears, knelt before the old nurse, kissed her hand, and asked to be forgiven. Needless to say that she was thenceforth fairly worshipped by the retainers of the family. She told me that that lesson was worth everything to her, and had taught her the principle of doing justice to those whose social rank made them incapable of compelling aggressors to do rightly towards them."[3]

In a delightful book, called *Juvenile Recollections Compiled for My Children** Mme Jelihovsky (H. P. B.'s sister Vera) tells these stories selected from the diary which she kept during her girlhood: [4] "The great country mansion

---

* Mme Jelihovsky wrote also My Youth, When I was Little, The Truth about Mme Blavatsky, as well as a serial entitled Helena Petrovna Blavatsky, which appeared in Lucifer (H. P. B.'s English magazine) in 1894 and 1895.

(*datche*) occupied by us at Saratow was an old and vast building, full of subterranean galleries, long abandoned passages, turrets, and most weird nooks and corners. It had been built by a family called Pantchoolidzef, several generations of whom had been governors at Saratow and Penja — the richest proprietors and noblemen of the latter province. It looked more like a mediaeval ruined castle than a building of the past century....

"We had been permitted to explore, under the protection of half a dozen male servants and a quantity of torches and lanterns, those awe-inspiring 'Catacombs.' True, we had found in them more broken wine bottles than human bones, and had gathered more cobwebs than iron chains, but our imagination suggested ghosts in every flickering shadow on the old damp walls. Still Helene would not remain satisfied with one solitary visit, nor with a second either.

" She had selected the uncanny region as a Liberty Hall, and a safe refuge where she could avoid her lessons. A long time passed before her secret was found out, and whenever she was found missing, a deputation of strong-bodied servant-men, headed by the *gendarme* on service in the Governor's Hall, was despatched in search of her, as it required no less than one who was not a serf and feared her little to bring her upstairs by force. She had erected for herself a tower out of old broken chairs and tables in a corner under an iron-barred window, high up in the ceiling of the vault, and there she would hide for hours, reading a book known as *Solomon's Wisdom*, in which every kind of popular legend was taught.

" Once or twice she could hardly be found in those damp subterranean corridors, having in her endeavours to escape detection lost her way in the labyrinth. For all this, she was not in the least daunted or repentant, for, as she assured us, she was never there alone, but in the company of her little ' hunch-backs' and playmates.

" Intensely nervous and sensitive, speaking aloud and often walking in her sleep, she used to be found at nights in the most out-of-the-way places, and to be carried back to her bed profoundly asleep. Thus she was missed from her room one night when she was hardly twelve, and the alarm having been given, she was searched for and found pacing one of the long subterranean corridors, evidently in deep conversation with someone invisible to all but herself.

" She was the strangest girl one has ever seen, one with a distinct dual nature... one mischievous, combative, and obstinate — everyway graceless; the other as mystical, and metaphysically inclined.... No schoolboy was ever more uncontrollable or full of the most unimaginable pranks and *espiègleries* than she was. At the same time, when the paroxysm of mischief-making had run its course, no old scholar could be more assiduous in his study; and she could not be prevailed upon to give up her books, which she would devour night and day as long as the impulse lasted. The enormous library of her grandparents seemed then hardly large enough to satisfy her cravings.

"Attached to the residence there was a large abandoned garden, a park rather, full of ruined kiosks, pagodas, and out-buildings which, running up hillward, ended in a virgin forest, whose hardly visible paths were covered knee-deep with moss, and with thickets in it which perhaps no human foot had disturbed for centuries. It was reputed the hiding-place for all the runaway criminals and deserters, and it was there that Helene used to take refuge when the 'Catacombs' had ceased to assure her safety....

"Fancy, or that which we all regarded in those days as fancy, was developed in the most extraordinary way, and from her earliest childhood, in my sister Helene.* For hours at a time she used to narrate to us younger children, and even to her seniors in years, the most incredible stories with the cool assurance and conviction of an eye witness, and one who knew what she was talking about.

"When a child, daring and fearless in everything else, she got often scared into fits through her own hallucinations. She felt certain of being persecuted by what she called 'the terrible glaring eyes,' invisible to everyone else, and often attributed by her to the most inoffensive inanimate objects; an idea that appeared quite ridiculous to the bystanders. As to herself, she would shut her eyes tight during such visions, and run away to hide from the ghostly glances thrown on her by pieces of furniture or articles of dress, screaming desperately, and frightening the whole household.

"At other times she would be seized with fits of laughter, explaining them by the amusing pranks of her invisible companions. She found these in every dark corner, in every bush of the thick park that surrounded our villa during the summer months; while in winter, when all our family emigrated back to town, she seemed to meet them again in the vast reception rooms of the first floor, entirely deserted from midnight till morning. Every locked

---

* Not fancy, but clairvoyance, the Theosophist would say.

"THE LOVELY MAIDEN"

door notwithstanding, Helene was found several times during the night hours in those dark apartments in a half-conscious state, sometimes fast asleep, and unable to say how she got there from our common bedroom on the top storey.

"She disappeared in the same mysterious manner in daytime also. Searched for, called and hunted after, she would be often discovered, with great pains, in the most unfrequented localities; once it was in the dark loft, under the very roof, to which she was traced, amid pigeons' nests, and surrounded by hundreds of those birds. She was 'putting them to sleep' (according to the rules taught in *Solomon's Wisdom*), as she explained. And indeed, pigeons were found, if not asleep, still unable to move, and as though stunned, in her lap at such times.

"At other times, behind the gigantic cupboards that contained our grandmother's zoological collection — the old Princess's museum of natural history having achieved a wide renown in Russia in those days — surrounded by relics of fauna, flora, and historical antiquities, amid antediluvian bones of stuffed animals and monstrous birds, the deserter would be found, after hours of search, in deep conversations with seals and stuffed crocodiles. If one could believe Helene, the pigeons were cooing to her interesting fairy tales, while birds and animals, whenever in solitary *tête-à-tête* with her, amused her with interesting stories, presumably from their own autobiographies.

"For her all nature seemed animated with a mysterious life of its own. She heard the voice of every object and form, whether organic or inorganic; and claimed consciousness and being, not only for some mysterious powers visible and audible for herself alone in what was to everyone else empty space, but even for visible but inanimate things, such as pebbles, mounds, and pieces of decaying phosphorescent timber.

"With a view of adding specimens to the remarkable entomological collection of our grandmother, as much as for our own instruction and pleasure, diurnal as well as nocturnal expeditions were often arranged. We preferred the latter, as they were more exciting, and had a mysterious charm to us.... We knew of no greater enjoyment. Our delightful travels in the neighbouring woods would last from 9 p.m. till 1, and often 2 a.m.

"We prepared for them with an earnestness that the Crusaders may have experienced when setting out to fight the infidel and dislodge the Turk from Palestine. The children of friends and acquaintances in town were invited — boys and girls from twelve to seventeen, and two or three dozen young serfs of both sexes, all armed with gauze nets and lanterns, as we were ourselves, strengthened our ranks. In the rear followed a dozen strong grownup servants, Cossacks, and even a *gendarme* or two, armed with real weapons for our safety and protection.

"It was a merry procession as we set out on it, with beating hearts and bent with unconscious cruelty on the destruction of the beautiful, large night-butterflies for which the forests of the Volga province are so famous. The foolish insects, flying in masses, would soon cover the glasses of our lanterns, and ended their ephemeral lives on long pins and cork burial-grounds four inches square.

"But even in this my eccentric sister asserted her independence. She would protect and save from death all those dark butterflies known as *sphynxes*, whose dark fur-covered heads and bodies bore the distinct image of a white human skull. 'Nature having imprinted on each of them the portrait of the skull of some dead hero these butterflies are sacred, and must not be killed,' she said, speaking like some heathen fetish-worshipper. She got very angry when we would not listen to her, but would go on chasing those 'dead heads,' as we called them ; and maintained that by so doing we disturbed the rest of the defunct persons whose skulls were imprinted on the bodies of the weird insects.

"No less interesting were our day-travels into regions more or less distant. At about ten versts from the Governor's villa there was a field, an extensive sandy tract of land, evidently once upon a time the bottom of a sea or a great lake, as its soil yielded petrified relics of fishes, shells, and teeth of some (to us) unknown monsters. Most of these relics were broken and mangled by time, but one could often find whole stones of various sizes on which were imprinted figures of fishes and plants and animals of kinds now wholly extinct, but which proved their undeniable antediluvian origin.

"The marvellous and sensational stories that we, children and schoolgirls, heard from Helene during that epoch were countless. I well remember when stretched at full length on the ground, her chin reclining on her two palms, and her two elbows buried deep in the soft sand, she used to dream aloud and tell us of her visions, evidently clear, vivid, and as palpable as life to her !...

"How lovely the description she gave us of the submarine life of all those beings, the mingled remains of which were now crumbling to dust around us! How vividly she described their past fights and battles on the spot where she lay, assuring us she saw it all; and how minutely she drew on the sand with her finger the fantastic forms of the long-dead sea-monsters, and made us almost see the very colours of the fauna and flora of those dead regions!*

"While listening eagerly to her descriptions of the lovely azure waves reflecting the sunbeams playing in rainbow light on the golden sands of the sea-bottom, of the coral reefs and stalactite caves, of the sea-green grass mixed with the delicate shining anemones, we fancied we felt ourselves the cool, velvety waters caressing our bodies, and the latter transformed into pretty and frisky sea-monsters; our imagination galloped off with her fancy to a full oblivion of the present reality.

"She never spoke in later years as she used to speak in her childhood and early girlhood. The stream of her eloquence has dried up, and the very source of her inspiration is now seemingly lost I She had a strong power of carrying away her audiences with her, of making them see actually, if even vaguely, that which she herself saw.

"Once she frightened all of us youngsters very nearly into fits. We had just been transported into a fairy world, when suddenly she changed her narrative from the past to the present tense, and began to ask us to imagine that all that which she had told us of the cool, blue waves with their dense populations was around us, only invisible and intangible, so far....

"'Just fancy! A miracle!' she said; 'the earth suddenly opening, the air condensing around us and re-becoming sea waves... Look, look... there, they begin already appearing and moving. We are surrounded with water, we are right amid the mysteries and the wonders of a submarine world!...'

"She had started from the sand, and was speaking with such conviction, her voice had such a ring of real amazement, horror, and her childish face wore such a look of wild joy and terror at the same time, that when suddenly covering her eyes with both hands, as she used to do in her excited moments, she fell down on the sand screaming at the top of her voice, 'There's the wave!... It has come!... The sea, the sea, we are drowning!' every one of us fell down on our faces, as desperately screaming and as

---

* Did she psychrometrise the fossils, or read their history in the astral records?

fully convinced that the sea had engulfed us, and that we were no more!

"It was her delight to gather round herself a party of us younger children at twilight, and after taking us into the large dark museum, to hold us there, spell-bound, with her weird stories. Then she narrated to us the most inconceivable tales about herself; the most unheard-of adventures of which she was the heroine, every night, as she explained. Each of the stuffed animals in the museum had taken her in turn into its confidence, had divulged to her the history of its life in previous incarnations or existences.

"Where had she heard of reincarnation, or who could have taught her anything of the superstitious mysteries of metempsychosis, in a Christian family? Yet she would stretch herself on her favourite animal, a gigantic stuffed seal, and caressing its silvery, soft white skin, she would repeat to us his adventures, as told to her by *himself*, in such glowing colours and eloquent style, that even grown-up persons found themselves interested involuntarily in her narratives. They all listened to, and were carried away by the charm of her recitals, the younger audience believing every word she uttered.

"If Helene loved to tell us stories, she was still more passionately fond of listening to other people's fairy tales. There was, among the numerous servants of the Fadeef family, an old woman, an under-nurse, who was famous for telling them. The catalogue of her tales was endless, and her memory retained every idea connected with superstition. During the long summer twilights on the grassy lawn under the fruit trees of the garden, or during the still longer winter evenings, crowding around the flaming fire of our nursery-room, we used to cling to the old woman, and felt supremely happy whenever she could be prevailed upon to tell us some of those popular fairy tales, for which our northern country is so famous.

"The adventures of 'Ivan Zarewitch,' of 'Kashtey the Immortal,' of the 'Grey Wolf,' the wicked magician travelling in the air in a self-moving sieve; or those of Meletressa, the Fair Princess, shut up in a dungeon until the Zarewitch unlocks the prison door with a golden key, and liberates her — delighted us all. Only, while all we children forgot those tales as easily as we had learned them, Helene never either forgot the stories or consented to recognise them as fictions.

"She thoroughly took to heart all the troubles of the heroes, and maintained that all their most wonderful adventures were quite natural. People *could* change into animals and take any form they liked, *if they only knew how*; men *could* fly, if they only wished so *firmly*. Such wise men had existed in all ages, and existed even in our own days, she assured us, making themselves known, of course, only to those who were worthy of knowing and seeing them, and who believed in, instead of laughing at, them....*

"As a proof of what she said, she pointed to an old man, a centenarian, who lived not far from the villa, in a wild ravine of a neighbouring forest, known as 'Baranig Bouyrak.' The old man was a real magician, in the popular estimation; a sorcerer of a good, benevolent kind, who cured willingly all the patients who applied to him, but who also knew how to punish with disease those who sinned. He was greatly versed in the knowledge of the occult properties of plants and flowers, and could read the future, it was said.

"He kept bee-hives in great numbers, his hut being surrounded by several hundreds of them. During the long summer afternoons he could be always found at his post, slowly walking among his favourites, covered as with a living cuirass, from head to foot, with swarms of buzzing bees, plunging both his hands with impunity into their dwellings, listening to their deafening noise, and apparently answering them — their buzzing almost ceasing whenever he addressed them in his (to us) incomprehensible tongue, a kind of chanting and muttering. Evidently the golden-winged labourers and their centenarian master understood each other's languages. Of the latter, Helene felt quite sure.

"'Baranig Bouyrak' had an irresistible attraction for her, and she visited the strange old man whenever she could find a chance to do so. Once there, she would put questions and listen to the old man's replies and explanations as to how to understand the language of bees, birds and animals,† with a passionate earnestness. The dark ravine seemed in her eyes a fairy kingdom. As to the centenarian 'wise-man,' he used to say of her constantly to us: 'This little lady is quite different from all of you. There are great events lying in wait for her in the future. I feel sorry in thinking that I will not live to see my predictions of her verified; but *they will all come to pass!*'"[4]

---

* This indicates her early knowledge or conviction of the existence of the Masters of Wisdom.
† One of the powers of the Raja Yogis. See Chapter XIV.

CHAPTER IV

Youth And Marriage

ery little is known of Helena von Hahn's youth, perhaps because it was so short — she was married before she attained seventeen. Mme Pissareff says of her: "One of her qualities which exercised a great attraction on her friends and at the same time seriously harmed her, was her well-pointed, brilliant humour, most kindly meant but sometimes ruffling to petty ambitions. Those who knew her in her earlier days remember her with delight — unswerving, impetuous, merry, sparkling with acute humour and witty conversation. She loved to joke, to tease, to create a commotion."[1]

The child who rode Cossack horses bareback and would never bend her will to authority of any kind carried over this trait into girlhood, and developed a violent distaste for conventions. She says: "I hated 'society' and the so-called 'world' as I hated hypocrisy in whatever form it showed itself; *ergo*, I ran amuck against society and the established proprieties."[2] "I hate dress, finery, and civilised society; I despise a ball room, and how much I despise it will be proved to you by the following fact. When hardly sixteen, I was being forced one day to go to a dancing party, a great ball at the Viceroy's. My protests were not listened to by my parents, who told me that they would have me dressed up — or rather, according to fashion, undressed — for the ball by servants by force, if I did not go willingly. I then deliberately plunged my foot and leg into a kettle of boiling water, and held it there till nearly boiled raw. Of course, I scalded it horribly, and remained at home for six months. I tell you, there is nothing of the woman in me. When I was young, if a young man had dared to speak to me of love, I would have shot him like a dog who bit me. Till nine years of age, in my father's regiment, the only nurses I knew were artillery soldiers and

Buddhist Calmucks."³

Her early marriage and precipitate flight from it puzzled friends of the family. Mme Pissareff hazards this guess: "Her marriage at the age of seventeen to an elderly and unloved man, with whom she could have nothing in common, can be explained only by a keen desire to gain more freedom. If one imagines the conditions of life of a young lady in provincial 'high life,' even in a good family, with all the prejudices and irksome etiquette of that time, one can easily understand how such conditions oppressed a nature so ardent, so difficult to limit, and so freedom-loving as the young Helena Petrovna's must have been."⁴

But according to her aunt, Mme Fadeef, no such serious motive underlay this youthful marriage; moreover, it is difficult to see how marriage to an important official would conduce to greater freedom from "dress, finery, and civilised society." Her aunt's story gives the marriage a casual, even accidental character:

"She had been simply defied one day by her governess, to find any man who would be her husband, in view of her temper and disposition. The governess, to emphasise the taunt, said that even the old man she found so ugly and had laughed at so much, calling him a 'plumeless raven,' even he would decline her for a wife! That was enough: three days after she made him propose, and then, frightened at what she had done, sought to escape from her joking acceptance of his offer. But it was too late."⁵

One may well ask: "Why too late?" Surely engagements of marriage had been broken before in Russia; why not this one? Mme Blavatsky in her old age, when Mr. Sinnett (in 1885, with the greatest difficulty) was extracting from her material for her memoirs, wrote to him: "Had you been in my skin, when the whole winter I was bombarded with family letters, warning me not to touch such or another family matter, not to lay sacrilegious hands on that or this *grave*, etc., you would then understand how nervous I felt about those *Memoirs*. Matters were such, that one sentence mentioning my prayers and supplications not to be married to old B —— would have brought down protests and denials from my cousins, who deem it their duty to prove that it was not my grandparents or aunt, but my father and I who had to be blamed for the ridiculous marriage."⁶

In another letter she wrote to him: "My aunt Mme Witte swore before the image of some St. Flapdoodle that she would *curse me* on her death-bed if I permitted any Memoirs* to be published, so long as all my relatives are yet living."[7]

"Details about my marriage? Well, now they say that I wanted to marry the old whistlebreeches *myself*. Let it be. My father was four thousand miles off. My grandmother was too ill. It was as I told you. I had engaged myself to spite the governess, never thinking I could no longer *disengage* myself. Well, Karma followed my sin. It is *impossible* to say truth without incriminating people that I would not accuse for the world, now that they are dead and gone. Rest it all on my back. There was a row already between my sister and aunt — the former accusing me of having slandered my dead relatives in the question of my marriage, and that my aunt had signed their and her own condemnation†. Let this alone"[8]

Finding her prayers unavailing with her family, the harassed girl endeavoured to induce her fiance to release her — but in vain. Her sister Vera (Jelihovsky) long afterward wrote: "At the age of seventeen, Helene married a man thrice her age.‡ Her husband was the Vice-Governor of the Province of Erivan, in Transcaucasia. He was in all respects an excellent man, with but one fault, namely, marrying a young girl who treated him without the least respect, and who told him quite openly beforehand that the only reason she had selected him from among others who sought to marry her was that she would mind less making him miserable than anyone else. 'You make a great mistake in marrying me,' she said to him before the marriage. 'You know perfectly that you are old enough to be my grandfather. You will make somebody unhappy, but it won't be me. As for me, I am not afraid of you, but I warn you that it is not you that will gain anything from our union.' He never could say that he did not get what he had bargained for."[9]

"Pressed to go on with the wedding, she seems to have consoled herself with the belief that she would be securing herself increased liberty of action

---

* See the *Memoirs of Count Witte*, in Chapter XXVI.

† In her account of the marriage quoted in this chapter. This aunt was to H. P. B. the dearest of all her relatives, except only her father. Perhaps the reason lay partly in the fact mentioned by her sister Vera, in a letter of 1886 to Countess Wachtmeister: "As for her childhood, I remember it but very little, being several years younger, and therefore having been bred apart from her and our youngest aunt, Miss Nadejda Fadeyeff, who can be a great deal more useful in this matter of your researches." (*Letters of H. P. Blavatsky to A. P. Sinnett*, 274.)

‡ "Mme Blavatsky believed that he was nearer seventy than sixty. He was himself reluctant to acknowledge more than about fifty." (*Incidents in the Life of Mme Blavatsky*, 41.)

as a married woman than ever she could compass as a girl. Her father was altogether off the scene, far away with his regiment.... The ceremony of the marriage, at all events, duly took place [at Djellallogly] on the 7th of July, 1848."[10] Her seventeenth birthday was on July 30-31, Russian, or August 12, English calendar.

To resume her aunt's story: "Hence the fatal step. All she knew and understood was — when *too late* — that she had been accepting, and was now forced to accept — a *master* she cared nothing for, nay, that she hated; that she was *tied* to him by the law of the country, hand and foot. A 'great horror' crept over her, as she explained later; one desire, ardent, irresistible, got hold of her entire being, led her on, so to say, by the hand, forcing her to act instinctively, as she would have done if, in the act of saving her life, she had been running away from a mortal danger.

"There had been a distinct attempt to impress her with the solemnity of marriage, with her future obligations and her duties to her husband and married life. A few hours later, at the altar, she heard the priest saying to her: 'Thou shalt honour and obey thy husband'; and at this hated word 'shalt' her young face — for she was hardly seventeen — was seen to flush angrily, then to become deadly pale. She was overheard to mutter in response, through her set teeth: 'Surely, I shall not.' And surely she has not. Forthwith she determined to take the law into her own hands, and — she left her 'husband' forever, without giving him any opportunity to ever even think of her as *his wife*. Thus Mme Blavatsky abandoned her country at seventeen, and passed ten long years* in strange and out-of-the-way places — in Central Asia, India, South America, Africa and Eastern Europe."[11]

Mr. Sinnett carries on the story thus: "Of course the theories concerning the married state entertained by General Blavatsky and his abnormally natured bride differed *toto ccelo*, and came into violent conflict from the day of the wedding — a day of unforeseen revelations, furious indignation, dismay, and belated repentance.... The day after the wedding she was conducted by the General to a place called Daretchichag, a summer retreat for the Erivan residents. She tried already on this journey to make her escape towards the Persian frontier, but the Cossack she sought to win over as her

---

* Says her sister, Mme Jelihovsky: "It was only at the expiration of ten years, the period necessary to render legal the separation from her husband, that Mme Blavatsky returned to Russia." (*Lucifer*, November, 1894.)

guide in this enterprise betrayed her instead to the General, and she was carefully guarded. The cavalcade duly reached the residence of the Governor — the scene of his peculiar honeymoon."[12]

Many years later a stray gleam is cast on this honeymoon. In 1874, when Mme Blavatsky went to Chittenden, Vermont, in the United States, in order to meet Colonel Olcott, then a reporter of the *New York Daily Graphic*, investigating Spiritualistic phenomena at the Eddy homestead, one of the "spirits" who appeared at a seance she attended was Safar Ali Bek. In an article she wrote for the newspapers concerning these phenomena, called "Marvellous Spirit Manifestations," she mentions "Safar Ali Bek, a young chief of a tribe of Khurds, who used to accompany me in my trips around Ararat in Armenia, and who on one occasion saved my life."

Colonel Olcott describes the incident as follows: "The last spirit to show himself that evening, was one of the most impressive figures of the whole four hundred or so I have seen. In 1851* Mme de Blavatsky was passing the summer at Daratschi-Tchag, an Armenian place of summer resort in the plain of Ararat. The name means 'The Valley of Flowers.' Her husband, being Vice-Governor of Erivan, had a bodyguard of some fifty Khourd warriors, among whom one of the strongest and bravest, named Safar Ali Bek, Ibrahim Bek Ogli (the son of Ibrahim), was detailed as the lady's personal escort. He rode after her everywhere on her daily equestrian excursions, and delighted to display his unusual skill as a cavalier.

"This very man walked out of Willian Eddy's cabinet in the form of a materialized spirit, dressed to the minutest detail as when she saw him last in Asia. Madame was playing the parlour-organ that evening, and as the back of the instrument was close against the platform, it brought her within three or four feet of each of the spirits as they stood outside the cabinet. There could be no mistaking her old Khourdish 'Nouker' and her recognition of him was immediate. He came out empty-handed; but just as I thought he was about to retire he bent forward, as if picking a handful of mould from the ground, made a gesture of scattering it, and pressed his hand to his bosom — a gesture familiar only to the tribes of Khourdistan; then he suddenly held in his right hand the most curious looking weapon I ever saw. It was a spear with a staff that might have been a dozen feet in length (perhaps more, for the butt seemed to extend into the cabinet)

---

* Not 1851, but 1848. During 1851 she was in England and America.

and a long steel head of peculiar shape, the base of which was surrounded with a ring of ostrich plumes. This weapon, Mme de B. tells me, is always carried by the Khourdish horsemen, who acquire a wonderful dexterity in handling it. One instant before, his hand was empty; the next, he grasps this spear, with its glittering steel barb and wavy plumes! Whence came it? From Chittenden township, master skeptic?"[13]

Mr. Sinnett resumes: "For three months the newly married couple remained under the same roof, each fighting for impossible concessions, and then at last, in connection with a quarrel more violent even than the rest, the young lady took horse on her own account and rode to Tiflis. Family councils followed, and it was settled that the unmanageable bride should be sent to join her father. He arranged to meet her at Odessa, and she was despatched in the care of an old man-servant and a maid, to catch at Poti a steamer that would take her to her destination.... It is not unreasonable to suppose that General Blavatsky himself was ready to acquiesce in the separation. He endeavoured, indeed, to obtain a formal divorce on the ground that his marriage had never been more than a form, and that his wife had run away; but Russian law at the time was not favourable to divorce, and the attempt failed."[14]

An article entitled "Heroic Women" appeared in the *New York Mercury* of January 18, 1875, which stated that Mme Blavatsky " at the age of seventeen married a Russian nobleman then in his seventy-third year. For many years they resided together at Odessa, and finally a legal separation was effected. The husband died recently in his ninety-seventh year. The widow is now a resident of the City of New York." To this Mme Blavatsky replied: "If I married a Russian nobleman, I never resided with him anywhere; for three weeks after the sacrifice I left him, for reasons plausible enough in my eyes, as in those of the 'puritan' world. I do not know if he died at the advanced age of ninety-seven, as since then this noble patriarch has vanished from my sight and memory"[15]

In "My Confession" she says: "In 1848, I, hating my husband, N. V. Blavatsky (it may have been wrong, but still such was the nature *God* gave me), left him, abandoned him — *a virgin* (I shall produce documents and letters proving this, although he himself is not such a swine as to deny it)."[16]

In an interview reported July 14, 1878, in the New York *Star*, under the caption "A Theosoph and a Citizen," she says: "I am a widow, a blessed widow, and I thank God. I wouldn't be a slave to God Himself, let alone man."

So she fled from her hated marriage, and disappeared for ten years. Says her sister Vera: "No one knew where she was, and we gave her up for dead."* Why had she been forced into this marriage? Was it family honour, or an opportunity to "settle" this troublesome, high-spirited girl? Whatever the motive, it was very cruel to poor Helena von Hahn, who thus sums up her bitter experience of marriage: "Woman finds her happiness in the acquisition of supernatural powers. Love is but a vile dream, a nightmare."†

---

* "She communicated privately with her father, and secured his consent to her vague programme of foreign travel.... He supplied his fugitive daughter with money, and kept her counsel in regard to her subsequent movements." (*Incidents in the Life of Mme Blavatsky*, 44, 45.)

† Found in her sketch-book, which she had begun not later than 1851, perhaps in tiie very year of her marriage; for in it she has noted her first meeting with her Master on her twentieth birthday, 1851. See Chapter VIII.

CHAPTER V

Disappearance

H.P.B.'s cousin, Count Sergius de Witte, in his *Memoirs* writes: "Helena soon abandoned her husband and came back to her grandfather. When she appeared in his spacious mansion, he immediately decided to send away the troublesome young person at the earliest possible moment to her father, who was an artillery colonel stationed in the vicinity of St. Petersburg. As there were no railways at that time within the territory of the Caucasus, the problem was not without its difficulties. It was solved in this wise.

"Two women and as many men, including grandfather's trusty steward, were selected from the large staff of domestic serfs, and under this convoy the future theosophic celebrity proceeded in the direction of Poti, enthroned in a capacious four-in-hand. From Poti it was planned to ship the fugitive by sea to some port connected by rail with the interior of Russia. When the company arrived at Poti, several steamers including an English craft lay in the harbour. Young Mme Blavatsky, so the story runs, immediately struck up an acquaintance with the captain of the English vessel. To make a long story short, one fine morning the convoy discovered to their horror that their mistress and charge had vanished into the air. Stowed away in an English ship, she was on her way to Constantinople."

Mr. Sinnett's narrative, in his *Incidents in the Life of Madame Blavatsky*, is to this effect: "She so contrived matters on the journey through Georgia that she and her escort missed the steamer at Poti. But a small English sailing vessel was lying in the harbour. Mme Blavatsky went on board this vessel — the *Commodore* she believes was the name, and by a liberal outlay of roubles, persuaded the skipper to fall in with her plans. The *Commodore* was bound first for Kertch, then to Taganrog in the Sea of Azof, and ultimately to Constantinople. Mme Blavatsky took passage for herself and servants, ostensibly for Kertch. On arriving there, she sent the servants ashore to procure apartments and prepare for her landing the following morning. But in the night, having now shaken herself free of the last restraints that connected her with her past life, she sailed away in the *Commodore*.

"The little voyage itself seems to have been full of adventures, which in dealing with a life less crowded with adventures than Mme Blavatsky's, one would stop to chronicle. The harbour police of Taganrog visiting the *Commodore* on her arrival, had to be so managed as not to suspect that an extra person was on board. The only available hiding-place — amongst the coals — was found unattractive by the passenger, and was assigned to the cabin-boy, whose personality she borrowed for the occasion, being stowed away in a bunk on pretence of illness. Later on, when the vessel arrived at Constantinople, further embarrassments had developed themselves, and she had to fly ashore precipitately in a caique with the connivance of the steward, to escape the persecutions of the skipper. At Constantinople, however, she had the good fortune to fall in with a Russian lady of her acquaintance the Countess Kisselev, with whom she formed a safe intimacy, and they travelled for a time in Egypt, Greece, and other parts of Eastern Europe."[1]

Mme A. L. Pogosky puts forward a hypothesis which may, or may not, throw some light on the disappearance (but not, in my opinion, on the marriage) of the fugitive bride. She says: "In the *Memories of Mme Ermoloff*, who knew all the circumstances of Mme Blavatsky's maiden life, we find a little detail not mentioned anywhere else, which may have had an important influence on her destiny. At the time there lived at Tiflis a Prince Galitzyne, a relative of the Viceroy of the Caucasus, who often visited the Fadeefs, and was greatly interested in this original young lady. He was considered, as Mme Ermoloff puts it, 'either a Freemason or a magician or a fortune-teller.' H. P. B.'s relatives replied to my enquiry, that Prince Galitzyne was indeed very often with the Fadeefs before Helena Petrovna's marriage; but whether he was an occultist or not they could not say, but thought it very likely.

"Immediately after the departure of Prince Galitzyne from Tiflis came the sudden decision of Helena Petrovna to marry a very unsuitable old gentleman, M. Blavatsky. Putting together these circumstances and the subsequent flight from the husband's house, it seems likely that, in conversing with the 'magician,' Prince Galitzyne, a man well-informed upon or at least interested in phenomena of mediumship and clairvoyance, Helena imbibed many hints affecting her decision to break with the life of a young lady in society. It is very probable that she told her sympathetic listener of her visions and of her 'Protector,' and received from him information and perhaps even the address of that Egyptian Copt who is quoted as her first teacher in Occultism.

"Confirmation of this lies in the fact that on reaching Kertch with her servants in her flight, she sends them back from the steamer, and instead of going to her father, as her relatives and servants believed, she travels to Egypt, not alone but with a friend, Countess Kisselev. It is possible that this meeting with a companion was mere chance, but it might have been previously arranged. If my surmise is true, all the character of her disappearance in the East changes; instead of being an aimless hunting for adventures, it appears in the light of a definite striving towards a definite aim."[2] That she was under the care and guidance of her Master, appears from a statement she made in a letter to General Lippitt, February 16, 1881, to the effect that "this power I have been acquainted with from childhood, but saw his face years before on a voyage (when M. Blavatsky was Governor at Erivan, capital of Armenia)."[3]

CHAPTER VI

Adventures In Egypt And Africa

Mr. Sinnett relates in *Incidents in the Life of Mme Blavatsky* that, "In Egypt, while travelling with the Countess Kisselev, Mme Blavatsky already began to pick up some occult teaching, though of a very different and inferior order from that she acquired later. At that time there was an old Copt at Cairo, a man very well and widely known, of considerable property and influence, and of a great reputation as a magician.* The tales of wonder told about him by popular report were very thrilling. Mme Blavatsky seems to have been a pupil who readily attracted his interest, and was enthusiastic in imbibing his instruction. She fell in with him again in later years, and spent some time with him at Boulak, but her acquaintance with him in the beginning did not last long, as she was only at that time in Egypt for about three months."[1]

Colonel Olcott relates one of her experiences, probably with this man: "She told me once in great glee of a *Máya* that had been put off on herself. She was travelling in the desert with a certain Coptic white magician who shall be nameless, and camping one evening expressed the ardent wish for a cup of French *café au lait*. 'Well, certainly, if you wish it so much' said the guardian guide. He went to the baggage-camel, drew water from the skin, and after a while returned, bringing in his hand a cup of smoking, fragrant coffee mixed with milk. H. P. B. thought this, of course, was a phenomenal production, since her companion was a high adept and possessed of very great powers. So she thanked him gratefully, and drank, and was delighted, and declared she had never tasted better coffee at the Café de Paris. The magician said nothing, but merely bowed pleasantly and stood as if waiting

* Paulos Metamon, of *Old Diary Leaves*, I, 23.

to receive back the cup. H. P. B. sipped the smoking beverage, and chatted merrily, and — but what is this ? The coffee has disappeared and naught but plain water remains in her cup ! It never was anything else ; she had been drinking and smelling and sipping the Máya of hot, fragrant Mocha."[2]

Mme Blavatsky describes many personal experiences and adventures under the editorial 'we' in *Isis Unveiled*. Here is one which occurred in Egypt : " Music is delightful to every person. Low whistling, a melodious chant, or the sounds of a flute will invariably attract reptiles in countries where they are found. We have witnessed and verified the fact repeatedly. In Upper Egypt, whenever our caravan stopped, a young traveller who believed he excelled on the flute amused the company by playing. The camel-drivers and other Arabs invariably checked him, having been several times annoyed by the unexpected appearance of various families of the reptile tribe, which generally shirk an encounter with men. Finally our caravan met with a party, among whom were professional serpent-charmers, and the virtuoso was then invited, for experiment's sake, to display his skill.

" No sooner had he commenced than a slight rustling was heard, and the musician was horrified at suddenly seeing a large snake appear in dangerous proximity to his legs. The serpent, with uplifted head and eyes fixed on him, slowly, and, as if unconsciously, crawled, softly undulating its body, and following his every movement. Then appeared at a distance another one, then a third and a fourth, which were speedily followed by others, until we found ourselves quite in a select company. Several of the travellers made for the backs of their camels, while others sought refuge in the *cantinier's* tent. But it was a vain alarm.

" The charmers, three in number, began their chants and incantations, and attracting the reptiles, were soon covered with them from head to foot. As soon as the serpents approached the men, they exhibited signs of torpor, and were soon plunged in a deep catalepsy. Their eyes were half closed and glazed, and their heads drooping. There remained but one recalcitrant, a large and glossy fellow, with a spotted skin. This *meloman* of the desert went on gracefully nodding and leaping, as if it had danced on its tail all its life, and keeping time to the notes of the flute. This snake would not be enticed by the 'charming' of the Arabs, but kept slowly moving in the direction of the flute-player, who at last took to his heels.

" The modern Psyllian then took out of his bag a half-withered plant, which he kept waving in the direction of the serpent. It had a strong smell of mint, and as soon as the reptile caught its odour, it followed the Arab, still erect upon its tail, but now approaching the plant. A few more seconds, and the 'traditional enemy' of man was seen entwined around the arm of his charmer, became torpid in its turn, and the whole lot were then thrown together in a pool, after having their heads cut off.

"Many believe that all such snakes are prepared and trained for the purpose, and that they are either deprived of their fangs, or have their mouths sewed up. There may be, doubtless, some inferior jugglers, whose trickery has given rise to such an idea.

But the *genuine* serpent-charmer has too well established his claims in the East, to resort to any such cheap fraud. They have the testimony on this subject of too many trustworthy travellers, including some scientists, to be accused of any such charlatanism. That the snakes, which are charmed to dance and to become harmless, are still poisonous, is verified by Forbes. 'On the music stopping too suddenly,' says he, 'or from some other cause, the serpent, who had been dancing within a circle of country-people, darted among the spectators, and inflicted a wound on the throat of a young woman, who died in agony in half an hour afterward.'" [3]

Other stories of Mme Blavatsky's adventures come from Mme Lydia de Paschkoff, through the humorous pen of David A. Curtis, a reporter for the *New York World*, April 24, 1878 : At the Eighth Avenue Lamasery, "Mme Blavatsky was entertaining, in better than royal style, a friend and compatriot, like herself a traveller in strange lands, like herself a firm believer in the occult, and a Russian Countess.,.. Besides Hierophant Olcott, there was a French diplomat, a reporter, and another and far profounder journalist. Two others should be mentioned, a Turk who smoked his own *nargileh* and drank coffee, and a table servant who passed round tea, tobacco, and sweetmeats. The one, a picture of the automatic chess-player, was ornamental; the other, the counterfeit of a Nubian god, was useful. Neither spoke....

"The Countess Paschkoff understands a little English, but does not speak it. It is perhaps to be regretted that the only record of her talk the reporter has, is derived from Colonel Olcott's running translation. This, notwithstanding the Hierophant's linguistic ability, can hardly be supposed to be literal. The lady spoke rapidly, vivaciously, musically, and throwing away her cigarette gesticulated gracefully. The Hierophant spoke sententiously, dropping into vernacular frequently, and using no gesture excepting when he stroked his ample beard....

"'I have seen the procession that goes every year to the shrine between Cairo and Alexandria. The dervishes go on camels and horses, and ride over the people that throw themselves down to make a road for them and no one is hurt. Then there are the dancing dervishes that spin around, till they go up in the air, and it takes three or four men to pull them down. And some of them stick knives through their legs and through their throats. The points of the knives come out on the other side. Blood runs down. They pull out the knives. They pass their hands over the wound. It is healed. There is not even a scar. Hoopla! I mean *Voila!*'...

"'I was once travelling between Baalbec and the river Orontes' continued the two speakers,' and in the desert I saw a caravan. It was Mme Blavatsky's. We camped together. There was a great monument standing there, near the village of El Maroun. It was between the Lebanus and the anti-Lebanus. On the monument were inscriptions that no one could ever read. Mme Blavatsky could do strange things with the "spirits" as I knew, and I asked her to find out what the monument was.

"'We waited until night. She drew a circle, and we went into it. (Mme Blavatsky, editing this article which she later copied in *The Theosophist*, here interpolates as a footnote: "Not so. It was the person — a Syrian who accompanied Mme Blavatsky, who drew the circle, not she, and the strange things he did do!") We built a fire and put much incense on it. Then she said many spells. (Footnote by Mme Blavatsky: "Rather he.") Then we put on more incense. Then she pointed with her wand at the monument. (Mme Blavatsky's footnote: "Something she never had.") We saw a great ball of white flame on it. There was a sycamore tree near by. We saw many little white flames on it. The jackals came and howled in the darkness a little way off. We put on more incense.

"'Then Mme Blavatsky commanded the spirit of the person to whom the monument was reared to appear. (Madame's footnote: "Mme Blavatsky never did anything of the kind. It was the Syrian ascetic again, who produced these wonders, and far more extraordinary were the phenomena than as given by the humorous writer.") Soon a cloud of vapour arose, and obscured the little moonlight there was. We put on more incense. The cloud took the indistinct shape of an old man with a beard, and a voice came, as it seemed from a great distance, through the image.

"'He said that the monument was once the altar of a temple that had long since disappeared. It was reared to a god that had long since gone to another world. "Who are you?" asked Mme Blavatsky. "I am... one of the priests of the temple," said the voice. Then Mme Blavatsky commanded him to show us the place as it was when the temple stood. He bowed, and for one instant we had a glimpse of the temple, and of a vast city filling the plain as far as the eye could reach. Then it was gone, and the image faded away. Then we built up big fires to keep off the jackals, and went to sleep.'

"'Yes, and she was finely scared, I can tell you' said Mme Blavatsky, laughing. The Countess then told many merry tales that were of the true Arabian Nights style, about the adventures of Mme Blavatsky and herself as they went around together, the former summoning spirits at will and doing magical feats out of pure fun; and finished with one about going into the Great Pyramid at night and performing incantations in the Queen's Chamber."[4]

Another stray glimpse of her African adventures appears in the report of an interview with Mme Blavatsky in *The Liberal Christian* of September 4, 1875, in which the reporter says: "Strange sights had she seen among tribes of sorcerers in Africa; a negro who by black art could submit to seventeen shots while the muzzle touched his body, causing each bullet to describe a triangle, spin into the air and finally bury itself in the earth; and a child whirled about in the air by invisible hands."[5]

A very interesting story of her Egyptian adventures appears in Colonel Olcott's *People from the Other World*, which is a compilation of all the articles he wrote for the *New York Daily Graphic* when he was reporting the Spiritualistic phenomena which took place at the home of the Eddy family at Chittenden, Vermont, in 1874. As soon as Mme Blavatsky attended the stances, a new type of materialised forms appeared — characters from Russia, Egypt, Africa, etc. Describing one of these the Colonel says:

"I saw one of the most singular creatures that ever excited the wonder of a 'circle.' He was a tall, spare negro, black as ink, and dressed in a curious costume, two features of which were very conspicuous. Upon his woolly head he had a coiffure that would make a sensation on Broadway. I could see an ornamental fillet, or band, and on top of his head four horns with bent tips, something like those of the chamois or some varieties of African antelope, such as the oryx. The points of the two in front were turned backwards, and those of the two in the rear forward, while a brass or gilt ball hung suspended from each tip.

"Mme Blavatsky did not recognise him at first, but he stepped forward a pace or two, and she then saw before her the chief of a party of African jugglers whom she encountered once in Upper Egypt, at a celebration of the feast of 'Ramazan.' The magical performances of his party upon that occasion make one of the most incredible stories in the history of either Magic or Spiritualism, and one feat deserves place in such a book of weird experiences as this.

"Mme de Blavatsky says that, in full sight of a multitude comprising several hundred Europeans and many thousand Egyptians and Africans, the juggler came out on a bare space of ground, leading a small boy, stark-naked, by the hand, and carrying a huge roll of tape that might be twelve or eighteen inches wide.

"After certain ceremonies, he twirled the roll about his head several times, and then flung it straight up into the air. Instead of falling back to earth after it had ascended a short distance, it kept on upward, unwinding and unwinding interminably from the stick, until it grew to be a mere speck, and finally passed out of sight. The juggler drove the pointed end of the stick into the ground, and then beckoned the boy to approach. Pointing upward, and talking in a strange jargon, he seemed to be ordering the little fellow to ascend the self-suspended tape, which by this time stood straight and stiff, as if it were a board whose end rested against some solid support up in mid-air. The boy bowed compliance and began climbing, using his hands and feet.... He went higher and higher until he, too, seemed to pass into the clouds and disappear.

"The juggler waited five or ten minutes, and then, pretending to be impatient, shouted up to his assistant as if to order him down. No answer was heard, and no boy appeared; so, finally, as if carried away with rage, the juggler thrust a naked sword into his breech-clout (the only garment on his person), and climbed after the boy. Up and up and up, hand over hand, and step by step, he ascended until the straining eyes of the multitude saw him no more. There was a moment's pause and then a wild shriek came down from the sky, and a bleeding arm, as if freshly cut from the boy's body, fell with a horrid thud upon the ground. Then came another, then the two legs one after the other, then the dismembered trunk, and last of all, the ghastly head, every part streaming with gore and covering the ground.

"A second lad now stepped forward and, gathering the mutilated fragments of his comrade into a heap, threw a dirty cloth over them and retired. Presently the juggler was seen descending as slowly and cautiously as he had ascended. He reached the ground at last, with his naked sword all dripping with blood. Paying no attention to the remains of his supposed victim, he went on rewinding his tape upon his stick, his audience meanwhile breaking out into cries of impatience and execration. When the tape was all rewound, he wiped his sword and, deliberately stepping to the bloody heap, lifted off the ragged quilt, and up rose the little tape-climber as hearty *as ever*, and bowed and smiled upon the amazed throng as though dismemberment were an after-breakfast pastime to which he had been accustomed from infancy."[6]

We may here add what Mme Blavatsky writes in *Isis Unveiled* about this phenomenon: "In the memoirs of the Emperor Jahangire, the performances of seven jugglers from Bengal, who exhibited before him, are thus described: '*Ninth*. They produced a man whom they divided limb from limb, actually severing his head from the body. They scattered these mutilated members along the ground, and in this state they lay some time. They then extended a sheet over the spot, and one of the men putting himself under the sheet, in a few minutes came from below, followed by the individual supposed to have been cut into joints, in perfect health and condition.'... We have in our possession a picture painted from such a Persian conjurer, with a man, or rather the various limbs of what was a minute before a man, scattered before him. We have seen such conjurers, and witnessed such performances more than once in various places."[7]

CHAPTER VII

Explorations In The Americas

According to Mr. Sinnett's account, Mme Blavatsky visited the American continents three times, as follows: in 1851 she travelled from Canada to Mexico, via New Orleans, also to the West Indies; from 1853 to 1855, she went from New York to San Francisco, crossing the Rocky Mountains with caravans of pioneers; lastly, she went to the United States in July, 1873, remaining until December, 1878, when she left for India, accompanied by Colonel Olcott. According to the list of her travels found by Mrs. Besant, she went to South America in 1851, and to the United States and Central America in 1853-55.

She never kept diaries; and, as Mr. Sinnett remarks: "Memory at a distance of time is a very uncertain guide." When he was trying to elicit information with which to compile her Memoirs, she once wrote impatiently: "To tell you about America! Why goodness me, I may as well try to tell you about a series of dreams I had in my childhood." No account of her adventures in America has come down to us; though, no doubt, there were plenty. Nevertheless, from data which she has given in *Isis Unveiled*, it will be seen that she was in Peru twice; for she says: "Several years after... we again visited Peru." At least we have the following accounts of the knowledge and traditions she collected, of the ancient peoples and their descendants who still dwell in the continents that were once part of the "Lost Atlantis."

"Stephens," she writes, "indulging in the anticipation 'that a key surer than that of the Rosetta-stone will be discovered' by which the American hieroglyphs may be read, says* that the descendants of the Caciques and

---
* In his Incidents of Travel in Central America, Chiapas and Yucatan.

the Aztec subjects are believed to survive still in the inaccessible fastnesses of the Cordilleras —'wildernesses which have never yet been penetrated by a white man.... living as their fathers did, erecting the same buildings.' He adds: 'I turn to that vast and unknown region, wherein fancy pictures that mysterious city seen from the topmost range of the Cordilleras, of unconquered, unvisited, and unsought aboriginal inhabitants.'

"Apart from the fact that this mysterious city has been seen from a great distance by daring travellers, there is no intrinsic improbability of its existence, for who can tell what became of the primitive people who fled before the rapacious brigands of Cortez and Pizarro? Dr. Tschuddi, in his work on Peru, tells us of an Indian legend that a train of 10,000 llamas, laden with gold to complete the Inca's ransom, was arrested in the Andes by tidings of his death, and the enormous treasure was so effectually concealed that not a trace of it has ever been found. He, as well as Prescott and other writers, informs us that the Indians to this day preserve their ancient traditions and sacerdotal caste, and obey implicitly the orders of rulers chosen among themselves, while at the same time nominally Catholics and actually subject to the Peruvian authorities. Magical ceremonies practised by their forefathers still prevail among them, and magical phenomena occur. So persistent are they in their loyalty to the past, that it seems impossible but that they should be in relations with some central source of authority which constantly supports and strengthens their faith, keeping it alive. May it not be that the sources of this undying faith lie in this mysterious city, with which they are in secret communication? Or must we think that all the above is again but a 'curious coincidence'?

"The story of this mysterious city was told to Stephens by a Spanish Padre in 1838-9. The priest swore to him that he had seen it with his own eyes, and gave Stephens the following details, which the traveller firmly believed to be true. 'The Padre of the little village near the ruins of Santa Cruz del Quiche, had heard of the unknown city at the village of Chajul.... He was then young, and climbed with much labour to the naked summit of the topmost ridge of the sierra of the Cordilleras. When arrived at a height of ten or twelve thousand feet, he looked over an immense plain extending to Yucatan and the Gulf of Mexico, and saw, at a great distance, a large city spread over a great space, and with turrets white and glittering in the sun.

"'Tradition says that no white man has ever reached this city; that the inhabitants speak the Maya language, know that strangers have conquered their whole land, and murder any white man who attempts to enter their territory.... They have no coin; no horses, cattle, mules, or other domestic animals except fowls, and the cocks they keep underground to prevent their crowing being heard.'

"Nearly the same was given to us personally about twenty years ago, by an old native priest whom we met in Peru, and with whom we happened to have business relations. He had passed all his life vainly trying to conceal his hatred toward the conquerors — 'brigands' he termed them; and, as he confessed, kept friends with them and the Catholic religion for the sake of his people, but he was as truly a sun-worshipper in his heart as ever he was. He had travelled in his capacity of a *converted* native missionary, and had been at Santa Cruz and, as he solemnly affirmed, had been also to see some of his people by a 'subterranean passage' leading into the mysterious city.

"We believe his account; for a man who is about to die will rarely stop to invent idle stories; and this one we have found corroborated in Stephens' *Travels*. Besides, we know of two other cities utterly unknown to European travellers; not that the inhabitants particularly desire to hide themselves; for people from Buddhistic countries come occasionally to visit them. But their towns are not set down on the European or Asiatic maps; and on account of the too zealous and enterprising Christian missionaries, and perhaps for more mysterious reasons of their own, the few natives of other countries who are aware of the existence of these two cities never mention them. Nature has provided strange nooks and hiding-places for her favourites; and unfortunately it is but far away from so-called civilized countries that man is free to worship the Deity in the way that his fathers did."[1]

The above will remind the reader of Sir Arthur Conan Doyle's story, *The Lost Continent*; and it may be of interest here to quote from an article called "The Book of the Azure Veil," which appeared in *Lucifer* of September, 1894: "Least known of all scriptures accessible to the West is *The Popul Vuh*. A Red man wrote it, some centuries ago, in Guatemala. He had knowledge. Like most men who have knowledge, his name is unknown in the West.... The author of *The Popul Vuh* belonged to a cultured people, who built great cities of hewn stone, with temples vast and imposing.... A few of these people still survive in a part of their country which the foot of no White man has ever pressed; there they follow in freedom and peace their priests who have the soul-sight, cling to the religion of their forefathers, and practise the magic of old.... All the Red men who have remained true to the ancient religion are still under their sway. One of their strong centres was in Guatemala, and of their Order was the author of *The Popul Vuh*"

Says Mme Blavatsky: "The ruins, which cover both Americas and are found on many West Indian islands, are all attributed to the submerged Atlanteans. As well as the hierophants of the old world, which in the days of Atlantis was almost connected with the new by land, the magicians of the now submerged country had a net-work of subterranean passages running in all directions. In connection with these mysterious catacombs, we will now give a curious story told us by a Peruvian long since dead, as we were travelling together in the interior of his country. There must be truth in it, as it was afterwards confirmed to us by an Italian gentleman who had seen the place and who, but for lack of means and time, would have verified the tale himself, at least partially. The informant of the Italian was an old priest, who had the secret divulged to him at confession, by a Peruvian Indian. We may add, moreover, that the priest was compelled to make the revelation, being at the time completely under the mesmeric influence of the traveller.

"The story concerns the famous treasures of the last of the Incas. The Peruvian asserted that since the well-known and miserable murder of the latter by Pizarro, the secret had been known to all the Indians, except the *Mestizos* who could not be trusted. It runs thus: The Inca was made prisoner, and his wife offered for his liberation a room full of gold, 'from the floor up to the ceiling, as high up as his conqueror could reach' before the sun should set on the third day. She kept her promise, but Pizarro broke his word, according to Spanish practice.

"Marvelling at the exhibition of such treasures, the conqueror declared that he would not release the prisoner, but would murder him, unless the Queen revealed the place whence the treasure came. He had heard that the Incas had somewhere an inexhaustible mine; a subterranean road or tunnel running many miles under ground, where were kept the accumulated riches of the country. The unfortunate Queen begged for delay, and went to consult the oracles. During the sacrifice, the chief priest showed her in the consecrated 'black mirror' the unavoidable murder of her husband, whether she delivered the treasures of the crown to Pizarro or not.

"Then the Queen gave the order to close the entrance, which was a door cut in the rocky wall of the chasm. Under the direction of the priest and magicians, the chasm was accordingly filled to the top with huge masses of rock, and the surface covered over so as to conceal the work. The Inca was murdered by the Spaniards, and his unhappy Queen committed suicide. Spanish greed overreached itself, and the secret of the buried treasures was locked in the breasts of a few faithful Peruvians.

"Our Peruvian informant added that, in consequence of certain indiscretions at various times, persons had been sent by different governments to search for the treasure under pretext of scientific exploration. They had rummaged the country through, but without realizing their object. So far this tradition is corroborated by the reports of Dr. Tschuddi and other historians of Peru. But there are certain additional details which we are not aware have been made public before now.

"Several years after hearing the story, and its corroboration by the Italian gentleman, we again visited Peru. Going southward from Lima, by water, we reached a point near Arica at sunset, and were struck by the appearance of an enormous rock, nearly perpendicular, which stood in mournful solitude on the shore, apart from the range of the Andes. It was the tomb of the Incas. As the last rays of the setting sun strike the face of the rock, one can make out, with an ordinary opera-glass, some curious hieroglyphics inscribed on the volcanic surface.

"When Cusco was the capital of Peru, it contained a temple of the sun, famed far and near for its magnificence. It was roofed with thick plates of gold, and the walls were covered with the same precious metal; the eave-troughs were also of solid gold. In the west wall the architects had contrived an aperture in such a way that when the sunbeams touched it, it focused them inside the building. Stretching like a golden chain from one sparkling point to another they encircled the walls, illuminating the grim idols, and disclosing certain mystic signs at other times invisible. It was only by understanding these hieroglyphics — identical with those which may be seen to this day on the tomb of the Incas — that one could learn the secret of the tunnel and its approaches.

"Among the latter was one in the neighbourhood of Cusco, now masked beyond discovery. This leads directly into an immense tunnel which runs from Cusco to Lima, and then, turning southward, extends into Bolivia. At a certain point it is intersected by a royal tomb. Inside this sepulchral chamber are cunningly arranged two doors; or rather, two enormous slabs which turn upon pivots, and close so tightly as to be only distinguishable from the other portions of the sculptured walls by the secret signs, whose key is in the possession of the faithful custodians. One of these turning slabs covers the southern mouth of the Liman tunnel — the other, the northern one of the Bolivian corridor. The latter, running southward, passes through Trapaca and Cobijo, for Arica is not far away from the little river called Payquina, which is the boundary between Peru and Bolivia.

"Not far from this spot stand three separate peaks which form a curious triangle; they are included in the chain of the Andes. According to tradition, the only practicable entrance to the corridor leading northward is in one of these peaks; but without the secret of its landmarks, a regiment of Titans might rend the rocks in vain in an attempt to find it. But even were someone to gain an entrance and find his way as far as the turning slab in the wall of the sepulchre, and attempt to blast it out, the superincumbent rocks are so disposed as to bury the tomb, its treasures, and — as the mysterious Peruvian expressed it to us — 'a thousand warriors' in one common ruin. There is no other access to the Arica chamber but through the door in the mountain near Payquina. Along the entire length of the corridor, from Bolivia to Lima and Cusco, are smaller hiding-places filled with treasures of gold and precious stones, the accumulations of many generations of Incas, the aggregate value of which is incalculable.

"We have in our possession an accurate plan of the tunnel, the sepulchre, and the doors, given to us at the time by the old Peruvian.* If we had ever thought of profiting by the secret, *it* would have required the co-operation of the Peruvian and Bolivian governments on an extensive scale. To say nothing of physical obstacles, no one individual or small party could undertake such an exploration without encountering the army of smugglers and brigands with which the coast is infested; and which, in fact, includes nearly the whole population. The mere task of purifying the mephitic air of the tunnel, which has not been entered for centuries, would also be a serious one. There, however, the treasure lies, and there the tradition says it will lie, till the last vestige of Spanish rule disappears from the whole of North and South America.

"The treasures exhumed by Dr. Schliemann at Mycenae have awakened

* It is in the Archives of the Theosophical Society.

popular cupidity, and the eyes of adventurous speculators are being turned toward the localities where the wealth of ancient peoples is supposed to be buried, in crypt or cave, or beneath sand or alluvial deposit. Around no other locality, not even Peru, hang so many traditions as around the Gobi Desert. In Independent Tartary this howling waste of shifting sand was once, if report speaks correctly, the seat of one of the richest empires the world ever saw.

"Beneath the surface are said to lie such wealth of gold, jewels, statuary, arms, utensils, and all that indicates civilization, luxury and fine arts, as no existing capital of Christendom can show to-day. The Gobi sand moves regularly from east to west before terrific gales that blow continually. Occasionally some of the hidden treasures are uncovered, but not a native dare touch them, for the whole district is under the ban of a mighty spell. Death would be the penalty. Bahti — hideous, but faithful gnomes — guard the hidden treasures of this prehistoric people, awaiting the day when the revolution of cyclic periods shall again cause their story to be known for the instruction of mankind.

"According to local tradition, the tomb of Ghengiz Khan still exists near Lake Tabasun Nor. Within lies the Mongolian Alexander, as though asleep. After three more centuries he will awake and lead his people to new victories and another harvest of glory. Though this prophetic tradition be received with ever so many grains of salt, we can affirm that the tomb itself is no fiction, nor has its amazing richness been exaggerated.

"The district of the Gobi wilderness and, in fact, the whole area of Independent Tartary and Thibet is jealously guarded against foreign intrusion. Those who are permitted to traverse it are under the particular care and pilotage of certain agents of the chief authority, and are in duty bound to convey no intelligence respecting places and persons to the outside world. But for this restriction, even we might contribute to these pages accounts of exploration, adventure, and discovery that would be read with interest. The time will come, sooner or later, when the dreadful sand of the desert will yield up its long-buried secrets, and then there will be unlooked-for mortifications for our modern vanity."[2]

That H. P. B. had an object in her American travels, there can be no doubt. She went to Mexico in 1851; she visited Peru twice, and speaks of having "business relations" with "an old native priest of Peru," and of "travelling together, in the interior of his country," with a "mysterious Peruvian." When, in 1872, her travels were finished and her life-work began, the first thing she did was to try to "spiritualise Spiritualism"; and it was only when that effort failed, that she was instrumental in founding the Theosophical Society.

CHAPTER VIII

Her Master

We come now to the subject of Helena Petrovna's Master. No argument or evidence on this subject can be offered in a biographical sketch. Statements in this book will be confined to her own declarations and the events of her life.

She wrote to Mr. Sinnett, when he was pressing her for materials for her Memoirs: "I saw Master in my visions ever since my childhood. In the year of the first Nepaul Embassy (when?)* saw and recognised him. Saw him twice. Once he came out of the crowd, then he ordered me to meet him in Hyde Park. I *cannot*, I *must not* speak of this."[1]

Of her second trip to London, she says: "Visit to London? I was in London and France with father in '44, not 1851. This latter year I was alone and lived in Cecil Street in furnished rooms at one time, then at Mivert's Hotel, but as I was with the old Countess Bagration, and when she went away remained with her Jezebel *demoiselle de compagnie*, no one knows *my* name there. Lived also in a big hotel somewhere between City and Strand or in the Strand, but as to names or numbers you might just as well ask me to tell you what was the number of the house you lived in during your last incarnation."[2]

Countess Wachtmeister, in her *Reminiscences of H.P. Blavatsky*,[3] gives the story of Helena Petrovna meeting her Master: "During her childhood she had often seen near her an Astral form, that always seemed to come in any moment of danger, and save her just at the critical point.† H.P.B. had learnt to look upon this Astral form as a guardian angel, and felt that she

---

* 1850-51, Jung Bahadur paid a visit to England.
† See Mme Pissareff's account of this, in Chapter I.

was under his care and guidance.

"When she was in London, in 1851, with her father, Colonel Hahn,* she was one day out walking when, to her astonishment, she saw a tall Hindu in the street with some Indian princes. She immediately recognised him as the same person that she had seen in the Astral. Her first impulse was to rush forward and speak to him, but he made her a sign not to move, and she stood as if spellbound while he passed on."

Countess Wachtmeister continues her account: "The next day she went into Hyde Park for a stroll, that she might be alone and free to think over her extraordinary adventure. Looking up, she saw the same form approaching her, and then her Master told her that he had come to London with the Indian princes on an important mission, and he was desirous of meeting her personally, as he required her co-operation in a work which he was about to undertake. He then told her how the Theosophical Society was to be formed, and that he wished her to be the founder. He gave her a slight sketch of all the troubles she would have to undergo, and also told her that she would have to spend three years in Tibet to prepare her for the important task.

"After three days' serious consideration and consultation with her father,† H. P. B. decided to accept the offer made to her, and shortly afterwards left London for India.

"In Würzburg a curious incident occurred [1885-6]. Mme Fadeef — H. P. B.'s aunt — wrote to her that she was sending a box to the Ludwigstrasse, containing what seemed to her a lot of rubbish. The box arrived, and to me was deputed the task of unpacking it. As I took out one thing after another and passed them to Mme Blavatsky, I heard her give an exclamation of delight, and she said: 'Come and look at this which I wrote in the year 1851, the day I saw my blessed Master'; and there in a scrapbook in faded writing, I saw a few lines in which H. P. B. described the above interview. This scrap-book we still have in our possession. I copy the lines:

> 'Nuit mémorable! Certaines nuits au clair de lune qui se couchait à Ramsgate 12 Aout:* 1851 lorsque je rencontrais M∴ le Maitre de mes reves!!

---

* An error, as will be seen by H. P. B.'s statement above.
† Her father did give his consent to the Master's plan.

* Le 12 Août c'est Juillet 31 style russe jour de ma naissance — *Vingt ans!'"*

"*Memorable night! On a certain night by the light of the moon that was setting at Ramsgate on August 12,* 1851 when I met M∴ the Master of my dreams!!*
August 12 is July 31 in the Russian calendar, the day of my birth — Twenty years!"

The "scrap-book" which the Countess Wachtmeister mentions is really a sketch-book, and is in the Archives of the Theosophical Society. The above is written beneath a sketch of some boats on a stretch of water,* The Countess goes on to say: "On seeing the manuscript I asked why she had written 'Ramsgate' instead of 'London,' and H.P.B. told me that it was a blind, so that anyone casually taking up her book would not know where she had met her Master, and that her first interview with him had been in London†, as she had previously told me."

---

* Facsimile, and account of the sketch-book in *The Theosophist* of January, 1935.
† For a third account of this meeting, see Chapter XIII.

CHAPTER IX

Seeking The Master

The Countess Wachtmeister remarks that, after meeting her Master, Mme Blavatsky left London for India. She was a long time on the way, however — considerably over a year, visiting (according to Mr. Sinnett's itinerary) Canada, New Orleans, Texas, and Mexico *en route*; and (according to Mrs. Besant's list) South America and the Pacific Islands, and arriving in Bombay only at the end of 1852.

She visited North America, says Mr. Sinnett, "prompted by a passionate enthusiasm for the North American Indians, contracted from the perusal of Fennimore Cooper's novels.... In 1851 she went in pursuit of the Red Indians of her imagination to Canada.... At Quebec (she believes it was) a party of Indians were introduced to her. She was delighted to encounter the sons of the forest, and even the daughters thereof, their squaws. With some of these she settled down for a long gossip over the mysterious doings of the medicine men. Eventually they disappeared, and with them various articles of Madame's personal property — especially a pair of boots that she greatly prized, and which the resources of Quebec in those days could not replace. The Red Indian of actual fact thus ruined the ideal she had constructed in her fancy. She gave up her search for their wigwams, and developed a new programme....

"Mexico looked an inviting region in which to risk her life next, and she made her way, in the meanwhile, to New Orleans.... Here the principal interest of her visit centred in the Voodoos, a sect of negroes, natives of the West Indies, and half-castes, addicted to a form of magic practices that no highly-trained occult student would have anything to do with, but which nevertheless presented attractions to Mme Blavatsky, not yet far advanced enough in the knowledge held in reserve for her to distinguish 'black' from 'white' varieties of mystic exercise.... She might have been drawn dangerously far into association with them;... but the strange guardianship that had so often asserted itself to her advantage during her childhood — which had by this time assumed a more definite shape, for she had now met as a living man the long familiar figure of her visions — again came to her rescue. She was warned in a vision of the risk that she was running with the Voodoos, and at once moved off to fresh fields and pastures new.

"She went through Texas to Mexico, and contrived to see a good deal of that insecure country, protected in these hazardous travels by her own reckless daring, and by various people who from time to time interested themselves in her welfare.... She passed through rough communities of all kinds, savage as well as civilised, and seems to have been guarded from harm, as assuredly she was guarded, by the sheer force of her own fearlessness, and her fierce scorn for all considerations however remotely associated with the 'magnetism of sex.'"[1]

Here it may be as well to add that she was also protected by the fact that she travelled in men's clothing. She wrote to Mr. Sinnett: "Suppose I were to tell that *I was in man's clothes* (for I was very thin then) which is solemn truth, what would people say? So I was in Egypt with the old Countess [Kisselev] who liked to see me dressed as *a man student*, 'gentleman student,' she said. Now you understand my difficulties? That which would pass with any other as eccentricity, oddity, would serve now only to *incriminate* me in the eyes of the world."[2]

"During her American travels, which lasted about a year, she was lucky enough to receive a considerable legacy, bequeathed to her by one of her godmothers. This put her splendidly in funds for a time, though it is much to be regretted on her account that the money was not served out to her in moderate installments, for the temperament, which the facts of her life so far even will have revealed, may easily be recognised as one not likely to go with habits of prudent expenditure.... She is wholly unable to explain how she ran through her 80,000 roubles, except that amongst other random purchases she bought land in America, the very situation of which she has long since totally forgotten, besides having, as a matter of course, lost all the papers that had any reference to the transaction."[3] Says Colonel Olcott: "She told me that she spent within two years a legacy of 85,000 roubles (about 170,000 rupees) left her by her grandmother, in desultory wandering over the world. A good part of the time she had with her a huge Newfoundland dog, which she led by a heavy gold chain."4

"She resolved, during her Mexican wanderings, that she would go to India, fully alive already to the necessity of seeking beyond the northern frontiers of that country for the further acquaintance of those great teachers of the highest mystic science, with whom the guardian of her visions was associated in her mind. She wrote, therefore, to a certain Englishman, whom she had met in Germany two years before, and whom she knew to be on the same quest as herself,* to join her in the West Indies, in order that they might go to the East together. He duly came, but the party was further augmented by the addition of a Hindu whom Mme Blavatsky met at Copan, in Mexico, and whom she soon ascertained to be what is called a 'chela' or pupil of the Masters, or adepts of oriental occult science. The three pilgrims of mysticism went out via the Cape to Ceylon, and thence in a sailing-ship to Bombay, where, as I make out the dates, they must have arrived at quite the end of 1852.

"A dispersion of the little party soon followed, each being bent on somewhat different ends. Madame would not accept the guidance of the chela, and was bent on an attempt of her own to get into Tibet, through Nepal. For the time her attempt failed, chiefly, she believes, through the opposition of the British Resident then in Nepal 5.

"On the 3rd of March, 1893," writes Colonel Olcott, "S. V. Edge and I met in the train between Nalhati and Calcutta, Major-General C. Murray (retired), late of the 70th Bengal Infantry, now Chairman of the Monghyr Municipality, who met H. P. B. in 1854 or '55,† at Punkabaree, at the feet of the Darjeeling Hills. He was then a Captain, commanding the Sebundy Sappers and Miners. She was trying to get into Tibet via Nepal 'to write a book'; and to do it, she wished to cross the Rungit river. Captain Murray had it reported to him by the guard that a European lady had passed that way, so he went after and brought her back. She was very angry, but in vain. She stopped with Captain and Mrs. Murray for about a month when,

---

* Is this the Captain Remington of whom Master K. H. wrote in 1880 : "There is a distinct section in our community who attend to our very rare accessions from another race and blood, and who brought across the threshold Captain Remington and two other Englishmen during this century"? (*The Mahatma Letters*, 19.)

† Confusion of dates ; should be 1853. She was not in India in 1854.

finding her plan defeated, she left, and Captain Murray heard of her as far as Dinajpore. She was then apparently about thirty years of age.

"The above facts were so interesting that I wrote them out in the railway carriage and got General Murray to append his certificate, as follows: 'The above memo is correct. C. Murray, Major-General'

"The British Resident probably did have something to do indirectly with her detention, for strict orders had been given by Captain Murray, in military command of that Frontier District, to permit no European to cross the Rungit, as they would be almost sure of being murdered by the wild tribes in that country.

"I got trace of another of her Tibetan attempts from a Hindu gentleman living at Bareilly, while on one of my North Indian official tours. The first time H.P.B. came to that station after our arrival in India, this gentleman recognised her as the European lady who had been his guest many years before, when she was going northward to try and enter Tibet via Kashmir. They had much pleasant chat about old times."[6]

This second attempt to enter Tibet through Kashmir occurred in 1856. When her first effort of 1853 had been frustrated, Mme Blavatsky "went down to Southern India then on to Java and Singapore, returning thence to England," says Mr. Sinnett. "1853, however, was an unfortunate year for a Russian to visit England. The preparations for the Crimean War were distressing to Mme Blavatsky's patriotism, and she passed over at the end of the year again to America, going this time to New York, and thence out West, first to Chicago, then an infant city compared to the Chicago of the present day, and afterwards to the Far West, and across the Rocky Mountains with emigrants' caravans, till ultimately she brought up for a time in San Francisco. Her stay in America was prolonged on this occasion to something like two years, and she then made her way for a second time to India via Japan and the Straits, reaching Calcutta in the course of 1855....

"During her travels in India in 1856 she was overtaken at Lahore by a German gentleman known to her father (Külwein), who — in association with two friends, having laid out a journey in the East on his own account, with a mystic purpose in view, in reference to which fate did not grant him the success that attended Mme Blavatsky's efforts — had been asked by Colonel Hahn to try if he could find his errant daughter."[7]

Says Mme Blavatsky herself: "Went to India in 1856 — just because I was longing for Master. Travelled from place to place, never said I was Russian, people taking me for what I liked. Met Külwein and his friend at Lahore somewhere. Were I to describe my visit to India only in that year, that would make a whole book,* but how can I now say the truth?"[8]

Mr. Sinnett proceeds: "The four compatriots travelled together for a time, and went through Kashmir to Leh† in Ladakh in company with a Tartar Shaman, who was instrumental in helping them to witness some psychological wonders at a Buddhist monastery.... The Tartar Shaman rendered Mme Blavatsky more substantial assistance in her efforts to penetrate Tibet than he was able to afford her companions. Investing her with an appropriate disguise, he conducted her successfully across the frontier, and far on into the generally inaccessible country." But let Mme Blavatsky relate these adventures in her own words.

---

* She did incorporate the story of this visit, perhaps also incidents of the previous one, in a book, *From the Caves and Jungles of Hindustan*, and they form Chapters XI, XII, XIII, and XIV of the present work.

† Misprinted as "Leli," in *Incidents in the Life of Mme Blavatsky*.

CHAPTER X

Adventures In Tibet

"Years ago, a small party of travellers were painfully journeying from Kashmir to Leh, a city of Ladahk (Central Tibet). Among our guides we had a Tartar Shaman, a very mysterious personage, who spoke Russian a little and English not at all, and who yet managed, nevertheless, to converse with us, and proved of great service. Having learned that some of our party were Russians, he had imagined that our protection was all-powerful, and might enable him to safely find his way back to his Siberian home, from which, for reasons unknown, some twenty years before he had fled, as he told us, via Kiatcha and the great Gobi Desert, to the land of the Tcha-gars.* With such an interested object in view, we believed ourselves safe under his guard.

"To explain the situation briefly: Our companions had formed the unwise plan of penetrating into Thibet, under various disguises, none of them speaking the language, although one, a Mr. K[ülwein], had picked up some Kasan Tartar, and thought he did. As we mention this only incidentally, we may as well say at once that two of them, the brothers N———, were very politely brought back to the frontier before they had walked sixteen miles into the weird land of Eastern Bod; and Mr. K———, an ex-Lutheran minister, could not even attempt to leave his miserable village near Leh, as from the first days he found himself prostrated with fever, and had to return to Lahore *via* Kashmere.

"But one sight seen by him was as good as if he had witnessed the reincarnation of Buddha itself. Having heard of this 'miracle' from some old

---

* Russian subjects were not allowed to cross the Tartar territory, neither the subjects of the Emperor of China to go to the Russian factories.

Russian missionary in whom he thought he could have more faith than in Abbé Hue, it had been for years his desire to expose the 'great heathen' jugglery, as he expressed it. K—— was a positivist, and rather prided himself on this anti-philosophical neologism. But his positivism was doomed to receive a deathblow.

"About four days' journey from Islamabad, at an insignificant mud village, whose only redeeming feature was its magnificent lake, we stopped for a few days' rest. Our companions had temporarily separated from us, and the village was to be our place of meeting. It was there that we were apprised by the Shaman that a large party of Lamaic 'Saints' on pilgrimage to various shrines, had taken up their abode in an old cave-temple and established a temporary Vihara* therein. He added that, as the 'Three Honourable Ones'† were said to travel along with them, the holy Bikshus (monks) were capable of producing the greatest miracles, Mr. K——, fired with the prospect of exposing this humbug of the ages, proceeded at once to pay them a visit, and from that moment the most friendly relations were established between the two camps.

"The Vihara was in a secluded and most romantic spot, secured against all intrusion. Despite the effusive attentions, presents, and protestations of Mr. K——, the Chief, who was Pase-Budhu (an ascetic of great sanctity), declined to exhibit the phenomenon of the 'incarnation' until a certain talisman in possession of the writer was exhibited. Upon seeing this, however, preparations were at once made, and an infant of three or four months was procured from its mother, a poor woman of the neighbourhood.

"An oath was first of all exacted from Mr. K—— that he would not divulge what he might see or hear, for the space of seven years. The talisman is a simple agate or carnelian‡ known among the Thibetans and others as

---

* Monastery.

† These are the representatives of the Buddhist Trinity — Buddha, Dharma, and Sangha ; or Fo, Fa, and Sengh, as they are called in Thibet.

‡ These stones are highly venerated among Lamaists and Buddhists ; the throne and sceptre of Buddha are ornamented with them, and the Dalai Lama wears one on the fourth finger of his right hand. They are found in the Altai Mountains, and near the River Yarkuh. Our talisman was a gift from the venerable high-priest, a Heiloung, of a Kalmuck tribe. Though treated as apostates from their primitive Lamaism, these nomads maintain friendly relations with their brother Kalmucks, the Chokhots of Eastern Thibet and Kokonor, and even with the Lamaists of Lha-Ssa. The ecclesiastical authorities, however, will have no relations with them. We have had abundant opportunities to become acquainted with this interesting people of the Astrakhan Steppes, having lived in their *kibitkas* in our early years, and partaken of the lavish hospitality of the Prince Tumene, their late chief, and his Princess....

A-yu, and naturally possessed, or had been endowed with very mysterious properties. It has a triangle engraved upon it, within which are contained a few mystical words.

"Several days passed before everything was ready; nothing of a mysterious character occurring meanwhile, except that, at the bidding of a Bikshu, ghastly faces were made to peep at us out of the glassy bosom of the lake, as we sat at the door of the Vihara upon its bank. One of these was the countenance of Mr. K——'s sister, whom he had left well and happy at home, but who, as we subsequently learned, had died some time before he had set out on the present journey. The sight affected him at first, but he called his scepticism to his aid, and quieted himself with theories of cloud-shadows, reflections of tree-branches, etc., such as people of his kind fall back upon.

"On the appointed afternoon, the baby being brought to the Vihara, was left in the vestibule or reception-room, as K—— could go no farther into the temporary sanctuary. The child was then placed on a bit of carpet in the middle of the floor, and everyone not belonging to the party being sent away, two 'mendicants' were placed at the entrance to keep out intruders. Then all the lamas seated themselves on the floor, with their backs against the granite walls, so that each was separated from the child by a space of, at least, ten feet. The chief, having had a square piece of leather spread for him by the *desservant*, seated himself at the farthest corner.

"Alone, Mr. K—— placed himself close to the infant, and watched every movement with intense interest. The only condition exacted of us was that we should preserve a strict silence, and patiently await further developments. A bright sunlight streamed through the open door. Gradually the 'Superior' fell into what seemed a state of profound meditation, while the others, after a short *sotto voce* invocation, became suddenly silent, and looked as if they had become completely petrified. It was oppressively still, and the crowing of the child was the only sound to be heard.

"After we had sat there a few moments, the movements of the infant's limbs suddenly ceased, and his body appeared to become rigid. K—— watched intently every motion, and both of us, by a rapid glance, became satisfied that all present were sitting motion less. The Superior, with his gaze fixed upon the ground, did not even look at the infant; but, pale and motionless, he seemed rather like a bronze statue of a Talapoin in meditation than a living being.

"Suddenly, to our great consternation, we saw the child, not raise itself, but, as it were, violently jerked into a sitting posture! A few more jerks, and then, like an automaton set in motion by concealed wires, the four months baby stood upon its feet! Fancy our consternation, and in Mr. K——'s case, horror. Not a hand had been outstretched, not a motion made, nor a word spoken; and yet, here was a baby-in-arms standing erect and firm as a man!

"The rest of the story we will quote from a copy of the notes written on this subject by Mr. K——, the same evening, and given to us, in case it should not reach its place of destination, or the writer fail to see anything more.

"'After a minute or two of hesitation,' writes K——, 'the baby turned his head and looked at me with an expression of intelligence that was simply awful! It sent a chill through me. I pinched my hands and bit my lips till the blood came, to make sure that I did not dream. But this was only the beginning. The miraculous creature, making, *as I fancied*, two steps towards me, resumed his sitting posture and, without removing his eyes from mine, repeated, sentence by sentence, in what I supposed to be Thibetan language, the very words, which I had been told in advance, are commonly spoken at the incarnations of Buddha, beginning with "I am Buddha; I am the old Lama; I am his spirit in a new body," etc.

"'I felt a real terror; my hair rose upon my head, and my blood ran cold. For my life I could not have spoken a word. There was no trickery here, no ventriloquism. The infant lips moved, and the eyes seemed to search my very soul with an expression that *made me think it was the face of the Superior himself*, his eyes, his very look that I was gazing upon. It was *as if his spirit had entered the little body, and was looking at me through the transparent mask of the baby's face.*

"'I felt my brain growing dizzy. The infant reached toward me, and laid his little hand upon mine. I started as if I had been touched by a hot coal; and, unable to bear the scene any longer, covered my face with my hands. It was but for a moment; but when I removed them, the little actor had become a crowing baby again; and a moment after, lying upon its back, set up a fretful cry. The Superior had resumed his normal condition, and conversation ensued.

"'It was only after a series of similar experiments, extending over ten days, that I realised the fact that I had seen the incredible, astounding phenomenon described by certain travellers, but always by me denounced as an imposture. Among a multitude of questions unanswered, despite my cross-examination, the Superior let drop one piece of information, which must be regarded as highly significant. "What would have happened," I inquired, through the Shaman, "if, while the infant was speaking, in a moment of insane fright, at the thought of its being the 'Devil,' I had killed it?" He replied that, if the blow had not been instantly fatal, the child *alone* would have been killed. "But," I continued, "suppose it had been as swift as a lightning-flash?" "In such case," was the answer, "you would have killed me also.""[1]

"We have mentioned a kind of carnelian stone in our possession, which had such an unexpected and favourable effect upon the Shaman's decision. Every Shaman has such a talisman, which he wears attached to a string, and carries under his left arm.

"'Of what use is it to you, and what are its virtues?' was the question we often offered to our guide. To this he never answered directly, but evaded all explanation, promising that as soon as an opportunity was offered, and we were alone, he would ask the stone *to answer for himself.* With this very indefinite hope, we were left to the resources of our own imagination.

"But the day on which the stone 'spoke' came very soon. It was during the most critical hours of our life; at a time when the vagabond nature of a traveller had carried the writer to far-off lands, where neither civilisation is known, nor security can be guaranteed for one hour. One afternoon, as every man and woman had left the *yourta* (Tartar tent) that had been our home for over two months, to witness the ceremony of the Lamaic exorcism of a Tshoutgour,* accused of breaking and spiriting away every bit of the poor furniture and earthenware of a family living about two miles distant, the Shaman, who had become our only protector in those dreary deserts, was reminded of his promise.

"He sighed and hesitated, but after a short silence, left his place on the sheepskin and, going outside, placed a dried-up goat's head with its prominent horns over a wooden peg, and then dropping down the felt curtain of the tent, remarked that now no living person would venture in, for the goat's head was a sign that he was 'at work.'

"After that, placing his hand in his bosom, he drew out the little stone,

---

* An elemental daemon, in which every native of Asia believes.

about the size of a walnut, and carefully unwrapping it, proceeded, as it appeared, to swallow it. In a few moments his limbs stiffened, his body became rigid, and he fell, cold and motionless as a corpse. But for a slight twitching of his lips at every question asked, the scene would have been embarrassing, nay — dreadful.

"The sun was setting, and were it not that dying embers flickered at the centre of the tent, complete darkness would have been added to the oppressive silence which reigned. We have lived in the prairies of the West, and in the boundless steppes of Southern Russia; but nothing can be compared with the silence at sunset on the sandy deserts of Mongolia; not even the barren solitudes of the deserts of Africa, though the former are partially inhabited, and the latter utterly void of life. Yet, there was the writer alone with what looked no better than a corpse lying on the ground. Fortunately, this state did not last long.

"'Mahandu!' uttered a voice, which seemed to come from the bowels of the earth, on which the Shaman was prostrated. 'Peace be with you... what would you have me do for you?'"

"Startling as the fact seemed, we were quite prepared for it, for we had seen other Shamans pass through similar performances.

"'Whoever you are,' we pronounced mentally, 'go to K——, and try to bring that person's thought here. See what that other party does, and tell... what we are doing and how situated.'

"'I am there,' answered the same voice. 'The old lady (Kokona) is sitting in the garden... she is putting on her spectacles and reading a letter.'

"'The contents of it, and hasten,' was the hurried order while preparing note-book and pencil. The contents were given slowly, as if, while dictating, the invisible presence desired to afford us time to put down the words phonetically, for we recognised the Valachian language of which we know nothing beyond the ability to recognise it. In such a way a whole page was filled.

"'Look west... toward the third pole of the *yourta*,' pronounced the Tartar in his natural voice, though it sounded hollow, and as if coming from afar. 'Her thought is here.'

"Then with a convulsive jerk, the upper portion of the Shaman's body seemed raised, and his head fell heavily on the writer's feet, which he clutched with both hands. The position was becoming less and less attractive, but curiosity proved a good ally to courage. In the west corner was standing, life-like but flickering, unsteady and mist-like, the form of a dear old friend, a Roumanian lady of Valachia, a mystic by disposition, but a thorough disbeliever in this kind of occult phenomena.

"'Her thought is here, but her body is lying unconscious. We could not bring her here otherwise,' said the voice.

"We addressed and supplicated the apparition to answer, but all in vain. The features moved, and the form gesticulated as if in fear and agony, but no sound broke forth from the shadowy lips; only we imagined — perchance it was a fancy — hearing as if from a long distance the Roumanian words: '*Non se pôte*!' (It cannot be done.)

"For over two hours, the most substantial, unequivocal proofs that the Shaman's astral soul was travelling at the bidding of our unspoken wish, were given us. Ten months later, we received a letter from our Valachian friend in response to ours, in which we had enclosed the page from the note-book, inquiring of her what she had been doing on that day, and describing the scene in full. She was sitting — she wrote — in the garden on that morning,* prosaically occupied in boiling some conserves; the letter sent to her was word for word the copy of the one received by her from her brother; all at once — in consequence of the heat, she thought — she fainted, and remembered distinctly *dreaming* she saw the writer in a desert place which she accurately described, and sitting under a 'gypsy tent,' as she expressed it. 'Henceforth,' she added, 'I can doubt no longer.'

"But our experiment was proved still better. We had directed the Shaman's inner *ego* to the same friend heretofore mentioned in this chapter, the Kutchi of Lha-Ssa, who travels constantly to British India and back. We *know* that he was apprised of our critical situation in the desert; for a few hours later came help, and we were rescued by a party of twenty-five horsemen who had been directed by their chief to find us at the place where we were, which no living man endowed with common powers could have known. The chief of this escort was a Shaberon, an 'adept' whom we had never seen before, nor did we after that, for he never left his *soumay* (lamasery), and we could have no access to it. But *he was a personal friend of the Kutchi.*

---

* The hour in Bucharest corresponded perfectly with that of the country in which the scene had taken place.

"The above will, of course, provoke naught but incredulity in the general reader. But we write for those who will believe; who, like the writer, understand and know the illimitable powers and possibilities of the human astral soul. In this case we willingly believe, nay, we know, that the 'spiritual double' of the Shaman did not act alone, for he was no adept, but simply a medium. According to a favourite expression of his, as soon as he placed the stone in his mouth, his 'father appeared, dragged him out of his skin, and took him wherever he wanted,' and at his bidding."[2]

CHAPTER XI

With The Master In India

Though she had penetrated into Tibet in 1856, Mme Blavatsky did not succeed in reaching her Master's *ashrama*. This does not imply not seeing him. He may have come to India, and she may have met him there, during both her visits of 1852-3 and 1855-7. Mr. Sinnett asserts on her authority that her occult training began in her twenty-fifth year, 1856 ; and he says that " she was directed by her occult guardian to leave the country [India] shortly before the troubles which began in 1857 "[1] ; namely, the Sepoy Rebellion.

She says : " Master ordered me to go to Java for a certain business. There were two whom I suspected always of being *chelas* there. I saw one of them in 1869 at the Mahatma's house and recognised him, but he denied."[2] This indicates that she was now definitely enrolled in her Master's service, and given commissions to execute for him here and there about the world.

Testimony as to her meeting and travelling with her Master in India comes from another source. In April, 1879, she and Colonel Olcott paid a visit to the Karli Caves, not far from Bombay. He gives an account of it in *Old Diary Leaves*, II,[3] and she in *From the Caves and Jungles of Hindustan*,[4] the latter being a collection of letters she wrote for the *Russky Vyestnik* at the time.

Colonel Olcott makes the party consist of " H. P. B., Mooljee Thakersey and me ; our servant Babula accompanied us." She says : " We were accompanied by three Hindu friends.... At the station our party was joined by two more natives, with whom we had been in correspondence for many a year.... One was a Brahman from Poona, the second a Moodeliar (landowner) from Madras, the third a Singhalese from Kegalla, the fourth a Bengali Zemindar, and the fifth a gigantic Rajput, whom we had known for a long time by the name of Gulab-Lal-Singh, and had simply called Gulab-Singh."*

Why this discrepancy in the two accounts? The reason appears in one of her letters to Mr. Sinnett, wherein she is expostulating with Sellin for questioning the truth of her story, *Can the Double Murder*? because she had altered a date. She claims the licence of the author, and says: "I wrote *stories*, on facts that happened hither and thither, with living persons, only changing names.... Was I writing my diary or confessions, to be honour-bound to give the facts as they happened, years and names?... It is like my *Russian Letters* from India, where while describing a fictitious journey or tour through India with Thornton's *Gazeteer* as my guide, I yet give there true *facts* and true personages, only bringing in together within three of four months' time, facts and events scattered all throughout years, as some of Master's phenomena. Is it a crime that?"[5]

One more explanatory incident, and we may launch forth on these adventures with the Master. V. S. Solovyoff was calling on her in Paris, May, 1884. "Are you here for long?" "I do not know myself yet; the Master sent me." "What master?" "My Master, the teacher, my Guru; you may call him Gulab Lai Singh, from the *Caves and Jungles of Hindustan*."[6]

After a day's exploration of the Karli Caves, and a visit to the Fair in progress nearby, the party settled down for the night on the verandah of one of the smaller chambers. Note the different treatment of this episode by the Colonel and H.P.B. He writes: "We had a warm supper served to us in the cave-porch, and then after admiring the moonlit panorama, and having a last smoke, all rolled ourselves in our blankets and lay down on the rock floor and slept quietly until morning. Babu Rao sat at the porch-door and tended a wood-fire burning as a protection against wild beasts.... The *Caves and Jungles* story about... the night attack on us by a huge tiger is all fiction."

She writes: "A supper was arranged after the Eastern fashion, on carpets spread upon the floor, and with thick banana leaves for plates and dishes. The noiselessly gliding steps of the servants, more silent than ghosts, their white muslins and red turbans, the limitless depths of space, lost in waves of moonlight, before us, and behind the dark vaults of ancient caves, dug out by unknown races, in unknown times, in honour of an unknown, prehistoric religion — all these, our surroundings, transported us into a strange

---

* In a marginal note of his copy of *Caves and Jungles*, Colonel Olcott has written here: "A Master — unseen."

world, and into distant epochs far different from our own."

The "distant epoch far different" was, no doubt, the occasion of a former visit to the Karli Caves, with a different party, including Gulab Lai Singh. She writes: "I shall dwell upon his personality because the most wonderful and diverse stories were in circulation about this strange man. It was asserted that he belonged to the sect of Raj-Yogis, and was an initiate of the mysteries of magic, alchemy, and various other occult sciences of India. He was rich and independent, and rumour did not dare to suspect him of deception, the more so because, though quite full of these sciences, he never uttered a word about them in public, and carefully concealed his knowledge from all except a few friends.

"He was an independent Takur from Rajistan, a province the name of which means the land of kings. Takurs are, almost without exception, descended from Surya (the sun), and are accordingly called Surya-vansa. They are prouder than any other nation in the world. They have a proverb: 'The dirt of the earth cannot stick to the rays of the sun.... England did not disarm the Rajputs, as she did the rest of the Indian nations, so Gulab-Singh came accompanied by vassals and shield-bearers.... (pp. 45-46)

"The Takurs of Rajputana, who are said to possess some of the underground libraries,* occupy in India a position similar to the position of European feudal barons of the Middle Ages. Nominally they are dependent on some of the native princes or on the British Government; but *de facto* they are perfectly independent. Their castles are built on high rocks, and besides the natural difficulty of entering them, their possessors are made doubly unreachable by the fact that long secret passages exist in every such castle, known only to the present owner and confided to his heir at his death. We have visited two such underground halls, one of them big enough to contain a village. No torture would ever induce the owners to disclose the secret of their entrance, but the Yogis and the initiated Adepts come and go freely, entirely trusted by the Takurs. A similar story is told concerning the libraries and subterranean passages of Karli.... (pp. 70-71)

"Kandala is nothing but a big village situated on the flat top of one of the mountains of the Sahiadra range, about 2200 feet above sea level. It is

---

* "Some of these libraries, filled with the most precious manuscripts, are in the possession of native princes and of pagodas attached to their territory, but the greater part are in the hands of the Jainas and of the Rajput Takurs, whose ancient hereditary castles are scattered all over Rajistan, like so many eagles' nests on high rocks." (Page 69)

surrounded by isolated peaks. One of them looks exactly like a long, one-storied building, with a flat roof and battlemented parapet. The Hindus assert that, somewhere about this hillock, there exists a secret entrance, leading into vast interior halls, in fact to a whole subterranean palace, and that there still exist people who possess the secret of this abode. A holy hermit, Yogi, and Magus, who had inhabited these caves for' many centuries' imparted this secret to Sivaji, the celebrated leader of the Mahratta armies. Like Tanhauser in Wagner's opera, the unconquerable Sivaji spent seven years in this mysterious abode, and therein acquired his extraordinary strength and valour." (pp. 59-60)

At this point in her narrative, H. P. B. adds two more to the party, quite without introduction, namely Miss X. and Mr. Y., the latter being an architect and the Colonel's secretary, and the former an elderly artistic lady. Presumably they also were members of that earlier party of which Gulab-Singh was one.

"In the cave every one slept soundly round the fire except myself. None of my companions seemed to mind in the least either the hum of the thousand voices of the Fair or the prolonged, far-away roar of the tigers rising from the valley, or even the loud prayers of the pilgrims who passed to and fro all night....

"Two of Gulab-Singh's servants, with traditional spears and shields of rhinoceros skin, who had been ordered to protect us from wild beasts, sat on the steps of the verandah of the cave. I was unable to sleep, and so watched with increasing curiosity everything that was going on. The Takur, too, was sleepless. Every time I raised my eyes, heavy with fatigue, the first object they fell upon was the gigantic figure of our mysterious friend.

"Having seated himself after the Eastern fashion, with his feet drawn up and his arms round his knees, the Rajput sat on a bench cut in the rock at one end of the verandah, gazing out into the silvery atmosphere. He was so near the abyss that the least incautious movement would expose him to great danger. But the granite goddess, Bhavani herself, could not be more immovable. The light of the moon before him was so strong that the black shadow under the rock which sheltered him was doubly impenetrable, shrouding his face in absolute darkness. From time to time the flame of the sinking fire leaping up shed its hot reflection on the dark bronze face, enabling me to distinguish its sphinx-like lineaments and its shining eyes, as unmoving as the rest of the features.

"'What am I to think? Is he simply sleeping, or is he in that strange state, that temporary annihilation of bodily life? Only this morning he was telling us how the Initiate Raj-Yogis were able to plunge into this state at will. Oh, if I could only go to sleep.'

"Suddenly a loud prolonged hissing, quite close to my ear, made me start, trembling with distinct reminiscences of cobras. The sound was strident, and evidently coming from under the hay upon which I rested. Then it struck one! two! It was our American alarum-clock, which always travelled with me. I could not help laughing at myself, and at the same time feeling a little ashamed of my involuntary fright.

"But neither the hissing, nor the loud striking of the clock, nor my sudden movement that made Miss X. raise her sleepy head, awakened Gulab-Singh, who still hung over the precipice. Another half hour passed. The far-away roar of the festivity was still heard, but everything round me was calm and still. Sleep fled further and further from my eyes. A fresh, strong wind arose before the dawn, rustling the leaves and then shaking the tops of the trees that rose above the abyss.

"My attention became absorbed by the group of three Rajputs before me — by the two shield-bearers and their master. I cannot tell why I was specially attracted at this moment by the sight of the long hair of the servants, which was waving in the wind, though the place they occupied was comparatively sheltered. I turned my eyes upon their Sahib, and the blood in my veins stood still. The veil of somebody's topi, which hung beside him, tied to a pillar, was simply whirling in the wind, while the hair of the Sahib himself lay as still as if it had been glued to his shoulders, not a hair moved, nor a single fold of his light muslin garment. No statue could be more motionless.

"'What is it then?' I said to myself. 'Is it delirium? Is this a hallucination, or a wonderful inexplicable reality?' I shut my eyes, telling myself I must look no longer. But a moment later I again looked up, startled by a crackling sound from above the steps. The long dark silhouette of some animal appeared at the entrance, clearly outlined against the pale sky. I saw it in profile. Its long tail was lashing to and fro. Both servants rose swiftly and noiselessly and turned their heads towards Gulab-Singh, as if asking for orders. But where was Gulab-Singh?

"In the place which, but a moment ago he occupied, there was no one. There lay the topi, torn from the pillar by the wind. I sprang up; a tremendous roar deafened me, filling the *vihara*, wakening the slumbering echoes, and resounding like the softened rumbling of thunder over all the borders of the precipice. Good heavens! A tiger!

"Before this thought had time to shape itself clearly in my mind, the sleepers sprang up and the men all seized their guns and revolvers, and then we heard the sound of crashing branches, and of something heavy sliding down into the precipice. The alarm was general.

"'What is the matter now?' said the calm voice of Gulab-Singh, and I again saw him on the bench of stone. 'Why should you be so frightened?'

"'A tiger! Was it not a tiger?' came in hasty, questioning tones from Europeans and Hindus. Miss X. trembled like one stricken with fever.

"'Whether it was a tiger, or something else, it is by this time at the bottom of the abyss,' answered the Rajput, yawning.

"'I wonder the Government does not destroy all these horrid animals,' sobbed Miss X., who evidently believed firmly in the omnipotence of her Executive.

"'But how did you get rid of the "striped one"?' insisted the Colonel. 'Has anyone fired a shot?'

"'You Europeans think that shooting is, if not the only, at least the best way to get rid of wild animals. We possess other means, which are sometimes more efficacious than guns,' explained Babu Narendro-Das-Sen. 'Wait till you come to Bengal, there you will have many opportunities to make acquaintance with tigers.'

"It was now getting light, and Gulab-Singh proposed to us to descend and examine the rest of the caves and the ruins of the fortress before the day became too hot, so at half-past three, we went by another and easier way to the valley. The Mahratti did not accompany us. He disappeared without informing us whither he was going....

"We were to spend the hottest hours of the day at the village of Vargaon. At about two p.m. when, in spite of the huge punkahs waving to and fro, we were grumbling at the heat, appeared our friend the Mahratta Brahman, whom we thought we had lost on the way. Accompanied by half a dozen Daknis (inhabitants of the Dekhan plateau), he was slowly advancing, seated almost on the ears of his horse, which snorted and seemed very unwilling to move. When he reached the verandah and jumped down, we saw the reason of his disappearance. Across the saddle was tied a huge tiger, whose tail dragged in the dust. There were traces of dark blood in his half-opened mouth. He was taken from the horse and laid down by the doorstep.

"Was it our visitor of the night before? I looked at Gulab-Singh. He lay on a rug in the corner, resting his head on his hand and reading. He knitted his brows slightly, but did not say a word. The Brahman who had just brought the tiger was silent too, watching over certain preparations, as if making ready for some solemnity. We soon learned that, in the eyes of the superstitious people, what was about to happen was a solemnity indeed. A bit of hair from the skin of the tiger that has been killed, neither by bullet nor by knife but by a 'word' is considered the best of all talismans against his tribe.

"'This is a very rare opportunity,' explained the Mahratti. 'It is seldom that one meets with a man who possesses the *word*. Yogis and Sadhus do not generally kill wild animals, thinking it sinful to destroy any living creature, be it even a cobra or a tiger, so they simply keep out of the way of noxious animals. There exists only one Brotherhood in India whose members possess all secrets, and from whom nothing in nature is concealed. Here is the body of the tiger to testify that the animal was not killed with a weapon of any kind, but simply by the *word* of Gulab-Singh. I found it very easily in the bushes exactly under our *vihara*, at the foot of the rock over which the tiger had rolled, already dead. Tigers never make false steps. Gulab-Lal-Singh, you are a Raj-Yogi, and I salute you!' added the proud Brahman, kneeling before the Takur.

"'Do not use vain words, Krishna Rao!' interrupted Gulab-Singh. 'Get up; do not play the part of a Shudra.'

"'I obey you, Sahib, but, forgive me, I trust my own judgment. No Raj-Yogi ever yet acknowledged connection with the Brotherhood, since the time Mount Abu came into existence.'

"And he began distributing bits of hair taken from the dead animal. No one spoke. I gazed curiously at the group of my fellow-travellers. The Colonel, President of our Society, sat with downcast eyes, very pale. His secretary, Mr. Y., lay on his back, smoking a cigar and looking straight above him, with no expression in his eyes. He silently accepted the hair and put it in his purse. The Hindus stood round the tiger, and the Singhalese traced mysterious signs on its forehead. Gulab-Singh continued quietly reading his book."

Mme Blavatsky's travels in the *Caves and Jungles of Hindustan* and Colonel Olcott's in *Old Diary Leaves* part company at the Caves of Karli. While he tells of the real tour of 1879 to Allahabad, Cawnpore, Bhurtpore, Jeypore, Amber, Agra, Saharanpore and Meerut, she, dealing with the jauntings of a past visit or visits in the 1850's, goes to Nassik to see the cave-temples; to Chandvad where are the cave-temples called Enkay-Tenkay; to Mandu, 'city of the dead'; and to the Bagh Caves, fifty miles from there.

The real tour of 1879 occupied only three weeks; Mme Blavatsky, after having covered nearly all of her itinerary in *Caves and Jungles*, says: "We had still seven weeks at our disposal. Where were we to go? How best to employ our time?" She and Colonel Olcott had no such leisure at their disposal. This evidently refers to her spacious past, when travelling was her occupation.

The mode of travel was very different in the two expeditions. In 1879 it was a hurried train journey; but she says in *Caves and Jungles*: "All day long we wandered across rivers and jungles, passing villages and ruins of ancient fortresses, travelling with the aid of bullock carts, elephants, horses, and very often being carried in *palks*. At nightfall we put up our tents and slept anywhere.... Many out-of-the-way paths and groves which most probably had never before been trodden by a European foot, were visited by us. Gulab-Singh was absent, but we were accompanied by a trusted servant of his, and the welcome we met with almost everywhere was certainly the result of the magic influence of his name. If the wretched, naked peasants shrank from us and shut their doors at our approach, the Brahmans were as obliging as could be desired."[7]

She evidently had an object in view on this expedition: the study of caves and cave-temples. One of her conclusions is rather startling. She says: "It is very remarkable that almost all the cave-temples of India are to be found inside conical rocks and mountains. It is as though the ancient builders looked for such natural pyramids purposely. I noticed this peculiarity at Karli, and it is to be met with only in India. Is it a mere coincidence, or is it one of the rules of the religious architecture of the remote past? And which are the imitators — the builders of the Egyptian pyramids, or the unknown architects of the caves of India? In pyramids as well as in caves, everything seems to be calculated with geometrical exactitude. In neither case are the entrances ever at the bottom, but always a certain distance from the ground.... Egypt has borrowed many things from India." Again she says of the caves at Nassik: "The first caves are dug out of a conical hillock about 280 feet from its base.... Farther on is a whole labyrinth of cells."* And of the caves of Enkay-Tenkay: "Twelve miles from Chandvad is a whole town of subterranean temples. Here again, the entrance is a hundred feet from the base,"[8] — and the hill is pyramidal.†

Now, while the above was the itinerary and purpose of one of her expeditions in India, another and very different one is sketched also in *Caves and Jungles*, merely outlined not described. "Benares, Prayaga (now Allahabad), Nassik, Hurdwar, Bhadrinath, Matura — these were the sacred places of prehistoric India which we were to visit one after the other; but to visit them, not after the usual manner of tourists, *à vol d'oiseau*, with a cheap guide-book in our hands and a cicerone to weary our brains, and wear out our legs."

Once more she lists this later itinerary, but somewhat differently: "We were to see Nassik, one of the few towns mentioned by Greek historians, its caves and the tower of Rama; to visit Allahabad, the metropolis of the moon dynasty;... Benares, the town of five thousand temples and as many monkeys; Cawnpur... the remains of the city of the sun, destroyed... 6000 years ago; Agra and Delhi; and then having explored Rajistan with its thousand Takur castles, fortresses, ruins, and legends, we were to go to Lahore, the, metropolis of the Punjab, and lastly, to stay for a while in Amritsar."[9]

It is noteworthy that Lahore ends the list here, and it was at Lahore that in 1856 she met Kulwein and his party, and they together made an attempt to enter Tibet through Kashmir and Ladakh. It is possible that we have here an outline of her movements during her two visits to India of 1852-3 and 1855-7.

---

* See also "The Caves of Bagh," of which the same is true.

† Compare this with the subterranean corridors and chambers of South America described in Chapter VII; also with the following passages from *The Secret Doctrine*: "The Great Dragon has respect but for the Serpents of Wisdom, the Serpents whose holes are now under the Triangular Stones." "The Serpents of Wisdom have well guarded their records, and the history of humanity is written in the heavens as well as on subterranean walls." "The Adepts or Wise Men of the Third, Fourth and Fifth Races dwelt in subterranean habitats, generally under some kind of pyramidal structure, if not actually under a pyramid."

CHAPTER XII
"The Caves Of Bagh"

n the chapter which bears this title in the *Caves and Jungles of Hindustan* Mme Blavatsky tells of another rescue by Gulab Singh, who had left the party but returned suddenly in this emergency. "Bagh," she says, "is situated on the road from Gujerat to Malva, in the defile of Oodeypur, which is owned accordingly by the Maharana of Oodeypur."[1]

"Like all the cave-temples of India, the Bagh caverns are dug out in the middle of a vertical rock.... Seventy-two steps cut out of the rock, and covered with thorny weeds and moss, are the beginning of the ascent to the Bagh caves;... join to this a number of mountain springs exuding through the pores of the stone, and no one will be astonished if I say that we simply felt faint under the weight of life and our archaeological difficulties But on reaching the top, we saw a whole enfilade of dark caves, through regular square openings, six feet wide. There was a curious ceiling over the square platform that once served as a verandah....

"Straight before the entrance, a door leads to another hall, which is oblong, with hexagonal pillars and niches containing statues in a tolerable state of preservation; goddesses ten feet and gods nine feet high. After this hall there is a room with an altar, which is a regular hexagon, having sides each three feet long, and protected by a cupola cut in the rock. Nobody was admitted here, except the initiates of the mysteries of the adytum. All round this room there are about twenty priests' cells.

"Absorbed in the examination of the altar, we did not notice the absence of the colonel, till we heard his loud voice in the distance calling to us: 'I have found a secret passage. Come along, let us find where it leads to!' Who was this 'colonel' of the earlier expedition? Colonel Olcott never visited the Caves of Bagh. Was it that 'Englishman whom she met in Germany two years before, whom she knew to be on the same quest as herself, and to whom she wrote [from America] to join her in the West Indies, that they might go to the East together'? And was this Captain Remington?

"Torch in hand, the colonel was far ahead of us, and very eager to proceed; but each of us had a little plan of his own, and so we were reluctant to obey his summons. The Babu [Narendro-Das-Sen] took upon himself to answer for the whole party: 'Take care, Colonel. This passage leads to the den of the glamour. Mind the tigers!'*

"But once fairly started on the way to discoveries, our president was not to be stopped. *Nolens volens* we followed him. He was right; he had made a discovery; and on entering the cell we saw a most unexpected tableau. By the opposite wall stood two torch-bearers with their flaming torches, as motionless as if they were transformed into stone caryatides; and from the wall, about five feet above the ground, protruded two legs clad in white trousers. There was no body to them; the body had disappeared, and but that the legs were shaken by a convulsive effort to move on, we might have thought that the wicked goddess of this place had cut the colonel into two halves; and having caused the upper half instantly to evaporate, had stuck the lower half to the wall, as a kind of trophy.

"'What is become of you, Mr. President? Where are you?' were our alarmed questions. Instead of answer, the legs were convulsed still more violently, and soon disappeared completely, after which we heard the voice of the colonel, as if coming through a long tube: 'A room, a secret cell. Be quick! I see a whole row of rooms. Confound it! my torch is out! Bring some matches and another torch!'

"But this was easier said than done. The torch-bearers refused to go on; as it was, they were already frightened out of their wits. Miss X. glanced with apprehension at the wall thickly covered with soot and then at her pretty gown. Mr. Y. sat down on a broken pillar and said he would go no farther, preferring to have a quiet smoke in the company of the timid torch-bearers.

"There were several vertical steps cut in the wall; and on the floor we saw a large stone of such curiously irregular shape that it struck me that

---

* "The Bagh tigers are no ordinary tigers, but the servants of the Sadhus, of the holy miracle-workers who have haunted the caves now for many centuries, and who deign sometimes to take the form of a tiger." (p. 206.)

it could not be natural. The quick-eyed Babu was not long in discovering its peculiarities, and said he was sure 'it was the *stopper* of the secret passage.' We all hurried to examine the stone most minutely, and discovered that, though it imitated as closely as possible the irregularity of the rock, its under surface bore evident traces of workmanship and had a kind of hinge to be easily moved. The hole was about three feet high, but not more than two feet wide.

"The muscular 'God's warrior' [Ram-Runjit-Das] was the first to follow the colonel.... The slender Babu joined him with a single monkey-like jump. Then, with the Akali pulling from above and Narayan pushing from below, I safely made the passage, though the narrowness of the hole proved most disagreeable, and the roughness of the rock left considerable traces on my hands.... Miss X. came next, under the escort of Mulji, but Mr. Y. stayed behind.

"The secret cell was a room of twelve feet square. Straight above, the black hole in the floor there was another in the ceiling, but this time we did not discover any 'stopper.' The cell was perfectly empty, with the exception of black spiders as big as crabs. Our apparition, and especially the bright light of the torches, maddened them; panic-stricken they ran in hundreds over the walls, rushed down, and tumbled on our heads, tearing their thin ropes in their inconsiderate haste.... Miss X. was seriously angry, and under pretext of giddiness said she would rejoin Mr. Y. below....

"As to us we climbed through the second opening, but this time under the leadership of Narayan, he disclosed to us that this place was not new to him; he had been here before, and confided to us that similar rooms, one on top of the other, go up to the summit of the mountain. Then, he said, they take a sudden turn, and descend gradually to a whole underground palace, which is sometimes temporarily inhabited. Wishing to leave the world for a while and to spend a few days in isolation, the Raj-Yogis find perfect solitude in this underground abode....

"The second cell was exactly like the first one; we easily discovered the hole in its ceiling, and reached the third cell. There we sat down for a while. I felt that breathing was becoming difficult to me, but I thought I was simply out of breath and tired, and so did not mention to my companions that anything was wrong. The passage to the fourth cell was almost stopped by earth mixed with little stones, and the gentlemen of the party were busy clearing it out for about twenty minutes. Then we reached the fourth cell.

"Narayan was right, the cells were one straight over the other, and the floor of the one formed the ceiling of the other. The fourth cell was in ruins. Two broken pillars lying one on the other presented a very convenient stepping-stone to the fifth storey. But the colonel stopped our zeal by saying that now was the time to smoke 'the pipe of deliberation' after the fashion of the Red Indians.

"'If Narayan is not mistaken,' he said, 'this going up and up may continue till to-morrow morning.'

"'I am not mistaken,' said Narayan almost solemnly. 'But since my visit here I have heard that some of these passages were filled with earth, so that every communication is stopped; and, if I remember rightly, we cannot go farther than the next storey.'

"'In that case there is no use trying to go any farther. If the ruins are so shaky as to stop the passages, it would be dangerous for us.'

"'I never said the passages were stopped by the hand of time. *They* did it.'

"'Who *they*? Do you mean glamour?'

"'Colonel' said the Hindu with an effort, 'don't laugh at what I say. I speak seriously'

"'My dear fellow, I assure you my intention is neither to offend you nor to ridicule a serious matter. I simply do not realise whom you mean when you say *they*.'

"'I mean the brotherhood... The Raj-Yogis. Some of them live quite close to here'

"By the dim light of the half-extinguished torches we saw that Narayan's lips trembled and that his face grew pale as he spoke. The colonel coughed, rearranged his spectacles and remained silent for a while.

"'My dear Narayan' at last said the colonel, 'I do not want to believe that your intention is to make fun of our credulity. But I can't believe either that you seriously mean to assure us that any living creature, be it an animal or an ascetic, could exist in a place where there is no air. I paid special attention to the fact, and so I am perfectly sure I am not mistaken; there is not a single bat in these cells, which shows that there is a lack of air. And just look at our torches! You see how dim they are growing. I am sure, that on climbing two or three more rooms like this, we should be suffocated!'

"'And in spite of these facts, I speak the truth,' repeated Narayan.[1] The caves farther on are inhabited by *them*. And I have seen them with my own eyes.'

"The colonel grew thoughtful, and stood glancing at the ceiling in a perplexed and undecided way. We all kept silent, breathing heavily.

"'Let us go back!' suddenly shouted the Akali [Ram-Runjit- Das].'My nose is bleeding.'

"At this very moment I felt a strange and unexpected sensation, and I sank heavily on the ground.... I vaguely realised that I had really fainted, and that I should die if not taken out into the open air. I could not lift my finger; I could not utter a sound; and in spite of it, there was no fear in my soul — nothing but an apathetic but indescribably sweet feeling of rest, and a complete inactivity of all the senses except hearing.... Is this death? was my indistinct wondering thought.

"Then I felt as if mighty wings were fanning me.... Then I experienced a new sensation: I rather *knew* than *felt* that I was lifted from the floor, and fell down and down some unknown precipice, amongst hollow rollings of a distant thunder-storm. Suddenly a loud voice resounded near me. And this time I think I did not hear, but felt it. There was something palpable in this voice, some thing that instantly stopped my helpless descent, and kept me from falling any farther. This was a voice I knew well, but whose voice it was I could not in my weakness remember.

"In what way I was dragged through all these narrow holes will remain an eternal mystery to me. I came to myself on the verandah below, fanned by fresh breezes, and as suddenly as I had fainted above in the impure air of the cell. When I recovered completely, the first thing I saw was a powerful figure clad in white, with a raven black Rajput beard, anxiously leaning over me. As soon as I recognised the owner of this beard, I could not abstain from expressing my feelings by a joyful exclamation: 'Where do *you* come from?' It was our friend Takur Gulab-Lal-Singh, who having promised to join us in the North-West Province, now appeared to us in Bagh, as if falling from the sky or coming from the ground.

"But my unfortunate accident, and the pitiable state of the rest of the daring explorers, were enough to stop any further questions and expressions of astonishment. On one side of me the frightened Miss X. using my nose as a cork for her sal-volatile bottle; on the other the 'God's warrior' covered with blood, as if returning from a battle with the Afghans; farther on poor Mulji with a dreadful headache. Narayan and the colonel, happily for our party, did not experience anything worse than a slight vertigo. As to the Babu, no carbonic-acid gas could inconvenience his wonderful Bengali nature. He said he was safe and comfortable enough, but awfully hungry.

"At last the outpour of tangled exclamations and unintelligible explanations stopped, and I collected my thoughts and tried to understand what had happened to me in the cave. Narayan was the first to notice that I had fainted, and hastened to drag me back to the passage. And at this very moment they all heard the voice of Gulab-Singh coming from the upper cell: '*Tumhare iha aneka kya kam tha*?' 'What on earth brought you here?'

"Even before they recovered from their astonishment, he ran quickly past them, and descending to the cell beneath called to them to 'pass him down the *bal*' (sister). This 'passing down' of such a solid object as my body, and the picture of the proceeding, vividly imagined, made me laugh heartily, and I felt sorry I had not been able to witness it. Handing him over their half-dead load, they hastened to join the Takur; but he had contrived to do without their help, though how he did it they were at a loss to understand. By the time they succeeded in getting through one passage Gulab-Singh was already at the next one, in spite of the heavy burden he carried; and they never were in time to be of any assistance to him. The colonel, whose main feature is a tendency to go into details, could not conceive by what proceedings the Takur had managed to pass my almost lifeless body so rapidly through all those narrow holes.

"'He could not have thrown her down the passage before going in himself, for every single bone in her body would have been broken,' mused the colonel. 'And it is still less possible to suppose that, descending first himself, he dragged her down afterwards. It is simply incomprehensible!' These questions harassed him for a long time afterwards, until they became something like the puzzle: which was created first, the egg or the bird?

"As to the Takur, when closely questioned, he shrugged his shoulders and answered that he really did not remember. He said that he simply did whatever he could to get me out into the open air; that all our travelling companions were there to watch his proceedings; he was under our eyes all the time; and that in circumstances when every second is precious, people do not think, but act.

"But all these questions arose only in the course of the day. As to the time directly after I was laid on the verandah, there were other things to puzzle all our party; no one could understand how the Takur happened to be on the spot exactly when his help was most needed, nor where he came from — and everybody was anxious to know. On the verandah they found me lying on a carpet, with the Takur busy restoring me to my senses, and Miss X. with her eyes wide open at the Takur, whom she decidedly believed to be a materialised ghost.

"However, the explanations our friend gave us seemed perfectly satisfactory, and at first did not strike us as unnatural. He was in Hardwar when Swami Dayanand sent us the letter which postponed our going to him. On arriving at Kandua by the Indore railway, he had visited Holkar; and learning that we were so near, he decided to join us sooner than he had expected. He had come to Bagh yesterday evening, but knowing that we were to start for the caves early in the morning, he went there before us and simply was waiting for us in the caves. 'There is the whole mystery for you,' he said.

"'Whole mystery?' exclaimed the colonel. 'Did you know, then, beforehand that we should discover the cells, or what?'

"'No, I did not. I simply went there myself because it is a long time since I saw them last. Examining them took me longer than I expected, and so I was too late to meet you at the entrance.'

"'Probably the Takur-Sahib was enjoying the freshness of the air in the cells,' suggested the mischievous Babu, showing all his white teeth in a broad grin.

"Our president uttered an energetic exclamation. 'Exactly! How on earth did I not think of that before? You could not possibly have any breathing air in the cells above the one you found us in. And besides, how did you reach the fifth cell, when the entrance of the fourth was nearly stopped and we had to dig it out?'

"'There are other passages leading to them. I know all the turns and corridors of these caves, and everyone is free to choose his way' answered Gulab-Singh; and I thought I saw a look of intelligence pass between him and Narayan, who simply cowered under his fiery eyes. 'However, let us go to the cave where breakfast is ready for us. Fresh air will do all of you good.'

"On our way we met with another cave, twenty or thirty steps south from the verandah, but the Takur did not let us go in, fearing new accidents for us. So we descended the stone steps I have already mentioned, and after descending about two hundred steps towards the foot of the mountain, made a short re-ascent again and entered the 'dining-room' as the Babu denominated it. In my *role* of interesting invalid, I was carried to it, sitting in my folding chair, which never left me in all my travels....

"We were met by the Takur's four servants, whom we remembered since our stay at Karli, and who bowed down in the dust to greet us. The carpets were spread, and the breakfast ready. Every trace of carbonic-acid gas had left our brains, and we sat down to our meal in the best of spirits. Our conversation soon turned on the Hardwar Mela [Fair], which our unexpectedly-recovered friend had left exactly five days ago....

"So we talked long after our breakfast under the cave vault was finished. But our talk was not so gay as it might have been, because we had to part with Ram-Runjit-Das, who was going to Bombay. [He had come, bearing the letter from Swami Dayanand.]*... Our new friend was a native of Amritsar, in the Punjab, and had been brought up in the 'Golden Temple' on the banks of Amrita-Saras, the 'Lake of Immortality.' The Head Guru, or instructor, of Sikhs resides there.

["Our Sannyasi was... a true Akali; one of the six hundred warrior-priests attached to the Golden Temple, for the purpose of serving God and protecting the Temple,† His personal appearance was in perfect accordance with his title of 'God's warrior.' His exterior was very remarkable and typical; he looked like a muscular centurion of ancient Roman legions, rather than a peaceable servant of the altar. He appeared mounted on a magnificent horse, and accompanied by another Sikh, who respectfully walked some distance behind him.... Our Hindu companions had discerned that he was an Akali when he was still in the distance. He wore a bright blue tunic without sleeves, exactly like that we see on the statues of Roman warriors. Broad steel bracelets protected his strong arms, and a shield protruded from behind his back. A blue conical turban covered his head.]

---

* This bracketed passage is from pp. 198-199.

† In October, 1880, Colonel Olcott and H. P. B. visited Amritsar and its Golden Temple; and there, says the Colonel: "I was greeted by one of the Masters, who for the moment was figuring among the guardians, and who gave each of us a fresh rose, with a blessing in his eyes." (*Old Diary Leaves*, II, 225.)

This was Master K. H., who wrote to Mr. Sinnett on October 29: "I had come for a few days, but now find that I myself cannot endure for any length of time the stifling magnetism of my own countrymen. I have seen some of our proud Sikhs drunk and staggering over the marble pavement of their sacred Temple.... I turn my face homeward to-morrow." (*The Mahatma Letters*, 12.)

"Now he was going to Bombay. The worthy Sikh shook hands with us in the European way, and then raising his right hand gave us his blessing, after the fashion of all the followers of Nanaka. But when he approached the Takur to take leave of him, his countenance suddenly changed. This change was so evident that we all noted it. The Takur was sitting on the ground, leaning on a saddle, which served him as a cushion. The Akali did not attempt either to give him his blessing or to shake hands with him. The proud expression of his face also changed, and showed confusion and anxious humility, instead of the usual self-respect and self-sufficiency. The brave Sikh knelt down before the Takur, and instead of the ordinary '*Namaste*!' —'Salutation to you!' — he whispered reverently, as if addressing the Guru of the Golden Lake : ' I am your servant, Sadhu-Sahib I Give me your blessing !'

"Without apparent reason or cause, we all felt self-conscious and ill at ease, as if guilty of some indiscretion. But the face of the mysterious Rajput remained as calm and dispassionate as ever. He was looking at the river before this scene took place, and slowly moved his eyes to the Akali, who lay prostrate before him. Then he touched the head of the Sikh with his index finger, and rose with the remark that we also had better start at once, because it was getting late.

"We drove in our carriage, moving slowly because of the deep sand which covers all this locality, and the Takur followed us on horseback all the way. He told us the epic legends of Hardwar and Rajistan, of the great deeds of the Hari-Kulas, the heroic princes of the Solar Race. *Hari* means sun, and *Kula*, family. Some of the Rajput princes belong to this family, and the Maharanas of Oodeypur are especially proud of their astronomical origin."

As the next story is a long and complicated one, it requires a chapter to itself, and shall bear the same title as in the *Caves and Jungles of Hindustan*.

CHAPTER XIII

"An Isle Of Mystery"

"When evening began to draw on, we were driving beneath the trees of a wild jungle; arriving soon after at a large lake, we left the carriages. The shores were overgrown with reeds — not the reeds that answer our European notions, but rather such as Gulliver was likely to meet with in his travels to Brobdingnag. The place was perfectly deserted, but we saw a boat fastened close to land. We had still about an hour and a half of daylight before us, and so we quietly sat down on some ruins and enjoyed the splendid view, whilst the servants of the Takur transported our bags, boxes, and bundles of rugs to the ferry-boat. Mr. Y. was preparing to paint the picture before us, which indeed was charming.

"'Don't be in a hurry to take down this view,' said Gulab-Singh. 'In half an hour we shall be on the islet, where the view is still lovelier. We may spend there the night and to-morrow morning as well.... I am going to treat you to a concert. To-night you shall be witness of a very interesting natural phenomenon connected with this island.'

"We all pricked up our ears with curiosity. 'Do you mean that island over there?' asked the colonel. 'Why should not we spend the night here, where we are so deliriously cool and where...'

"'Where the forest swarms with playful leopards, and the reeds shelter snug families of the serpent race, were you going to say, colonel?' interrupted the Babu, with a broad grin. 'Don't you admire this merry gathering, for instance? Look at them! There is the father and the mother, uncles, aunts, and children. I am sure I could point out even a mother-in-law.'

"Miss X. looked in the direction he indicated and shrieked, till all the echoes of the forest groaned in answer. Not farther than three steps from her, there were at least forty grown-up serpents and baby snakes. They amused themselves by practising somersaults, coiled up, then straightened again and interlaced their tails, presenting to our dilated eyes a picture of perfect innocence and primitive contentment. Miss X. could not stand it any longer and fled to the carriage, whence she showed us a pale, horrified face. The Takur, who had arranged himself comfortably beside Mr. Y. in order to watch the progress of his painting, left his seat and looked attentively at the dangerous group, quietly smoking his *gargari* — Rajput narghile — the while.

"'If you do not stop screaming, you will attract all the wild animals of the forest in another ten minutes' said he. 'None of you have anything to fear. If you do not excite an animal, he is almost sure to leave you alone and most probably will run away from you.'

"With these words he lightly waved his pipe in the direction of the serpentine family-party. A thunderbolt falling in their midst could not have been more effectual. The whole living mass looked stunned for a moment, and then rapidly disappeared among the reeds with loud hissing and rustling.

"'Now this is pure mesmerism, I declare,' said the colonel, on whom not a gesture of the Takur was lost. 'How did you do it, Gulab-Singh? Where did you learn this science?'

"'They were simply frightened away by the sudden movement of my chibook, and there was no science and no mesmerism about it. Probably by this fashionable word you mean what we Hindus call *vashi-karana-vidya* — that is to say, the science of charming people and animals by the force of the will. However, as I have already said, this has nothing to do with what I did.'

"'But you do not deny, do you, that you have studied this science and possess this gift?'

"'Of course I *don't*. Every Hindu of my sect* is bound to study the mysteries of physiology and psychology amongst other secrets left to us by our ancestors. But what of that? I am very much afraid, my dear colonel,' said the Takur with a quiet smile, 'that you are rather inclined to view the simplest of my acts through a mystical prism. Narayan has been telling you all

---

* " My sect " in the sense in which the Lord Buddha said : " It is the custom of my race, " when he returned to his kingdom after his illumination, " shorn, with the mendicant's sad-coloured cloth."

kinds of things about me behind my back. Now, is it not so ?' And he looked at Narayan who sat at his feet, with an indescribable mixture of fondness and reproof. The Dekhan colossus dropped his eyes and remained silent.

"'You have guessed rightly,' absently answered Mr. Y., busy over his drawing apparatus. 'Narayan sees in you something like his late deity Shiva; something just a little less than Para-brahm. Would you believe it? He seriously assured us — in Nassik it was — that the Raj-Yogis, and amongst them yourself — though I must own I still fail to understand what a Raj-Yogi is, precisely — can force anyone to see, not what is before his eyes at the given moment, but what is only in the imagination of the Raj-Yogi. If I remember rightly, he called it *Máya*. Now this seems to me going a little too far !'

"'Well! You did not believe, of course, and laughed at Narayan?' asked the Takur, fathoming with his eyes the dark green depths of the lake.

"'Not precisely. Though, I dare say, I did just a little bit' went on Mr. Y. absently, being fully engrossed by the view.... 'I dare say I am too sceptical on this kind of question...'

"'However, there are any number of people who do not doubt, because they have had proof that this phenomenon really occurs,' remarked the Takur, in a careless tone which showed that he had not the slightest desire to insist upon this topic. However, his remark excited Mr. Y.

"'No doubt there are !' he exclaimed. 'But what does that prove? Besides them, there are equal numbers of people who believe in the materialisation of spirits. But do me the kindness of not including me among them !...'

"Mr. Y. was growing altogether too excited, and the Takur dropped the subject and talked of something else.... The Babu and Mulji left us to help the servants to transport our luggage to the ferry boat.... The Takur went on smoking, and as for me, I sat in my folding chair, looking lazily at everything round me, till my eyes rested on Gulab-Singh and were fixed, as if by a spell.

"'Who and what is this mysterious Hindu?' I wondered in my uncertain thoughts. 'Who is this man, who unites in himself two such distinct personalities; the one exterior, kept for strangers, for the world in general; the other interior, moral and spiritual, shown only to a few intimate friends? But even these intimate friends — do they know much beyond what is generally known? They see in him a Hindu who differs very little from the rest of educated natives, perhaps only in his perfect contempt for the social conventions of India and the demands of Western civilisation. And that is all — unless I add that he is known in Central India as a sufficiently wealthy man, and a Takur, a feudal chieftain of a Raj, one of the hundreds of similar Rajes. Besides, he is a true friend of ours, who offered us his protection in our travels, and volunteered to play the part of mediator between us and the suspicious uncommunicative Hindus. Beyond all this, we know absolutely nothing about him. It is true, though, that I know a little more than the others; but I have promised silence, and silent I shall be. But the little I know is so strange, so unusual, that it is more like a dream than a reality.'

"A good while ago, more than twenty-seven years, I met him in the house of a stranger in England, whither he came in the company of a certain dethroned Indian prince. Then our acquaintance was limited to two conversations; their unexpectedness, their gravity, and even severity, produced a strong impression on me then; but in the course of time, like many other things, they sank into oblivion and Lethe. About seven years ago, he wrote to me to America, reminding me of our conversation and of a certain promise I had made. Now we saw each other once more in India, his own country, and I failed to see any change wrought in his appearance by all these long years.

"I was, and looked, quite young when I first saw him;* but the passage of years had not failed to change me into an old woman. As to him, he appeared to me twenty-seven years ago a man of about thirty, and still looked no older, as if time were powerless against him. In England, his striking beauty, especially his extraordinary height, together with his eccentric refusal to be presented to the Queen — an honour many a high-born Hindu has sought, coming over on purpose — excited the public notice and the attention of the newspapers. The newspapermen of those days, when the influence of Byron was still great, discussed the 'wild Rajput' with untiring pens, calling him 'Raja-Misanthrope' and 'Prince Jalma-Samson' and inventing fables about him all the time he stayed in England.

"I forgot every exterior circumstance... sitting and staring at him in no wise less intensely than Narayan.... The magic circle of my revolving thoughts grew too much for me. 'What does all this mean?' I exclaimed to myself. 'Who is this being whom I saw so many years ago, jubilant with manhood

---

* Master Morya once wrote about a youthful portrait of her: "That's her, as I knew her first — " the lovely maiden V (*The Mahatma Letters*, 254.)

and life, and now see again, as young and as full of life, only still more austere, still more incomprehensible. After all, maybe it is his brother, or even his son?' thought I, trying to calm myself, but with no result. 'No, there is no use doubting; it is himself, it is the same face, the same little scar on the left temple. But, as a quarter of a century ago, so now; no wrinkles on those beautiful features; not a white hair in this thick jet-black mane; and in moments of silence, the same expression of perfect rest on that face, calm as a statue of living bronze. What a strange expression, and what a wonderful Sphinx-like face!'

"'Not a very brilliant comparison, my old friend!' suddenly spoke the Takur, and a good-natured laughing note rang in his voice, whilst I shuddered and grew red like a naughty schoolgirl. 'This comparison is so inaccurate that it decidedly sins against history in two important points. *Primo*, the Sphinx is a lion; so am I, as indicates the word Singh in my name; but the Sphinx is winged and I am not. *Secondo*, the Sphinx is a woman, as well as a winged lion; but the Rajput Singhs never had anything effeminate in their characters. Besides, the Sphinx is the daughter of Chimera, or Echidna, who were neither beautiful nor good; and so you might have chosen a more flattering and a less inaccurate comparison!'

"I simply gasped in my utter confusion, and he gave vent to his merriment, which by no means relieved me.

"'Shall I give you some good advice?' continued Gulab-Singh, changing his tone for a more serious one. 'Don't trouble your head with such vain speculations.... You already know every detail you ever will learn. So leave the rest to our respective fates.' And he rose because the Babu and Mulji informed us that the ferry was ready to start.

"'Just let me finish,' said Mr. Y. 'Have nearly done. Just an additional touch or two.'

"'Let us see your work. Hand it round!' insisted the colonel, and Miss X. joined us, still half asleep. Mr. Y. hurriedly added a few more touches to his drawing, and rose to collect his brushes and pencils. We glanced at his fresh wet picture, and opened our eyes in astonishment. There was no lake on it, no woody shores, no velvety evening mists that covered the distant island at this moment. Instead of all this, we saw a charming view; thick clusters of shapely palm-trees scattered over the chalky cliffs of the littoral; a fortress-like bungalow with balconies and a flat roof, an elephant standing at its entrance, and a native boat on the crest of a foaming billow.

"'Now what is this view, sir?' wondered the colonel. 'As if it was worth your while to sit in the sun, and detain us all, to draw fancy pictures out of your head!'

"'What on earth are you talking about?' exclaimed Mr. Y. 'Do you mean to say you do not recognise the lake?'

"'Listen to him — the lake! Where is the lake, if you please? Were you asleep, or what?'

"By this time all our party gathered round the colonel, who held the drawing. Narayan uttered an exclamation, and stood still, the very image of bewilderment past description.

"'I know the place,' he said at last. 'This is Dayri-Bol, the country-house of the Takur-Sahib. I know it. Last year during the famine I lived there for two months.'

"I was the first to grasp the meaning of it all, but something prevented me from speaking at once. At last Mr. Y. finished arranging and packing his things, and approached us in his usual lazy, careless way, but his face showed traces of vexation. He was evidently bored by our persistency in seeing a sea, where there was nothing but the corner of a lake. But, at the first sight of his unlucky sketch, his countenance suddenly changed. He grew so pale, and the expression of his face became so piteously distraught that it was painful to see. He turned and re-turned the piece of Bristol-board, then rushed like a madman to his drawing portfolio and turned the whole contents out. Evidently failing to find what he was looking for, he glanced again at his sea-view, and suddenly covering his face with his hands totally collapsed. We all remained silent, exchanging glances of wonder and pity, heedless of the Takur, who stood on the ferry-boat, vainly calling to us to join him.

"'Look here, Y.,' timidly spoke the colonel. 'Are you sure you remember drawing this view?'

"'Yes, I do remember. Of course I made this sketch, but I made it from nature. I painted only what I saw. And it is that very certainty that upsets me so.'

"'But why should you be upset, my dear fellow? Collect yourself! What happened to you is neither shameful nor dreadful. It is only the result of the temporary influence of one dominant will over another less powerful.'

"'That is exactly what I am most afraid of.... Good gracious! Am I to believe that these confounded Hindus really possess the mystery of this trick? I tell you, colonel, I shall go mad if I don't understand it all!'

"'No fear of that, Mr. Y.' said Narayan, with a triumphant twinkle in his eyes. 'You will simply lose the right to deny Yoga-Vidya, the ancient science of my country.'

"Mr. Y. did not answer him. He made an effort to calm his feelings, and bravely stepped on the ferry-boat with firm foot. Then he sat down apart from us all, obstinately looking at the surface of the water, and struggling to seem his usual self....

"The island was a tiny one, and so overgrown with tall reeds that from a distance it looked like a pyramidal basket of verdure. With the exception of a colony of monkeys, who bustled away to a few mango trees at our approach, the place seemed uninhabited. In this virgin forest of thick grass there was no trace of human life.... The *grass* under which we stood, like insects under a rhubarb leaf, waved its feathery many-coloured plumes much above the head of Gulab-Singh (who stood six feet and a half in his stockings) and of Narayan, who measured hardly an inch less. From a distance it looked like a waving sea of black, yellow, blue, and especially of rose and green. On landing, we discovered that it consisted of separate thickets of bamboos, mixed with the gigantic sirka reeds, which rose as high as the tops of the mangoes.

"It is impossible to imagine anything prettier and more graceful than the bamboos and sirka. The isolated tufts of bamboos show, in spite of their size, that they are nothing but grasses, because the least gush of wind shakes them, and their green crests begin to nod like heads adorned with long ostrich plumes. There were some bamboos there fifty or sixty feet high. From time to time we heard a light metallic rustle in the reeds, but none of us paid much attention to it.

"Whilst our coolies and servants were busy clearing a place for our tents, pitching them and preparing the supper, we went to pay our respects to the monkeys, the true hosts of the place. Without exaggeration there were at least two hundred. While preparing for their nightly rest, the monkeys behaved like decorous and well-behaved people; every family chose a separate branch and defended it from the intrusion of strangers lodging on the same tree, but this defence never passed the limits of good manners.

"...We cautiously passed from one tree to another, afraid of frightening them away; but evidently the years spent by them with the fakirs, who left the island only a year ago, had accustomed them to human society. They were sacred monkeys, as we learned, and so had nothing to fear from men. They showed no signs of alarm at our approach, and having received our greeting, and some of them a piece of sugar-cane, they calmly stayed on their branch-thrones, crossing their arms, and looking at us with a good deal of dignified contempt in their intelligent hazel eyes.

"The sun had set, and we were told that the supper was ready.... As the last golden ray disappeared on the horizon, a gauzelike veil of pale lilac fell over the world.... The phosphoric candles of the fireflies began to twinkle here and there, shining brightly against the black trunks of the trees, and lost again on the silvery background of the opalescent evening sky. But in a few minutes more, thousands of these living sparks, precursors of Queen Night played round us, pouring like a golden cascade over the trees, and dancing in the air above the grass and the dark lake.

"And behold! here is the queen in person. Noiselessly descending upon earth, she reassumes her rights. With her approach, rest and peace spread over us; her cool breath calms the activities of the day. Like a fond mother, she sings a lullaby to nature, lovingly wrapping her in her soft black mantle.... Nature sleeps, but man is awake, to be a witness to the beauties of this solemn evening hour. Sitting round the fire, we talked, lowering our voices as if afraid of awaking night. We were only six; the colonel, the four Hindus and myself, because Mr. Y. and Miss X. could not resist the fatigue of the day and had gone to sleep....

"We were waiting for the 'concert' which the Takur had promised us. 'Be patient,' he said, 'the musicians will not appear before the moon rises.' The fickle goddess was late: she kept us waiting till after ten o'clock. Just before her arrival... a sudden wind rose.... In the general silence, we heard again the same musical notes, which we had passed unheeded when we first reached the island, as if a whole orchestra were trying their musical instruments before playing some great composition. All round us, and over our heads, vibrated strings of violins, and thrilled the separate notes of a flute.

"In a few moments came another gust of wind tearing through the reeds, and the whole island resounded with the strains of hundreds of Aeolian harps. And suddenly there began a wild unceasing symphony. It swelled in the surrounding woods, filling the air with an indescribable melody. Sad and solemn were its prolonged strains, like the *arpeggios* of some funeral march; then changing into a trembling thrill, they shook the air like the song of a nightingale, and died away in a long sigh. They did not quite cease, but grew louder again, ringing like hundreds of silver bells; then changing from the heart-rending howl of a wolf deprived of her young, to the precipitate rhythm of a gay tarantella, forgetful of every earthly sorrow; from the articulate song of a human voice to the vague majestic accords of a violoncello; from merry child's laughter to angry sobbing. And all this was repeated on every side by mocking echo....

"The colonel and I glanced at each other in great astonishment.... The Hindus smiled.... The Takur smoked his *gargari* as peacefully as if he had been deaf. There was a short interval, after which the invisible orchestra started again with renewed energy. The sounds poured and rolled in unrestrainable, overwhelming waves.... Listen! A storm in the open sea, the wind tearing through the rigging, the swish of the maddened waves rushing over each other, or the whirling snow wreaths on the silent steppes. Suddenly the vision is changed; now it is a stately cathedral and the thundering strains of an organ rising under its vaults. The powerful notes now rush together, now spread out through space, break off, intermingle, and become entangled like the fantastic melody of a delirious fever, some musical fantasy born of the howling and whistling of the wind.

"Alas! the charm of these sounds is soon exhausted, and you begin to feel that they cut like knives through your brain. A horrid fancy haunts our bewildered heads; we imagine that the invisible artists strain our own veins, and not the strings of imaginary violins; their cold breath freezes us, blowing their imaginary trumpets, shaking our nerves and impeding our breathing.

"'For God's sake stop this, Takur! This is really too much,' shouted the colonel, at the end of his patience, and covering his ears with his hands. 'Gulab-Singh, I tell you must stop this.'

"The three Hindus burst out laughing; and even the grave face of the Takur lit up with a merry smile.

"'Upon my word,' said he, 'do you really take me for the great Parabrahm? Do you think it is in my power to stop the wind, as if I were Marut, the lord of storms, in person? Ask for something easier than the instantaneous uprooting of all these bamboos.'

"'I beg your pardon; I thought these strange sounds were some kind of psychological influence.'

"'So sorry to disappoint you, my dear colonel.... Don't you see that this wild music is a natural acoustic phenomenon? Each of the reeds round us — and there are thousands on this island — contains a natural musical instrument; and the musician, Wind, comes here daily to try his art after nightfall — especially during the last quarter of the moon.'

"'The wind!' murmured the colonel. 'Oh, yes! But this music begins to change into a dreadful roar. Is there no way out of it?'

"'I at least cannot help it. But keep up your patience, you will soon get accustomed to it. Besides, there will be intervals when the wind falls.'

"We were told that there are many such natural orchestras in India. The Brahmans know well their wonderful properties, and calling this kind of reed *vina-devi*, the lute of the gods, keep up the popular superstition and say the sounds are divine oracles. The sirka grass and the bamboos always shelter a number of tiny beetles, which make considerable holes in the tiny reeds. The fakirs of the idol-worshipping sects add art to this natural beginning, and work the plants into musical instruments. The islet we visited bore one of the most celebrated *vina-devis*, and so, of course, was proclaimed sacred.

"'To-morrow morning,' said the Takur, 'you will see what deep knowledge of all the laws of accoustics was in the possession of the fakirs. They enlarged the holes made by the beetle according to the size of the reed, sometimes shaping it into a circle, sometimes into an oval. These reeds in their present state can be justly considered as the finest illustration of mechanism applied to accoustics. However, this is not to be wondered at, because some of the most ancient Sanskrit books about music minutely describe these laws, and mention many musical instruments which are not only forgotten, but totally incomprehensible in our days.'

"All this was very interesting, but still, disturbed by the din, we could not listen attentively.

"'Don't worry yourselves,' said the Takur. 'After midnight the wind will fall, and you will sleep undisturbed. However, if the too close neighbourhood of this musical grass is too much for you, we may as well go nearer the shore. There is a spot from which you can see the sacred bonfires on the opposite shore....'

"We arrived at a small glade some distance from the bamboo forest. The sounds of the magic orchestra reached us still, but considerably weakened, and only from time to time.... We sat down, and only then I realised how tired and sleepy I was — and no wonder, after being on foot since four in the morning."

CHAPTER XIV

Hatha Yogis And Raja Yogis

Natives of India are truly wonderful people. However unsteady a thing may be, they are sure to walk on it, and sit on it, with the greatest comfort. They think nothing of sitting whole hours on the top of a post.... They also feel perfectly safe with their toes twisted round a thin branch and their bodies resting on nothing, as if they were crows perched on a telegraph wire.

"'Salaam, sahib!' said I once to an ancient naked Hindu of low caste, seated in the above described fashion. 'Are you comfortable, uncle? And are you not afraid of falling down?'

"'Why should I fall?' seriously answered the 'uncle'... 'I do not breathe, mem-sahib.'

"'What do you mean? A man cannot do without breathing!' exclaimed I, a good deal astonished by this wonderful bit of information.

"'Oh, yes, he can. I do not breathe just now, and so I am perfectly safe. But soon I shall have to fill up my breast again with fresh air, and then I will hold on to the post, otherwise I should fall.'

..."In those days we were still inexperienced,* and inclined to resent this kind of information as coming very near to mockery. But later on we learned that his description of the process necessary to keep up this bird-like position was perfectly accurate.

"In Jubblepore we saw much greater wonders. Strolling along the bank of the river, we reached the so-called Fakirs' Avenue; and the Takur invited us to visit the courtyard of the pagoda. This is a sacred place, and neither Europeans nor Mussulmans are admitted inside. But Gulab-Singh said

---

* Apparently this happened on her first visit to India, in 1852-3.

something to the chief Brahman, and we entered without hindrance.

"The yard was full of devotees and of ascetics. But our attention was especially attracted to three ancient, perfectly naked fakirs. As wrinkled as baked mushrooms, as thin as skeletons, crowned with twisted masses of white hair, they sat or rather stood in the most *impossible* postures, as we thought.

"One of them, literally leaning only on the palm of his right hand, was poised with his head downwards and his legs upwards; his body was as motionless as if he were the dry branch of a tree.... Another fakir stood on a 'sacred stone of Shiva,' a small stone about five inches in diameter. One of his legs was curled up under him, and the whole of his body was bent backwards into an arc; his eyes were fixed on the sun. The palms of his hands were pressed together as if in prayer.... We were at a loss to imagine by what means this man came to be master of such equilibrium.

"The third of these wonderful people sat crossing his legs under him; but how he could sit was more than we could understand, because the thing on which he sat was a stone lingam, not higher than an ordinary street post and hardly more than five or seven inches in diameter. His arms were crossed behind his back, and his nails had grown into the flesh of his shoulders. 'This one never changes his position,' said one of our companions. 'At least, he has not changed for the last seven years.'...

"'And if I were to push one of these fakirs?' I asked. 'I dare say the least touch would upset them.'

"'Try!' laughingly advised the Takur. 'In this state of religious trance, it is easier to break a man to pieces than to remove him from his place.'

"To touch an ascetic in the state of trance is a sacrilege in the eyes of the Hindus; but evidently the Takur was well aware that, under certain circumstances, there may be exceptions to every Brahmanical rule. He had another aside with the chief Brahman, who followed us, darker than a thunder-cloud; the consultation did not last long, and after it was over Gulab-Singh declared to us that none of us was allowed to touch the fakirs, but that he personally had obtained this permission, and so was going to show us something still more astonishing.

"He approached the fakir on the little stone, and carefully holding him by his protruding ribs, lifted him and put him on the ground. The ascetic remained as statuesque as before. Then Gulab-Singh took the stone and showed it to us, asking us however not to touch it, for fear of offending the crowd. The stone was round, flattish with rather an uneven surface. When lain on the ground it shook at the least touch.

"'Now you see that this pedestal is far from being steady. And you have seen that, under the weight of the fakir, it is as immovable as if it were planted in the ground.'

"When the fakir was put back on the stone, he and it at once resumed their appearance as of one single body, solidly joined to the ground, and not a line of the fakir's body had changed.... What I have described is a fact, but I do not take upon myself to explain it.

"At the gates of the pagoda we found our shoes, which we had been told to take off before going in. We put them on again, and left this 'holy of holies' of the secular mysteries, with our minds still more perplexed than before.

"In the Fakirs' Avenue we found Narayan, Mulji and the Babu, who were waiting for us. The chief Brahman would not hear of their entering the pagoda. All the three had long before released themselves from the iron claws of caste; they openly ate and drank with us, and for this offence they were regarded as excommunicated, and despised by their compatriots much more than by the Europeans themselves. Their presence in the pagoda would have polluted it forever, whereas the pollution brought by us was only temporary....

"The Hindus are strange and original, but their religion is still more original. It has its dark points, of course.... In spite of them the Hindu religion possesses something so deeply and mysteriously irresistible that it attracts and subdues even unimaginative Englishmen. The following incident is a curious instance of this fascination:

"N. C. Paul, G.B.M.C, wrote a small, but very interesting and very scientific pamphlet. He was only a regimental surgeon in Benares, but his name was well known among his compatriots as a very learned specialist in physiology. The pamphlet was called *A Treatise on the Yoga Philosophy*, and produced a sensation amongst the representatives of medicine in India, and a lively polemic between the Anglo-Indian and native journalists. Dr. Paul spent thirty-five years in studying the extraordinary facts of Yogism, the existence of which was for him beyond all doubt. He not only described them, but *explained* some of the most extraordinary phenomena, for instance, *levitation*.... It was his great friendship with Captain Seymour chiefly which helped him to penetrate some mysteries which, till then, were supposed to be impenetrable.

"The history of this English gentleman is truly incredible, and produced, about twenty-five years ago, an unprecedented scandal in the records of the British army in India. Captain Seymour, a wealthy and well-educated officer, accepted the Brahmanical creed and became a Yogi. Of course, he was proclaimed mad, and having been caught, was sent back to England. Seymour escaped, and returned to India in the dress of a Sannyasi. He was caught again, and shut up in some lunatic asylum in London. Three days after, in spite of the bolts and the watchmen, he disappeared from the establishment.

"Later on his acquaintances saw him in Benares, and the Governor-General received a letter from him from the Himalayas.*

In this letter he declared that he never was mad, in spite of his being put into a hospital; he advised the Governor-General not to interfere with what was strictly his own private concern, and announced his firm resolve never to return to civilized society. 'I am a Yogi,' he wrote, 'and I hope to obtain before I die what is the aim of my life — to become a Raj-Yogi.' After this letter he was left alone, and no European ever saw him except Dr. Paul who, it is reported, was in constant correspondence with him, and even went twice to see him in the Himalayas, under the pretext of botanic excursions.

"I was told that the pamphlet of Dr. Paul was ordered to be burned 'as being offensive to the science of physiology and pathology.' At the time I visited India, copies of it were very great rarities. Out of a few copies still extant, one is to be found in the library of the Maharaja of Benares, and another was given to me by the Takur.

"This evening we dined at the refreshment rooms of the railway station. Our arrival caused an evident sensation. Our party occupied the whole end of a table, at which were dining many first-class passengers, who all stared at us with undisguised astonishment. Europeans on an equal footing with Hindus! Hindus who condescended to dine with Europeans! These were two rare and wonderful sights indeed. The subdued whispering grew into loud exclamations. Two officers who happened to know the Takur took him aside and, having shaken hands with him, began an animated conversation,

---

* He is probably one of the "other two Englishmen" of whom Master K. H. said in 1880: "There is a section in our community who attend to our very rare accessions from another race and blood, and who brought across the threshold Captain Remington and two other Englishmen during this century." (*The Mahatma Letters*, 19.)

as if discussing some matter of business; but, as we learned afterwards, they simply wanted to gratify their curiosity about us....

"The train for Allahabad was to leave at eight p.m. and we were to spend the night in the railway carriage. We had ten reserved seats in a first-class carriage, and had made sure that no strange passengers would enter it, but, nevertheless, there were many reasons which made me think I could not sleep this night. So I obtained a provision of candles for my reading lamp, and making myself comfortable on my couch, began reading the pamphlet of Dr. Paul, which interested me greatly.

"Amongst many other interesting things, Dr. Paul explains very fully and learnedly the mystery of the periodical suspension of breathing, and some other seemingly impossible phenomena practised by the Yogis.... However, all these are physical phenomena produced by the Hatha-Yogis. Each of them ought to be investigated by physical science, but they are much less interesting than the phenomena of the region of psychology. Dr. Paul has next to nothing to say on this subject.

"During the thirty-five years of his Indian career, he met only three Raj-Yogis; but in spite of the friendliness they showed to the English doctor, none of them consented to initiate him into the mysteries of nature, a knowledge of which is ascribed to them.... "The gifts of the Raj-Yogis are much more interesting and a great deal more important for the world, than the phenomena of the lay Hatha-Yogis. These gifts are purely psychic: to the knowledge of the Hatha-Yogis the Raj-Yogis add the whole scale of mental phenomena. Sacred books ascribe to them the following gifts: foreseeing future events; understanding of all languages; the healing of diseases; the art of reading other people's thoughts; witnessing at will everything that happens thousands of miles from them; understanding the language of animals and birds; *Prâkâmya*, or the power of keeping up youthful appearance during incredible periods of time; the power of abandoning their own bodies and entering other people's frames; *Vashitva*, or the gift to kill and to tame wild animals with their eyes; and lastly, the mesmeric power to subjugate anyone, and to force anyone to obey the unexpected orders of the Raj-Yogi."

CHAPTER XV
Adventures In India, Burma, Siam And China

"We believe in no Magic which transcends the scope and capacity of the human mind, nor in 'miracle' whether divine or diabolical, if such imply a transgression of the laws of nature instituted from all eternity. Nevertheless, we accept the saying of the gifted author of *Festus*, that the human heart has not yet fully uttered itself, and that we have never attained or even understood the extent of its powers"[1]

"Many years of wandering among 'heathen' and 'Christian' magicians, occultists, mesmerists, and the *tutti quanti* of white and black art, ought to be sufficient, we think, to give us a certain right to feel competent to take a practical view of this doubted and very complicated question. We have associated with fakirs, the holy men of India, and seen them when in intercourse with the *Pitris*. We have watched the proceedings and *modus operandi* of the howling and dancing dervishes; held friendly communications with the marabouts of European and Asiatic Turkey; and the serpent-charmers of Damascus and Benares have but few secrets that we have not had the fortune to study"[2]

"We witnessed once in India a trial of psychical skill between a holy *gossein** and a sorcerer,† ... We had been discussing the relative powers of the fakir's *Pitris* — pre-Adamite spirits — and the juggler's invisible allies. A trial of skill was agreed upon, and the writer was chosen as a referee. We were taking our noonday rest, beside a small lake in Northern India. Upon the surface of the glassy water floated innumerable aquatic flowers, and

* Fakir, beggar.
† Juggler.

large shining leaves. Each of the contestants plucked a leaf.

"The fakir, laying his upon his breast, folded his hands across it, and fell into a momentary trance. He then laid the leaf, with its surface downward, upon the water. The juggler pretended to control the 'water-master,' the spirit dwelling in the water; and boasted that he would compel the *power* to prevent the *Pitris* from manifesting any phenomena upon the fakir's leaf in *their* element. He took his own leaf and tossed it upon the water, after going through a form of barbarous incantation. It at once exhibited a violent agitation, while the other leaf remained perfectly motionless.

"After a lapse of a few seconds, both leaves were recovered. Upon that of the fakir was found — much to the indignation of the juggler — something that looked like a symmetrical design traced in milk-white characters, as though the juices of the plant had been used as a corrosive writing fluid. When it became dry, and an opportunity was afforded to examine the lines with care, it proved to be a series of exquisitely-formed Sanskrit characters; the whole composed a sentence embodying a high moral precept. The fakir, let us add, could neither read nor write. Upon the juggler's leaf, instead of writing, was found the tracing of a most hideous, impish face. Each leaf, therefore, bore an impression or allegorical reflection of the character of the contestant, and indicated the quality of spiritual beings with which he was surrounded."[3]

"This is how an English paper describes the astounding *trick* of plant-growth, as performed by Indian *jugglers*. 'An empty flower pot was placed upon the floor by the juggler, who requested that his comrades might be allowed to bring up some garden mould from the little plot of ground below. Permission being accorded, the man went, and in two minutes returned with a small quantity of fresh earth tied up in a corner of his chudder, which was deposited in the flower-pot and lightly pressed down.

"'Taking from his basket a dry mango-stone, and handing it round to the company that they might examine it and satisfy themselves that it was really what it seemed to be, the juggler scooped out a little earth from the centre of the flower-pot and placed the stone in the cavity. He then turned the earth lightly over it, and, having poured a little water over the surface, shut the flower-pot out of view by means of a sheet thrown over a small triangle.

"'And now, amid a full chorus of voices and rat-tat-tat of the tabor, the stone germinated; presently a section of the cloth was drawn aside, and gave to view a tender shoot, characterised by two long leaves of a blackish-brown colour. The cloth was readjusted, and the incantation resumed. Not long was it, however, before the cloth was a second time drawn aside, and it was then seen that the two first leaves had given place to several green ones, and that the plant now stood nine or ten inches high.

"'A third time, and the foliage was much thicker, the sapling being about thirteen or fourteen inches in height. A fourth time and the little miniature tree, now about eighteen inches in height, had ten or twelve mangoes about the size of walnuts hanging about its branches. Finally, after the lapse of three or four minutes, the cloth was altogether removed and the fruit, having the perfection of size, though not of maturity, was plucked and handed to the spectators, and on being tasted was found to be approaching ripeness, being sweetly acid.'*

"We may add to this, that we have witnessed the same experiment in India and Tibet, and that more than once we provided the flower-pot ourselves, by emptying an old tin of some Liebig's extract. We filled it with earth with our own hands, and planted in it a small root handed to us by the conjurer, and until the experiment was ended never removed our eyes from the pot, which was placed *in our own room*. The result was invariably the same as above described."[4]

"In the West a 'sensitive' has to be entranced before being rendered invulnerable by the presiding 'guides' and we defy any 'medium,' in his or her normal physical state, to bury the arms to the elbows in glowing coals. But in the East, whether the performer be a holy lama or a mercenary sorcerer (the latter class being generally termed 'jugglers') he needs no preparation or abnormal state to be able to handle fire, red-hot pieces of iron, or melted lead. We have seen in Southern India these 'jugglers' keep their hands in a furnace of burning coals until the latter were reduced to cinders.

"During the religious ceremony of Siva-Ratri, or the vigil-night of Siva, when the people spend whole nights in watching and praying, some of the Sivaites called in a Tamil juggler, who produced the most wonderful phenomena by simply summoning to his help a spirit whom they called *Kutti-Sâttan* — the little *démon*. But, far from allowing people to think he was *guided* or 'controlled' by this gnome — for it was a gnome, if it was

---

* A Western parallel to this, which took place at a seance, is related in Mme d'Esperance's *Shadowland*, p. 261.

anything — the man, while crouching over his fiery pit, proudly rebuked a Catholic missionary who took this opportunity to inform the bystanders that the miserable sinner 'had sold himself to Satan.'

"Without removing his hands and arms from the burning coals within which he was coolly refreshing them, the Tamil only turned his head and gave one arrogant look at the flushed missionary. 'My father and my father's father,' he said, 'had this "little one" at their command. For two centuries the Kutti is a faithful servant in our home, and now, sir, you would make people believe that *he* is my master! But they know better.' After this, he quietly withdrew his hands from the fire, and proceeded with the other performances."[5]

"Upon one occasion we witnessed in Bengal an exhibition of willpower that illustrates a highly interesting phase of the subject. An adept in magic made a few passes over a piece of common tin, the inside of a dish-cover, that lay conveniently by; and while regarding it attentively for a few moments, seemed to grasp the imponderable fluid* by handfuls and throw it against the surface.

When the tin had been exposed to the full glare of light for about six seconds, the bright surface was suddenly covered, as with a film. Then patches of a darker hue began coming out on its surface; and when in about three minutes the tin was handed back to us, we found imprinted upon it a picture, or rather a photograph, of the landscape that stretched out before us; faithful as nature itself, and every colour perfect. It remained for about forty-eight hours and then slowly faded away.

"This phenomenon is easily explained. The will of the adept condensed upon the tin a film of *akasha* which made it for the time being like a sensitised photographic plate. Light did the rest. Such an exhibition as this of the potency of the will to effect even objective physical results, will prepare the student to comprehend its efficacy in the cure of disease by imparting the desired virtue to inanimate objects which are placed in contact with the patient."[6]

"Every animal is more or less endowed with the faculty of perceiving, if

---

* A subtle fluid communicated from one individual to another, or to substances which are touched.... "A magnetic emanation unconsciously produced is sure to be overpowered by any stronger one.... But when an intelligent and powerful will directs the blind force, and concentrates it upon a given spot, the weaker emanation will often master the stronger. A human will has the same effect on the A kasha." (Isis Unveiled, p. 463.)

not spirits, at least something which remains for the time being invisible to common men, and can only be discerned by a clairvoyant. We have made hundreds of experiments with cats, dogs, monkeys of various kinds, and once with a tame tiger. A round black mirror, known as the 'magic crystal,' was strongly mesmerised by a native Hindu gentleman, formerly an inhabitant of Dindigul, and now residing in a more secluded spot, among the mountains known as the Western Ghats. He had tamed a young cub, brought to him from the Malabar coast, in which part of India the tigers are proverbially ferocious; and it is with this interesting animal that we made our experiments.

"Like the ancient Marsi and Psylli, the renowned serpent-charmers, this gentleman claimed to be possessed of the mysterious power of taming any kind of animal. The tiger was reduced to a chronic *mental numbness*, so to say; he had become as inoffensive and harmless as a dog. Children could tease and pull him by the ears, and he would only shake himself and howl like a dog.

"But whenever forced to look into the 'magic mirror,' the poor animal was instantly excited to a sort of frenzy. His eyes became full of a *human* terror; howling in despair, unable to turn away from the mirror to which his gaze seemed riveted as by a magnetic spell, he would writhe and tremble till he was convulsed with fear at some vision which to us remained unknown. He would then lie down, feebly groaning, but still gazing in the glass. When it was taken away from him, the animal would lie panting and seemingly prostrated for about two hours. What did he see? What spirit-picture from his own invisible *animal-world* could produce such a terrific effect on the wild and naturally ferocious and daring beast? Who can tell? Perhaps *he* who produced the scene.

"The same effect on animals was observed during spiritualistic seances with some holy mendicants; the same when a Syrian, half-heathen and half-Christian, from Kunankulam (Cochin State), a reputed sorcerer, was invited to join us for the sake of experimenting.

"We were nine persons in all — seven men and two women, one of the latter a native. Beside us, there were in the room, the young tiger intensely occupied on a bone; a *wânderoo*, or lion-monkey which, with its black coat and snow-white goatee and whiskers, and cunning sparkling eyes, looked the personification of mischief; and a beautiful golden oriole, quietly cleaning its radiant-coloured tail on a perch, placed near a large window of the verandah.

"In India 'spiritualistic stances' are not held in the dark, as in America; and no conditions but perfect silence and harmony are required. It was in the full glare of daylight streaming through the opened door and windows, with a far-away buzz of life from the neighbouring forests and jungles, sending us the echo of myriads of insects, birds, and animals. We sat in the midst of a garden in which the house was built, and instead of breathing the stifling atmosphere of a stance-room, we were amid the fire-coloured clusters of the erythxina — the coral tree — inhaling the fragrant aromas of trees and shrubs, and the flowers of the bignonia, whose white blossoms trembled in the soft breeze.

"In short, we were surrounded with light, harmony, and perfumes. Large nosegays of flowers and shrubs, sacred to the native gods, were gathered for the purpose, and brought into the rooms. We had the sweet basil, the Vishnu-flower, without which no religious ceremony in Bengal will ever take place; and the branches of the *Ficus Religiosa*, the tree dedicated to the same bright deity intermingling their leaves with rosy blossoms of the sacred lotus and the Indian tuberose, profusely ornamented the walls.

"While the 'blessed one' — represented by a very dirty, but nevertheless really holy fakir — remained plunged in self-contemplation, and some spiritual wonders were taking place under the direction of his will, the monkey and the bird exhibited but few signs of restlessness. The tiger alone visibly trembled at intervals, and stared around the room, as if his phosphorically-shining green orbs were following some invisible presence as it floated up and down. That which was as yet unperceived by human eyes, must have therefore been *objective* to him. As to the *wdnderoo*, all its liveliness had fled; it seemed drowsy, and sat crouching and motionless. The bird gave few, if any, signs of uneasiness.

"There was a sound as of gently flapping wings in the air; the flowers went travelling about the room, displaced by invisible hands; and, as a glorious azure-tinted flower fell on the folded paws of the monkey, it gave a nervous start, and sought refuge under its master's white robe. These displays lasted for an hour, and it would be too long to relate all of them; the most curious of all being the one which closed that season of wonders. Somebody complaining of the heat, we had a shower of delicately perfumed dew. The drops fell fast and large, and conveyed a feeling of inexpressible refreshment, drying the instant after touching our persons.

"When the fakir had brought his exhibition of *white* magic to a close, the 'sorcerer,' or conjurer, as they were called, prepared to display his power. We were treated to a succession of the wonders that the accounts of travellers have made familiar to the public; showing among other things, the fact that animals naturally possess clairvoyant faculty, and even, it would seem, the ability to discern between the good and the bad spirits.

"All the sorcerer's feats were preceded by fumigations. He burned branches of resinous trees and shrubs, which sent up volumes of smoke. Although there was nothing about this calculated to affright an animal using only his natural eyes, the tiger, monkey, and bird exhibited an indescribable terror. We suggested that the animals might be frightened at the blazing brands, the familiar custom of burning fires round the camp to keep off wild beasts, recurring to our mind.

"To leave no doubt upon this point, the Syrian approached the crouching tiger with a branch of the Bael-tree (the wood-apple, sacred to Siva) and waved it several times over his head, muttering meanwhile his incantations. The brute instantly displayed a panic of terror beyond description. His eyes started from their sockets like blazing fire-balls; he foamed at the mouth; he flung himself upon the floor, as if seeking some hole in which to hide himself; he uttered scream after scream, that awoke a hundred responsive echoes from the jungle and the woods. Finally, taking a last look at the spot from which his eyes had never wandered, he made a desperate plunge, which snapped his chain, and dashed through the window of the verandah, carrying a piece of the framework with him. The monkey had fled long before, and the bird fell from the perch as though paralysed.

"We did not ask either the fakir or sorcerer for an explanation of the method by which their respective phenomena were effected. If we had unquestionably they would have replied as did a fakir to a French traveller, who tells his story in a recent number of a New York newspaper, called the *Franco-American*, as follows: '... I have only one means.' 'What is it?' 'The will. Man, who is the end of all intellectual and material forces, must dominate over all. The Brahmans know nothing besides this.'[7]

"We have seen in India a small brotherhood of fakirs settled round a little lake, or rather a deep pool of water, the bottom of which was literally carpeted with enormous alligators. These amphibious monsters crawl out, and warm themselves in the sun, a few feet from the fakirs, some of whom may be motionless, lost in prayer and contemplation. So long as one of these holy beggars remains in view, the crocodiles are harmless as kittens. But we would never advise a foreigner to risk himself alone within a few yards of these monsters. The poor Frenchman, Pradin, found an untimely grave in one of these terrible Saurians, commonly called by the Hindus Moudela"[8]

"At the great festivals of Hindu pagodas, at the marriage feasts of rich high-castes, everywhere where large crowds are gathered, Europeans find *guni* — or serpent-charmers, fakir-mesmerizers, thaum-working sannyasi, and so-called 'jugglers.' To deride is easy — to explain, rather more troublesome — to science impossible. The British residents of India and the travellers prefer the first expedient. But let anyone ask of these Thomases how the following results — which they cannot and do not deny — are produced.

"When crowds of *guni* and fakirs appear with their bodies encircled by *cobras-de-capello*, their arms ornamented with bracelets of *corallilos* — diminutive snakes inflicting certain death in a few seconds — and their shoulders with necklaces of *trigonocephali*, the most terrible enemy of naked Hindu feet, whose bite kills like a flash of lightning, the sceptic witness smiles and gravely proceeds to explain how these reptiles, having been thrown in cataleptic torpor, were all deprived by the *guni* of their fangs. 'They are harmless and it is ridiculous to fear them.'

"'Will the Sahib caress one of my *nag*?' asked once a *guni*, approaching our interlocutor who had been thus humbling his listeners with his herpetological achievements for a full half-hour. Rapidly jumping back — the brave warrior's feet proving no less nimble than his tongue — Captain B.'s angry answer could hardly be immortalized by us in print. Only the *gunI's* terrible body-guard saved him from anns uncereremonious thrashing. Besides, say a word, and for a half-rupee any professional serpent-charmer will begin creeping about and summon around in a few moments numbers of untamed serpents of the most poisonous species, and will handle them and encircle his body with them.

"On two occasions in the neighbourhood of Trinkemal a serpent was ready to strike at the writer, who had once nearly sat on its tail; but both times, at a rapid whistle of the *guni* whom we had hired to accompany us, it stopped — hardly a few inches from our body, as if arrested by lightning, and slowly sinking its menacing head to the ground, remained stiff and motionless as a dead branch, under the charm of the *kilna*, the Hindu appellation for the peculiar mantram of charm which prevents the serpent from biting"⁹

"The poor heathen have no such impedimenta [as modern scientists] but — will European science believe it — nevertheless produce the very same phenomena. Upon one occasion, when, in a case of exceptional importance, an 'oracle' was required, we saw the possibility of what we had previously vehemently denied — namely, a simple mendicant cause a sensitive flame to give responsive flashes without a particle of apparatus. A fire was kindled of branches of the Bael-tree, and some sacrificial herbs were sprinkled upon it. The mendicant sat nearby, motionless, absorbed in contemplation.

"During the intervals between the questions, the fire burned low and seemed ready to go out; but when the interrogatories were propounded, the flames leaped, roaring, skyward, flickered, bowed, and sent fiery tongues flaring towards the east, west, north, or south; each motion having its distinct meaning in a code of signals well understood. Between whiles it would sink to the ground, and the tongues of flame would lick the sod in every direction, and suddenly disappear, leaving only a bed of glowing embers.

"When the interview with the flame-spirits was at an end, the Bikshu (mendicant) turned towards the jungle where he abode, keeping up a wailing, monotonous chant, to the rhythm of which the sensitive flame kept time, not merely like Professor Tyndall's, when he read the *Faerie Queene*, by simple motions, but by a marvellous modulation of hissing and roaring, until he was out of sight. Then, as if its very life were extinguished, it vanished, and left a bed of ashes before the astonished spectators."¹⁰

"The Yogis of the olden times, as well as modern lamas and *Talapoins*, use a certain ingredient with a minimum of sulphur, and a milky juice which they extract from a medicinal plant. They must certainly be possessed of some wonderful secrets, as we have seen them healing the most rebellious wounds in a few days; restoring broken bones to good use in as many hours as it would take days to do by means of common surgery. A fearful fever contracted by the writer near Rangoon, after a flood of the Irrawaddy River, was cured in a few hours by the juice of a plant called, if we mistake not, *Kukushan*, though there may be thousands of natives ignorant of its virtues who are left to die of fever. This was in return for a trifling kindness we had done to a *simple mendicant*; a service which can interest the reader but little." [11]

"A prevalent belief in some parts of Russia, particularly Georgia (Caucasus) and in India, is that in case the body of a drowned person cannot be otherwise found, if a garment of his be thrown into the water it will float until directly over the spot, and then sink. We have even seen the experiment successfully tried with the sacred cord of a Brahman. It floated hither and thither, circling about as though in search of something, until suddenly darting in a straight line for about fifty yards, it sank, and at that exact spot the divers brought up the body. This phenomenon is explained by the law of the powerful attraction existing between the human body and objects that have been long worn upon it. The oldest garment is most effective for the experiment; a new one is useless" [12]

"There is not perhaps, on the face of the whole globe, a more imposing mass of ruins than Nagkon-Wat, the wonder and puzzle of European archaeologists who venture into Siam. When we say ruins, the expression is hardly correct; for nowhere are there buildings of such tremendous antiquity to be found in a better state of preservation than Nagkon-Wat, and the ruins of Angkorthom, the great temple.

"Hidden far away in the province of Siamrap — Eastern Siam — in the midst of a most luxuriant tropical vegetation, surrounded by almost impenetrable forests of palms, cocoa-trees, and betel-nut, 'the general appearance of the wonderful temple is beautiful and romantic, as well as impressive and grand' says Mr. Vincent, a recent traveller....

"We have seen Nagkon-Wat under exceptionally favourable circumstances, and can, therefore, certify to the general correctness of Mr. Vincent's description.... For our part, we may add, that there are on the walls several repetitions of Dagon, the man-fish of the Babylonians, and of the Kabeirian gods of Samothrace. This may have escaped the notice of the few archaeologists who have examined the place; but upon stricter inspection they will be found there, as well as the reputed father of the Kabeiri — Vulcan, with his bolts and implements.... It is easy to see that the excavators of Ellora, the builders of the old Pagodas, the architects of Copan and of the ruins of Central America, those of Nagkon-Wat, and those of the Egyptian remains were, if not of the same race, at least of the same religion — the one taught in the oldest Mysteries."[13]

"A Brahmana at Golaghat, Assam, was robbed. Despite all efforts, he could neither detect the thief nor recover his stolen property. He therefore resolved to have recourse to some magic contrivance known in Assam as 'Huka-Mella,' or 'the running-stick.' He sent for a famous conjurer of the name of Mahidar. The man came. The first thing he did was to cut a rod in the Brahmana's garden; he then placed himself on the threshold of the house, waiting for someone to pass. After a while a clerk in the Commissioner's office chanced to pass that way. The sorcerer called the young man, whose name was Rochpar; and having explained matters, asked him if he would be willing to help the Brahmana to regain his stolen property. Rochpar consented, and took the rod which the sorcerer, after muttering some conjuration over it, gave him.

"But scarcely had he touched it than he was compelled to run by some strange force. He screamed that the stick seemed to have grown into the flesh of his hand, and was dragging him along. Naturally the Brahmana and a great crowd of people followed the clerk, eager to see what would happen. Arrived at a small tank, Rochpar pushed the stick into the middle of the shallow water and said: 'Dig here!' The water was drawn off, and the stolen property dug out of the mud....

"I have come to know this kind of sorcery myself. My brooch and gold watch having been stolen (in India), they were found on the very same day by a girl five years old, to whose hand a fakir had tied such a stick. The child was used for this purpose all over the country. The fakir or Bawa (father) did not accept a remuneration for his service."[14]

In *The Theosophist* of August, 1900, Colonel Olcott publishes a corroboration of Mme Blavatsky's visit to China, which is worth presenting. "Through the kindness of an Indian Prince, we have received a letter written by a gentleman from Simla who was travelling in China, to an Indian friend. The reference to H. P. B. makes it specially interesting. We omit the names from the original letter, which is in our possession.

"Rung Jung, Mahan, China,
January 1, 1900.

"Dear ——

"Your letter addressed through His Highness, Rajah Sahab Hira

Singh, reached me while traversing the Spiti Mts. Now I have crossed these Mts. and am in the territory of Mahan, China. This place is known by the name of Rung Jung, and lies within the territory of the Chinese Empire. The place has a great cave and is surrounded by high mts. It is the chief haunt of lamas and the favourite resort of Mahatmas. Great Rishis have chosen it on account of its antiquity and beautiful scenery.

"The place is suited for divine contemplation. A man can nowhere find a place better suited for focussing one's mind. The great Lama Kut Te Hum is the guru of all lamas, and has absorbed his attention in the form of *samadhi* for the last two and a half months. He is expected to be out of *samadhi* after some three and a half months, so it is my chief desire to wait here for that period, and personally converse with him. His *chelas* also are ever meditating and trying to absorb themselves in the great Divide.

"From conversation with them, I came to know that Mme Blavatsky had visited this place and meditated here for some time. Formerly I had doubts as to her arrival here, but all my misgivings have now been removed, and I feel confident of her divine contemplation at this holy and sacred place.

"The lesson and *Updesha* I received from these lamas show that the views of the Theosophical Society are not merely visionary and theoretical, but are practical schemes. But after long experience I felt that it is difficult to practise Yoga in the plains of Hindustan; that it is possible to do so only in these high mountains. Formerly I used to contemplate for two or three hours per day, and that even with difficulty; now I can sit easily for eight or nine hours and even more. I am, nowadays, quite healthy and feel myself better than before.

"A Bengali Babu named —— is here with me, and has come here for the sake of contemplation, and we two will together proceed to Llasa. These Lamas have got with them a valuable library, which I cannot describe to you within this short space."

CHAPTER XVI

The Home-Coming At Pskoff

This long-deferred home-coming, in the town of Pskoft, H. P. B.'s sister Vera describes: "We were not expecting her to arrive for some weeks to come; but, curiously enough, no sooner did I hear her ring at the door-bell than I jumped up, knowing that she had arrived. As it happened, there was a party going on that evening in my father-in-law's house, in which I was living.* His daughter was to be married that very evening, the guests were seated at table, and the ringing of the door-bell was incessant. Nevertheless I was so sure that it was she who had arrived that, to the astonishment of everyone, I hurriedly rose from the wedding feast and ran to open the door, not wishing the servants to do so.

"We embraced each other, overcome with joy, forgetting for the moment the strangeness of the event. I took her at once to my room, and that very evening I was convinced that my sister had acquired strange powers. She was constantly surrounded, awake or asleep, with mysterious movements, strange sounds, little taps which came from all sides — from the furniture, from the window-panes, from the ceiling, from the floor, and from the walls. They were very distinct and seemed intelligent into the bargain; they tapped three times for 'yes,' twice for 'no.'"[1]

"The relatives of Mme Blavatsky's sister were leading a very fashionable life, and received a good deal of company in those days. Her presence attracted a number of visitors, no one of whom ever left her unsatisfied; for the raps which she evoked gave answers, composed of long discourses in several languages, some of which were unknown to the *medium*, as she

---

* Vera, then Mme Yahontoff, was staying at Pskoff with General N. A. Yahontoff, her late husband's father. She married M. Jelihovsky some time afterward.

was called.

"The poor 'medium' became subjected to every kind of test, to which she submitted very gracefully, no matter how absurd the demand, as a proof that she did not bring about the phenomena by juggling. It was her usual habit to sit very quietly and quite unconcerned on the sofa, or in an arm-chair, engaged in some embroidery, and apparently without taking the slightest interest or active part in the hubbub which she produced round herself. And the hubbub was great indeed.

"One of the guests would be reciting the alphabet, another putting down the answers received, while the mission of the rest was to offer mental questions, which were always and promptly answered.... During that time, conversations and discussions in a loud tone were carried on around her. Mistrust and irony were often shown, but she bore it all very coolly and patiently, a strange or puzzling smile or an ironical shrugging of the shoulders being her only answer....

"To put an end to all this, she allowed herself to be subjected to the most stupid demands; she was searched, her hands and feet were tied with string.... At times she would wickedly revenge herself by practical jokes on those who doubted her. Thus, for example, the raps which came one day inside the glasses of the young Professor ——, while she was sitting at the other side of the room, were so strong that they fairly knocked the spectacles off his nose, and made him become pale with fright.

"At another time, a lady, an *esprit fort*, very vain and coquettish, to her ironical question as to what was the best conductor for the production of raps, and whether they could be done anywhere, received a strange and puzzling answer. The word 'Gold' was rapped out, and then came the words, 'We will prove it to you immediately.' The lady kept smiling with her mouth slightly open. Hardly had the answer come, than she became very pale, jumped from her chair, and covered her mouth with her hand. Her face was convulsed with fear and astonishment. Why? Because she had felt the raps in her mouth, as she confessed later on. Those present looked at each other significantly. Previous even to her own confession, all had understood that the lady had felt a violent commotion and raps *in the gold* of her artificial teeth! And when she rose from her place and left the room with precipitation, there was a homeric laugh among us at her expense."[2]

"As usual, those nearest and dearest to H. P. B. were, at the same time, the most sceptical as to her occult powers. Her brother Leonide and her father stood out longer than all against the evidence, until at last the doubts of the former were greatly shaken by the following fact. The drawing-room of the Yahontoffs was full of visitors. Some were occupied with music, others with cards, but most of us, as usual, with phenomena.

"Leonide de Hahn did not concern himself with anything in particular, but was leisurely walking about, watching everybody and everything. He was a strong, muscular youth, saturated with the Latin and German wisdom of the University, and believed so far in no one and nothing. He stopped behind the back of his sister's chair, and was listening to her narratives of how some persons, who called themselves 'mediums,' made light objects so heavy that it was impossible to lift them; and others which were naturally heavy become again remarkably light.

"'And you mean to say you can do it?' ironically asked the young man of his sister.

"'Mediums can, and I have done it occasionally; though I cannot always answer for its success… I will try, I will simply fix this chess-table and try. He who wants to make the experiment, let him lift it now, and then try *again after I shall have fixed it.*

"'Do you mean to say that you will not touch the table at all?'

"'Why should I touch it?' answered Mme Blavatsky, with a quiet smile.

"Upon hearing the extraordinary assertion, one of the young men went determinedly to the small chess-table, and lifted it as though it were a feather.

"'All right' she said. 'Now kindly leave it alone, and stand back!'

"The order was obeyed at once, and a great silence fell upon the company. All, holding their breath, anxiously watched for what Mme Blavatsky would do next. She merely fixed her large eyes upon the chess-table, and kept looking at it with an intense gaze. Then, without removing her gaze, she silently, with a motion of her hand, invited the same young man to remove it. He approached, and grasped the table by its leg with great assurance. The table *could not be moved*! Folding his hands in a Napoleonic way, he slowly said: 'Well, this is a good joke!'

"'Indeed, it is a good one!' echoed Leonide. A suspicion had crossed his mind that the young visitor was acting in secret confederacy with his sister and fooling them.

"'May I also try?' he suddenly asked her.

"'Please do, my dear' was the laughing response.

"'Her brother upon this approached smiling, and seized in his turn the diminutive table by its leg with his strong muscular arm. But the smile instantly vanished to give place to an expression of mute amazement. He stepped back a little and examined very carefully the, to him, well-known chess-table. Then he gave it a tremendous kick, but the little table did not even budge. Suddenly applying to its surface his powerful chest, he enclosed it within his arms, trying to shake it. The wood cracked, but would yield to no effort. Its three feet seemed screwed to the floor. Then Leonide Hahn lost all hope, and abandoning the ungrateful task, stepped aside, and frowning, exclaimed but these two words: 'How strange!'...

"The loud debate had meanwhile drawn the attention of several visitors, and they came pouring in from the drawing-room into the large apartment where we were. Many of them, old and young, tried to lift up, or even to impart some slight motion to, the obstinate little chess-table. They failed, like the rest of us.

"Upon seeing her brother's astonishment, and perchance desiring finally to destroy his doubts, Mme Blavatsky, addressing him with her usual careless laugh, said, 'Try to lift the table now, once more!'

"Leonide H. approached the little thing very irresolutely, grasped it again by the leg, and pulling it upwards, came very near to dislocating his arm, owing to the useless effort; the table was lifted like a feather this time!"[3]

CHAPTER XVII
Rougodevo

"My father," says Mme Jelihovsky, "a man of vast intellectual power, and most learned, had all his life been a sceptic, a 'Voltarien' as we say in Russia. He was compelled by force of circumstances to change his convictions, and before long passed days and nights writing, under the dictation of *messieurs les esprits*, the genealogy of his ancestors,* the 'gallant knights of Hahn-Hahn von Rotterhahn.'"[1]

The circumstances of his conversion are given by Mr. Sinnett in his *Incidents in the Life of Mme Blavatsky*, as related by Mme Jelihovsky, thus: "It occurred in St. Petersburg a few months later, when Mme Blavatsky had already left Pskoff with her father and sister, and when all three were living in a hotel. They had come to St. Petersburg on business, on their way to Mme Yahontoff's property at Rougodevo, in the district of Novorgeff, about two hundred versts from St. Petersburg, where they had decided to pass the summer. All their forenoons were occupied with business, their afternoons and evenings with making and receiving visits, and there was no time for, or even mention of, phenomena.

"One night they received a visit from two old friends of their father.... Both were much interested in recent Spiritualism, and were, of course, anxious to see something. After a few successful phenomena, the visitors declared themselves positively amazed, and quite at a loss what to make of Mme Blavatsky's powers. They could neither understand nor account, they said, for her father's indifference in presence of such manifestations.

"There he was, coolly laying out his '*grande patience*' with cards, while

---
* A full account is given in *Incidents in the Life of Mme Blavatsky*, by A. P. Sinnett, pp. 75-77.

phenomena of such a wonderful nature were occurring round him. The old gentleman, thus taken to task, answered that it was all bosh, and that he would not hear of such nonsense; such occupation being hardly worthy of serious people, he added. The rebuke left the two old gentlemen unconcerned. They began, on the contrary, to insist that Colonel Hahn should, for old friendship's sake, make an experiment, before denying the importance, or even the possibility of his daughter's phenomena.

"They offered him to test the *intelligences* and their power, by writing a word in another room, secretly from them all, and then asking the raps to repeat it. The old gentleman, more probably in the hope of a failure that would afford him the opportunity of laughing at his two old friends, than out of a desire to humour them, finally consented. He left his cards, and proceeding to an adjoining room, wrote a word on a bit of paper; after which, conveying it to his pocket, he returned to his *patience*, and waited silently, laughing behind his grey moustache.

"'Well, our dispute will now be settled in a few moments' said K——w. 'What shall you say, however, old friend, if the word written by you is correctly repeated? Will you not feel compelled to believe in such a case?'

"'What I might say, *if* the word were correctly guessed, I could not tell at present' he sceptically replied. 'One thing I could answer, however, from the time I can be made to believe your alleged Spiritism and its phenomena, I shall be ready to believe in the existence of the devil, undines, sorcerers and witches — in the whole paraphernalia, in short, of old women's superstitions; and you may prepare to offer me as an inmate of a lunatic asylum.'

"Upon delivering himself thus, he went on with his *patience*, and paid no further attention to the proceedings.... The younger sister was repeating the alphabet; the old general marked the letters down; while Mme Blavatsky did nothing at all — apparently....

"By means of raps and alphabet we got *one word*, but it proved such a strange one, so grotesquely absurd as having no relation to anything that might be supposed to have been written by her father, that Jl of us who had been in expectation of some complicated sentence looked at each other, dubious whether we ought to read it aloud. To our question, whether it was all, the raps became more energetic in the affirmative sounds. We had several triple raps, which meant in our code — Yes!... Yes, yes, yes!!!

"Remarking our agitation and whispering, Mme B's father looked at us over his spectacles, and asked: 'Well I Have you any answer? It must be something very elaborate and profound indeed!'

"He arose, and laughing in his moustache, approached us. His younger daughter, Mme Yahontoff, then went to him and said, with some little confusion: 'We got only one word.' And what is it? 'Zaitchik.'

"It was a sight indeed to witness the extraordinary change that came over the old man's face at this *one* word! He became deadly pale. Adjusting his spectacles with a trembling hand, he stretched it out while hurriedly saying: 'Let me see it! Hand it over. Is it really so?'

"He took the slips of paper, and read in a very agitated voice: 'Zaitchik. Yes, Zaitchik; so it is. How very strange!'

"Taking out of his pocket the paper he had written upon in the adjoining room, he handed it in silence to his daughter and guests. They found on it both the question offered and the answer that was anticipated. The words read thus:

"'What was the name of my favourite war-horse which I rode during my first Turkish campaign?' and lower down, in parenthesis, ('Zaitchik').

"We felt fully triumphant, and expressed our feeling accordingly. This solitary word, Zaitchik, had an enormous effect upon the old gentleman. As it often happens with inveterate sceptics, once he found that there was indeed *something* in his eldest daughter's claims, and that it had nothing to do whatever with deceit and juggling, having been convinced of this one fact, he rushed into the region of phenomena with all the zeal of an ardent investigator."[2]

"Having settled in our property at Rougodevo, we found ourselves as though suddenly transplanted into an enchanted world, in which we got gradually so accustomed to see self-moving furniture, things transferred from one place to another, in the most inexplicable way, and to the strong interference with, and presence in, our matter-of-fact daily life of some unknown, to us, yet *intelligent* power, that we all ended by paying very little attention to it, though the phenomenal facts struck everyone else as being simply miraculous..."[3]

"All the persons living on the premises, with the household members, saw constantly, often in full noon-day, vague human shadows walking about the rooms, appearing in the garden, in the flower-beds in front of the house, and near the old chapel. My father (once the greatest sceptic), Mlle Leontine, the governess of our younger sister, told me many a time, that they had just met and seen such figures quite plainly...."⁴

"Not only H. P. B., but even her little sister, Lisa, a child of nine years old, saw more than once strange forms gliding noiselessly along the corridors of the old house.... The child, strange to say, feared the restless ghosts no more than her elder sister; the former taking them innocently for living persons, and concerned but with the interesting problems: where they had come from, who they were, and why no one except her 'old' sister and herself ever consented to notice them. She thought this very rude — the little lady. Luckily for the child, and owing perhaps to the efforts of her sister, Mme Blavatsky, the faculty left her very soon, never to return during her subsequent life."⁵

"The quiet life of the sisters at Rougodevo was brought to an end by a terrible illness which befell Mme Blavatsky. Years before, perhaps during her solitary travels in the steppes of Asia, she had received a remarkable wound. We could never learn how she had met with it. Suffice to say that the profound wound reopened occasionally, and during that time she suffered intense agony, often bringing on convulsions and a death-like trance.*

"The sickness used to last from three to four days, and then the wound would heal as suddenly as it had reopened, as though an invisible hand had closed it, and there would remain no trace of her illness. But the affrighted family was ignorant at first of this strange peculiarity, and their despair and fear were great indeed.

"A physician was sent for to the neighbouring town; but he proved of little use, not so much indeed through his ignorance of surgery, as owing to a remarkable phenomenon which left him almost powerless to act, through sheer terror at what he had witnessed. He had hardly examined the wound of the patient prostrated before him in complete unconsciousness, when suddenly he saw a large, dark hand between his own and the wound he was going to anoint. The gaping wound was near the heart, and the hand kept moving at several intervals from the neck down to the waist. To make his terror worse, there began suddenly in the room such a terrific noise, such a chaos of noises and sounds from the ceiling, the floor, window-panes and every bit of furniture in the apartment, that he begged he might not be left

---

* Colonel Olcott says this wound reopened while H. P. B. was at Chittenden, at the Eddy homestead, in 1874. He describes it as a stiletto wound, just below the heart.

alone in the room with the insensible patient.

"In the spring of 1860, both sisters left Rougodevo for the Caucasus, on a visit to their grandparents, whom they had not seen for long years."[6]

CHAPTER XVIII

In The Caucasus

n the summer of 1860, we left the Government of Pskoff, for the Caucasus, to pay a visit to our grandparents, the Fadeews, and Mme Witte, our aunt, our mother's sister, who had not seen Hélène for more than eleven years. On our way there, at the town of Zadonsk, in the Government of Voronege, we learnt that the Metropolitan of Kieff, the Venerable Isadore, whom we had known well when we were children at Tiflis, where he had been the head of the Exarchate of St. George, happened to be in the town, passing through on his way to St. Petersburg, and was for the moment officiating in the monastery.

"We were most eager to see him; he remembered us, and sent us word to say that he would be very pleased to see us after Mass. We made our way to the Archi-Episcopal Church, but not without misgivings on my part. As we were on our way there, I said to my sister: 'Do please take care that your little devils keep themselves quiet while we are with the Metropolitan.'

"She began laughing and saying that she would like nothing better, but that she could not answer for them. Alas! I knew it but too well. And so I was not astonished, but all the same suffered agonies when I heard the tapping begin as soon as ever the venerable old man began to question my sister about her travels. One! two! One! two! three! Surely he could not but notice these importunate individuals who seemed determined to join the party and take part in the conversation; in order to interrupt us they made the furniture, the looking-glasses, our cups of tea, even the rosary of amber beads, which the saintly old man was holding in his hand, move and vibrate.

"He saw our dismay at once, and taking in the situation at a glance, enquired which of us was the medium. Like a true egotist, I hastened to fit the cap on my sister's head. He talked to us for more than an hour, asking my sister question after question out loud, and asking them mentally of her attendants, and seemed profoundly astonished and well pleased to have seen the phenomena. On taking leave of us, he blessed my sister and myself, and told us that we had no cause to fear the phenomena.

"'There is no force,' he said, 'that both in its essence and in its manifestation does not proceed from the Creator. So long as you do not abuse the gifts given you, have no uneasiness. We are by no means forbidden to investigate the hidden forces of nature. One day they will be understood and utilized by man, though that is not yet. May the blessing of God rest on you, my child!'

"He again blessed Helene and made the sign of the cross. How often must these kindly words of one of the chief Heads of the Orthodox Greek Church have been recalled to the memory of H. P. Blavatsky in later years, and she ever felt gratefully towards him."[1]

General P. S. Nikolaeff describes the Tiflis (Caucasus) home of the Fadeefs in his *Reminiscences of Prince A. T. Bariatinsky*, as follows: "They were living in those years in the ancient mansion of Prince Tchavtchavadze, the great building itself carrying the imprint of something weird or peculiar about it.... A long, lofty and gloomy hall was hung with the family portraits of the Fadeefs and the Princes Dolgorouky. Farther on was a drawing-room, its walls covered with Gobelin tapestry, a present from the Empress Catherine; and near at hand was the apartment of Mlle N. A. Fadeef — in itself one of the most remarkable of private museums. There were brought together arms and weapons from all the countries of the world; ancient crockery, cups and goblets, archaic utensils, Chinese and Japanese idols, mosaics and images of the Byzantine epoch, Persian and Turkish carpets, and fabrics worked with gold and silver, statues, pictures, paintings, petrified fossils, and finally a very rare and most precious library.

"The emancipation of the serfs had altered in no way the daily life of the Fadeefs. The whole enormous host of their *valetaille* (ex-serfs) had remained with the family as before their freedom, only now receiving wages; and all went on as before with the members of that family — that is to say, luxuriously and plentifully (it means in their usual hospitable and open way of living). I loved to pass my evenings in that home.

"At precisely a quarter to eleven o'clock, the old General, brushing along the *parquets with* his warmly muffled-up feet, retired to his apartments. At that same moment, hurriedly and in silence, the supper was brought in on trays, and served in the interior rooms; and immediately after this the drawing-room doors would be closely shut, and an animated conversation take place on every topic. Modem literature was reviewed and criticised, contemporary social questions from Russian life discussed; at one time it was the narrative of some visitor, a foreign traveller; or an account given of a recent skirmish by one of its heroes, some sunburnt officer just returned from the battlefield (in the Caucasus Mountains), would be eagerly listened to; at another time the antiquated old Spanish Mason (then an officer in the Russian army) Quartano, would drop in and give us thrilling stories from the wars of Napoleon the Great.

"Or again, 'Radda Bay' — H. P. Blavatsky, the granddaughter of General A. M. Fadeef — would put in an appearance, and was made to call forth from her past some stormy episode of her American life and travels; when the conversation would be sure to turn suddenly upon mystic subjects, and she herself commence to 'evoke spirits' And then the tall candles would begin to burn low, hardly flickering toward the end; the human figures on the Gobelin tapestry would seem to waken and move; and each of us feel queer from an involuntary creeping sensation; and this generally lasted until the eastern portion of the sky began to pale on the dark face of the southern night"[2]

Mme Jelihovsky says: "Mme Blavatsky resided at Tiflis less than two years, and not more than three in the Caucasus";[3] but later in her serial in *Lucifer*, she wrote: "Helena Petrovna for the next four years continued to live in the Caucasus" Her narrative goes on: "The last year she passed roaming about in Imeretia, Georgia and Mingrelia....

"It was but natural that the princes and landed 'noblemen' who lived in their 'castles' scattered through, and stuck like nests in thick foliage in the dense woods and forests of Mingrelia and Imeretia, and who, hardly half a century back, were nearly all half-brigands when not full-blown highwaymen, who are fanatical as Neapolitan monks, and ignorant as Italian noblemen — that they should, we say, have viewed such a character as was then Mme Blavatsky in the light of a witch, when not in that of a beneficent magician.

"If she cured and helped those who believed themselves sincerely bewitched, it was only to make herself cruel enemies of those who were supposed to have bewitched and spoiled the victims.... Thus, while people of the class of the Princes Gouriel and Dadiani and AbashedsS were ranked among her best friends, some others — all those who had a family hatred of the above named — were, of course, her sworn enemies....

"She avoided society, showing her scorn of its idols, and was therefore treated as a dangerous iconoclast. All her sympathies went toward that tabooed portion of humanity which society pretends to ignore and avoid while secretly running after its more or less renowned members — the necromancers, the obsessed, the possessed, and such-like mysterious personages. The native *Koodiani* (magicians, sorcerers), Persian thaumaturgists, and old Armenian hags — healers and fortune-tellers — were the first she generally sought out and took under her protection.

"Finally public opinion became furious, and society — that mysterious somebody in general, and nobody in particular — made an open levee of arms against one of its members who dared to defy its time-honoured laws and act as no *respectable* person would — namely, roaming in the forests alone, on horseback, and preferring smoky huts and their dirty inmates to brilliant drawing-rooms and their frivolous denizens.... The whole country was talking of her. The superstitious Gouriel and Mingrelian nobility began very soon to regard her as a magician, and people came from afar to consult her about their private affairs"[4]

In a letter to Mr. Sinnett, H. P. B. says: "Ask her (Vera) what she knows of my powers when I was in Imeretia and Mingrelia, in the virgin forests of Abhasia and the Black Sea coast — whether people, independent princes and archbishops and nobility, did not flock from everywhere to ask me to heal and protect them, do this and the other."[5]

"Ever in search of occupation," writes Mme Jelihovsky, "always active and full of enterprise, she established herself for some time in Imeretia, then in Mingrelia, on the shores of the Black Sea, where she connected herself with the trade in the high-class woods with which that region abounds. Later on she moved southwards to Odessa, where our aunts had gone to live after the death of our grandparents. There she placed herself at the head of an artificial flower factory, but soon left that for other enterprises, which in turn she quickly abandoned, notwithstanding the fact that they generally turned out well."⁶

Perhaps it is to this time that a certain statement, made in *The Liberal Christian* of September 4, 1875 (U.S.A.), applies: "Marvellous were her narratives of her attempts at commerce, selling a cargo of cocoanuts which an unseaworthy ship could not bring away."⁷

Her sister continues in *Lucifer*: "She was never troubled by any dread of doing anything derogatory to her position, all honest trades seemed to her equally good. It is curious to note, however, that she did not light on some occupation which would have better suited her talents than these commercial enterprises; that, for instance, she did not take instead to literature or to music, which would have better served to display her grand intellectual powers, especially as in her younger days she had never had anything to do with commerce."

Her cousin, Count Witte, says in his *Memoirs*: "She was heard of next from Odessa. At the time, our entire family was settled in that city (my grandparents and father had died at Tiflis), and my brother and I attended the university there. It was then that my versatile cousin opened in succession an ink factory and retail shop and a store of artificial flowers.

"I was specially impressed by the extraordinary facility with which she acquired skill and knowledge of the most varied description. Her abilities in this respect verged on the uncanny. A self-taught musician,* she was able to give pianoforte concerts in London and Paris, and although entirely ignorant of the theory of music, she conducted a large orchestra. Consider also that although she never seriously studied any foreign languages, she spoke several of them with perfect ease.

"I was also struck by her mastery of the technique of verse. She could write pages of smoothly flowing verse without the slightest effort, and she could compose essays in prose on every conceivable subject. Besides, she possessed the gift of hypnotising both her hearers and herself into believing the wildest inventions of her fantasy. She had, no doubt, a literary talent. The Moscow editor, Katkov, famous in the annals of Russian journalism, spoke to me in the highest terms of praise about her literary gifts, as evidenced in the tales entitled *From the Caves and Jungles of Hindustan*, which she contributed to his magazine, *The Russian Messenger* (Russky Vyestnik)."†

---

* Hardly. She had received lessons in childhood, both at home and in London.
† First published in English after her death, in 1892; though the tales had appeared in a Russian

Ultimately she bought a house at Ozoorgetty, a military settlement in Mingrelia, a small town, lost among old forests that had neither roads nor conveyances, except of the most primitive. In her little home at Ozoorgetty, Mme Blavatsky fell very ill. Says Mme Jelihovsky in her narrative to Mr. Sinnett: "It was one of those mysterious nervous diseases that baffle science, and elude the grasp of everyone but a very expert psychologist. She began — as she repeatedly told her friends — 'to lead a double life.' What she meant by it, no one of the good people of Mingrelia could understand. This is how she herself describes the state:

"Whenever I was called by name, I opened my eyes upon hearing it, and was myself, my own personality in every particular. As soon as I was left alone, however, I relapsed into my usual, half-dreamy condition, and became *somebody else* (who, namely, Mme B. will not tell). I had simply a mild fever that consumed me slowly but surely, day after day, with entire loss of appetite, and finally of hunger, as I would feel none for days, and often went a week without touching any food whatever, except a little water; so that in four months I was reduced to a living skeleton.

"In cases where I was interrupted, when in my other self, by the sound of my present name being pronounced, and while I was conversing in my dream life — say at half a sentence either spoken by me or those who were with my *second me* at the time — and opened my eyes to answer the call, I used to answer very rationally, and understood all, for I was never delirious. But no sooner had I closed my eyes again than the sentence which had been interrupted was completed by my other self, continued from the word, or even half the word, it had stopped at. When awake, and *myself*, I remembered well *who I was* in my second capacity, and what I had been and was doing. When somebody else, i.e., the personage I had become, I know I had no idea of who was H. P. Blavatsky! I was in another far-off country, a totally different individuality from myself, and had no connection at all with my actual life."[8]

Perhaps the following, written by H. P. B. many years later, throws fight on this abstruse subject: "This power is latent in man, and not in solitary units of the human family only, though this mystery of *dual* life in every man, woman and child may remain unknown to them ninety-nine times out of a hundred. This ignorance is due to our Western modes of life....

edition as early as 1883.

"For who of us knows, or has any means of knowing *Self*, while he lives in the lethal atmosphere of whether Society or Proletariat? Who, taught from babyhood that he is born in sin, helpless as a reed, whose only true support is the 'Lord' — can think of testing his own powers, when even their presence in him is a thought that could never enter his mind? Between the eternal struggle for more gold, more honours, more power in the higher classes, and the 'struggle for existence,' for bread and life, in the lower ones, there is no time or room for the manifestation of the 'inner man' in us.

"Thus from birth to death that ego slumbers, paralysed by the external man, and asserts itself only occasionally in dreams, in casual visions, and strange 'coincidences' — unbidden and unheeded. The *Psychic* or higher self has to be first of all entirely ridden of the soporific influence of the *Personal Self*, before it can proclaim obviously its existence and actual presence in man.*

"But once this condition is fulfilled, then truly 'he who reigns within himself and rules passions, desires and fears is more than a king' — as Milton says: for he *is an adept already*; the *shell* alone between the inner man and the world of objective as subjective manifestation, is to be overcome; and when it offers no better resistance than a merely passive one, then the higher self is as free as on the day on which that shell will be left behind him forever.†

"But there are individuals who seem born with this capacity, for certain mysterious objects of karma, and whose *inner* selves are so strong as to actually reduce to nought the resistance of their personal or provisional bodies."⁹

To resume the story of H. P. B.'s illness: "The only physician of the place, the army surgeon, could make nothing of her symptoms; but as she was visibly and rapidly declining, he packed her off to Tiflis to her friends. Unable to go on horseback, owing to her great weakness, and a journey in a cart being deemed dangerous, she was sent off in a large native boat along the river — a journey of four days to Kutais — with four native servants only to take care of her....

"In that solitary boat, on a narrow river, hedged on both sides by centenarian

---

* This is probably what H. P. B. means when she says that there are millions of soulless men in the world.

† She once wrote to Mr. Wm. L. Judge: "Yes, there are 'two persons' in me. But what of that? So there are two in you; only mine is conscious and responsible — and yours is not." — The Path, July, 1892.

forests, her position must have been precarious. The little stream they were sailing along was, though navigable, rarely, if ever, used.... It appears that as they were gliding slowly along the narrow stream, cutting its way between two steep and woody banks, the servants were several times during three consecutive nights frightened out of their senses by seeing, *what they swore was their mistress*, gliding off from the boat, and across the water in the direction of the forests, while the body of that same mistress was lying prostrate on her bed at the bottom of the boat.

"Twice the man who towed the canoe, upon seeing the 'form,' ran away shrieking, and in great terror. Had it not been for a faithful old servant who was taking care of her, the boat and the patient would have been abandoned in the middle of the stream. On the last evening, the servant swore he saw two figures, while the third — his mistress, in flesh and bone — was sleeping before his eyes. No sooner had they arrived at Kutais, where Mme Blavatsky had a distant relative residing, than all the servants, with the exception of the old butler, left her, and returned no more.

"It was with great difficulty that she was transported to Tiflis. A carriage and a friend of the family were sent to meet her; and she was brought into the house of her friends apparently dying. She never talked upon that subject with anyone....

"One afternoon, very weak and delicate still after the illness just described, Mme Blavatsky came in to her aunt's, N. A. Fadeef's room. After a few words of conversation, remarking that she felt tired and sleepy, she was offered to rest upon the sofa. Hardly had her head touched the cushion when she fell into a profound sleep. Her aunt had quietly resumed some writing she had interrupted to talk to her niece, when suddenly soft but quite audible steps in the room behind her chair made her rapidly turn her head to see who was the intruder, as she was anxious that Mme Blavatsky should not be disturbed.

"The room was empty! There was no other living person in it but herself and her sleeping niece; yet the steps continued audibly, as though of a heavy person treading softly, the floor creaking all the while. They approached the sofa, and suddenly ceased. Then she heard stronger sounds as though someone was whispering near Mme Blavatsky, and presently a book on a table near the sofa was seen by N. A. Fadeef to open, and its pages kept turning to and fro, as if an invisible hand were busy at it. Another book was snatched from the library shelves, and flew in that same direction.

"More astonished than frightened — for everyone in the house had been trained in and become quite familiar with such manifestations — N. A. Fadeef arose from her arm-chair to awaken her niece, hoping thereby to put a stop to the phenomena; but at the same moment a heavy arm-chair moved at the other end of the room, and rattling on the floor, glided toward the sofa. The noise it made awoke Mme Blavatsky who, upon opening her eyes, inquired of the invisible presence what was the matter. A few more whisperings, and all relapsed into quietness and silence, and there was nothing more of the sort during the rest of the evening."[10]

CHAPTER XIX
Psychic Development In Russia

"Spiritism (or Spiritualism) was then just looming on the horizon of Europe. During her travels, the psychological peculiarities of Mme Blavatsky's childhood and girlhood had developed, and she returned already possessed of occult powers which were in those days attributed to mediumship."[1]

"At last, to the incessant questions of her sister, she confessed that these manifestations had never ceased to follow her everywhere, as in the early days of her infancy and youth. That such raps could be increased or diminished, and at times even made to cease altogether, by the mere force of her will, she also acknowledged, proving her assertion generally on the spot. Of course, the good people of Pskoff, like the rest of the world, knew what was then occurring, and had heard of Spiritualism and its manifestations. There had been mediums in Petersburg, but they had not penetrated as far as Pskoff, and its guileless inhabitants had never heard the rappings of the so-called 'spirits.'"[2]

"When addressed as a medium," says Mme Jelihovsky, "Mme Blavatsky used to laugh and assure us that she was no medium, but only a *mediator* between mortals and beings whom we knew nothing about. But I could never understand the difference.... My sister had passed most of her time, during her many years' absence from Russia, travelling in India where, as we are now informed, spiritual theories are held in great scorn, and the so-called (by us) mediumistic phenomena are said to be caused by quite another agency than that of spirits; mediumship proceeding, they say, from a source, to draw from which my sister thinks it degrading to her human dignity; in consequence of which ideas she refuses to acknowledge such a force in herself."³

"It is impossible to give in detail even a portion of what was produced in the way of such phenomena during the stay of Mme Blavatsky amongst us in the town of Pskoff. But they may be mentioned under general classification as follows:

1. Direct and perfectly clear written and verbal answers to mental questions — or 'thought-reading.'
2. Prescriptions for different diseases, in Latin, and subsequent cures.
3. Private secrets, unknown to all but the interested party, divulged, especially in the case of those persons who mentioned insulting doubts.
4. Change in weight of furniture and of persons, at will.
5. Letters from unknown correspondents, and immediate answers written to queries made, and found in the most out-of-the-way mysterious places.
6. Appearance and *apport* of objects unclaimed by anyone present.
7. Sounds as of musical notes, in the air wherever Mme Blavatsky desired they should resound."⁴

"We soon arrived at the conviction that the forces at work, as Mme Blavatsky constantly told us, had to be divided into several distinct categories. While the lowest on the scale of invisible beings produced most of the physical phenomena, the very highest of the agencies at work condescended but rarely to a communication or intercourse with strangers. The last-named 'invisibles' made themselves manifestly seen, felt and heard only during those hours when we were alone in the family, and when great harmony and quiet reigned among us... when no one cared to make experiments or sought useless tests and when there was no one to convince or enlighten....

"In the majority of cases the phenomena were sporadic, seemingly quite independent of her will, apparently never heeding anyone's suggestion, and generally appearing in direct contradiction with the desires expressed by those present. We used to feel extremely vexed whenever there was a chance to convince some highly intellectual investigator, but through H.P.B.'s obstinacy or lack of will nothing came out of it....

"I well remember how, during a grand evening party, when several families had come from afar off, in some cases from distances of hundreds of miles, on purpose to witness some phenomena... Mme Blavatsky, though assuring us she did all she could, gave them no result to ponder upon. This lasted for several days.* The visitors had left dissatisfied, and in a spirit as sceptical as it was uncharitable.

"Hardly, however, had the gates been closed after them, the bells of their horses yet merrily tinkling in the last alley of the entrance park, when everything in the room seemed to become endowed with life. The furniture acted as though every piece of it was animated and gifted with voice and speech, and we passed the rest of the evening and the greatest part of the night as though we were between the enchanted walls of the magic palace of some Sheherazade....

"At one moment as we sat at supper in the dining-room, there were loud accords played on the piano which stood in the adjoining apartment, and which was closed and locked, and so placed that we could all of us see it from where we were through the large open doors.

"Then at the first command and look of Mme Blavatsky, there came rushing at her through the air her tobacco-pouch, her box of matches, her pocket handkerchief, or anything she asked for, or was made to ask for. Then, as we were taking our seats, all the lights in the room were suddenly extinguished, both lamps and wax candles, as though a mighty rush of wind had swept through the whole apartment; and when a match was instantly struck, there was all the furniture — sofas, arm-chairs, tables, cupboards and large sideboard — standing upside down, as though turned over noiselessly by some invisible hands, and not an ornament of the fragile carved work nor even a plate broken.

"Hardly had we gathered our senses together after this miraculous performance, than we heard again *someone* playing on the piano a loud and intelligible piece of music, a long *marche de bravoure* this time. As we rushed with lighted candles to the instrument (I mentally counting all the persons to ascertain that all were present) we found, as we had anticipated, the piano locked, the last sounds of the final chords still vibrating in the air, from beneath the heavy closed lid"⁵

"She was what would be called in our days 'a good writing medium'; that is to say, she could write out the answers herself while talking with those around her upon quite indifferent topics.... From the first, almost from her childhood, and certainly in the days mentioned above, Mme Blavatsky, as

---

* H. P. B. explained this by describing herself as tired and disgusted with the ever-growing public thirst for "miracles."

she tells us, would in such cases see either the actual present thought of the person putting the questions, or its paler reflection — still quite distinct for her — of an event, or a name, or whatever it was, as though hanging in a shadow-world around the person, generally in the vicinity of the head. She had but to copy it consciously, or allow her hand to do so mechanically. At any rate, she never felt herself helped or led on by an external power, i.e., no 'spirits' helped her in this process after she returned from her first voyage, she avers....

"Whenever the thought of a person had to be communicated through raps, the process changed. She had to read, first of all, sometimes to interpret, the thought of the querist; and having done so, remember it well after it had often disappeared; watch the letters of the alphabet as they were read or pointed out; prepare the will current that had to produce the raps at the right letter, and then have it strike at the right moment the table or any other object chosen to be the vehicle of sounds or raps."[6]

"It often happened that my sister, being occupied with her reading, we — our father, the governess and myself — unwilling to disturb her, communicated with the invisible power *mentally* and in silence, simply thinking out our questions, and writing down the letters rapped out either on the walls or the table near us.... It is most extraordinary that our *silent* conversations, with that *intelligent* force that had ever manifested itself in my sister's presence, were found by us the most successful during her sleep or when she was very ill."[7]

"She had long since given up communication through raps[*] and preferred — what was a far more rapid and satisfactory method — to answer people either verbally or by means of direct writing. This was always done in full consciousness and simply, as she explained, by watching people's thoughts as they evolved out of their heads in spiral luminous smoke, sometimes in jets of what might be taken for some radiant material, and settled in distinct pictures and images around them.

"Often such thoughts and answers to them would find themselves impressed in her own brain, couched in words and sentences in the same way as original thoughts do. But, as far as we are able to understand, the former visions are always more trustworthy, as they are independent and distinct from the seer's own impressions, belonging to pure clairvoyance,

[*] Speaking of the time when she was in Mingrelia.

and not to thought-transference, which is a process always liable to get mixed up with one's own more vivid impressions.

"At times during such process (of direct writing), Mme Blavatsky seemed to fall into a kind of coma, or magnetic sleep, with eyes wide open, though even then her hand never ceased to move, and she continued its writing. When thus answering mental questions, the answers were rarely unsatisfactory;" to which H. P. B. herself adds in a footnote: "Very naturally, since it was neither 'magnetic sleep' nor coma, but simply a state of intense concentration, an attention only too necessary during such concentration, when the least distraction leads to a mistake. People knowing but of mediumistic clairvoyance, and not of our philosophy and mode of operation, often fall into such error."

"Her occult powers all this while, instead of weakening, became every day stronger, and she seemed finally to subject to her will every kind of manifestation.... Meanwhile sporadic phenomena were gradually dying away in her presence. They still occurred, but very rarely, though they were always very remarkable."[8]

"As soon as she was restored to life and health [after her mysterious illness], Mme Blavatsky left the Caucasus, and went to Italy. Yet it was before her departure from the country in 1863, that the nature of her powers seems to have changed."[9]

"At the date at which we write (1885), every phenomenon independent of her will... has for more than twenty years entirely ceased. At what time this complete change in her occult powers was wrought, we are unable to say, as she was far away from our observation, and spoke of it but rarely — never unless distinctly asked in our correspondence to answer the question.... We believe her statement to have been entirely true when she wrote to us: 'Now (in 1866) I shall never be subjected to external influences.'"[10]

"'I believe this statement,' said her sister, Mme Jelihovsky, in a conversation at Paris, 'the more so as for nearly five years we had a personal opportunity of following the various and gradual phases in the transformations of that force. At Pskoff and Rougo-devo it happened very often, that she could not control, nor even stop, its manifestations. After that she appeared to master it more fully every day; until after her extraordinary and protracted illness at Tiflis, she seemed to defy and subject it entirely to her will.

"'This was proved by her stopping such phenomena at her will, and by previous arrangement, for days and weeks at a time. Then when the term was over, she could produce them at her command and leaving the choice of what should happen to those present. In short, it is the firm belief of all that, *where a less strong nature would have been surely wrecked in the struggle, her indomitable will found somehow or other the means of subjecting the world of the invisibles — to the denizens of which she has ever refused the name of 'spirits' and souls — to her own control.*'" [11]

CHAPTER XX

Third Attempt To Reach Tibet

As soon as she was fully recovered from her mysterious illness in the Caucasus, Mme Blavatsky left Russia — "and went to Italy" we are told in *Incidents in the Life of Mme Blavatsky*; she herself says: "Left Tiflis about '64 and went to Servia, travelled about in Karpat, all as I explain in my story about the Double;"[1] "left again for foreign parts, first for Greece and then for Egypt," says Mme Jelihovsky in *Lucifer*.

"All her life was passed in restlessness and travelling; she was ever, as it were, seeking some unknown goal, some task which it was her duty to discover and to fulfill. Her wandering life and unsettled ways did not end until she found herself face to face with the scientific, the humanitarian and spiritual problems presented by Theosophy; then she stopped short like a ship which, after years of wandering, finds itself in port, the sails are furled, and for the last time the anchor is let go.

"Mr. Sinnett, her biographer, alleges that for many years ere she left definitely for America [1873], Mme Blavatsky had had spiritual relations with those strange beings, whom she later called her Masters, the Mahatmas of Ceylon and Tibet, and that it was only in direct obedience to their commands that she travelled from place to place, from one country to another.... We her nearest relations, for the first time heard her mention these enigmatic beings in 1874, when she was established in New York."[2]

But some years earlier, in her *Memoirs*, Mme Jelihovsky had written: "Everyone considered the manifestations taking place in my sister's presence as caused by the 'spirits' and through her mediumistic power; she herself *has constantly denied it*.... She asserts *now as then* that quite another power influenced her then as it does now, namely the power acquired by the Hindu sages — the Raj-Yogis. She assures me that even the shadows she used to see, and saw during her whole life, were no ghosts or spirits of deceased persons, but simply the astral bodies of her all-powerful Hindu friends."[3] "What's in a name?" Whether H. P. B. called them " Raj-Yogis" or " Mahatmas," she meant the same Persons.

In *Lucifer* of January, 1895, Mme Jelihovsky quaintly remarks: "As for myself, I have never seen them, nevertheless I have no right to doubt their existence, testified to by persons whose truthfulness cannot be questioned. All the same, these apparitions have always seemed to me very problematical, and this opinion I have never hesitated to express to my sister, on which she would reply: 'As you like, my dear... I wish you better understanding.'"

In Dr. Besant's itinerary, Mme Blavatsky is said to have gone to Egypt and Persia in 1863, and to have crossed Central Asia to Tibet in 1864. These dates should be set forward by a year. As, according to her sister Vera, she went " first to Greece" before embarking on this third attempt to reach her Master's home in Tibet, it may be that she was accompanied by, or at least received instructions from, Illarion, a fellow-student of occultism, who lived at Cyprus, " A Greek gentleman I have known since 1860," she says. From Greece she proceeded to Egypt; to reach Persia from thence, she would need to cross Syria. Of her activities there, either at this time or when she returned in 1871, she sketches a few pictures in *Isis Unveiled*:

"Whoever desires to assure himself that there now exists a religion which has baffled, for centuries, the impudent inquisitiveness of missionaries and the persevering inquiry of science, let him violate, if he can, the seclusion of the Syrian Druzes. He will find them numbering over 80,000 warriors, scattered from the plain east of Damascus to the western coast. They covet no proselytes, shun notoriety.... There was never a case of an *initiated* Druze* becoming a Christian. As to the uninitiated, they are never allowed to even see the sacred writings, and none of them have the remotest idea where these are kept....

"The characteristic dogma of the Druzes is the absolute unity of God. He is the essence of life, and although incomprehensible and invisible, is to be known through *occasional manifestations in human form*. Like the Hindus, they hold that He was incarnated more than once on earth. Hamsa was the *precursor* of the last manifestation to be (the tenth avatar), not the

* Called an *Okhal*.

inheritor of Hakem, who is yet to come. Hamsa was the personification of the 'Universal Wisdom.' Boha-eddin, in his writings, calls him Messiah.... Hamsa, like Jesus, was a mortal man; and yet 'Hamsa' and 'Christos' are synonymous terms as to their inner and hidden meaning. Both are symbols of the *Nous*, the divine and higher soul of man — his spirit. The doctrine taught by the Druzes on that particular question of the duality of spiritual man, consisting of one soul mortal, and another immortal, is identical with that of the Gnostics, the older Greek philosophers, and other initiates....

"Their stages or degrees of promotion after initiation are five.... Their ideas on Transmigration are Pythagorean and kabalistic....

The life of man they divide into soul, body, and the intelligence, or mind. It is the latter which imparts and communicates to the soul the divine spark from its Hamsa (Christos).... They have seven great commandments, which are imparted equally to all the uninitiated....

"The morality of the Druzes is strict and uncompromising. Nothing can tempt one of these Lebanon Unitarians to go astray from what he is taught to consider his duty. *Their ritual being unknown to outsiders*, their would-be historians have hitherto denied them one. Their 'Thursday meetings' are open to all, but no interloper has ever participated in the rites of initiation which take place occasionally on Fridays in the greatest secrecy. Women are admitted to them as well as men, and they play a part of great importance at the initiation of men. The probation, unless some extraordinary exception is made, is long and severe.... (p. 312)

"Before we close the subject, we may add that if a stranger ask for admission to a 'Thursday meeting' he will never be refused. Only, if he is a Christian, the *Okhal* will open a *Bible* and read from it; and if a Mahometan, he will hear a few chapters of the *Koran*, and the ceremony will end with this. They will wait until he has gone, and then, shutting well the doors of their convent, take to their own rites and books, passing for this purpose into their subterranean sanctuaries. (p. 315)

"Outside the East we have met one initiate («id only one), who, for some reasons best known to himself, does not make a secret of his initiation into the Brotherhood of Lebanon. It is the learned traveller and artist, Professor A. L. Rawson, of New York City."[4] (p. 312.)

Professor Rawson, in an article called "Two Mme Blavatskys," says: "There is no doubt in my mind that Mme Blavatsky was made acquainted with many, if not quite all, of the rites, ceremonies and instructions practised among the Druzes of Mount Lebanon in Syria; for she speaks to me of things that are only known by the favoured few who have been initiated. In my visits to the Levant, her name has frequently been met with, in Tripolis, Beirut, Deir el Kamer, Damascus, Jerusalem and Cairo. She was well known to a merchant of Jiddah, who has a ring with her initials, which he said was a present to him from her. His servant, a camel-driver formerly, says he was dragoman and camelji to Mme Blavatsky from Jiddah to Mecca. I inquired of the Shereef of Mecca, but heard nothing of her there. She may have been *incog*, while there for prudential reasons. My visit was made as a Mohammadan divinity student, and secretary to Kamil Pasha, in whose company I journeyed."[5]

Of the Yezidis, she writes in *Isis Unveiled*: "We have met few sects which truly practise sorcery. One such is the Yezidis, considered by some a branch of the Koords, though we believe erroneously. These inhabit chiefly the mountainous and desolate regions of Asiatic Turkey, about Mosul, Armenia, and are found even in Syria and Mesopotamia. They are called and known everywhere as devil-worshippers.... They recognise the present wickedness of the chief of the 'black powers'; but at the same time they dread his power, and so try to conciliate to themselves his favours. He is in constant quarrel with Allah, they say, but a reconciliation can take place between the two any day....

"During their prayer-meetings, they join hands and form immense rings with their Sheik or an officiating priest in the middle, who claps his hands and intones every verse in honour of Sheitan (Satan). Then they whirl and leap in the air. When the frenzy is at its climax, they often wound and cut themselves with their daggers, occasionally rendering the same service to their neighbours. But their wounds do not heal and cicatrize as easily as in the case of lamas and holy men; for but too often they fall victims to these self-inflicted wounds. While dancing... they coax and praise Sheitan and entreat him to manifest himself in his works by 'miracles.' As their rites are chiefly accomplished during night, they do not fail to obtain manifestations of a varied character, the least of which are enormous globes of fire which take the shapes of the most uncouth animals.

"Lady Esther Stanhope, whose name was for many years a power among the Masonic fraternities of the East, is said to have witnessed personally several of these Yezidean ceremonies. We were told by an *Ockhal* of the sect of Druzes, that after having been present at one of the Yezidis' 'Devil's masses,' as they are called, this extraordinary lady, so noted for personal courage and daring bravery, fainted and notwithstanding her usual Emir's male attire, was recalled to life and health with the greatest difficulty. Personally, we regret to say, all our efforts to witness one of these performances failed."[6]

Mme Blavatsky gives an interesting pen-picture of an incident of her travels in Persia, in *Isis Unveiled:* " In the eastern portion of Turkey and Persia have dwelt, from time immemorial, the warlike tribes of the Koordistan. This people of purely Indo-European origin, and without a drop of Semitic blood in them (though some ethnologists seem to think otherwise), notwithstanding their brigandlike disposition unite in themselves the mysticism of the Hindu and the practices of the Assyro-Chaldean magians, vast portions of whose territory they have helped themselves to, and will not give up, to please either Turkey or even all Europe.

"Nominally Mahometans of the sect of Omar, their rites and doctrines are purely magical and magian. Even those who are Christian Nestorians, are Christians but in name. The Kaldany, numbering nearly 100,000 men, and with their two Patriarchs, are undeniably rather Manicheans than Nestorians. Many of them are Yezids.

["We have twice assisted at the strange rites of the remnants of that sect of fire-worshippers known as the Guebers who assemble from time to time at Baku, on the 'field of fire.' This ancient and mysterious town is situated near the Caspian Sea. It belongs to Russian Georgia. About twelve miles north-east from Baku, stands the remnant of an ancient Guebre temple, consisting of four columns, from whose empty orifices issue constantly jets of flame which gives it therefore the name of Temple of the Perpetual Fire. The whole region is covered with lakes and springs of naphtha. Pilgrims assemble there from distant parts of Asia, and a priesthood, worshipping the divine principle of fire, is kept by some tribes scattered hither and thither about the country."] (p. 632 footnote.)

"One of these tribes is noted for its fire-worshipping predilections. At sunrise and sunset the horsemen alight and, turning towards the sun, mutter a prayer; while at every new moon they perform mysterious rites throughout the whole night. They have a tent set apart for the purpose; and its thick, black, woollen fabric is decorated with weird signs, worked in bright red and yellow.

"In the centre is placed a kind of altar, encircled by three brass bands, to which are suspended numerous rings by ropes of camel's hair, which every worshipper holds with his right hand during the ceremony. On the altar burns a curious, old-fashioned silver lamp, a relic found possibly among the ruins of Persepolis. This lamp, with three wicks, is an oblong cup with a handle to it, and is evidently of the class of Egyptian sepulchral lamps, once found in such profusion in the subterranean caves of Memphis, if we may believe Kiercher. It widened from its end toward the middle, and its upper part was of the shape of a heart; the apertures for the wicks forming a triangle, and its centre being covered by an inverted heliotrope attached to a gracefully curved stalk proceeding from the handle of the lamp. This ornament clearly bespoke its origin. It was one of the sacred vessels used in sun-worship. The Greeks gave the *heliotrope* its name from its strange propensity to ever incline towards the sun. The ancient Magi used it in their worship; and who knows but Darius had performed the mysterious rites with its triple light illuminating the face of the king-hierophant!

"If we mention the lamp at all, it is because there happened to be a strange story in connection with it. What the Koords do during their nocturnal rites of lunar-worship, we know but from hearsay; for they conceal it carefully, and no stranger could be admitted to witness the ceremony. But every tribe has one old man, sometimes several, regarded as 'holy beings,' who know the past, and can divulge the secrets of the future. These are greatly honoured, and generally resorted to for information in cases of theft, murder, or danger.

"Travelling from one tribe to the other, we passed some time in company with these Koords. As our object is not autobiographical we omit all details that have no immediate bearing upon some occult fact, and even of these have room but for a few. We will then simply state that a very expensive saddle, a carpet, and two Circassian daggers, richly mounted and chiselled in gold, had been stolen from the tent; and that the Koords, with the chief of the tribe at the head, had come, taking Allah for their witness that the culprit could not belong to their tribe. We believed it, for it would have been unprecedented among these nomad tribes of Asia, as famed for the sacredness in which they hold their guests, as for the ease with which they plunder and occasionally murder them, when once they have passed the boundaries of their *aotil*.

"A suggestion was then made by a Georgian belonging to our caravan, to have resort to the light of the *Koodian* (sorcerer) of their tribe. This was arranged in great secrecy and solemnity, and the interview appointed to take place at midnight, when the moon would be at its full. At the stated hour, we were conducted to the above-described tent.

"A large hole, or square aperture, was managed in the arched roof of the tent, and through it poured in vertically the radiant moonbeams, mingling with the vacillating triple flame of the little lamp. After several minutes of incantations, addressed as it seemed to us to the moon, the conjurer, an old man of tremendous stature whose pyramidal turban touched the top of the tent, produced a round looking-glass of the kind known as 'Persian mirrors.' Having unscrewed its cover, he proceeded to breathe on it for over ten minutes, and wipe off the moisture from the surface with a package of herbs, muttering incantations the while *sotto voce*. After every wiping, the glass became more and more brilliant, till its crystal seemed to radiate refulgent rays in every direction.

"At last the operation was ended; the old man, with the mirror in his hand, remained as motionless as if he had been a statue. 'Look, Hanoum, look steadily,' he whispered, hardly moving his lips. Shadows and dark spots began gathering, where one moment before nothing was reflected but the radiant face of the full moon. A few more seconds, and there appeared the well-known saddle, carpet, and daggers, which seemed to be rising as from deep, clear water, and becoming with every instant more definitely outlined. Then a still darker shadow appeared hovering over these objects, which gradually condensed itself, and then came out, as visibly as at the small end of a telescope, the full figure of a man crouching over them.

"'I know him,' exclaimed the writer. 'It is the Tartar who came to us last night, offering to sell his mule.'

"The image disappeared, as if by enchantment. The old man nodded assent, but remained motionless. Then he muttered again some strange words, and suddenly began a song. The tune was slow and monotonous, but after he had sung a few stanzas in the same unknown tongue, without changing either rhythm or tune, he pronounced, *recitative-like*, the following words, in his broken Russian: 'Now, Hanoum, look well, whether we will catch him — the fate of the robber — we will learn this night' etc.

"The same shadows began gathering, and then almost without transition we saw the man lying on his back, in a pool of blood, across the saddle, and two other men galloping off at a distance. Horror-stricken, and sick at the sight of this picture, we desired to see no more. The old man, leaving the tent, called some of the Koords standing outside, and seemed to give them instructions. Two minutes later, a dozen horsemen were galloping off at full speed, down the side of the mountain on which we were encamped.

"Early in the morning, they returned with the lost objects. The saddle was all covered with coagulated blood, and of course abandoned to them. The story they told was, that coming in sight of the fugitive, they saw disappearing over the crest of a distant hill two horsemen; and upon riding up, the Tartar thief was found dead upon the stolen property, exactly as we had seen him in the magical glass. He had been murdered by the two banditti, whose evident design to rob him was interrupted by the sudden appearance of the party sent by the old Koodian."[7]

CHAPTER XXI

Buddhist Lamaseries And Convents

Although it was not until 1864 that Mme Blavatsky finally reached the goal she had set for herself; namely, her Master's *ashrama*, yet she had been in Tibet before that time. In a criticism of Mr. Arthur Lillie's pamphlet, *Buddha and Early Buddhism*, she says: "I have lived at different periods in Little Tibet as in Great Tibet, and these combined periods form more than seven years. Yet, I have never stated either verbally or over my signature that I had passed seven consecutive years in a convent. What I have said and repeat now is, that I have visited Tzi-gadze, the Tdashoo-Hlumpo territory and its neighbourhood, and that I have been farther in, and in such places of Tibet as have never been visited by other Europeans...." [1]

"Again,' she (I) now tells us that she was never a Thibetan nun'!!! When have I ever told anyone such an absurdity? When have I said that I had been one? Had I claimed to be one, then indeed, if the writer knew anything about Thibet or Thibetans, he might rush into print; for he would have the right to doubt my statement and expose my imposture, since that would have been one. A nun in Thibet, a regular 'ani,' once consecrated, never leaves her convent except for pilgrimages, so long as she remains in the Order.

"Nor have I ever received any instruction 'under the roof' of the monks; nor has anyone ever claimed such a thing on my behalf, or to my knowledge. I might have lived in male lamaseries, as thousands of lay men and women do; and I might have received my 'instruction' there. Anyone can go to Darjeeling and receive, a few miles from there, teaching from Thibetan monks, and 'under their roofs.' But I have never so claimed, for the simple reason that *neither of the Mahatmas* whose names are known in the

West *are monks*...

"I close by informing Mr. Lillie that years before he had an idea of Buddhists and Thibetans, I was quite familiar with the Lamaism of Thibetan Buddhists. I passed months and years of my childhood among the Lamaist Calmucks of Astrakhan, and with their great priest. However 'heretical' in their religious terminology, the Calmucks have still the same identical terms as the other Lamaists of Thibet (from whence they came). As, however, I had visited Semipalatinsck and the Ural Mountains with an uncle of mine, who has possessions in Siberia, on the very borderland of the Mongolian countries where the 'Terachan Lama' resides, and had made numerous excursions beyond the frontiers, and knew all about Lamas and Thibetans before I was fifteen; therefore I could hardly have ever thought 'that Chinese was the language of Thibet.'...

"But possibly this does not count; I should have learned my Buddhism and Lamaism in Mr. Lillie's school, rather than in Astrakhan, Mongolia or Thibet, if I thought of setting up as an authority for such critics as those in *Light*.... Well, so be it. I leave them to feed their censers with their own incense. I shall waste no more time in trying to correct their hydra-headed 'mistakes,' for when one is slain ten more spring up from the dead carcass"[2]

There came recently (1927) through one of the greatest living students of Tibet and its philosophies, Mr. W. Y. Evans-Wentz, a corroboration of H. P. B.'s sojourn in that country. He writes in his *Tibetan Book of the Dead*: "As regards the esoteric meaning of the Forty-nine Days of Bardo, compare H. P. Blavatsky, *The Secret Doctrine* (London, 1888) I — 238, 411; II — 617, 627-8. The late Lama Kazi Dawa Samdup was of opinion that, despite the adverse criticisms directed against H. P. Blavatsky's works, there is adequate internal evidence in them of their author's intimate acquaintance with the higher *lamaistic* teachings, into which she claimed to have been initiated."[3]

Mme Blavatsky has given a detailed and interesting account of Buddhist monasteries and convents in Mongolia, Tibet, and Nepal, together with some of her experiences there, in *Isis Unveiled*, from which the following extracts have been collected: "Both in Western and Eastern Tibet, as in every other place where Buddhism predominates, there are two distinct religions.... The Buddhism of Nepal, being the one which may be said to have diverged less than any other from the primeval ancient faith, the Lamaism of Tartary, Mongolia, and Thibet, may be thus shown to be the purest

Buddhism; for, we say it again, Lamaism is but an external form of rites.

"The Upasakas and Upasakis, or male and female semi-monastics and semi-laymen, have equally with the lama monks themselves, to strictly abstain from violating any of Buddha's rules, and must study *Meipo** and every psychological phenomenon. Those who become guilty of any of the 'five sins' lose all right to congregate with the pious community. The most important of these is *not to curse upon any consideration, for the curse returns upon the one that utters it, and often upon his innocent relatives who breathe the same atmosphere with him.*

"To love each other and even our bitterest enemies; to offer our lives even for animals, to the extent of abstaining from defensive arms; to gain the greatest of victories by conquering one's self; to avoid all vices; to practise all virtues, especially humility and mildness; to be obedient to superiors, to cherish and respect parents, old age, learning, virtuous and holy men; to provide food, shelter, and comfort for men and animals; to plant trees on the roads and dig wells for the comfort of travellers; such are the moral duties of Buddhists. Every Ani, or Bikshuni (nun), is subjected to these laws...."[4]

"Many of the lamaseries contain schools of magic, but the most celebrated is the collegiate monastery of the Shu-tukt, to which there are attached over 30,000 monks, the lamasery forming quite a little city. Some of the female nuns possess marvellous psychological powers. We have met some of these women on their way from Lha-Ssa to Candi,† the Rome of Buddhism, with its miraculous shrines and Gautama's relics. To avoid encounters with Mussalmans and other sects, they travel by night alone, unarmed, and without the least fear of wild animals, *for these will not touch them*. At the first glimpse of dawn, they take refuge in caves and *viharas*, prepared for them by their co-religionists at calculated distances; for notwithstanding the fact that Buddhism has taken refuge in Ceylon, and nominally there are but few of the denomination in British India, yet the secret *Byauds* (Brotherhoods) and Buddhist *viharas* are numerous, and every Jain feels himself obliged to help, indiscriminately, Buddhist or Lamaist.

"Ever on the look-out for occult phenomena, hungering after sights, one of the most interesting that we have seen was produced by one of these poor

---

* Magic.

† Kandy, Ceylon.

travelling Biskshunis. It was years ago, and at a time when all such manifestations were new to the writer. We were taken to visit the pilgrims by a Buddhist friend, a mystical gentleman born at Kashmir, of Katchi parents, but a Buddha-Lamaist by conversion, and who generally resides at Lha-Ssa.

"'Why carry about this bunch of dead plants?' inquired one of the Bikshunis, an emaciated, tall and elderly woman, pointing to a large nosegay of beautiful, fresh and fragrant flowers in the writer's hands.

"'Dead?' we asked, inquiringly. 'Why, they have just been gathered in the garden.'

"'And yet, they are dead,' she gravely answered. 'To be born in this world, is this not death? See, how these herbs look when alive in the world of eternal light, in the gardens of our blessed Foh.'

"Without moving from the place where she was sitting on the ground, the Ani took a flower from the bunch, laid it in her lap, and began to draw together, by large handfuls as it were, invisible material from the surrounding atmosphere. Presently a very, very faint nodule of vapour was seen, and this slowly took shape and colour, until poised in mid-air, appeared a copy of the bloom we had given her. Faithful to the last line and the last petal it was, and lying on its side like the original, but a thousand-fold more gorgeous in hue and exquisite in beauty, as the glorified human spirit is more beauteous than its physical capsule.

"Flower after flower to the minutest herb was thus reproduced and made to vanish, reappearing at our desire, nay, at our simple thought. Having selected a full-blown rose, we held it at arm's length, and in a few minutes our arm, hand, and the flower, perfect in every detail, appeared reflected in the vacant space, about two yards from where we sat. But while the flower seemed immeasurably beautified and as ethereal as the other spirit flowers, the arm and hand appeared like a mere reflection in a looking-glass, even to a large spot on the forearm, left on it by a piece of damp earth which had stuck to one of the roots. Later we learned the reason why."[5]

"What is generally known as Shamanism is very little; and that has been perverted, like the rest of the non-Christian religions. It is called the 'heathenism' of Mongolia, and wholly without reason, for it is one of the oldest religions of India. It is spirit-worship, or belief in the immortality of the souls, and that the latter are still the same men they were on earth, though their bodies have lost their objective form, and man has exchanged his physical for a spiritual nature.

"In its present shape, it is an offshoot of primitive theurgy, and a practical blending of the visible with the invisible world. Whenever a denizen of earth desires to enter into communication with his invisible brethren, he has to assimilate himself to their nature, i.e., he meets these beings half-way, and furnished by them with a supply of spiritual essence, endows them in his turn with a portion of his physical nature, thus enabling them sometimes to appear in a semi-objective form. It is a temporary exchange of natures, called theurgy.

"Shamans are called sorcerers, because they are said to evoke the 'spirits' of the dead for purposes of necromancy. The true Shamanism — striking features of which prevailed in India in the days of Megasthenes (300 B.C.) — can no more be judged by its degenerated scions among the Shamans of Siberia, than the religion of Gautama-Buddha can be interpreted by the fetishism of some of his followers in Siam and Burmah. It is in the chief lamaseries of Mongolia and Thibet that it has taken refuge; and there Shamanism, if so we must call it, is practised to the utmost limits of intercourse allowed between man and 'spirit.'

"The religion of the lamas has faithfully preserved the primitive science of *magic*, and produces as great feats now as it did in the days of Kublai-Khan and his barons. The ancient mystic formula of the King Srong-ch-Tsans-Gampo, the '*Aum mani padme houm*,' effects its wonders now as well as in the seventh century.* Avalo-kitesvara, highest of the three Boddhisattvas, and patron saint of Thibet, projects his shadow, full in the view of the faithful, at the lamasery of Dga-G'Dan, founded by him; and the luminous form of Son-Ka-pa, under the shape of a fiery cloudlet that separates itself from the dancing beams of the sunlight, holds converse with a great congregation of lamas, numbering thousands; the voice descending from above, like the whisper of the breeze through foliage. Anon, say the Thibetans, the beautiful appearance vanishes in the shadows of the sacred trees in the park of the lamasery.

"At Garma-Khian (the mother-cloister) it is rumoured that bad and unprogressed spirits are made to appear on certain days, and *forced* to give

---

* *Aum* (mystic Sanscrit term of the Trinity), *mani* (holy jewel), *padme* (in the lotus, *padma* being the name for lotus), *houm* (be it so). The six syllables in the sentence correspond to the six chief powers of nature emanating from Buddha (the abstract deity, not Gautama), who is the seventh, and the Alpha and Omega of Being.

an account of their evil deeds; they are compelled by the lamaic adepts to redress the wrongs done by them to mortals. This is what Hue naively terms 'personating evil spirits', i.e., devils. Were the sceptics of various European countries permitted to consult the accounts printed daily at Moru,* and in the 'City of Spirits,' of the business-like intercourse which takes place between the lamas and the invisible world, they would certainly feel more interest in the phenomena described so triumphantly in the spiritualistic journals.

"At Buddha-lla, or rather Foht-lla (Buddha's Mount), in the most important of the many thousand lamaseries of that country, the sceptre of the Boddhiscat is seen floating unsupported in the air, and its motions regulate the actions of the community. Whenever a lama is called to account in the presence of the Superior of the monastery, he knows beforehand it is useless for him to tell an untruth; the 'regulator of justice' (the sceptre) is there, and its waving motion, either approbatory or otherwise, decides instantaneously and unerringly the question of his guilt. We do not pretend to have witnessed all this personally — we wish to make no pretensions of any kind. Suffice it, with respect to any of these phenomena, that what we have not seen with our own eyes has been so substantiated to us that we indorse its genuineness."[6]

"Within the cloisters of Tashi-Lhumpo and Si-Dzang, these powers, inherent in every man, called out by so few, are cultivated to their utmost perfection. Who, in India, has not heard of the Banda-Chan Rambout-chi, the *Houtouktou* of the capital of Higher Thibet? His brotherhood of Khe-lan was famous throughout the land; and one of the most famous 'brothers' was a Peh-ling (an Englishman) who had arrived one day during the early part of this century from the West, a thorough Buddhist, and after a month's preparation was admitted among the Khe-lans. He spoke every language, including the Thibetan, and knew every art and science, says the tradition. His sanctity and the phenomena produced by him, caused him to be proclaimed a *shaberon* after a residence of but a few years. His memory lives to the present day among the Thibetans, but his real name is a secret with the *shaberons* alone."

---

* Moru (the pure) is one of the most famous lamaseries of Lha-Ssa, directly in the centre of the city. There the Shaberon, the Dalai Lama, resides the greater portion of the winter months; during two or three months of the warm season his abode is Foht-lla. At Mom is the largest typographical establishment of the country.

"A number of lamas in Sikkim produce *meipo* — 'miracle' — by magical powers. The late Patriarch of Mongolia, Gegen Chutuktu, who resided at Urga, a veritable paradise, was the sixteenth incarnation of Gautama, therefore a Boddhisattva. He had the reputation of possessing powers that were phenomenal, even among the thaumaturgists of the land of miracles *par excellence*.

"Let no one suppose that these powers are developed without cost. The lives of most of these holy men, miscalled idle vagrants, cheating beggars, who are supposed to pass their existence in preying upon the easy credulity of their victims, are miracles in themselves. Miracles, because they show what a determined will and perfect purity of life and purpose are able to accomplish, and to what degree of preternatural asceticism a human body can be subjected and yet live and reach a ripe old age. No Christian hermit has ever dreamed of such refinement of monastic discipline; and the aerial habitation of a Simon Stylite would appear child's play before the fakir's and the Buddhist's inventions of will-tests.

"But the theoretical study of magic is one thing; the possibility of practising it, quite another. At Bras-ss-Pungs, the Mongolian college where over three hundred magicians (*sorciers*, as the French missionaries call them) teach about twice as many pupils from twelve to twenty, the latter have many years to wait for their final initiation. Not one in a hundred reaches the highest goal; and out of the many thousand lamas occupying nearly an entire city of detached buildings clustering around it, not more than two per cent become wonderworkers.

"One may learn by heart every line of the 108 volumes of Kadjur,* and still make but a poor practical magician. There is but one thing which leads surely to it, and this particular study is hinted at by more than one Hermetic writer. One, the Arabian alchemist Abipili, speaks thus: 'I admonish thee, whoever thou art that desirest to dive into the inmost parts of nature; if that thou seekest thou findest not *within thee*, thou wilt *never find it without thee*. If thou knowest not the excellency of thine own house, why dost thou seek after the excellency of other things? O Man, Know Thyself; in thee is hid the treasure of treasures.'"[8]

A vivid description of the Temple of the Teshu Lama at Tchigadze comes

---

* The Buddhist great canon, containing 1083 works in several hundred volumes, many of which treat of magic.

from an unexpected source. Dr. Franz Hartmann, writing to Mme Blavatsky while she was living at Ostende (1886), told her of the psychometrising of an "occult letter"* by a German peasant woman, living near Kempton.

"Ah," she exclaimed, "what is this? I never saw anything so beautiful in my life! I see before me a high but artificially made elevation or hill, and upon that hill a building which looks like a temple, with a high Chinese roof. The temple is of a splendid white, as if it were made of pure white marble, and the roof is resting upon three pillars. On the top there is a shining sun — but no! — it only looks like a sun; it seems to be some kind of animal.... There is a beautiful walk of smooth stones and some steps leading to the temple, and I am going up to it. Now I am there, and lo! the floor is a lake, in which the light of that sun on the top of the roof is reflected! But no — I am mistaken; it is no water at all; it is a kind of yellowish marble, which shines like a mirror. Now I see it plainly! It is a square marble floor, and in the centre there is a dark round spot....

"Now I am in the temple, and I see two gentlemen looking at something on the wall. One is a very fine-looking gentleman, but he is dressed quite differently from the people in this country. He is dressed in a loose flowing robe of pure white, and the fore-part of his shoes is pointed upward. The other one is smaller and bald-headed; he wears a black coat and silver buckles.... It (a vase) stands in the corner, and there are ornamental paintings on it....

"There are some paintings and drawings on the wall. Below the ceiling, where the roof begins, there is a field, or panel, on which there are some curious figures. Some look like a 15 and one like a V, and others like squares and ciphers.... They look as if they were numbers, but I do not think they are. They may be some strange letters or characters. Above that field or panel there is another one, on which there are some square pictures or plates, with some very queer things painted on them. They are movable; at least, I think they are....

"Now these gentlemen are going out, and I am following them. There are a great many trees looking like pine-trees. I think they are pines. There are others with big fleshy leaves and spikes, something like prickly-pears. There are mountains and hills and a lake. They are taking me away from that temple.... There is a big ravine, and there are some trees which I take to

---

* A letter from the Master which Dr. Hartmann had received at Adyar.

be olive-trees. Now I have arrived at a place where I can see a wide expanse of country. The two gentlemen have gone away.

"Here is some antiquity looking like an old ruined wall, and something like what I saw on that paper you showed me. I believe you call it a Sphinx. There is a sort of pillar, and on the top of it a statue whose upper part looks like a woman, while the lower part of her body seems to be a fish. She seems to be holding some moss in her hands, or resting them upon it.... What a funny sight! There are lots of queer people! They are little women and children. They have *soles* tied to their feet! They are collecting something from the shore and putting it into baskets. Now the whole scene dissolves into a cloud"[9]

To this Mme Blavatsky replied by letter: "This looks like the temple of the Teschu Lama, near Tchigadze — made of the 'Madras cement' -like material; it does shine like marble and is called the snowy 'Shakang' (Temple) — as far as I remember. It has no 'sun or cross' on the top, but a kind of algiorno dagoba, triangular, on three pillars, with a dragon of gold and a globe. But the dragon has a swastika on it.... I don't remember any 'gravel walk' — nor is there one, but it stands on an elevation (artificial) and a stone path leading to it, and it has steps — how many I do not remember (I was never allowed inside); saw from the outside, and the interior was described to me.

"The floors of nearly all Buddha's (Songyas) temples are made of yellow polished stone, found in those mountains of Oural and in Northern Thibet towards Russian territory. I do not know the name but it looks like yellow marble. The 'gentleman' in white may be Master, and the 'bald-headed gentleman' I take to be some old 'shaven-headed' priest....

"In those temples there are always movable 'pictures' on which various geometrical and mathematical problems are placed for the disciples who study astrology and symbolism. The 'vase' must be one of many Chinese queer vases about in temples, for various objects. In the corners of the temples there are numerous statues of various deities (Dhyanis). The roofs are always (almost always) supported by rows of wooden pillars dividing the roof into three parallelograms, and the mirror 'Melong' of burnished steel (round like the sun) is often placed on the top of the Kiosque on the roof. I myself took it once for the sun.

"Also on the cupolas of the dagobas, there is sometimes a graduated pinnacle, and over it a disk of gold placed vertically, and a pear-shaped point, and often a crescent supporting a globe and the swastika upon it. Ask her whether it is this she saw: *Om tram ah hri hum*, which figures are roughly drawn sometimes on the Melong 'mirrors' — (a disc of brass) against evil spirits — for the mob.

"Or perhaps what she saw was a row of slips of wood (little cubes) on which such things were seen. (She illustrates.) If so, then I will know what she saw. 'Pinewoods' are all round such temples, the latter built expressly where there are such woods, and prickly pear, and trees with Chinese fruits that the priests use for making inks. A lake is there, surely, and mountains plenty — if where Master is; if near Tchigadze — only little hillocks. The statues of Meilha Gualpo, the androgyne Lord of Salamanders or the Genii of the Air, looks like this 'sphinx'; but her lower body is lost in clouds, not fish; and she is not beautiful, only symbolical. Fisherwomen do use soles alone, like the sandals, and they wear all fur caps. That's all; will this do?"[10]

CHAPTER XXII

In The Master's Ashrama At Last

Why was she so many weary years reaching her goal? Why the long search and the repeated failure to find? "Ever since 1851 when I saw my Master bodily and personally for the first time, I have never denied or even doubted Him," she cries. But that confidence in Him was not enough. "Before the soul can stand in the presence of the Masters, its feet must be washed in the blood of the heart," says *Light on the Path*.

"Remember *my* seven years' preliminary initiation, trials, danger, and fighting with all the Incarnated Evils and legions of Devils," she writes to Colonel Olcott in 1875, " and think before you accept." And again in the same letter: "I am an *initiated* wretch and I know what a curse the word 'Try'* has proved to me in my life, and how I often trembled and feared to misunderstand their orders and bring on myself punishment for carrying them too far or not far enough."[1]

Perhaps the chief obstacle in her path was that same Dolgouroky temper which had caused so much trouble in her childhood and youth. It had to be brought within bounds, and only she could do it. Colonel Olcott remarks: "I asked (the Master) why a permanent control was not put upon her fiery temper, and why she should not always be modified into the quiet, self-centred sage that she became under certain obsessions. The answer was that such a course would inevitably lead to her death by apoplexy; the body was vitalised by a fiery and impetuous spirit, one which from childhood brooked

---

* "Try" might well be called the slogan of the Masters who communicated with Colonel Olcott in New York. Thus: "He who seeks Us finds Us. Try.... Don't give up thy club. Try," etc. Mahatma K. H. writes to Mr. Sinnett: "You know our motto, and that its practical application has erased the word 'impossible' from the occultist's vocabulary. If he wearies not of trying, he may discover that most noble of all facts, his true SELF."

no restraint; and if vent were not allowed for the excessive corporeal energy, the result must be fatal.

"I was told to look into the history of her kinsfolk, the Russian Dolgourokis, and I would understand what was meant. I did so and found that this princely and warlike family, tracing back to Rurik (ninth century) had always been distinguished by extreme courage, a daring equal to every emergency, a passionate love of personal independence, and a fearlessness of consequences in the carrying out of its wishes. Prince Yakob, a Senator of Peter the Great, was a type of the family character. Disliking an imperial ukase, he tore it to pieces in full council of the Senate, and when the Tsar threatened to kill him, he replied: 'You have but to imitate Alexander, and you will find a Clitus in me.'*

"This was H. P. B.'s character to the life, and she more than once told me that she would not be controlled by any power on earth or out of it. The only persons she actually reverenced were the Masters, yet even towards them, she was occasionally so combative that in certain of her moods the gentler ones could not, or did not, approach her. To get herself into the frame of mind when she could have open intercourse with them had — as she had pathetically assured me — cost her years of the most desperate self-restraint. I doubt if any person ever entered upon the Path against greater obstacles or with more self-suppression."[2]

"There was another and supreme reason why the Masters dare not control and compel H. P. B.'s innate character to be softened and refined into the higher ideal of the benevolent and gentle sage, independently of her own volition. To do so would have been an unlawful interference with her personal Karma.... To have interfered with that by benumbing the violent temper and suppressing the other personal defects of character, would have been a grievous wrong to her without hastening her evolution one whit; it would have been something like the keeping of a hypnotic sensitive perpetually under the hypnotiser's will, or an invalid permanently stupefied by a narcotic."[3]

"Of course, a brain so liable to disturbance was not the best adapted to the supremely delicate business of the mission she had taken upon herself;

---

* Probably this is the ancestor about whom H. P. B. wrote to Mr. Sinnett: "She (Vera) was furious with me for telling that story about the ancestor which she says is a family secret, 'a skeleton in the family cupboard' or how is it, the expression?" — *Letters* of H. P. B. to A. P. Sinnett, 156.

but the Masters told me that it was far and away the best now available, and that they must get all they could out of it. She was to them loyalty and devotion personified, and ready to dare and suffer all for the sake of the Cause. Gifted beyond all other persons of her generation with innate psychical powers, and fired with an enthusiasm that ran into fanaticism, she supplied the element of fixity of purpose, which conjoined with a phenomenal degree of bodily endurance, made her a most powerful, if not a very docile and equable agent. With less turbulence of spirit she would, probably, have turned out less faulty literary work, but instead of lasting seventeen years under the strain, she would doubtless have faded out of the body ten years earlier, and her later writings have been lost to the world."[4]

Of H.P.B.'s life in the home of her Master, we catch but few glimpses. One of the most intimate of these is contained in the following reminiscence written by her in 1886: "I was again (a scene of years back) in Mahatma K. H.'s* house. I was sitting in a corner on a mat, and he was walking about the room in his riding dress, and Master [M.] was talking to someone behind the door.

"'I remind can't' — I pronounced in answer to a question of His about a dead aunt. He smiled and said: 'Funny English you use.' Then I felt ashamed, hurt in my vanity, and began thinking (mind you, in my dream or vision which was the exact reproduction of what had taken place word for word sixteen years ago). 'Now I am here and speaking nothing but English in verbal phonetic language, I can perhaps learn to speak better with Him.'

"To make it clear: with Master I also used English, which whether bad or good was the same for Him, as He does not speak it but understands every word I say *out of my head*, and I am made to understand Him — *how* I could never tell or explain if I were killed *but I do*. With D. (jwal) K. (ul) I also speak English, he speaking it better even than Mah. K. H.

"Then in my dream still, *three months after*, as I was made to feel in that vision — I was standing before Mah. K. H., near the old building taken down He was looking at; and as Master was not at home, I took to Him a few sentences I was studying in Senzar in His sister's room, and asked Him to tell me if I had translated them correctly and gave Him a slip of paper with these sentences written in English.

---

* He spent a year at Leipzig University in the middle of the 70*[3]. See my *The 'Brothers' of Mme Blavatsky*, p. 63; also my article in *The Theosophist*, November, 1929, called "Master Koot Hoomi."

RAVINE IN TIBET

"He took and read them, and correcting the interpretation read them over, and said: 'Now your English is becoming better. *Try to pick out of my head even the little I know of it.*' And He put His hand on my forehead in the region of memory and squeezed His fingers on it (and I felt even the same trifling pain in it as then, and the cold shiver I had experienced); and since that day He did so with my head daily, for about two months.

"Again the scene changes, and I am going away with Master who is sending me off back to Europe. I am bidding good-bye to His sister and her child, and all the chelas. I listen to what the Masters tell me. And then come the parting words of Mah. K. H., laughing at me as He always did, and saying: 'Well, if you have not learned much of the Sacred Sciences and practical Occultism — *and who could expect a woman to* — you have learned, at any rate, a little English. You speak it now *only a little worse* than I do!' and He laughed.

"Again the scene changes. I am in 47th Street, New York, writing *Isis*, and His voice dictating to me. In that dream or retrospective vision, I once more re-wrote all *Isis* and could now point out all the pages and sentences Mah. K. H. dictated — as those that Master did — in my bad English, when Olcott tore his hair out by handfuls, in despair to ever make out the meaning of what was intended. I again saw myself night after night in bed — writing *Isis* in my dreams at New York, positively *writing it in my sleep*, and felt sentences by Mah. K. H. impressing themselves on my memory.

"Then as I was awakening from that vision (in Würzburg now) I heard Mah. K. H.'s voice: 'And now put two and two together, poor blind woman. The bad English and the construction of sentences you *do* know, even that you have learned *from me*.... Take off the slur thrown upon you by that misguided, conceited man (Hodgson); explain the truth to the few friends who will believe you — for the public never will to that day that the secret doctrine comes out.'

"I awoke, and it was like a flash of lightning; but I still did not understand what it referred to. But an hour after there comes Hubbe-Schleiden's letter to the Countess [Wachtmeister], in which he says, that unless I explain how it is that such similarity is found and proven by Hodgson between my faulty English and Master K. H.'s certain expressions, the construction of sentences and peculiar Gallicisms I stand accused for ever of deceit forgery (!!) and what not.

"Of course I have learned my English from Him! This Olcott even shall understand. You know, and I told it to many friends and enemies, I was taught dreadful Yorkshire by my nurse, called Governess. From the time my father brought me to England, when fourteen, thinking I spoke beautiful English, and people asked him if he had me educated in Yorkshire or Ireland, and laughed at my accent and way of speaking — I gave up English altogether, trying to avoid speaking it as much as I could.

"From fourteen till I was over forty, I never spoke it, let alone writing; and forgot it entirely. I could read — which I did very little — I could not speak it. I remember how difficult it was for me to understand a well written book in English, so far back only as 1867 in Venice. All I knew when I came to America in 1873 was to speak a little, and this Olcott and Judge and all who knew me then can testify to. I wish people saw an article I once attempted to write for the *Banner of Light*, when instead of *sanguine* I put *sanguinary*, etc.

"I learned to write it through ISIS, that's sure; and Prof. A. Wilder, who came weekly to help Olcott arranging chapters and writing Index, can testify to it. When I had finished it (and this ISIS is *the third part only* of what I wrote and destroyed), I could write as well as I do now, not worse nor better. What wonder then that *my* English and the Mahatma's show similarity! Olcott's and mine do also in our Americanisms, that I picked up from him these ten years."⁵

Besides English, Mme Blavatsky while with the Adepts in Tibet studied Senzar, as she mentioned above, in order that she might communicate with them safely when once more at work in the world. Of this ancient language she says: "Zen-(d)-zar, the sacerdotal language in use among the Initiates of archaic India. Found now in several undecipherable inscriptions, it is still used and studied unto this day in the secret communities of the Eastern adepts, and called by them — according to locality — Zend-zar and Brahma or Deva-Bashya."⁶

Again she says in *The Secret Doctrine*: "*Isis Unveiled* begins with a reference to an 'old book.'... This very old book is the original work from which the many volumes of Kiu-ti were compiled.... Tradition says it was taken down in *Senzar*, the secret sacerdotal tongue, from the words of Divine Beings, who dictated it to the Sons of Light, in Central Asia, at the very beginning of our Fifth Race; for there was a time when its language (the Senzar) was known to Initiates of every nation, when the forefathers of the Toltec understood it as easily as the inhabitants of the lost Atlantis [the Fourth Race], who inherited it in their turn from the sages of the Third Race, the Manushis, who learnt it direct from the Devas of the Second and First Races."[7]

The Tiravellum Mahatma, in "Replies to Enquiries Suggested by Esoteric Buddhism," says: "It is not enough to have studied stray fragments of Sanskrit literature.... To comprehend correctly and make out the inner meaning of most of them, one has to read these texts with the help of the esoteric light and after having mastered the language of the Brahmanic Secret Code."[8]

Mme Blavatsky speaks of the "esoteric Senzar Catechism"[9] which probably she studied while living with the Masters, as so much of *The Secret Doctrine* she was to write in future years hinged on a knowledge of it. There were other phases to be mastered too, cypher, etc. She says elsewhere: "The sacerdotal language (Senzar), besides an alphabet of its own, may be rendered into several modes of writing in cypher characters which partake more of the nature of ideographs than syllables." And again: "The Senzar and Sanskrit and other occult tongues, besides other potencies, have a number and colour and distinct syllable for every letter, and so also has ancient Hebrew."

Colonel Olcott mentions in *Old Diary Leaves* that, "when H.P.B. wrote to the Masters or they to her, on business that was not to be communicated to third parties, it was in an archaic language, said to be 'Senzar' which resembles Tibetan, and which she wrote as fluently as she did Russian, French or English."[10] And he tells how, wishing to communicate with her Master while on a train, April, 1879, in India, "she wrote something on a page of her pocket-book in two kinds of character, the upper half Senzar — the language of all her personal writings from the Mahatmas — the lower half English, which she allowed me to read,"[11] and flung it from the window.

In 1884 she wrote to Mr. Sinnett that "Coulomb stole a 'queer-looking paper' and gave it to the missionaries with the assurance that this was a cipher used by the Russian spies (!!). They took it to the Police Commissioner, had the best experts examine it, sent it to Calcutta, for five months moved heaven and earth to find out what the cipher meant and — now give up in despair. 'It is one of your flapdoodles' says Hume. 'It is one of my *Senzar* MSS.' I answer. I am perfectly confident of it, for one of the sheets of my book with numbered pages is missing. I defy anyone but a Tibetan occultist to make it out, if it is."[12]

Another subject " Upasaka "* was set to learn was " Precipitation." She says : " I have often seen M. sit with a book of most elaborate Chinese characters that he wanted to copy, and a blank book before him, and he would put a pinch of black lead dust before him and then rub it slightly on the page ; and then over it precipitate ink ; and then, if the image of the characters was all right and correct in his mind, the characters copied would be all right ; and if he happened to be interrupted, then there would be a blunder, and the work would be spoilt."[13]

In order to make the subject of precipitation a little clearer, let us anticipate by some years and quote from letters post-dating this sojourn of hers in Tibet. Thus she writes to Mr. Sinnett from Wurzburg in 1886 : " Has Master K. H. himself written all *His* letters ? How many *chelas* have been precipitating them — heaven only knows."[14]

Of this process of precipitation, Master K. H. tells Mr. Sinnett : " I have to *think* it over, to photograph every word and sentence carefully in my brain, before it can be repeated by 'precipitation.' As the fixing on chemically prepared surfaces of the images formed by the camera requires a previous arrangement within the focus of the object to be represented, for otherwise — as often found in bad photographs — the legs of the sitter might appear out of all proportion with the head, and so on ; so we have to arrange our sentences, and impress every letter to appear on paper, in our minds before it becomes fit to be read. For the present that is *all* I can tell you.

When science will have learned more about the mystery of the *lithophyl* (or lithobiblion) and how the impress of leaves comes originally to take place on stones, then I will be able to make you better understand the process. But you must know and remember one thing : we but follow and *servilely copy nature* in her works."[15]

"When the Master orders a *chela* to 'precipitate' a note or letter in His handwriting — because of the intense desire of some one individual to that effect, a desire or prayer which, according to occult law, the Masters feel, and if the 'addressee' is worthy, they are bound to notice one or the other — he

---

* Tibetan for disciple, or chela.

gets according to his deserts," says H. P. B. "When the Master — who certainly cannot descend to our level — gives such an order to a *chela*, the latter acts according to the best of his ability; and if he in any way perverts the meaning, so much the worse for that *chela*, and him or her who troubled the Master with his or her petty worldly affairs. But each time when the desire for Master's interference is intense and sufficiently pure (though foolish in Their sight) the Master's sacramental phrase is: 'Satisfy so and so' — to the *chela*."[16]

Master K. H. says: "Another of our customs, when corresponding with the outside world, is to entrust a *chela* with the task of delivering the letter or any other message; and if not absolutely necessary — to never give it a thought. Very often our letters — unless something very important and secret — are written in our handwritings* by our *chelas*. Thus last year some of my letters to you were *precipitated*, and when sweet and easy precipitation was stopped — well, I had but to compose my mind, assume an easy position, and — think, and my faithful 'Disinherited' had but to copy my thoughts, making only occasionally a blunder."[17]

Was it this "copying" of the Master's thoughts that Mme Blavatsky was learning while in Mingrelia, when her sister said "she seemed to fall into a kind of coma," but which she herself declared to be "no coma but a state of intense concentration, when the least distraction leads to a mistake."[18] Master K. H. thus describes the process:

"The recent experiments of the Psychic Research Society will help you greatly to comprehend the rationale of this mental telegraphy. You have observed in the journal of that body, how thought transference is cumulatively effected. The image of the geometrical or other figure which the active brain has had impressed upon it, is gradually imprinted upon the recipient brain of the passive subject, as the series of reproductions illustrated in the cut shows.

"Two factors are needed to produce a perfect and instantaneous mental telegraphy — close concentration in the operator and complete receptive passivity in the reader subject. Given a disturbance of either condition, and the result is proportionately imperfect. The reader does not see the image

---

* For specimens of their handwritings, see *The Mahatma Letters*, xliii, xlv, xlvii. Also *The Theosophist*, September, 1933 to February, 1934, or Mr. C. Jinarajadasa's book, *Did Mme Blavatsky Forge the Mahatma Letters*.

as in the telegrapher's brain, but as arising in his own. When the latter's thoughts wander, the psychic current becomes broken, the communication disjointed and incoherent."[19]

Mme Blavatsky, commenting on such precipitations by *chelas* (especially *chelas* unfamiliar with the English language), says: "How many a time was I (no Mahatma) shocked and startled, burning with shame when shown notes written in Their handwritings (a form of writing adopted for the T.S. and used by *chelas*, only *never without Their special permission or order* to that effect) exhibiting mistakes in science, grammar and thoughts, expressed in such language that it perverted entirely the meaning originally intended....

"It is very rarely that Mahatma K. H. (*dictated verbatim*) and when He did there remained the few sublime passages found in Mr. Sinnett's letters from Him. The rest, He would say, write so and so, and the *chela* wrote, often without knowing a word of English, as I am now made to write Hebrew and Greek and Latin, etc.* Two or three times, perhaps more, letters were precipitated *in my presence*, by *chelas* who could not speak English, and who took ideas and expressions out of my head."[20]

So much for precipitations *from* the Masters, but it was also necessary for the *chela* to learn how to send messages *to* Them. Of this she says: "Now to 'send on' a letter, two or three processes are used:

1. To put the envelope sealed on my forehead; and then, warning the Master to be ready for the communication, have the contents reflected by my brain carried off to His perception by the *current formed by Him*. This, if the letter is in a language I know; otherwise, if it is in an unknown tongue,

2. To unseal it, read it *physically* with my eyes, without understanding even the words, and *that which my eyes see* is carried off to the Master's perception and reflected in it in His own language, after which to be sure no mistake is made, I have to burn the letter with a stone I have (matches and common fire would never do), and the ashes caught by the current become more minute than atoms would be, and are *remoterialized* at any distance where the Master may be."[21]

These studies of Mme Blavatsky, while in her Master's ashrama in Tibet, pertain to her exoteric training; preparing her for future usefulness when she should return to the outer world. Her occult training, the preparation of

---

* 1886, while she was writing *The Secret Doctrine*.

her various vehicles, to act as transmitting wires for communications from the Masters to the busy world of men, had been going on (as we have seen) for years. The phenomena she produced and the experiences she passed through while in Russia from 1859 to 1863 bear witness to this.

When this occult training began is indicated in a passage by Mr. Sinnett in his *Incidents in the Life of Mme Blavatsky*. He says ; "To make this clear and intelligible, I must give her explanation. She never made a secret that she had been, ever since her childhood, and until nearly the age of twenty-five, a very strong *medium* ; though after that period, owing to regular psychological and physiological training, she was made to lose this dangerous gift, and every trace of mediumship *outside her will*, or beyond her direct control, was overcome."[22] The age, then, at which her definite training at the hands of the Master began was twenty-five ; and this is the time of her second visit to India, 1855 to 1857. When, at last, in 1864, she made her way to her Master's home, this inner training was, no doubt, intensified and hastened ; but of that phase we shall not know till we in turn experience it.

CHAPTER XXIII
Flying Visit To Europe

Mrs. Besant's itinerary* lists a "flying visit" of Mme Blavatsky to Italy in 1867. It seems to have been a very crowded visit. First she went with the crippled child she had adopted to Bologna, in the hope of saving its life. Not succeeding as she had hoped, she took the boy back to Russia, "whom I did not succeed to bring back alive to the governess chosen for him by the Baron," she says. He died and was buried in a small town in southern Russia. "Without notifying my relatives of my having returned to Russia... I returned to Italy on the same passport," she continues.

"Then comes Venice, Florence, Mentana. The Garibaldis (the sons) are alone to know the whole truth; and a few more Gari-baldians with them. What I did, you know partially; you do not know all. My relatives do, my sister does not."[1] "I *was* at Mentana during the battle of October, 1867, and left Italy in November of that year. Whether I was *sent* there, or found myself there by accident, are questions that pertain to my private life."[2]

In her first scrap-book, she has annotated an article called "Heroic Women," in which she is spoken of as "a petticoated Staff Officer of Garibaldi," as follows: "Every word is a lie. Never was on 'Garibaldl's staff.' Went with friends to Mentana to help shooting the Papists and got shot myself. Nobody's business, least of all a d—— reporter's."

Says Colonel Olcott: "She told me of her having been present as a volunteer... with Garibaldi at the bloody battle of Mentana. In proof of her story she showed me where her left arm had been broken in two places by a sabre-stroke, and made me feel in her right shoulder a musket-bullet still imbedded in the muscle, and another in her leg. She also showed me

---
* See Chronological Table.

a scar just below the heart where she had been stabbed with a stiletto. This wound reopened a little while she was at Chittenden, and it was to consult me about it that she was led to show it to me*.... I have sometimes been even tempted to suspect that none of us, her colleagues, ever knew the normal H. P. B. at all; but that we just dealt with an artificially animated body, a sort of perpetual psychic mystery, from which the proper *jiva* was killed out at the battle of Mentana (November 2, 1867),† when she received those five wounds and was picked up out of a ditch for dead."³

She (or the body) recovered from the wounds at Florence. She says: "The Hospodar (of Servia) was killed in the beginning of 1868 I think (see Encyclopaedia), when I was in Florence after Mentana, and on my way to India with Master from Constantinople.... Why, you knew from the first that Mentana was October 1867. I was in Florence about Christmas, perhaps a month before.... Then I went from Florence to Antemari and toward Belgrad, where in the mountains I had to wait (as ordered by Master) to Constantinople passing through Serbia and the Karpat Mountains, waiting for a certain‡ he sent after me.... Please do not speak of Mentana, and do not speak of master I implore you."⁴

Her reference to the death of the Hospidar introduces a subject of considerable interest; namely, her collaboration with Master Hilarion in the writing of stories. It is he of whom Mahatma K. H. says, "the adept who writes stories with H. P. B."⁵ One of his tales appeared in *The Theosophist* of January, 1880. It is entitled "The Ensouled Violin," and signed "By Hilarion Smerdis, F.T.S., Cyprus,§ October 1, 1879." It was incorporated in her *Nightmare Tales*, issued in 1892.

Another, "Can the Double Murder?" is based on the death of the Hospidar of Serbia, and is to be found in *The Theosophist* of January, 1883; but its first appearance was in the *New York Sun* in the 1870's, as one of a series of "weird stories" which H. P. B. published there, under the *nom de plume* of "Hadji Mora." Was this a veiled reference to her pilgrimage to Mecca? Perhaps even the name she bore on that occasion?

As Mme Blavatsky was an actor, or at least an eye-witness, in one of the

---

* The last-named was an older wound; it had reopened at Rougodevo, in 1859 or 1860.

† Colonel Olcott gives the correct date, November 2, not October, 1867.

‡ Word omitted in the text.

§ H. P. B. sometimes called him "the Cyprian Adept"

scenes of this latter story, here is a condensed version of her tale: "One morning in 1867, Eastern Europe was startled by news of the most terrifying description. Michael Obrenovitch, reigning Prince of Serbia; his aunt, the Princess Catherine, or Katinka as she was called; and her daughter, had been murdered in broad daylight near Belgrade, in their own garden, the assassin or assassins remaining unknown.... It was rumoured that the bloody deed was perpetrated by the Prince Kara-Gueorguevitch, an old pretender to the modest throne of Serbia, whose father had been wronged by the first Obrenovitch.... A young relative of the victim, greatly beloved by his people, a mere child, taken for the purpose from a school in Paris, was brought over in ceremony to Belgrade, and proclaimed Hospodar of Serbia (Milan, now King of Serbia.)*...

"In the turmoil of political excitement, the tragedy of Belgrade was forgotten, by all but an old Serbian matron who had been attached to the Obrenovitch family and who, like Rachel, would not be consoled for the death of her children. After the proclamation of the young Obrenovitch, the nephew of the murdered man, she had sold out her property and disappeared, but not before taking a solemn vow on the tombs of the victims to avenge their deaths.

"The writer of this truthful narrative had passed a few days at Belgrade about three months before the horrid deed was perpetrated, and knew the Princess Katinka. She was kind, gentle, and lazy at home; abroad she seemed a Parisian in manners and education. The old Serbian lady seldom left her house, going out but to see the Princess occasionally. Crouched on a pile of pillows and carpeting, clad in the picturesque national dress, she looked like the Cumaean Sibyl in her days of calm repose. Strange stories were whispered about her occult knowledge, and thrilling accounts circulated sometimes among the guests assembled round the fireside of my modest inn.

"The old lady, whom I will, then, call Gospoja P——, was generally attended by another personage, destined to be the principal actress in our tale of horror. It was a young gypsy girl from some part of Roumania, about fourteen years of age. Where she was born and who she was, she seemed to know as little as anyone else. I was told that she had been brought one

---

* H. P. B.'s cousin, Count Witte, states in his Memoirs that she "afterwards became the manager of the Royal Choir maintained by King Milan of Serbia."

day by a party of strolling gypsies and left in the yard of the old lady, from which moment she became an inmate of the house. She was nicknamed the 'sleeping girl,' as she was said to be gifted with the faculty of apparently dropping asleep wherever she stood, and speaking her dreams aloud. The girl's heathen name was Frosya.

"About eighteen months* after the news of the murder had reached Italy (where I was at the time), I was travelling over the Banat in a small waggon of my own, hiring a horse whenever I needed it, after the fashion of this primitive, trusting country. I met on my way an old Frenchman, a scientist, travelling alone after my own fashion; but with the difference that while he was a pedestrian, I dominated the road from the eminence of a throne of dry hay, in a jolting waggon. I discovered him one fine morning, slumbering in a wilderness of shrubs and flowers, and had nearly passed over him, absorbed as I was in contemplation of the surrounding glorious scenery. The acquaintance was soon made, no great ceremony of mutual introduction being needed. I had heard his name mentioned in circles interested in mesmerism, and knew him to be a powerful adept of the school of Dupotet.

"'I have found,' he remarked in the course of the conversation, after I had made him share my seat of hay, one of the most powerful subjects in this lovely Thebaide. I have an appointment to-night with the family. They are seeking to unravel the mystery of a murder by means of the clairvoyance of the girl. She is wonderful; very very wonderful.'

"'Who is she?' I asked.

"'A Roumanian gypsy. She was brought up, it appears, in the family of the Serbian reigning Prince who reigns no more, for he was very mysteriously murdered. Hol-la-a-h! Take care! Diable, you will upset us over the precipice!' he hurriedly exclaimed, unceremoniously snatching from me the reins, and giving the horse a violent pull.

"'Do you mean the Prince Obrenovitch?' I asked, aghast.

"'Yes; I do, and him precisely. To-night I have to be there, hoping to close a series of stances, by finally developing a most marvellous manifestation of the hidden power of the human spirit, and you may come with me. I will introduce you; and besides, you can help me as an interpreter, for they do not speak French.'

---

* She says, in her letter to Mr. Sinnett quoted above; "I met the Gospoja with Frosya about a month or two after the murder."

"As I was pretty sure that if the somnambula was Frosya, the rest of the family must be Gospoja P——, I readily accepted. At sunset we were at the foot of the mountain, leading to the old castle, as the Frenchman called the place. It fully deserved the poetical name given to it.

"There was a rough bench in the depths of one of the shadowy retreats; and as we stopped at the entrance of this poetical place and the Frenchman was gallantly busying himself with my horse, on the suspicious-looking bridge which led across the water to the entrance gate, I saw a tall figure slowly rise from the bench and come towards us. It was my old friend, Gospoja P——, and looking more pale and more mysterious than ever. She exhibited no surprise at seeing me, but simply greeting me after the Serbian fashion — with a triple kiss on both cheeks — took hold of my hand and led me straight to the nest of ivy. Half-reclining on a small carpet spread on the tall grass, with her back leaning against the wall, I recognised our Frosya.

"She was dressed in the national costume of the Vallachian women: a sort of gauze turban intermingled with various gilt medals and beads on her head, white shirt with opened sleeves and petticoats of variegated colours. Her face looked deadly pale, her eyes were closed, and her countenance presented that stony, sphinx-like look which characterises in such a peculiar way the entranced clairvoyant somnambulas. If it were not for the heaving motion of her chest and bosom, ornamented with rows of medals and necklaces, which feebly tinkled at every breath, one might have thought her dead, so lifeless and corpse-like was her face.

"The Frenchman informed me that he had sent her to sleep just as we were approaching the house, and that she now was as he had left her the previous night. He then began busying himself with the *sujet*, as he called Frosya. Paying no further attention to us, he shook her by the hand, and then making a few rapid passes stretched out her arm and stiffened it. The arm, as rigid as iron, remained in that position. He then closed all her fingers but one — the middle finger — which he caused to point at the evening star that twinkled in the deep blue sky. Then he turned round and went from right to left, throwing out some of his fluid here, again discharging it at another place, and busying himself with his invisible but potent fluids, like a painter with his brush when giving the last touches to a picture....

"Meanwhile the night had come, and the moon illuminated the landscape with a pale, ghastly light. The nights in the Banat are nearly as beautiful as in the East, and the Frenchman had to go on with his experiments in the open air, as the pope of the church had prohibited such in his tower, which was used as the parsonage, for fear of filling the holy precincts with the heretical devils of the mesmeriser, which he remarked he would be unable to exorcise on account of their being foreigners.

"The old gentleman had thrown off his travelling blouse, rolled up his shirt sleeves, and now striking a theatrical attitude began a regular process of mesmerisation. Under his quivering fingers, the odyle fluid actually seemed to flash in the moonlight. Frosya was placed with her figure facing the moon, and every motion of the entranced girl was discernible as in daylight. In a few minutes large drops of perspiration appeared on her brow, and slowly rolled down her pale face, glittering in the moonbeams. Then she moved uneasily about and began chanting a low melody, to the words of which the Gospoja, anxiously bending over the unconscious girl, was listening with avidity and trying to catch every syllable. With her thin finger on her lips, her eyes nearly starting from their sockets, her frame motionless, the old lady seemed herself transfixed into a statue of attention.

"Suddenly Frosya, as if lifted by some supernatural force, rose from her reclining posture and stood erect before us, motionless and still again, waiting for the magnetic fluid to direct her. The French-man silently taking the old lady's hand, placed it in that of the somnambulist, and ordered her to put herself *en rapport* with the Gospoja.

"'What sayest thou, my daughter?' softly murmured the Serbian lady, 'Can your spirit seek out the murderers?'

"'Search and behold,' sternly commanded the mesmeriser, fixing his gaze upon the face of the subject.

"'I am upon my way — I go,' faintly whispered Frosya, her voice not seeming to come from herself, but from the surrounding atmosphere.

"At this point something so extraordinary took place that I doubt my ability to describe it. A luminous shadow, vapour-like, appeared closely surrounding the girl's body. At first about an inch in thickness, it gradually expanded, and gathering itself, suddenly seemed to break off from the body altogether, and condense itself into a kind of semi-solid vapour, which very soon assumed the likeness of the somnambulist herself. Flickering about the surface of the earth, the form vacillated for two or three seconds, then glided noiselessly towards the river. It disappeared like a mist, dissolved in the moonbeams which seemed to absorb and imbibe it altogether!

"I had followed the scene with an intense attention. The mysterious operation known in the East as the invocation of the *scin-lecca* was taking place before my own eyes. To doubt was impossible, and Dupotet was right in saying that mesmerism was the conscious magic of the ancients, and spiritualism the unconscious effect of the same magic upon certain organisms.

"As soon as the vaporous double had soaked itself through the pores of the girl, the Gospoja had by a rapid motion of the hand which was left free, drawn from under her pelisse something which looked suspiciously like a small stiletto, and placed it as rapidly in the girl's bosom. The action was so quick that the mesmeriser, absorbed in his work, had not remarked it, as he afterward told me. A few minutes elapsed in dead silence. We seemed a group of petrified persons. Suddenly a thrilling and transpiercing cry burst from the entranced girl's lips. She bent forward, and snatching the stiletto from her bosom, plunged it furiously around her in the air, as if pursuing imaginary foes. Her mouth foamed, and incoherent wild exclamations broke from her lips, among which discordant sounds I discerned several times two familiar Christian names of men. The mesmeriser was so terrified that he lost all control over himself, and instead of withdrawing the fluid, he loaded the girl with still more.

"'Take care' I exclaimed, 'stop! You will kill her or she will kill you!' But the Frenchman had unwittingly raised subtle potencies of nature over which he had no control. Furiously turning round, the girl struck at him a blow which would have killed him had he not avoided it by jumping aside, receiving but a severe scratch on the right arm. The poor man was panic-stricken. Climbing with an extraordinary agility for a man of his bulky form on the wall above her, he fixed himself on it astride and gathering the remnants of his will power, sent in her direction a series of passes. At the second, the girl dropped the weapon and remained motionless.

"'What are you about?' hoarsely shouted the mesmeriser in French, seated like some monstrous night-goblin on the wall. 'Answer me, I command you.'

"'I did — but what she — whom you ordered me to obey — commanded me to do,' answered the girl in French, to my utter amazement.

"'What did the old witch command you to do?' irreverently asked he.

"'To find them — who murdered — kill them — I did so — and they are no more! Avenged — avenged I They are ——'

"An exclamation of triumph, a loud shout of infernal joy, rang loud in the air; and awakening the dogs of the neighbouring villages, a responsive howl of barking began from that moment like a ceaseless echo of the Gospoja's cry.

"'I am avenged, I feel it, I know it! My warning heart tells me that the fiends are no more.' And she fell panting on the ground, dragging down in her fall the girl, who allowed herself to be pulled down as if she were a log of wood.

"'I hope my subject did no further mischief to-night. She is a dangerous as well as a very wonderful subject,' said the Frenchman.

"We parted. Three days after that I was at T. [emesvar]; and as I was sitting in the dining-room of a restaurant waiting for my lunch, I happened to pick up a newspaper. The first lines I read ran thus:

"'Vienna, 186—, Two Mysterious Deaths. Last evening at 9.45 as P—— was about to retire, two gentlemen-in-waiting suddenly exhibited great terror, as though they had seen a dreadful apparition. They screamed, staggered, and ran about the room holding up their hands as if to ward off the blows of an unseen weapon. They paid no attention to the eager questions of their master and suite; but presently fell writhing upon the floor, and expired in great agony. Their bodies exhibited no appearance of apoplexy nor any external marks of wounds; but strange to relate, there were numerous dark spots and long marks upon the skin, as though they were stabs and slashes made without puncturing the cuticle. The autopsy revealed the fact that beneath each of these mysterious discolorations there was a deposit of coagulated blood. The greatest excitement prevails, and the faculty are unable to resolve the mystery....'"

Writing to Mr. Sinnett about this incident in her life, H. P. B. says: "Left Tiflis about '64 and went to Serbia, travelled about in the Karpat.... The Hospodar was killed in the beginning of 1868 I think (see Encyclopaedia), when I was in Florence after Mentana, and on my way to India with Master from Constantinople.

"If you take as your ground to stand upon my novel, the 'Double Murder' then you are wrong. I knew the Gospoja and Frosya and the Princess Katinka and even the Gospoda Michael Obrenovitch far earlier.*... What had

---

* That is, during her earlier visit of 1864, whereas the murder of the Hospidar took place after

happened in Vienna was told to me after my incident with Gospoja using Frosya for it. Why every detail is true — as far as I am concerned and the actors in it.... Mentana was October, 1867. I was in Florence about Christmas, perhaps a month before, when the poor Michael Obrenovitch was killed. Then I went... to Serbia and the Karpat Mountains; and it is there that I met the Gospoja with Frosya about a month or two after the murder, I believe....

"I made up these details and true personages into a story for the *Sun* (N.Y.) under the *nom de plume* of 'Hadji Mora'... I simply wrote *facts*, about personages known to me personally, and only of Mme Popesco who had told me what had happened after I had seen the evocation, I put the author in her place. And now Sellin comes out and cross-examines me — were you there? I say *no*, for I was on my way to India, but it was told to me and I made a story out of it.... The story *is* true.

"Only I was not going to publish the name of Mme Popesco, who gave me the last act (four years later) and who read it in some Vienna number *immediately suppressed*.... That's why I said I read it in a Temesvar coffee house.... Mme Popesco gave it to me to read in her diary into which she had copied that event, which putting dates together I considered as having happened on that same night....

"I never gave my series of sensational stories in the N.Y. *Sun* for infallible and Gospel truths. I wrote *stories*, on facts that happened hither and thither, with living persons, only changing names (not in the 'Double Murder' though, where I was fool enough to put real personages); and this was put up and arranged for me by Illarion, and he says and said again only that day I quarrelled with Sellin — 'As every word of the evocation of Frosya by Gospoja is true, so the scenes in Vienna and double murder *are true*, as Mme Popescu told you.' I thought you knew it."[6]

It was probably on this return journey to India *with her Master* that there occurred the incident mentioned by Mme Blavatsky in a letter to her relatives in Russia. It is given by her niece, Mrs. Vera Johnston (daughter of Mme Vera Jelihovsky) in *The Path* of January, 1895:

"There was naturally considerable fear in the minds of H.P.B.'s nearest relatives as to the character of this mysterious Hindu teacher. They could not help regarding him more of a 'heathen sorcerer' than anything else.

Mentana, 1868.

And this view H. P. B. took pains to combat. She told them that her Master had a deep respect for the spirit of Christ's teachings. She had once spent seven weeks in a forest not far from the Karakoram Mountains, where she had been isolated from the world, and where her teacher alone visited her daily, whether astrally or otherwise she did not state.

"But whilst there she had been shown in a cave-temple a series of statues representing great teachers of the world, amongst others: A huge statue of Jesus Christ, represented at the moment of pardoning Mary Magdalene; Gautama Buddha offers water in the palm of his hand to a beggar, and Ananda is shown drinking out of the hands of a Pariah prostitute."

It is just possible that the route which she pursued in leaving Tibet for Italy has come to light. "Major Cross, who with his wife, Dr. Cross, and their daughter, have been visiting Toronto... gave a long, graphic and intensely interesting account of his travels in north-western Tibet, during which he traced the progress of a white woman in 1867, through the most difficult country to a lamasery far north, through the recollections of various old people who were impressed by the personality of this unusual visitor. He identified her with Mme Blavatsky, and the date was settled by those he talked with as having been ten years after the Mutiny. Major Cross said he was not a Theosophist, but could not help being interested in the story of Mme Blavatsky's journey, as it had been related to him.... He is manager or factor of tea and other estates of the Dalai Lama of Tibet, to which he is returning."[7]

CHAPTER XXIV

From The Master's Ashram A To The World

fter recovering from the wounds received at the battle of Mentana, sometime in 1868, H. P. B. returned to Tibet. She relates that she first met the Master Koot Hoomi in that year, so it would seem that he was away during her former stay in her Master's home. The following from " Mme Blavatsky on Mr. Lillie's Delusions," written in 1884, will be of interest:

"As to his [Mr. Lillie's] trying to insinuate that there is no Mahatma Koot Hoomi at all, the idea alone is absurd. He will have to dispose before he does anything more, of a certain lady in Russia whose truthfulness and impartiality no one who knows her would ever presume to question, who received a letter from that Master so far back as 1870. Perchance a forgery also? As to my having been in Tibet, at Master Koot Hooml's house, I have better proof in store — when I believe it needed....

"I had never seen Mr. Sinnett's correspondent [Master K. H.] before 1868.... If Mr. Lillie tells us that Koot Hoomi is not a Tibetan name, we answer that we have never claimed it to be one. Everyone knows that the Master is a Punjabi whose family was settled for years in Cashmere. But if he tells us that an 'expert at the British Museum ransacked the Tibetan dictionary for the words "Kut" and "Humi" and found no such words'; then I say, 'Buy a better dictionary' or 'Replace the expert by a more expert one.' Let Mr. Lillie try the glossaries of the Moravian Brothers and their alphabets."[1]

The letter to which reference is made by H. P. B. was received by Mme N. A. Fadeef, her aunt, who wrote to Colonel Olcott from Paris in 1884: "What happened to me in the case of a letter received phenomenally by me, when my niece was in the other side of the world, and when in fact nobody knew where she was. That is what was precisely causing us worry. All our researches ended in nothing. We were prepared to believe her dead when, I think, about the year 1870 or a little after that, I received a letter from him whom you call, I believe, Koot-Hoomi, which was brought in the most incomprehensible and mysterious manner to my house, by a messenger of Asiatic features, who disappeared under my very eyes. This letter, which requested me not to be afraid and which advised me of her being in safety, I have still in Odessa. As soon as I return, I'll send it to you, and will be very glad if it will be of any use to you."

She duly sent the letter, and it is now in the Archives of the Theosophical Society. On the lower left corner of the envelope is pencilled in Russian: "Received at Odessa, November 7, about Helinka, probably from Tibet. November n, 1870. Nadejda F." The letter is in French, in the "handwriting" of Master Koot Hoomi. This is a translation:

"To the Honourable,
    Most Honourable Lady,
        Nadyejda Andreewna Fadeew,
            Odessa.

"The noble relations of Mme H. Blavatsky have no cause whatsoever for grief. Their daughter and niece has not left this world at all. She is living, and desires to make known to those whom she loves that she is well and quite happy in the distant and unknown retreat she has selected for herself. She has been very ill, but is so no longer; for under the protection of the Lord Sangyas* she has found devoted friends who guard her physically and spiritually. The ladies of her house should therefore remain tranquil. Before eighteen moons shall have risen, she will return to her family."† [2]

"I did come back from India in one of the early steamers." [3] "November, 1869? Well, maybe for all I know or remember. We did not land. What I know is, that it was the *year* of the opening of the [Suez] Canal, soon after and when the Empress of France was there. Whether she had been there some months before or was there *then* —I could not tell. But my remembrances hang on the fuss made about it on board, and constant

---

* Lord Buddha.
† This is the first of all the "Mahatma Letters."

conversations, and that either *our* steamer or one going with it was the *third* that crossed it.

"My aunt received letter November n, 1870 from the Master. I crossed, if I remember, in December. Went to Cyprus, then in April, I think, got blown up in steamship *Eumonia*; went to Cairo from Alexandria in October '71. Returned to Odessa May, '72 — '18 moons' after receipt of M.'s letter by my aunt. Then if she has put the right year it was a year after first opening that I crossed."[4]

The official opening of the Suez Canal was on November 16, 1869, and on the 17th sixty-eight ships passed through. It would seem that the ship in which H. P. B. crossed in 1870 (the year *after* the opening) had been the third in this procession of sixty-eight. Elsewhere she says:

"I first went to Greece and saw Illarion, in *what place* I cannot and must not say. Then to Piree and from that port to Spezzia, in view of which we were blown up. Then I went to Egypt, first to Alexandria, where I had no money and won a few thousand francs on the No. 27 — (don't put this) — and then went to Cairo where I stopped from October or November, 1871 to April, 1872, only four or five months, and returned to Odessa in July, as I went to Syria and Constantinople first and some other places. I had sent Mme Sebir with the monkeys beforehand, for Odessa is only four or five days from Alexandria."[5]

The S.S. *Eumonia* carried gunpowder and fireworks. Of its 400 passengers only sixteen escaped. The Greek Government afforded these passage to their destination; and so H. P. B. arrived at Cairo in straits until she should receive a remittance from Russia. She went to the Hotel d'Oriente, where Mme Coulomb (Miss Emma Cutting) was very kind to her, under these trying circumstances.

H. P. B. "wrote from Cairo to tell her friends that she had been shipwrecked and... had to wait in Egypt for some time; meanwhile she determined to establish a *Soctbti Sptrite* for the investigation of mediums and phenomena according to Allen Kardec's theories and philosophy.... To accomplish this she was ready to go to any amount of trouble."[6]

Dr. A. L. Rawson, in an article in *Frank Leslie's Popular Magazine* of February, 1892, says that "Paulos Metamon, a celebrated Coptic magician, who had several very curious books full of astrological formulas, magical incantations and horoscopes which he delighted in showing his visitors, *after a proper introduction*, advised delay."⁷ This was H.P.B.'s old Coptic friend, but she did not follow his advice.

"A few weeks later," continues Mr. Sinnett's account, "a new letter was received [by her relatives]. In this one she showed herself full of disgust for the enterprise, which had proved a perfect failure. She had written, it seems, to England and France for a medium, but without success. *En désespoir de cause*, she had surrounded herself with amateur mediums — French female Spiritualists, mostly beggarly tramps, when not adventuresses in the rear of M. de Lesseps' army of engineers and workmen on the Canal of Suez.

"'They steal the Society's money,' she wrote, 'they drink like sponges, and now I caught them cheating most shamefully our members who come to investigate the phenomena, by bogus manifestations. I had very disagreeable scenes with several persons who held me alone responsible for all this. So I ordered them out, and I will bear myself the costs and money laid out for hire of premises and furniture. My famous *Société Spirite* has not lasted a fortnight — it is a heap of ruins, majestic, but as suggestive as those of the Pharaoh's tombs....

"'To wind up the whole comedy with a drama, I got nearly shot by a madman — a Greek who had been present at the only two public seances we held, and got possessed, I suppose, by some vile spook.'"⁸ The Archives MS. gives the following additional details. "He premised by running about the bazaars and streets of Cairo with a cocked revolver, screaming that I had sent him during three nights running a host of she-demons, of spirits who were attempting to choke him.

"He rushed into my house with his revolver, and finding me in the breakfast room, declared that he had come to shoot me, but would wait till I had done with my meal. It was very kind of him, for in the meanwhile I *forced* him to drop his pistol and to rush out once more out of the house. He is now shut up in a lunatic asylum, and I swear to put an end forever to such stances — they are too dangerous and I am not practised and strong enough to control the wicked spooks that may approach my friends during such sittings.

"I had told you before now that this kind of promiscuous seances with mediums in the circle, are a regular whirlpool — a maelstrom of bad magnetism, during which time the so-called spirits (vile Kiki-mora!) feed upon us, suck in sponge-like our vital powers, and draw us down to their own plane of being. But you will never understand this without going over again a portion at least, if not the whole range of writings that exist upon the subject."⁹

How dangerous, not only to sitters but also to medium, is shown in the following account, written by H.P.B. from Cairo to her sister Vera: "A friend of mine, a young English lady and a medium, stood writing mechanically on bits of paper, leaning upon an old Egyptian tomb. The pencil had begun tracing perfect gibberish... when suddenly and as I was looking from behind her back, they changed into what I thought were Russian letters. My attention having been called elsewhere, I came back just in time to prevent her from destroying that slip of paper, as she had done the rest. Possessing myself of the rejected slip, fancy my astonishment on finding it contained in Russian an evident apostrophe to myself!

"'*Barishnya*, (little or young miss) dear *barishnya*, help, oh help me, a miserable sinner! I suffer; drink, drink, give me a drink!...'*

"The gentle girl had hardly written the Russian words addressed to me, when she was seized with a trembling, and asked for a drink. When water was brought, she threw it away, and went on asking for a drink. Wine was offered her — she greedily drank it, and began drinking one glass after another until, to the horror of all, she fell into convulsions, and cried for 'Wine — a drink!' till she fainted and was carried home in a carriage. She had an illness after this that lasted for several weeks."¹⁰

Mr. Sinnett states that: "New slanders and scandals were set on foot. The sceptics who had, moved by idle curiosity, visited the *Sociiti Spirite* and witnessed the whole failure, made capital of the thing. Ridiculing the idea of phenomena, they had as a natural result declared such claims to be fraud and charlatanry all round. Conveniently inverting the facts of the case, they even went the length of maintaining that, instead of paying the mediums and expenses of the Society, it was Mme Blavatsky who had herself been paid, and had attempted to palm off juggler tricks as genuine phenomena.

"The groundless inventions and rumours thus set on foot by her enemies, mostly the discharged 'French women mediums' did not prevent Mme Blavatsky from pursuing her studies and proving to every honest investigator that her extraordinary powers of clairvoyance and clairaudience were *facts*, over which she possessed an undeniable control. Also that her power,

* For the story of the "spook" himself, read p. 128, *Incidents in the Life of Mme Blavatsky*.

by simply looking at them, of setting objects in motion without any direct contact with them, and sometimes at a great distance, instead of deserting her or diminishing, had increased with years.

"A Russian gentleman, M. G. Yakovlef, who happened to visit Egypt at that time, wrote: 'Once I showed her a closed medallion containing the portrait of one person and the hair of another, which was made at Moscow and of which very few know; and she told me, without touching it, "Oh, it is your godmother's portrait and your cousin's hair. Both are dead," and she proceeded to describe them as though she had both before her eyes. How could she know!'"[11]

Dr. Rawson in his article says that H.P.B. had told Countess Kazinoff, "that she had solved at least one of the mysteries of Egypt, and proved it by letting a live serpent loose, from a bag she had concealed in the folds of her dress."[12]

Colonel Olcott states: "From an eye-witness I had it that while H.P.B. was in Cairo the most extraordinary phenomena would occur in any room she might be sitting in; for example, the table-lamp would quit its place on one table and pass through the air to another, just as if carried in someone's hand; this same mysterious Copt would suddenly vanish from the sofa where he was sitting, and many such marvels."[13]

As to one of her letters to her sister at the time, Mr. Sinnett remarks that "a portion of it consists of fly-sheets torn out from a note-book and these were all covered with pencil-writing. The strange events they had recorded had been all put down on the spot — some under the shadow of the great Pyramid of Cheops, and some of them inside the Pharaoh's Chamber. It appears that Mme Blavatsky had gone there several times, once with a large company, some of whom were Spiritualists. Some wonderful phenomena were described by some of her companions as having taken place in broad daylight in the desert when they were sitting under a rock; whilst other notes in Mme Blavatsky's writing recorded the strange sight she saw in the Cimmerian darkness of the King's Chamber when she had passed a night alone comfortably settled inside the sarcophagus."[14]

Having executed her various commissions — she speaks of Greece, Syria, Constantinople and "some other places" — she visited her family, then settled at Odessa, but not for long. In 1872 and 1873 she toured Europe as "Madame Laura," pianist. At some time she conducted the Royal Choir

"HER HANDS WERE MODELS FOR THE SCULPTOR"

of King Milan of Servia, according to the statement of her cousin, Count Witte, in his *Memoirs*. Dr. Corson says: "My mother described to me how H.P.B. would sit down and improvise at the piano with great skill, showing remarkable efficiency for one who played but at odd times, as the spirit might move her."[15] This was at Ithaca, New York, in 1875.

Colonel Olcott writes: "She was a splendid pianist, playing with a touch and expression that were simply superb. Her hands were models — ideal and actual — for a sculptor, and never seen to such advantage as when flying over the keyboard to find its magical melodies. She was a pupil of Moscheles; and when in London as a young girl, with her father, played at a charity concert with Mme Clara Schumann and Mme Arabella Goddard in a piece of Schumann's for three pianos. Some weeks after the above was published, I learned from a member of her family that shortly before coming to America, H.P.B. had made some concert tours in Italy and Russia under the pseudonym of 'Madame Laura.'

"During the time of our relationship she played scarcely at all.... There were times when she was occupied by one of the Mahatmas, when her playing was indescribably grand. She would sit in the dusk sometimes, with nobody else in the room beside myself, and strike from the sweet-toned instrument improvisations that might well make one fancy he was listening to the Gandharvas, or heavenly choristers. It was the harmony of heaven."[16]

H.P.B. writes to Mr. Sinnett: "Went March, 1873, from Odessa to Paris — stopped with my cousin Nicolas Hahn (son of Uncle Gustave Hahn, father's brother, and the Countess Adlerberg, his mother) at Rue de L'Universite II, I believe; then, in July the same year went as ordered to New York. From that time let the public know all. It's all opened."[17]

Dr. L.M. Marquette, of New York, who met her during this Paris sojourn, states in a letter to Colonel Olcott of December 6, 1875: "I was with her almost daily; and in fact, spent a good part of my time with her when I was not in the hospitals or attending the lectures.... She passed her time in painting and writing, seldom going out of her room. She had few acquaintances, but among the number were M. and Mme Leymarie."[18]

Mme Blavatsky having left Odessa to settle in Paris, her family were naturally puzzled by her sudden departure for New York. Her sister Vera says: "We, her nearest relations, for the first time heard her mention those enigmatic beings [the Masters] in 1873-4, when she was established in New

York. The fact is that her departure from Paris for America was as sudden as it was inexplicable, and she would never give us the explanation of what led her to do so until many years later; she then told us that these same Masters had ordered her to do so, without at the time giving any reason. She gave us as her reason for not having spoken of them to us, that we should not have understood, that we should have refused to believe, and very naturally so."[19]

"H. P. B. told me," says Colonel Olcott, "that she had come to Paris intending to settle down for some time under the protection of a relative of hers, but one day received from the 'Brothers' a peremptory order to go to New York to await further orders. The next day she had sailed, with little more than money enough to pay her passage."[20]

A characteristic incident occurred, which Mr. William Q. Judge related in the *New York Times* of January 6, 1889, thus: "She reached Havre with a first class ticket to New York, and only one or two dollars over. Just as she was going aboard the steamer, she saw a poor woman accompanied by two little children, who was sitting on the pier, weeping bitterly.

"'Why are you crying?' she asked.

"The woman replied that her husband had sent to her from America money to enable her and the children to join him. She had expended it all in the purchase of steerage tickets that turned out to be valueless counterfeits. Where to find the swindler who had so heartlessly defrauded her she did not know, and she was quite penniless in a strange city.

"'Come with me,' said Mme Blavatsky, who straightway went to the agent of the steamship company and induced him to exchange her first-class ticket for steerage tickets for herself, the poor woman and the children. Anybody who has ever crossed the ocean in the steerage among a crowd of emigrants will appreciate the magnitude of such a sacrifice to a woman of fine sensibilities, and there are few but Mme Blavatsky who would have been capable of it."[21]

CHAPTER XXV

The Metrovitch Incident

Mr. Sinnett wished to include "the Metrovitch incident" in his *Memoirs*, which were ultimately not called Memoirs but *Incidents in the Life of Mme Blavatsky*. However she was adamant.

"I WILL NOT WRITE ANYTHING about the 'Metrovitch incident' nor any other *incident* of the sort, where politics and secrets of dead people are mixed up. This is my last and final determination. If you can make the *Memoirs* interesting in some other way, do so and I will help you. Anything you like after 1875. My life was a public and an opened life since then, and except during my hours of sleep *I was never alone*. I defy the whole world to *prove* any of the accusations brought against me during that time."[1]

Even after she had received a letter addressed to her as "Mme Metrovitch," she still refused. "Here's a new letter with blackmail and bullying in it.... What the blackguardly *clique* means, I do not know, but what the Coulomb means I see clear for it is an old, old story.... Now this address:

'Mme Metrovitch otherwise
Mad. Blavatsky.'

is a written *libel* and a bullying bit of *chantage*, blackmail or whatever you call it. People with a mouth and a tongue cannot be stopped from saying that every man who ever approached me, from Meyen-dorff down to Olcott, was my lover.... But I do believe that when a *lawyer* or *lawyers*, on the authority of Mme Coulomb's infernal gossip *writes* such an insult, implying not only prostitution, but *bigamy* and *aliases* — it is a defamation. If you please show *this* to the lawyer (ours) and do make him stop it at once, by saying that unless *they*... write an excuse I will prosecute them and bring them in for libel."²

[Mme Coulomb was] " no friend of mine, only a casual acquaintance with whom since I left Cairo in 1871 I had never any correspondence, and whose very name I had forgotten! In that infamous letter* I am made, nevertheless, to say that I had left my husband, *loved and lived with* a man (whose wife was my dearest friend and who died in 1870, a man who died too, a year after his wife, and was buried by me at Alexandria) *had three children by him and others*!!! (sic) and etc., etc., winding [up] the whole confession by asking her not to speak of me as she knew me, and so on : sentences strung together, to show that I *had never known the Masters, never was in Tibet*, was in fact an impostor.

"It was only wasting time to argue upon all this. Those who believe the published letters [of the Coulomb attack in 1884] genuine, have no reason to disbelieve in that one, and if there are such fools in this world — or people so cunning as to play the part of a fool — who can believe me capable of writing *such a suicidal confession*, to such a woman, a perfect stranger to me with the exception of a few weeks I had known her at Cairo — well these people are welcome to do so."³

"I deliver myself into your hands and ask you only to remember that the *Memoirs* are sure to throw out like a volcano some fresh mud and flames. Do not awake the sleeping dogs more than necessary. That I was never Mme Metrovitch or even Mme Blavatsky is something the proofs of which I will carry to my grave — and it's no one's business."⁴

The story contained in her letters to Mr. Sinnett, as to her friendship with the Metrovitches, is as follows : " You say, 'Thus, for example, we must bring in the whole of that Metrovitch incident.' I say *we must not*. These *Memoirs* will not bring *my vindication*. This I know as well as I knew that *The Times* would not notice my letter against Hodgson's Report [on behalf of the Society for Psychical Research]. Not only will they fail to do so, 'if they are made sufficiently complete,' but if they appeared in six volumes and ten times as interesting — they will never vindicate me ; simply because 'Metrovitch' is only one of the many incidents that the enemy throws at my head.

"If I touch this 'incident' and vindicate myself fully, a Solovioff, or some other blackguard will bring out the Meyendorff and 'the three children

---

* A letter alleged (in 1884) by Mme Coulomb to have been received by herself from H. P. B. in 1882.

incident.' And if I were to publish his [Meyendorff's] letters (in Olcott's possession) addressed to his 'darling Nathalie' in which he speaks of her raven black hair* — '*Long comme un beau manteau de roi*' ... as de Musset expresses it of his Marquesa d'Amedl's hair — then I would be simply dealing a slap on the face of a dead martyr, and call forth the convenient shadow of someone else from the long gallery of my supposed lovers."[5]

This "long gallery of supposed lovers" arose partly through confusing Mme H. P. Blavatsky with others as above; for instance, with a Mme Heloise Blavatsky — "a non-existing personage, who had joined the Black Hussars during the Hungarian revolution, her sex being found out only in 1849," says Mme N. A. Fadeef, who continues: "Her friends [H. P. B.'s] were as much surprised as pained to read fragments from her supposed biography which spoke of her as a person well known in *high life*, as well as *low*, of Vienna, Berlin Warsaw, and Paris, and mixed her name with events and anecdotes whose scene was laid in those cities, at various epochs when her friends had every possible proof of her being far away from Europe. These anecdotes referred to her indifferently, under the several Christian names of Julie, Nathalie, etc., which were those really of other persons of the same surname."[6]

The question of her identity, as well as the truth of certain adventures she related in *Isis Unveiled*, arising in America after the publication of that book, Dr. A. L. Rawson of New York wrote: "Having had some peculiar experience, I am qualified somewhat to sympathise with Mme Blavatsky in her unpleasant position under the fire of certain critics, who question her personal experience in different countries, and who even go so far as to throw suspicion upon her very identity.

"Only last week a letter passed under my eyes containing enquiries to this effect, written in Aden, in Arabia: Is the Mme Blavatsky the real Mme Blavatsky who was so well known in Cairo, Aden and elsewhere a few years since? For if she is, she must have revived, for the real Mme Blavatsky died at her friend's residence six or seven miles from that city in 1868. The real Mme Blavatsky was a Russian lady of family and fortune, and of considerable literary ability and reputation. She had a large amount of written materials with her at the time of her death. These materials disappeared, together with her amanuensis, who had been a constant and trusted

---

* Mme H. P. Blavatsky's hair was very light brown.

companion. Is it not possible this amanuensis has assumed the name, rank, and character of the deceased lady?

"Good fortune favours the diligent, and Mme Blavatsky is one of the most earnest workers in the literary world. The many columns of correspondence from her pen show that; and now there comes upon the scene, as if by magic, Mme Lydie de Paschkoff, a Russian Countess, member of the Geographical Society of France, of a notable family, great fortune, and a traveller for many years. Mme Paschkoff fortunately knew the Mme Nathalie Blavatsky who died in Aden, and also knows, and has known for many years, Mme H. P. Blavatsky, having met her in Syria, in Egypt, and elsewhere in the East.

"Others of my acquaintance have met Mme Blavatsky in the far East; others have heard of her residence there; for instance, the eminent physician and surgeon, David E. Dudley, M.D. of Manila, Philippine Islands, who spent some months in this city recently, and is now on his way to return to his Eastern home; Mr. Frank A. Hill, of Boston, Mass., who "was in India some years since. Both these gentlemen corroborate many of her statements."[7]

"From 17 to 40 I took care during my travels to sweep away all traces of myself wherever I went. When I was at Barri in Italy studying with a local witch — I sent my letters to Paris to post from there to my relatives. The only letter they received from me from India was when I was leaving it, the first time. Then from Madras in 1857; when I was in South America I wrote to them through, and posted *in London*. I never allowed people to know *where* I was and *what* I was doing.

"Had I been a common p—— they would have preferred it to my studying occultism. It is only when I returned home that I told my aunt that the letter received from K. H. by her was no letter from a *spirit* as she thought. When she got the proofs that they were living men, she regarded them as devils or *sold to Satan*. Now you have seen her. She is the shyest, the kindest, the meekest individual. All her life, her money and all is for others. Touch her religion, and she becomes like a fury. I never speak to her about the Masters."[8]

Elsewhere H. P. B. says: "I shall tell everything I did, for the twenty years and more that I laughed at the *qu'en dira-t-on** and covered up all traces

---

* "What will they say?"

of what I was *really* occupied in; i.e. the *sciences occultes*, for the sake of my family and relations, who would at that time have cursed me. I will tell how from my eighteenth year I tried to get people to talk about me, and say that this man and that was my lover, and *hundreds* of them."[9]

To resume her story of the Metrovitches: "Now why should I bring out the Metrovitch incident? Suppose I said the *whole* truth about him? What is it? Well, I knew the man in 1850, over whose apparently dead corpse I stumbled in Pera, at Constantinople, as I was returning home one night from Bougakdira to Missire's hotel. He had received three good stabs in his back from one, or two, or more Maltese ruffians and a Corsican, who were paid for it by the Jesuits. I had him picked up, after standing over his still breathing corpse for about four hours, before my guide could get *mouches* to pick him up. The only Turkish policeman meanwhile who chanced to come up asking for a *baksheesh* and offering to roll the supposed corpse into a neighbouring ditch, then showing a decided attraction to my own rings, and bolting only when he saw my revolver pointing at him.

"Remember, it was in 1850, and in Turkey. Then I had the man carried to a Greek hotel over the way, where he was recognised and taken sufficiently care of, to come back to life. On the next day he asked me to write to his wife and *Sophie Cruvelli* (the Duchess's dear friend, now Vicomtesse de Vigier at Nice and Paris, and at the time his mistress; No. I scandal). I wrote to his wife and did not to the Cruvelli. The former arrived from Smyrna where she was, and we became friends.

"I lost sight of them after that for several years and met him again at Florence, where he was singing at the Pergola *with his wife*. He was a Carbonaro, a revolutionist of the worst kind, a fanatical rebel, a Hungarian from Metrovitz, the name of which town he took as a *nom de guerre*. He was the natural son of the Duke of Lucea, as I believe, who brought him up. He hated the priests, fought in all the rebellions, and escaped hanging by the Austrians only because — well, it's something I need not be talking about.

"Then I found him again in Tiflis in 1861, again with his wife, who died after I had left, in 1865,* I believe; then my relatives knew him well, and was friends with my cousins Witte. Then, when I took the poor child to Bologna to see if I could save him, I met him again in Italy, and he did all

---

* She says elsewhere, "died in 1870"; which is more likely, as she also says: "When his wife died, he came to Odessa in 1870."

he could for me, more than a brother. Then the child died; and as it had no papers nor documents, and I did not care to give my name in food to the kind gossips, it was he, Metrovitch, who undertook all the job, who buried *the aristocratic Baron's* child — *under his, Metrovitch's* name, saying' he did not care,' in a small town of Southern Russia in 1867.

"After this, without notifying my relatives of my having returned to Russia to bring back the unfortunate little boy whom I did not succeed to bring back alive to the governess chosen for him by the Baron, I simply wrote to the child's father to notify him of this pleasant occurrence for him, and returned to Italy with the same passport....

"Now, shall I, in the illusive hope of justifying myself, begin by exhuming these several corpses — the child's mother, Metrovitch, his wife, the poor child himself, and all the rest? Never. It would be as mean and sacrilegious as it would be useless. *Let the dead sleep*, I say. We have enough avenging shadows around us.... Touch them not, for you would only make them share the slaps in the face and the insults I am receiving, but you would not succeed to screen me in any way. I do not want to lie, and I am not permitted to tell the truth. What shall we, what can we, do?

"The whole of my life except the weeks and months I passed with the Masters, in Egypt or in Tibet, is so inextricably full of events with whose secrets and real actuality the dead and living are concerned, and I made only responsible for their outward appearance, that to vindicate myself I would have to step on a hecatomb of the dead and cover with dirt the living. *I will not do so.*

"For, *firstly*, it will do me no good except adding to other epithets I am graced with, that of a slanderer of *post mortem* reputation, and accused perhaps of *chantage* and blackmail; and secondly I am an Occultist, as I told you. You speak of my 'susceptibilities' with regard to my relatives; I say it is *Occultism*, not susceptibilities. I know the effect it would have on the dead, and want to forget the living. This is my last and final decision: I WILL NOT TOUCH THEM.

"And now, to another aspect of the thing. I am repeatedly reminded of the fact, that as a public character, a woman who, instead of pursuing her womanly duties, sleeping with her husband, breeding children, wiping their noses, minding her kitchen, and consoling herself with matrimonial assistants on the sly and behind her husband's back, I have chosen a path that has led me to notoriety and fame; and that therefore I had to expect all that befell me. Very well, I admit it and agree.

"But I say at the same time to the world: 'Ladies and gentlemen, I am in your hands and subject and subordinate to the world's jury, *only since I founded the T. S.* Between H. P. Blavatsky from 1875 and H. P. B. from 1830 to that date, is a veil drawn and you are in no way concerned with what took place behind it, before I appeared as a public character. It was my *private life* holy and sacred, to all but the slanderous and venomous mad-dogs who poke their noses under cover of the night into every family's and every individual's private lives.'

"To those hyenas who will unearth every tomb by night, to get at the corpses and devour them, I owe no explanations. If I am prevented by circumstances from killing them, I have to suffer, but no one can expect me to stand on Trafalgar Square and to be taking into my confidence all the city roughs and cabmen that pass. And even these, have more my respect and confidence than your reading and literary public, your 'drawing-room' and Parliament ladies and gentlemen. I would rather trust an honest, half-drunk cabman than I would the former.

"I have lived little in the world even in my own country, but I know it — especially for the last decade — better than *you know* them perhaps, though you have been moving in the midst of that cultured and refined lot for the last 25 years of your life. Well, humbled down as I am, slandered, vilified, and covered with mud, I say that it would be beneath my dignity to throw myself on their mercy and judgment. Had I even been all they accuse me of; had I had lovers and children by the bushels; who among all that lot is *pure enough to throw at me openly and publicly* the first stone?

"A Bibiche who was caught, is in company with hundreds of others who have not been so exposed, but — they are no better than she is. The higher spheres of Society, from Grand Duchesses and Princesses of blood down to their *camiristes* — all are honeycombed with secret sensuality, licentiousness and prostitution. Out of ten women, married and unmarried, if you find one who is pure — I am ready to proclaim the present world comparatively holy, yet, with very few exceptions all the women are liars to themselves as to others. Men are all no better than animals and brutes in their lower natures. And it is *they*, such *a lot*, that I am going to ask to sit in judgment over me, to address them tacitly and virtually, by describing certain events in my life in the *Memoirs*, to 'please give me the benefit of the doubt.'

"'Dear ladies and gentlemen, you who have never failed to sin behind a shut door, you who are all tainted with the embraces of other women's husbands and other men's wives, you not one of whom is exempt from the pleasure of keeping a skeleton or two in your family closets — please take my defence.' No Sir, I die rather than do it! As Hartmann truly remarked, it is far more important what I myself think of me, than what the world does. It is that which I *know* of myself that will be my judge hereafter, not what a reader who buys for a few shillings my life, '*a made-up one*' as he will always think — believes of me.

"If I had daughters whose reputations I might damage by failing to justify my behaviour, I would perhaps resort to such an indignity. As I have none, and that three days after my death all the world save a few Theosophists and friends will have forgotten my name — let all go, I say.

"The moral of the above and conclusion: you are welcome to stun the public with the recital of my life day after day ever since the T. S. was founded, and the public is entitled to it."[10]

"Agardi Metrovitch was my most faithful devoted friend ever since 1850. With the help of Ct. Kisseleff I had saved him from the gallows in Austria. He was a Mazzinist, had insulted the Pope, was exiled from Rome in 1863 — he came with his wife to Tiflis, my relatives knew him well, and when his wife died, a friend of mine too — he came to Odessa in 1870. There my aunt, miserable beyond words, as she told me, at not knowing what had become of me, begged him to go to Cairo, as he had business in Alexandria, and to try and bring me home. He did so.

"There some Maltese, instructed by the Roman Catholic monks, prepared to lay a trap for him and to kill him. I was warned by Illarion, then *bodily* in Egypt, and made Agardi Metrovitch come direct to me and never leave the house for ten days. He was a brave and daring man and could not bear it, so he went to Alexandria *quand même*, and I went after him with my monkeys, doing as Illarion told me, who said he saw death for him and that he had to die on April 19th (I think).

"All this mystery and precaution made Mme C. [oulomb] open her eyes and ears, and she began gossiping and bothering me to tell her whether it was true — what people said — that I was secretly married to him; she was not daring enough I suppose to say that people believed him most charitably *worse* than a husband. I sent her to grass, and told her that people might say and believe whatever they liked, as I didn't care. This is the *germ* of all the later gossip.

"Now whether he was poisoned, poor man, as I always suspected, or died of typhoid fever, I cannot say. One thing I know. When I arrived to Alexandria, to force him to go back on the steamer that brought him, I arrived too late. He had gone to Ramleh on foot, had stopped on his way to drink a glass of lemonade at the hotel of a Maltese who was seen talking with two monks, and when he arrived at Ramleh fell down senseless. Mme Paschkoff heard of it and telegraphed to me.

"I went to Ramleh and found him in a small hotel, in typhoid fever I was told by the doctor, and *with a monk* near him. I kicked him out, knowing his aversion to priests — had a row and sent for the police to drag away the dirty monk, who showed me his fist. Then I took care of him for ten days — an agony incessant and terrible during which he saw his wife apparently and called loudly for her. I never left him, for I knew he was going to die as Illarion had said, and so he did.

"Then no church would bury him, saying he was a *Carbonaro*. I appealed to some Free Masons, but they were afraid. Then I took an Abyssinian — a pupil of Illarion, and with the hotel servant, we dug him a grave under a tree on the sea shore, and I hired *fellahs* to carry him in the evening, and we buried his poor body. I was then a Russian subject, and had a row for it with the Consul at Alexandria (the one at Cairo was always my friend). That's all.

"The Consul told me that I had no business to be friends with revolutionaries and Mazzinists, and that people said he was my lover. I answered that since he (Ag. Metrovitch) had come from Russia with a regular passport, was a friend of my relatives and had done nothing against *my country*, I had a right to be friends with him, and with whomsoever I chose. As to the dirty talk about me, I was accustomed to it and could only regret that my reputation clashed with facts — ' *avoir la reputation sans en avoir les plaisirs*' — (if any) has always been my fate.

"Well, this is what Coulomb now got hold of. Last year Olcott wrote to my aunt about this poor man, and she answered him telling him that they all had known Metrovitch and his wife, whom he adored, and who had just died when she asked him to go to Egypt, etc. But all this is flapdoodle.

What I want to know is — has a lawyer *a right* to insult me in a letter, as this Remnant has — and have I, or have I not the right to *threaten him* at least with proceedings?

"Please see to it, I ask you as a friend, otherwise I will have to write myself to some lawyer and begin an action, which I can do without going to England. I have no desire to begin an action myself, as you know, but I want these lawyers to know that I have a right to, if I choose. Perhaps they believe, indeed, the fools, that I was *secretly* married to poor Metrovitch, and that it is a skeleton in the family cupboard?"[11]

One rejoices that, in spite of Mme Blavatsky's reticence, the truth has at last been made known through the publication of her letters to Mr. Sinnett, as to the part she played in the life of Agardi Metrovitch; especially since an impossible account of it has appeared in the *Memoirs* of her cousin, Count Sergius de Witte.

Of the one real love in her life, not "a love affair," she said in *My Confession*: "I loved one man deeply, but still more I loved occult science, believing in magic, wizards, etc. I wandered with him here and there, in Asia, in America, and in Europe."[12] This declaration eliminates Agardi Metrovitch; for, even according to Count Witte's narrative, she never was outside Europe with Metrovitch, save in Egypt at his death.

CHAPTER XXVI

Count Witte's Version

Now that Mme Blavatsky's contemporaries are dead, existing slanders of her good name are to be found in documents; and chief of these, perhaps, is the brief and garbled story in the *Memoirs* of her cousin. Having described her flight from her husband,* he continues:

"The subsequent developments of her amazing career appear as follows: At Constantinople she entered a circus as an equestrienne and it was there that Mitrovich, one of the celebrated bassos of the time, fell in love with her. She gave up the circus and accompanied the singer to one of the European capitals where he was engaged to sing. Shortly afterward grandfather was the recipient of letters from the singer Mitrovich, who asserted that he had been married to Yelena and styled himself 'grandson.' The famous basso apparently was not disconcerted by the fact that she had not been properly divorced from her husband, the Vice-Governor of Erivan.

"Several years later, a new 'grandson' accrued to my grandparents. A certain Englishman from London informed them, in a letter bearing an American stamp, that he had been married to Mme Blavatski, who had gone with him on a business trip to United States.

"Next she appears in Europe and becomes the right hand of the celebrated medium of the sixties, Hume. Then her family caught two glimpses of her dazzling career. They learned from the papers that she gave pianoforte concerts in London and Paris, and afterward became the manager of the Royal Choir maintained by King Milan of Serbia.

"In the meantime some ten years had passed. Grown tired, perhaps, of her adventures, the strayed sheep decided to return to the fold. She succeeded

---
* See Chapter V.

at the end of that period in getting grandfather's permission to return to Tiflis. She promised to mend her ways, and even to go back to her legitimate husband. It was during that visit that I saw her first.

"Her face, apparently once of great beauty, bore all the traces of a tempestuous and passionate life, and her form was marred by an early obesity. Besides, she paid but scant attention to her appearance, and preferred loose morning dresses to more elaborate apparel. But her eyes were extraordinary. She had enormous, azure-coloured eyes and when she spoke with animation, they sparkled in a fashion which is altogether indescribable. Never in my life have I seen anything like that pair of eyes.

"It was this apparently unattractive woman that turned the heads of a great many society people in Tiflis. She did it by means of spiritualistic stances, which she conducted in our house.... Although a young boy, my attitude toward these performances was decidedly critical, and I looked on them as mere sleight-of-hand tricks.... It was Hume, I believe, to whom Mme Blavatski owed her occult knowledge.

"Mme Blavatski made her peace with her husband and went as far as establishing a home at Tiflis, but it was not given her to walk in the path of righteousness for any length of time. One fine morning she was accosted in the street by Mitrovich. The famous basso was now declining, artistically and otherwise. After a brilliant career in Europe, he was forced to accept an engagement at the Italian Opera of Tiflis. The singer apparently had no doubts as to his rights to my cousin, and did not hesitate to assert his claims. As a result of the scandal, Mme Blavatski vanished from Tiflis and the basso with her.

"The couple went to Kiev, where under the guidance of his 'wife,' Mitrovich, who by this time was approaching sixty, learned how to sing in Russian and appeared with success in such Russian operas as *Life for the Czar, Russalka*, etc. The office of Governor-General of Kiev was held at that time by Prince Dundukov-Korsakov. The Prince, who at one time served in the Caucasus, had known Yelena Petrovna in her maiden days.

"I am not in a position to say what was the nature of their relationship, but one fine morning the Kievans discovered a leaflet posted on the doors and telegraph posts, which contained a number of poems very disagreeable for the Governor-General. The author of this poetic outburst was no other person than Mme Blavatski herself, and as the fact was patent, the couple had to clear out.

"She was heard of next from Odessa, where she emerged in the company of her faithful basso. At the time, our entire family was settled in that city (my grandparents and father had died at Tiflis), and my brother and I attended the university there. The extraordinary couple must have found themselves in great straits. It was then that my versatile cousin opened in succession an ink factory and retail shop and a store for artificial flowers. In those days she often came to see me, and I visited her store several times, so that I had an opportunity of getting better acquainted with her....

"Mme Blavatski's adventures in the field of commerce and industry proved, of course, dismal failures. It was then that Mitrovich accepted an engagement to sing at the Italian Opera at Cairo, and the couple set out for Egypt. By that time they represented a rather sorry plight, he a toothless lion perennially at the feet of his mistress, an aged lady, stout and slovenly.

"Off the African coast their ship was wrecked, and all the passengers found themselves in the waves. Mitrovich saved his mistress, but was drowned himself. Mme Blavatski entered Cairo in a wet skirt and without a penny to her name. How she extracted herself from that situation I do not know, but she was next discovered in. England, where she founded the Theosophical Society.

"To strengthen the foundations of the new cult, she travelled to India, where she studied the occult science of the Hindus. Upon her return, she became the centre of a large group of devotees of the theosophic doctrine, and settled in Paris as the acknowledged head of the theosophists. Shortly afterward she fell ill and died."

There is so little truth in this whole story that it is hardly worth considering. In extenuation it should be remembered that the author was a mere boy of ten or eleven when his mysterious cousin first returned home in 1859, and he was a university student at the time of her second return to Russia in 1872. Because of his youth, she appeared old to the lad — he speaks of her as 'an aged lady' when she was only thirty-nine or forty.

Count Witte's chronology is vague, perhaps because his *Memoirs* were written in his old age. Many of his statements are misleading or even wide of the facts. Mme Blavatsky says in *My Confession* that she spent three and a half days with General Blavatsky at Tiflis in 1863; but this scarcely warrants her cousins's statement that she "established a home with him

THE METROVITCHES IN "FAUST"

at Tiflis."

Even if, as she says, she encouraged tales of lovers to cover her real aim, and making due allowance for the exuberant imagination of youth on the part of Witte, the declaration that her grandfather received notification of *two* " grandsons" by marriage within a few years of each other, is difficult to accept outside "university student" circles; more especially as both her aunt and her sister Vera declare that the family heard nothing of her during those ten years of her first absence and thought her dead.

To say, for instance, that "It was Hume to whom Mme Blavatsky owed her occult knowledge" is the height of absurdity. Her years of travel in search of the occult in every form, and her long course of training at the direction of her Master both before and during her stay at His *ashrama*, make her connection with the medium Hume, if she had any, as a candle to the sun.

Of Mme Blavatsky's "adventures in the field of commerce," her cousin says they "proved, of course, dismal failures"; while her sister Vera declared that "they generally turned out well."

As to the incident at Kiev during the Governorship of Prince Dandoukov-Korsakov, it is effectively disposed of by the following:

1. A letter of Mme Blavatsky to Colonel Olcott (1884): "For them who know me from my childhood I am the personification of chastity; and hearing what was said about me by Smirnof, what Coulomb told you about me (Master told them all her lies about the poor dead child *whose mother my aunt and sister both knew*), about that poor dead man who lies buried in Alexandria, about Sebir and how she, to thank me for saving her from starvation, said lies about me in Odessa and Cairo too, to my uncle when he went there during the last Russo-Turkish war, etc., etc.... Dandoukouf behaved like a true friend and gentleman. He telegraphed to Mme de Barren to quiet me; that he received my letter and would immediately —'the day after to-morrow' send me all the official documents needed from the police and *himself* officially to show how Smirnof lied."

2. June, 1884, the documents of Prince Dandoukof, Commander-in-Chief and General-Governor of the Caucasus, sent as an official duty and a personal pleasure. Encloses Certificate of the Police Department of Tiflis, stating that Mme Blavatsky has never during her residence at Tiflis made herself liable to any accusation.[1]

Count Witte appears not to know of the existence of the real wife of Agardi Metrovitch; at least he makes no mention of her at all, though she was well known to other members of the family. Mme Blavatsky speaks of her as "my best friend, who died in 1870"; and in her sketch-book has drawn two portraits of this friend, executed with loving and appreciative touch. One is alone, the other represents Mme Metrovitch as "Marguerite" praying before a crucifix, while her husband as "Mephistopheles" whispers seductions in her ear. Beneath is written: "Teresina Signora Mitrovitch (Faust) Tiflis 7 Avril 1862." It was probably drawn after Mme Blavatsky had attended a performance of theirs at Tiflis.

One has but to compare the two stories of the death of Metrovitch to know which is the truth. After drowning Metrovitch, and having Mme Blavatsky enter Cairo "in a wet skirt," Count Witte says: "She was next discovered in England where she founded the Theosophical Society." As everyone knows, the Theosophical Society was founded in New York. Again he states that "she settled in Paris as the acknowledged head of the theosophists." Every Theosophist knows that when, in 1885, she finally went to Europe from India, she resided for a short time in Italy, Germany, and Belgium, and settled at last in London, where she died on May 8, 1891. The absolute inaccuracy of these statements furnish a criterion by which to judge Count Witte's whole story of Mme Blavatsky's life.

CHAPTER XXVII

The Child

V. S. Solovyoff says: "This is how it came: she had wished to save the honour of a friend, and had adopted the child of this friend as her own. She never parted from him, she educated him herself, and called him her son in the face of the world. Now he was dead."[1]

It would seem that she had already adopted this child in 1862; for there exists in the Archives of the Theosophical Society a "Passport to the wife of Civil Counsellor Blavatsky, attache of the Viceroy of the Caucasus, and their infant ward Youry, to proceed to the Provinces of Tauris, Cherson and Pskoff, for the term of one year." It is dated August 23, 1862 — the year she spent roaming about Imeretia and Mingrelia.

She may have taken the child much earlier; for she says: "In 1858 I was in London; there came out some story about a child, not mine (there will follow medical evidence...). One thing and another was said of me; that I was depraved, possessed with a devil, etc."[2] Possibly she had already taken charge of the child in 1858. He was a little hunchback and often ill. "Yourotita" is the diminutive by which Mme Nadejda Fadeef mentions him in a letter.

When Mr. Sinnett was asking her for material for her *Memoirs*, she protested: "The incident of the child! I better be hung than mention it. Do you know if, even withholding *names*, what it would lead to? To a hurricane of dirt thrown at me. When I told you that even my own father suspected me, and had it not been for the doctor's certificate* would have never forgiven me, perhaps. After he pitied and loved that poor cripple child.... Well, my dear Mr. Sinnett, if you would ruin me (though it is hardly possible now)

---

* Evidently refers to "what Professors Bodkin and Pirogoff said at Pskoff in 1862." See p. 187.

we shall mention this 'incident.' Do not mention any, this is my advice and prayer. I have done too much toward proving and swearing it was mine — and have overdone the thing. The doctor's certificate will go for nothing. People will say we bought or bribed the doctor, that's all."[3]

"It is *simply impossible* that the plain undisguised truth should be said about my life. Impossible even to touch upon the child.

There's the Baron Myendorffs and all Russian aristocracy that would rise against me if in the course of contradictions (which are sure to follow) the Baron's name should be mentioned. I gave my *word of honour* and shall not break it — TO THE DEAD."[4]

The implication in the above statement is that the child was the son of Baron Meyendorff; indeed, she says so specifically in the account of its death: "Then, when I took the poor child to Bologna to see if I could save him, I met him [Metrovitch] in Italy and he did all he could for me, more than a brother. Then the child died; and as it had no papers nor documents, and I did not care to give my name in food to the kind gossips, it was he, Metrovitch, who undertook all the job, who buried the *aristocratic Baron's child* — *under his, Metrovitch's, name*, saying 'he did not care,' in a small town of Southern Russia in 1867. After this, without notifying my relatives of my having returned to Russia to bring back the unfortunate little boy, whom I did not succeed to bring back alive to the governess chosen for him by the Baron, I simply wrote to the child's father to notify him of this pleasant occurrence for him, and returned to Italy on the same passport."[5]

In America the slanderous story of the child took a different form. In 1890 Mme Blavatsky brought a charge of libel against the *New York Sun*. She wrote as follows to the editor of *The Path*, Wm. Q. Judge: "For some fifteen years I have calmly stood by and seen my good name assailed by the newspaper gossips who delight to dwell upon the personal peculiarities of those who are well known, and have worked on for the spread of Theosophical ideas, feeling confident that, though I might be assailed by small minds who try their best to bring me into reproach, the Society which I helped to found would withstand the attacks and, indeed, grow under them. This latter has been the case. It may be asked by some members why I have never replied to those attacks which were directed against Occultism and Phenomena. For two reasons: Occultism will remain forever, no matter how assailed, and Occult Phenomena can never be proved in a Court of

Law during this century....

"But now a great metropolitan daily paper in New York, with no knowledge of the facts in the case, throws broadcast before the public many charges against me, the most of which meet their refutation in my life for over a decade. But as one of them reflects strongly upon my moral character, and brings into disrepute the honourable name of a dead man, an old family friend, it is impossible for me to remain silent....

"This daily paper accuses me of being a member of the *demimonde* in 1858 and 1868, and of having improper relations with Prince Emil Wittgenstein, by whom the paper says I had an illegitimate son. The first part of the charge is so ridiculous as to arouse laughter, but the second and third hold others up to reprobation. Prince Wittgenstein, now dead, was an old friend of my family, whom I saw for the last time when I was eighteen years old, and he and his wife remained until his death in close correspondence with me. He was a cousin of the late Empress of Russia, and little thought that upon his grave would be thrown the filth of a modern New York newspaper. This insult to him and to me I am bound by all the dictates of my duty to repel, and am also obliged to protect the honour of Theosophists who guide their lives by the teachings of Theosophy; hence my appeal to the Law and to a jury of my fellow-Americans. I gave up my allegiance to the Czar of Russia in the hope that America would protect her citizens; may that hope not prove vain!"[6]

Mr. Judge inserted the following editorial in his *Path* of November, 1892: "In July, 1890, the *Sun* published a news article in which gross charges were made against the character of H. P. Blavatsky, and charging Colonel Olcott, Wm. Q. Judge and others with assisting her in fraud and with living upon the Society. It was intended to be a general sweeping attack on all who were in the Society, having been written by an enemy who once was counted in the ranks of our members.... Two suits for libel were begun by Mme Blavatsky and Mr. Judge, against the *Sun* and Dr. E. Coues of Washington.... The suits went on the calendar of the courts of New York.... In 1891 H. P. B. died, and as her action was for a personal injury to character, her demise worked a determination of the suit begun in her name, and by that fact the paper was at once released from any fear of that action. This should be noted in view of what follows. On the 26th September, 1892, the *Sun* published the following in its editorial columns:

"'We print on another page an article in which Mr. Wm. Q. Judge deals with the romantic and extraordinary career of the late Mme Helena P. Blavatsky, the Theosophist. We take occasion to observe that on July 20, 1890, we were misled into admitting to the *Sun's* columns an article by Dr. E. F. Coues of Washington, in which allegations were made against Mme Blavatsky's character, and also against her followers, which appear to have been without solid foundation. Mr. Judge's article disposes of all questions relating to Mme Blavatsky as represented by Dr. Coues, and we desire to say that his allegations respecting the Theosophical Society and Mr. Judge personally are not sustained by evidence, and should not have been printed.' In view of the fact that no suit was then pending, this reflects credit on the paper. Thus ends this libel."[7]

There is a letter of H. P. B.'s in the Archives of the Theosophical Society, carefully preserved by Colonel Olcott, which deals with her doctor's examination when she was ill in Europe in 1885. The first page of the letter is missing; page two begins in the midst of a sentence thus: " he brought his instruments, looking-glass or mirror to look *inside* and other horrors. When he did he asked in amazement, 'Were you ever married?' 'Yes' I said, 'but never had any children' — not wanting to go into physiological particulars. 'No, surely' he answered, 'how could you since for all I can see, *you must have never had connection with your husband*.' I said this to Mrs. Sinnett, and Mme Tidesco who had assisted at the operation corroborated. Sinnett pounced upon me. 'Have a certificate, Old Lady, have one!' I understood why, and yesterday when the Professor came again, I asked him whether he could give me *such a certificate*, saying that some enemies said I had children and had been immoral. He consented readily....

" He says, I have from birth the uterus crooked or hooked inside out, and that I could not, not only *never have children*, but that it is now the cause of my suffering with the bladder... and that if I had ever tried (thanks!) to be *immoral* with anyone, I would have had each time an inflammation and great suffering. There! So much for the Coulomb's three children; my marriage with Mitra, etc., etc. I sent the certificate to Sinnett, for he says *he needs it*. It is a great shame, but a great triumph likewise."

The medical certificate is as follows: "The undersigned testifies as requested, that Mme Blavatsky of Bombay — New York, corresponding secretary of the Theosophical Society, is at the present time under the medical treatment of the undersigned. She suffers from *Antefiexio Uteri*, most probably from the day of her birth, as proved by minute examination; she has never borne a child, nor has she had any gynaecological illness.

(Signed) Dr. Leon Oppenheim.

Wurzburg, 3 *November*, 1885.
Attested by Hübbe Schleiden
Franz Gebhard."

It was pointed out to Countess Wachtmeister (then living in H.P.B.'s home) that the wording of this certificate was not clear, that "gynaecological illness" was rather vague; whereupon Dr. Oppenheim, at her request, wrote a second certificate much more to the point: "I hereby certify that Mme Blavatsky has never been pregnant with child and so consequently can never have had a child. Oppenheim."

Accompanying this certificate in the Society's Archives is a letter of which only one page, number four, is left; it reads: "Here's your stupid new certificate with your dreams of *virgo intacta* in a woman who had all her guts out, womb and all, by a fall from horseback. And yet the doctor looked, examined *three* times, and says what the Professor Bodkin and Pirogoff said at Pskoff in 1862. I could never have had connection with *any* man without an inflammation, because I am lacking something and the place is filled up with some crooked cucumber."

There is another, a covering letter (for this second certificate) from Countess Wachtmeister.

10th February. [1886]

Dear Friend and Brother,

Here is the certificate you desire to have. It was in Mme Blavatsky's presence that I asked for it, for I felt I had no right to make such a demand without her permission.

You see the word *pregnant* embraces the whole meaning, for without being pregnant she could have neither miscarriage nor child. The first certificate was badly translated. In the original held by Mr. Sinnett, the word miscarriage has been translated into 'women's disease.' The Doctor then told me that, though no doctor can positively certify whether a woman has lived with her husband or not, on account of the virginity being lost by a fall or hard exercise, to the best of his belief Mme Blavatsky had not lived with a man — so you see all the slander and calumny against her goes for nothing. The Doctor also said that in his experience he had examined girls of 10 or 12 years of age, knowing them to be pure and virtuous children, yet their virginity was gone owing to a fall....

C. WACHTMEISTER.[8]

With this heritage from her past, H. P. B. set her face from travel to work, "from apprenticeship to duty."

CHAPTER XXVIII

Poor And Penniless In New York

MR. WILLIAM KINGSLAND, in his *The Real H. P. Blavatsky*, says that now, in 1873, H. P. B. has completed her *Wanderjahre*, has served her apprenticeship in the outer world — in many lands, races, communities, societies (from the most primitive to the most aristocratic); she has also sought and found many occult experiences, which were then regarded by science as altogether unworthy of attention, and by religion as lying in the province of the Devil and his minions. "What," he asks, "may we consider to be the outcome of all this restless, stormy, strange and exceptional life?" The answer is: Work for the Masters in the world. She began that work tentatively by organising the *Sociité Spirite* in Cairo. The attempt failed. Colonel Olcott wisely remarks: "I fell heir to the wasted chances of her Cairo group in 1871."[1]

We have seen how she arrived in New York, July 7th, almost penniless, having sailed the day after she received "orders" to that effect. "She wrote to her father for funds to be sent her in care of the Russian Consul at New York, but this could not arrive for some time; and as the Consul refused her a loan, she had to set to work to earn her daily bread. She told me that she had taken lodgings in one of the poorest quarters of New York — Madison Street — and supported herself by making cravats or artificial flowers — I forget which now* — for a kind-hearted Hebrew shop-keeper. She always spoke to me with gratitude about this little man.

Miss Anna Ballard, a veteran journalist and life-member of the New York Press Club, tells how she met H. P. B. "not more than a week after she

---

* She had owned a factory for making artificial flowers in the Caucasus, says her sister Vera; so the latter is more probable.

landed in July, 1873. I was then a reporter on the staff of the *New York Sun*, and had been detailed to write an article on a Russian subject. In the course of my search after facts, the arrival of this Russian lady was reported to me by a friend, and I called upon her.... She told me that she had no idea of leaving Paris until the evening before she sailed, but why she came or who hurried her off she did not say, I remember perfectly well her saying with an air of exultation, " I have been to Tibet." Why she should think that a great matter, more remarkable than any other of the travels in Egypt, India and other countries she told me about, I could not make out, but she said it with special emphasis and animation. I now know, of course, what it means.'"[2]

Another lady who knew H. P. B. in her first difficult days in New York was Elizabeth G. K. Holt who has fortunately written at some length about it: " In those days there were no women in business ; a few were beginning to be heard clamouring for their 'rights'; but the women who had to go out into the world to earn a living were teachers, telegraphers, sewers of various kinds, and workers at small trades which paid very badly. The typewriter had not yet been invented. A lady travelling alone was not received in the better hotels.... It was probably this difficulty of finding proper accommodation that led H. P. B. to the house in which I met her. I have always wondered how she, a stranger coming to New York, had discovered it.*

" The house was unique and a product of that particular era. It was hard then for respectable women workers of small means to find a fitting place in which to live ; so it happened that some forty of them launched a small experiment in co-operative living. They rented a new tenement house, 222 Madison Street, one of the first built in New York, I think. It was a street of small two-storey houses occupied by their owners, who were proud of their shade-trees, and kept their front and back yards in order....

" My mother and I had spent the summer of 1873 at Saratoga. In order to be ready for school when it opened, I was sent home in August to the Madison Street house, where we had a friend who would take me under her protection ; and there I found Mme Blavatsky. She had a room on the second floor, and my friend had a duplicate room next to her, so that they became very friendly neighbours. Being a co-operative family, we all knew one another familiarly, and kept a room next the street-door as a common sitting-room or office, a meeting-place for members, and a place where

---

* Having been in New York at least twice before, she was not a stranger to it.

mail and messages were cared for.

"Mme Blavatsky sat in the office a large part of her time, but she seldom sat alone; she was like a magnet, powerful enough to draw round her everyone who could possibly come. I saw her, day by day, sitting there rolling her cigarettes and smoking incessantly. She had a conspicuous tobacco pouch, the head of some fur-bearing animal, which she wore round the neck. She was certainly an unusual figure. I think she must have been taller than she looked, she was so broad; she had a broad face and broad shoulders; her hair was a lightish brown and crinkled like that of some negroes. Her whole appearance conveyed the idea of power. I read somewhere lately an account of an interview with Stalin; the writer said that when you entered the room you felt as if there was a powerful dynamo working. You felt something like that when you were near H.P.B....

"Madame referred often to her life in Paris; for one thing she told us that she had decorated the Empress Eugenie's private apartments. I thought of her as dressed in blouse and trousers, mounted on a ladder and doing the actual work, and I think this is what she told us; but I cannot be sure whether she said that she did the actual painting, frescoing, etc. or whether she merely designed it. Later she gave practical demonstration that she had ability in the arts. I had a piano, and Madame sometimes played, usually because somebody pressed her to do so.

"She described their past life to the people who asked her to do so, and these accounts must have been accurate, they made such a profound impression. I never heard that she told them their future, but she may have done so without my knowing it.... She was considered to be a Spiritualist, though I never heard her say she was one.... When my friend, Miss Parker, asked Madame to put her in communication with her dead mother, Madame said it was impossible, as her mother was absorbed in higher things and had progressed beyond reach. The spirits she spoke about continually were the *diaki*, tricksy little beings, evidently counterparts of the fairies of Irish folk-lore, and certainly non-human from her description of them and their activities....

"I never looked upon Madame as an ethical teacher. For one thing, she was too excitable; when things went wrong with her, she could express her opinion about them with a vigour which was very disturbing. I would say here that I never saw her angry with any person or thing at close range.

Her objections had an impersonality about them.... In mental or physical dilemma, you would instinctively appeal to her, for you felt her fearlessness, her un-conventionality, her great wisdom and wide experience and hearty good will — her sympathy with the under dog.

"An instance of this kind comes to mind. Undesirable people were beginning to move into the street, and the neighbourhood was changing rapidly. One evening one of our young girls, coming home late from work, was followed and greatly frightened; she flung herself breathless into a chair in the office. Madame interested herself at once, expressed her indignation in most vigorous terms, and finally drew from some fold in her dress a knife (I think she used it to cut her tobacco, but it was sufficiently large to be a formidable weapon of defence) and said she had *that* for any man who molested her.

"At this time Madame was greatly troubled about money; the income she had received regularly from her father in Russia had stopped, and she was almost penniless. She had some idea that this condition was caused by the machinations of some person or persons in touch with her father, and she expressed herself about these persons with customary vigour. Some of the more conservative people in our house suggested that she was, after all, an adventuress, and the want of money was only what might be expected; but my friend, Miss Parker, whom she took with her to the Russian Consul, assured me that she was really a Russian Countess, that the Consul knew of her family, and had promised to do all he could to get in touch with them and find out what was the difficulty. I may say here that the holding up of her income was caused by the death of her father and the consequent time required to settle up his affairs.

"The owner of our house was a Mr. Rinaldo, who personally collected his rents, and so became acquainted with our people. Like everyone else, he became interested in H. P. B. and introduced two young friends of his to her. They came very often to see her, and were of practical aid to her, in suggesting and giving her work. They got her to design picture advertising-cards for themselves and others. I think these gentlemen had a collar and shirt factory, for the card I remember best was of little figures (*diaki* perhaps), dressed in collars and shirts of their manufacture. I think these were the first picture advertising-cards used in New York.* Madame also

---

* For illustration of these or similar cards, see *Old Diary Leaves*, I, p. 472.

tried ornamental work in leather, and produced some very fine and intricate examples, but they did not sell, and she abandoned the leather work.

"About this time she completed the unfinished novel *Edwin Drood* which Charles Dickens had not completed when he died in 1870. I am under the impression that these Jewish friends of Madame were Spiritualists, and that they urged her to complete the book with spirit-aid. She had a long table in her private room and I saw her for days, perhaps weeks, steadily writing page after page of manuscript.*...

"Shortly after this and while Madame was still without income she met and became intimate with a French lady, a widow, whose name I have forgotten; for though she became a familiar visitor to the house she was usually called 'the French Madame,'† while H.P.B. remained ever 'the Madame.' It was this lady who afterward went with H.P.B. to the Eddy farm.

"At this time she lived a short distance away in Henry Street. She offered to share her home with H.P.B. until the latter's money difficulties had passed. This offer was accepted, and Madame left our house. Many of our people, however, and notably Miss Parker, kept in close touch with her, and attended Sunday evening meetings inaugurated by the two ladies, from which I was shut out....

"One of the stories about the *diaki* dates from this time. One morning Madame did not appear for breakfast, and her friend finally went to her bedroom to see what was the matter; there she found H.P.B. unable to rise because her night-gown was securely sewed to the mattress, and sewed in such a manner that it would have been impossible for Madame to have done it herself, and so thoroughly had the sewing been done that the stitches had to be cut before Madame could rise. This was the work of the *diaki*.

"Shortly after this Madame received money from Russia, and moved to the north-east corner of 14th Street and Fourth Avenue. The house was very unpretentious, with a liquor saloon on the street floor, and the two upper floors let as furnished rooms. To this house Miss Parker took me.... There I found Madame in a poorly furnished top-floor room; her bed was an iron cot, and beside her bed on a table was a small cabinet with three drawers.

---

* She merely translated into Russian the work of a Mr. James, a medium. She wrote to Alexander Aksakoff, a noted Russian publisher, October 28, 1874, offering her translation of James's work.

† This may be the Mme Magnon who later visited H.P.B. in Philadelphia.

"Madame was in a state of great excitement. Earlier in the day her room had been on fire; she said it had been purposely set on fire to rob her. After the fire was out, and the firemen and curious strangers had gone, she found that her valuable watch and chain had been stolen. When she complained to the proprietor of the saloon, who was her landlord, he intimated that she had never had a watch to lose. She told us that she asked 'Them' to give her some proof which she could show her landlord and convince him that she really had lost her property; immediately there appeared before her a sheet of paper all grey with smoke except for white spots, the size and shape of a watch and chain, indicating that after the fire had darkened the paper, the watch and chain had been lifted from it, revealing the white spots which they had covered.

"She went on to tell us that when she needed money, she had only to ask 'Them' for it, and she would find what she needed in one of the drawers of the little cabinet on her table. I could not understand this. I had always heard the 'They' and 'Them' explained by the people who were round her, as referring to her 'Spirit Guides'; naturally I thought she spoke of them. I knew nothing of Occultism, its pledges, nor of the selflessness it demands of its followers.

"Some time after this, I heard that she went to Ithaca, to give to Professor Corson, of Cornell University, a ring entrusted to her by some of her mysterious directors, which would identify her as an authentic messenger from them. But my visit to H. P. B. was the last time I saw her; from that time on her life has been well known and described by others."[3]

Colonel Olcott carries forward the narrative of 1873: "In October her ever-indulgent, forbearing and beloved father died;* and on the 29th of the month she received a cable dispatch from Stavropol, from her sister 'Elise' conveying the news and informing her as to the amount of her heritage, adding that a draft of 1000 roubles had been sent to her. In due course of post she received all the money, and then shifted her quarters to better neighbourhoods in New York city — Union Square, East Sixteenth Street, Irving Place, etc., and it was in the last-named I found her upon returning from the Eddy Homestead."[4]

---

* This is an error. He died July 15. See next chapter. She received the cable so late, perhaps, because her whereabouts were not known to her family in Russia.

CHAPTER XXIX

Meeting Of The Founders Of The Theosophical Society

The account of their meeting at the Eddy Homestead which Colonel Olcott wrote at the time (1874) to the *New York Daily Graphic* may be read in full in his *People from the Other World*. Briefly it is this: "The arrival of a Russian lady of distinguished birth and rare educational and natural endowments, on the 14th of October... was an important event in the history of the Chittenden manifestations. This lady — Madam Helene P. de Blavatsky — has led a very eventful life, travelling in most of the lands of the Orient,* searching for antiquities at the base of the Pyramids, witnessing the mysteries of Hindoo temples, and pushing with an armed escort far into the interior of Africa. The adventures she has encountered, the strange people she has seen, the perils by land and sea she has passed through, would make one of the most romantic stories ever told by a biographer. In the whole course of my experience, I never met so interesting and, if I may say it without offence, eccentric a character."[1]

Eighteen years later, he opened in *The Theosophist* his serial, "The Oriental Series," now in book-form as *Old Diary Leaves*, with a chapter on the "First Meeting of the Founders"; and there he says: "Since I am to tell the story of the birth and progress of the Theosophical Society, I must begin at the beginning, and tell how its two founders first met. It was a very prosaic incident: I said: '*Permettez moi, Madame,*' and gave her a light for her cigarette; our acquaintance began in smoke, but it stirred up a great and permanent fire.

---

* He says elsewhere in the book that she had travelled thrice round the world unaccompanied.

"The circumstances which brought us together were peculiar... One day, in the month of July, 1874, I was sitting in my law office thinking over a heavy case in which I had been retained by the Corporation of the City of New York, when it occurred to me that for years I had paid no attention to the Spiritualist movement.... I went round the corner and bought a copy of the *Banner of Light*. In it I read an account of certain incredible phenomena... which were said to be occurring at a farmhouse in the township of Chittenden, in the State of Vermont. I saw at once that if it were true... this was the most important fact in modern physical science. I determined to go and see for myself. I did so, found the story true, stopped three or four days, and then returned to New York. I wrote an account of my observations to the *New York Sun*,... A proposal was then made to me by the Editor of the *New York Daily Graphic* to return to Chittenden in its interests, accompanied by an artist to sketch under my orders, and to make a thorough investigation of the affair....

"On September 17th I was back at the 'Eddy Homestead'... I stopped in that house of mystery, surrounded by phantoms, and having daily experiences of a most extraordinary character, for about twelve weeks.... Twice a week there appeared in the *Daily Graphic* my letters about the 'Eddy ghosts' illustrated with sketches drawn by the artist, Mr. Kappes. It was the publication of these letters which drew Mme Blavatsky to Chittenden, and so brought us together....

"The dinner hour at Eddy's was noon, and it was from the entrance door of the bare and comfortless dining-room that Kappes and I first saw H.P.B. She had arrived shortly before noon with a French Canadian lady,* and they were at table as we entered. My eye was first attracted by a scarlet Garibaldian shirt the former wore, as in vivid contrast with the dull colours around. Her hair was then a thick blonde mop, worn shorter than the shoulders, and it stood out from her head, silken-soft and crinkled to the roots, like the fleece of a Cotswold ewe. This and the red shirt were what struck my attention before I took in the picture of her features. It was a massive Calmuck face, contrasting in its suggestion of power, culture and imperiousness, as strangely with the commonplace visages about the room as her red garment did with the grey and white tones of the walls and woodwork and the dull costumes of the rest of the guests.

* Perhaps Mrs. Magnon.

"All sorts of cranky people were continually coming and going at the Eddy's to see the mediumistic phenomena, and it only struck me on seeing this eccentric lady that this was but one more of the sort. Pausing on the door-sill, I whispered to Kappes, 'Good gracious! look at *that* specimen, will you'... Dinner over, the two went outside and Mme Blavatsky rolled herself a cigarette, for which I offered her a light as a pretext to enter into conversation".[2]

It is to be noted that Colonel Olcott was a confirmed and enthusiastic protagonist for Spiritualism; whereas H.P.B. came fresh from her Cairo failure with mediums, and having her clairvoyant powers in full working order. In the same number of the *Daily Graphic* in which her anti-Beard letter appeared later, there was published a short biography in which she said of herself: "In 1858, I returned to Paris and made the acquaintance of Daniel Home, the Spiritualist... Home converted me to Spiritualism.... After this I went to Russia. I converted my father to Spiritualism."[3]

"I had never known nor even seen a medium," she says elsewhere, "nor ever found myself in a seance room, before March, 1873, when I was passing through Paris on my way to America. It was in August of that year that I learned *for the first time in my life*, what was the philosophy of the Spiritualists.... Very true, I had had a general and very vague idea of the teachings of Allan Kardec since 1870. But when I heard stated the claims of the American Spiritualists about the 'Summer Land,' etc., I rejected the whole thing point blank... I say again, I was never a Spiritualist.... I have always known the reality of mediumistic phenomena, and defended the reality; that is all. If to have the whole long series of phenomena happen through one's organism, will, or any other agency, is to be a 'Spiritualist,' then I was one, perhaps, fifty years ago; i e. I was a Spiritualist before the birth of modern Spiritialism.

"In the beginning of 1872, on my arrival from India, I had tried to found a Spiritist Society at Cairo, after the fashion of Allan Kardec (I knew of no other), to try for phenomena, as a preparative for occult science. I had two French pretended mediums, who treated us to bogus manifestations, and who revealed to me such mediumistic tricks as I never dreamed possible. I put an end to the stances immediately, and wrote to Mr. Burns to see whether he could not send out an English medium. He never replied, and I returned to Russia soon afterward."[4]

After her visit to the Eddys, H. P. B. wrote an account of the phenomena which occurred for the *Daily Graphic*. The article was called "Marvellous Spirit Manifestations, a Reply to Dr. Beard." It may be read in full in *A Modern Panarion*, under the title "The Eddy Manifestations." Her description of the "spirits" which follows is quoted from this article.

"I remained fourteen days at the Eddys. In that short period of time I saw and recognised fully out of 119 apparitions 7 'spirits' I admit that I was the only one to recognise them, the rest of the audience not having been with me in my numerous travels throughout the East; but their various costumes were plainly seen and closely examined by all.

"The first was a Georgian boy, dressed in the historical Caucasian attire. I recognised and questioned him in Georgian upon circumstances known only to myself. I was understood and answered. Requested by me in his mother-tongue (upon the whispered suggestion of Colonel Olcott) to play the 'Lezguinka' a Circassian dance, he did so immediately upon the guitar."

This is Colonel Olcott's version in his *People from the Other World*: "Then the first of the Russian lady's spirit-visitors made his appearance. He was a person of middle height, well shaped, dressed in a Georgian (Caucasian) jacket, with loose sleeves and long pointed oversleeves, an outer long coat, baggy trousers, leggings of yellow leather, and white skull-cap, or fez, with tassel. She recognised him at once as Michalko Guegidze, late of Kutais, Georgia, a servant of Mme Witte, a relative, and who waited upon Mme de Blavatsky in Kutais....

"The next evening a new spirit, 'Hassan Agha' came to Mme de Blavatsky. He was a wealthy merchant of Tiflis whom she knew well. He had a sneaking fancy for the Black Art, and sometimes obliged his acquaintance by divining for them with a set of conjuring stones, procured from Arabia at a great price.... Hassan's dress was a long yellowish coat, Turkish trousers, a *bishmet* or vest, and black Astrachan cap, *pappaha*, covered with the national *bashlik* or hood, with its long tasseled ends thrown over each shoulder."

H. P. B. says of him: "Second, a little old man appeared. He is dressed as Persian merchants generally are. His dress is perfect as a national costume. Everything is in its right place, down to the 'babouches' that are off his feet, he stepping out in his stockings. He speaks his name in a loud whisper. It is 'Hassan Agga,' an old man whom I and my family have known for twenty years in Tiflis. He says, half in Georgian and half in Persian that he has got a 'dead secret to tell me,' and comes at three different times, vainly seeking to finish his sentence.

"Third, a man of gigantic stature emerges forth, dressed in the picturesque attire of the warriors of Khurdistan. He does not speak, but bows in the Oriental fashion, and lifts up his spear ornamented with bright coloured feathers, shaking it in token of welcome. I recognised him immediately as 'Safer Ali Bek,' a young chief of a tribe of Kurds who used to accompany me in my trips around Ararat in Armenia on horseback, and who on one occasion saved my life. More, he bent to the ground as though taking up a handful of mould and scattering it around, presses his hand to his bosom — a gesture familiar only to the tribes of Khurdistan.*

"Fourth, a Circassian comes out. I can imagine myself at Tiflis, so perfect is the costume of 'noukar,' a man who either runs before or behind one on horseback. This one speaks. More, he corrects his name, which I pronounced wrong on recognising him and when I repeated he bowed, smiling, and said in the purest gutteral Tartar which sounds so familiar to my ears: 'Tchock yachtchl' (All right), and goes away.

"Fifth, an old woman appears, with a Russian headgear. She comes and addresses me" in Russian, calling me by an endearing term that she used in my childhood. I recognise an old servant of my family, a nurse of my sister.

Sixth, a large powerful negro next appears on the platform. His head is ornamented with a wonderful coiffure, something like horns bound about with white and gold. His looks are familiar to me, but I do not at first recollect where I have seen him. Very soon he begins to make some vivacious gestures, and his mimicry helps me to recognise him. It is a conjurer from Central Africa. He grins and disappears.†

"Seventh, and last, a large grey-haired gentleman comes out, attired in the conventional suit of black. The Russian decoration of St. Ann hangs suspended by a red moire ribbon with two black stripes as every Russian will know, belonging to the said decoration. This ribbon is worn round his neck. I feel faint, for I think I recognize my father, but the latter was a great deal taller. In my excitement I address him in English, and ask him, 'Are you my father?' He shakes his head in the negative, and answers as plainly as any mortal man can speak and in Russian, 'No, I am your uncle' The word

---

* See Colonel Olcott's description of this "spirit" in Chapter IV.

† For Colonel Olcott's description, see Chapter VI.

'Diadia' was heard and remembered by all the audience. It means 'Uncle'"

Mme Blavatsky did not recognise all the "spirits" who came to her. Colonel Olcott says: "Among the most noticeable forms to present themselves was one who seemed to be either a Hindoo coolie or an Arab athlete. He was dark-skinned, of short stature, a lean, wiry, active form, with no more superfluous fat on his frame than has a greyhound in working condition. The artist, writing to me of him says: 'He left a more vivid impression on my mind than any other spirit. I can see him now, perfectly — long, mere bone and sinew, with a cat-like suppleness. For dress, a closely-fitting vest, seemingly cotton, drawers tucked into what might have been socks or gaiters, a sash about his loins, and upon his head a dark red handkerchief' He came to visit Mme de Blavatsky, and made her a profound obeisance; but she failed to recognise him."

H. P. B. says: "Most decidedly I have seen forms called 'spirits' at Eddy's, and recognised them; even to the form of *my uncle*. But in some cases I had thought of them, and *wanted* to see them. The objectivation of their astral forms was no proof at all that they were dead. I was making experiments, though Colonel Olcott knew nothing of it; and so well did some of them succeed that I actually evoked among them the form of one *whom I believed dead* at the time, but who, it now appears, was up to last year alive and well, viz., 'Michalko,' my Georgian servant! He is now with a distant relative at Kutais, as my sister informed me two months ago in Paris. He had been reported, and I thought him, dead, but he had got well at the hospital. So much for '*spirit*' identification."*

"Even the materialised form of my uncle at the Eddy's was a picture; for it was I who sent it out from my own mind, as I had come out to make experiments without telling it to any one. It was like an empty outer envelope of my uncle that I seemed to throw on the medium's astral body. I saw and followed the process, I knew Will Eddy was a genuine medium, and the phenomenon was as real *as it could be*; and therefore when days of trouble came upon him, I defended him in the papers.

"In short, for all the years of experience in America, I never succeeded in identifying, in one single instance, those I wanted to see. It is only in my dreams and personal visions that I was brought into direct contact with

---

* Her Reply to Arthur Lillier quoted above. This is similar to the Tekla Lebendorff experience of her childhood, described in Chapter II.

my own blood relatives and friends, those between whom and myself there had been a strong mutual *spiritual* love. For certain psycho-magnetic reasons, too long to be explained here, *the shells of those spirits* who loved us best will not, with very few exceptions, approach us. They have no need of it since unless they were irretrievably wicked, they have us with them in Devachan, that state of bliss in which the *monads* are surrounded with all those, and that, which they have loved — objects of spiritual aspiration as well as human entities.

"'Shells' once separated from their higher principles have nought in common with the latter. They are not drawn to their relatives and friends, but rather to those with whom their terrestrial, sensuous affinities are the strongest. Thus the shell of a drunkard will be drawn to one who is either a drunkard already or has the germ of this passion in him, in which case they will develop it by using his organs to satisfy their craving; one who died full of sexual passion for a still living partner will have its shell drawn to him or her etc."[5]

"It stands to reason that this mere earthly refuse, irresistibly drawn to the earth, cannot follow the soul and spirit — these highest principles of man's being. With horror and disgust I often observed how a reanimated shadow of this kind separated itself from the inside of the medium; how, separating itself from his astral body and clad in someone else's vesture, it pretended to be someone's relation, causing the person to go into ecstasies and making people open wide their hearts and their embraces to these shadows they sincerely believed to be their dear fathers and brothers, resuscitated to convince them of life eternal, as well as to see them.... Oh, if they only knew the truth, if they only believed! If they saw, as I have often seen, a monstrous bodiless creature seizing hold of someone present at these Spiritualistic stances. It wraps a man as if with a black shroud and slowly disappears in him as if drawn into his body by each of his living pores."[6]

In a letter to her relatives, Mme Blavatsky thus summarises her experiences at the Eddy's: "We cannot avoid, in some way or another, assimilating our dead.... This process is common to humanity in general. It is a natural one.... But there is another law, an exceptional one, and which manifests itself among mankind sporadically and periodically: the law of forced post-mortem assimilation, during the prevalence of which epidemic the dead invade the domain of the living from their respective spheres — though, fortunately, only within the limits of the regions they lived in, and in which they are buried. In such cases the duration and intensity of the epidemic depend on the welcome they receive.... Such a periodical visitation is now occurring in America. It began [1847] with innocent children — the little Misses Fox — playing unconsciously with this terrible weapon. And, welcomed and passionately invited to 'come in,' the whole dead community seemed to have rushed in, and got a more or less strong hold of the living.

"I went on purpose to a family of strong mediums — the Eddys — and watched for over a fortnight, making experiments which, of course, I kept to myself.... I saw and watched these soulless creatures, the shadows of their terrestrial bodies, from which in most cases soul and spirit had fled long ago, but which throve and preserved their semi-material shadows at the expense of the hundreds of visitors that came and went, as well as of the mediums.

"And I remarked, under the advice and guidance of my Master, that (1) those apparitions which were genuine were produced by the 'ghosts' of those who had lived and died within a certain area of those mountains; (2) those who had died far away were less entire, a mixture of the real shadow and of that which lingered in the personal aura of the visitor for whom it purported to come; (3) the purely fictitious ones, or as I call them, the reflections of the genuine ghosts or shadows of the deceased personality. To explain myself more clearly, it was not the spooks that assimilated the medium, but the medium, W. Eddy, who assimilated unconsciously to himself the pictures of the dead relatives and friends from the aura of the sitters.

"It was ghastly to watch the process! It made me often sick and giddy; but I had to look at it, and the most I could do was to hold the disgusting creatures at arm's length. But it was a sight to see the welcome given to these *umbrae* by the Spiritualists! They wept and rejoiced round the medium, clothed in these empty materialised shadows; rejoiced and wept again, sometimes broken down with an emotion, a sincere joy and happiness that made my heart bleed for them. 'If they could but see what I see,' I often wished. If they only knew that these simulacra of men and women are made up wholly of the terrestrial passions, vices, and worldly thoughts, of the residuum of the personality that was; for these are only such dregs that could not follow the liberated soul and spirit, and are left for a second death in the terrestrial atmosphere, that can be seen by the average medium and the public. [They are left in the *shell* of the earth, for its (to us) invisible astral form is the region in which the *umbrae* linger after death — a grand truth given out in the exoteric doctrine of Hades by the ancient Latins.] At times I used to see one of such phantoms, quitting the medium's astral body, pouncing upon one of the sitters, expanding so as to envelop him or her entirely, and then slowly disappearing within the living body as though sucked in by its every pore."[7]

A very different phenomenon occurred on October 24, at Chittenden. Colonel Olcott's version is this: "The evening was as bright as day with the light of the moon.... In the dark circle, as soon as the light was extinguished, 'George Dix,'* addressing Mme de Blavatsky said: 'Madame, I am now about to give you a test of the genuineness of the manifestations of this circle, which I think will satisfy not only you, but a skeptical world beside. I shall place in your hands the buckle of a medal of honour worn in life by your brave father, and buried with his body in Russia. This has been brought to you by your uncle, whom you have seen materialised this evening.'

"Presently I heard the lady utter an exclamation and, a light being struck, we all saw Mme de B. holding in her hand a silver buckle of a most curious shape, which she regarded with speechless wonder. When she had recovered herself a little she announced that this buckle had indeed been worn by her father, with many other decorations; that she identified it by the fact that the point of the pin had been carelessly broken off by herself many years ago; and that, according to universal custom, this with all his other medals and crosses must have been buried with her father's body.

"The medal to which the buckle belongs was one which was granted by the late Czar to his officers after the Turkish campaign of 1828. The medals were distributed at Bucharest, and a number of the officers had buckles similar to this one made by the rude silversmiths of that city. Her father died July 15, 1873, and she being in this country could not attend the obsequies. As to the authenticity of this present so mysteriously received, she possessed ample proof in a photographic copy of her father's oil portrait, in which this very buckle appears, attached to its own ribbon and medal"[8]

It is evident that this gift was entirely unexpected by H.P.B., and not one of her experiments. Her version, given in a letter dated December 3, 1874, to Alexander N. Aksakoff (editor of the Leipzig *Psychische Studien*,

---

* A "spirit" who frequently appeared — a "guide."

to whom she sent articles for publication), is as follows: "In a dark circle a spirit brought me my father's Turkish war medal of 1828, saying: 'I bring you, Helene Blavatsky, the badge of honour received by your father for the war of 1828. We took this medal *through the influence of your uncle* who appeared to you this night — from your father's grave at Stavropol, and bring it to you as a remembrance of us in whom you believe and have faith.'"[9] Needless to say, the "us in whom you believe and have faith" does not refer to the "spirits," but to the Masters. Only H. P. B. understood the true inwardness of this gift.

"The medium, Home, who was well known in Russia, accused Mme Blavatsky, first in letters to various persons and then in print, of being a fraudulent medium, on the ground of Olcott's letters and books, and attacked her private life.... All this was brought about chiefly by the medal and clasp brought from the tomb of her father, M. Hahn. Home showed with good reason that it was not customary in Russia to put orders of merit in the grave, and further that the medal and clasp seemed to be creations of pure fancy."[10] Replying to this, H. P. B. wrote to M. Aksakoff:

"I was not at my father's funeral. But at this moment the medal and clasp which were brought me are hanging on my neck; and at the stake, on my death-bed, on the rack, I could only say one thing: it is my father's *clasp*. The medal I do not remember. Of the clasp I myself broke the end in Rougodevo, and I have seen it a hundred times in my father's hands. If it is not his clasp, then it must be that the spirits are really devils, and can materialise what they like, and drive people out of their senses. But I know that if my father's principal decorations were not buried with him, still as he always wore the medal which he had received for twenty-five years of service and the one he had for the Turkish War, even when he was retired and in half-dress, it is likely that they would not take them off him.... But I shall write to Markoff who was present at the funeral, and to my brother at Stavropol, because I wish to know the truth.... Everyone heard the spirit's speech, forty persons besides myself. So, then, it would seem that I had laid some plot or other with the mediums! Very well, let them think so. How on earth do I interfere with Home?* I am not a medium,

I never was and never will be a professional one. I have devoted my whole

---

* Mr. Epes Sargent, in a letter to H. P. B. of July 29,1876, says that Home "has subsided. A shot from his cousin Aksakoff had this salutary effect."

life to the study of the ancient cabbala and occultism, the ' occult sciences.'... My position is very cheerless; simply helpless. There is nothing left but to start for Australia and change my name for ever."[11]

The defence of William Eddy in the newspapers, of which H. P. B. spoke above, inaugurated her journalistic career in America, and is the opening article of her scrap-books (which she began in 1874 and carried on through life — these, with Colonel Olcott's Diaries faithfully kept year by year, being the chief sources of knowledge of their activities and of the history of the Society they founded). The article appeared in the *Daily Graphic*, and is called " Marvellous Spirit Manifestations, a Reply to Dr. Beard."* She solicits the use of their columns " to reply to an article of Dr. Beard in relation to the Eddy family in Vermont.... Dr. Beard writes thus : 'When your correspondent [Colonel Olcott] returns to New York, I will teach him on any convenient evening, how to do all that the Eddys do.' He, in denouncing them and their Spiritual manifestations in a most sweeping declaration, would aim a blow at the entire Spiritual world of to-day.... I do not know Dr. Beard personally... but what I do know is that he may never hope to equal, much less to surpass, such men and *savants* as Crookes, Wallace, or even Flammarion, all of whom have devoted years to the investigation of Spiritualism. All of them came to the conclusion that, supposing even the well-known phenomenon of materialisation of spirits did not prove the identity of the persons whom they purported to represent, it was not, at all events, the work of mortal hands, still less was it a fraud. [Here follow her experiences at the Eddys' as chronicled above.] I hereby challenge Dr. Beard finally and publicly to the amount of $500 to produce before a public audience and under the same conditions the manifestations herein attested, or failing this, to bear the ignominious consequences of his proposed expose." (He did not take up the challenge.)

A reporter of the *New York Times* of January 2, 1885, recalling evenings at " The Lamasery," in 1877, writes of Mme Blavatsky as expressing her opinion on Spiritualism thus : " The phenomena that are presented are perhaps often frauds. Perhaps not one in a hundred is a genuine communication of spirits, but that one cannot be judged by the others. It is entitled to scientific examination, and the reason the scientists don't examine it is because they are afraid. The mediums cannot deceive me. I know more about it than

---

* For a facsimile of this page of her Scrap-book I, see *The Theosophist*, January, 1930.

they do. I have lived for years in different parts of the East, and have seen more wonderful things than they can do.

"The whole universe is filled with spirits. It is nonsense to suppose that we are the only intelligent beings in the world. I believe there is latent spirit in all matter. I believe almost in spirits of the elements. But all is governed by natural laws. Even in case of apparent violation of these laws, the appearance comes from a misunderstanding of the laws. In cases of certain nervous diseases, it is recorded of some patients, that they have been raised from their beds by some undiscoverable power, and it has been impossible to force them down. In such cases it has been noticed that they float feet first with any current of air that may be passing through the room. The wonder of this ceases when you come to consider that there is no such thing as the law of gravitation, as it is generally understood. The law of gravitation is only to be rationally explained in accordance with magnetic laws, as Newton tried to explain it, but the world would not accept it. The world is fast coming to know many things that were known centuries ago, and were discarded through the superstition of theologians."[12]

H. P. B. had a delightful habit of commenting personally on articles as she pasted them in her scrap-books, and even of illustrating them by sketches or appropriate pictures. Above the cutting of her anti-Beard article she has written: "(H. P. B.'s first letter)" and as a footnote to the list of the seven "spirits" seen by her: "They may be the *portraits* of the dead people they represent (they certainly are not spirits or souls), yet a real phenomenon produced by the Elementaries. H. P. B."

Note the meticulous phrasing; "portraits" and "pictures" she terms the manifestations. She is studying these appearances carefully. Spiritualists, reading her article, promptly jumped to the conclusion that she was with them, heart and soul, and entirely failed to see the fine distinctions she drew. She wrote another letter to the *Graphic* referring to Dr. Beard's criticism,* and at the end of the cutting in her scrap-book she has written: "So much in defence of phenomena. As to whether these spirits are *ghosts* is another question. H. P. B."

Her first letter is signed: "H. P. Blavatsky. 124, East Sixteenth Street, New York City, October 27, 1874"; and the second: "23, Irving Place, New York City, November 10th, 1874." After an article on "Unpractical Spirits" on

---

* Called "Dr. Beard Criticised" in *A Modern Panarion*.

page 4 of her scrap-book, she has written: "Irvin Frances Fern. Bravo! A great occultist. He is right, but we have to defend phenomena and prove it true, before we teach them philosophy."

To return to "H. P. B.'s 1st letter" on the first page of her first scrap-book, she has ornamented the top of the page with two quaint little figures of a man and a woman, and written above them:

"The curtain is raised. H. S. O.'s acquaintance on October 14, 1874, with H. P. B. at Chittenden. H. S. O. is a rabid Spiritualist, and H. P. Blavatsky is an *occultist*, who laughs at the supposed agency of spirits!" To this she has added in pencil: "(but all the same pretends to be one herself)" and below the two figures she has pencilled: "The two rising suns of Future Theosophy."* These pencil writings are larger and fainter than the ink notes, and would seem to be of a later date, as there was no Theosophical Society in 1874. Or was this a prophecy?

---

* Facsimile in *The Theosophist* of January, 1930 and in *The Golden Book of the T.S.*, p. 6.

CHAPTER XXX

"The Philadelphia Fiasco" — H. P. B. Supports Spiritualism

Says Colonel Olcott: "We became greater friends day by day, and by the time she was ready to leave Chittenden she had accepted from me the nickname 'Jack' and so signed herself in her letters to me from New York. When we parted it was as good friends likely to continue the acquaintance thus pleasantly begun."[1]

What he did not know was that his acquaintance had been deliberately sought by H. P. B., acting under orders. She once wrote: "In March, 1873, we were directed to proceed from Russia to Paris. In June we were told to proceed to the United States, where we arrived July 6th*... In October, 1874, we received an intimation to go to Chittenden, Vermont, where, at the famous homestead of the Eddy family, Colonel Olcott was engaged in making investigation."[2]

The Colonel continues: "In November, 1874, signing her letter 'Jack the Pappoose' she wrote to ask me to get her an engagement to write weird stories for a certain journal, as she would soon be 'hard up' and gave me a rollicking account of her family pedigree and connexions on both sides; talking like a democrat, yet showing but too plainly that she felt she, if any one, had reason to be proud of her lineage. She writes me how the *Daily Graphic* people had interviewed her about her travels and asked for her portrait. In her second letter, dated six days later, signed 'Jack Blavatsky' she tells me: 'I speak to you as a true friend to yourself and as a Spiritualist anxious to save Spiritualism from a danger.'[3]

---
* July 7 really. See Chapter XXXVIII.

"In November, 1874, when my researches were finished, I returned to New York and called upon her at her lodgings at Irving Place, where she gave me some stances of table-tipping and rapping, spelling out messages of sorts, principally from an invisible intelligence calling itself 'John King.' This pseudonym is one that has been familiar these forty years past, all over the world. It was first heard of in 1850, in the 'spirit room' of Jonathan Koons of Ohio, where it pretended to be a ruler of a tribe or tribes of spirits. Later on, it said it was the earth-haunting soul of Sir Henry Morgan, the famous buccaneer, and as such it introduced itself to me.

"It showed its face and its turban-wrapped head to me at Philadelphia, during the course of my investigations of the Holmes mediums, in association with the late respected Robert Dale Owen, General F. J. Lippitt and Mme Blavatsky; and both spoke and wrote to me frequently. It had a quaint handwriting, and used queer old-English expressions. I thought it a veritable John King then. But now, after seeing what H. P. B. could do in the way of producing *mayavic* illusions and in the control of elementals, I am persuaded that 'John King' was a humbugging elemental, worked by her as a marionette and used as a help toward my education.... He was first John King, an independent personality, then John King, messenger and servant — never the equal — of the living adepts, and finally an elemental pure and simple, employed by H. P. B. and a certain other expert in the working of wonders."[4]

"I reached Philadelphia on the 4th of January, 1875.... I took rooms at the private hotel of Mrs. Martin, in Girard Street, where our friend, Mme de Blavatsky, was also quartered. My acquaintance with Mme de B. has recently become more intimate in consequence of her having accepted the offer of A. Aksakoff the eminent St. Petersburg publisher, former tutor to the Czarowitch, to translate my Chittenden letters into the Russian language for publication in the capital of the Czar. I gradually discovered that this lady... is one of the most remarkable mediums in the world. At the same time, her mediumship is totally different from that of any other person I have ever met; for instead of being controlled by spirits to do their will, it is she who seems to control them to do her bidding.... Whether Mme de B. has been admitted behind the veil or not can only be surmised, for she is very reticent upon the subject, but her startling gifts seem impossible of explanation upon any other hypothesis. She wears upon her bosom the mystic jewelled emblem of an Eastern Brotherhood and is probably the only representative in this country of this fraternity....

"The first evening I spent in Philadelphia, I had a very long conversation through rappings with what purported to be the spirit who calls himself 'John King.' Whoever this person may be... he has been the busiest and most powerful spirit, or what you please to call it, connected with Modern Spiritualism. In this country and Europe we read of his physical feats, his audible speaking, his legerdemain, his direct writing, his materializations.... Mme de B. encountered him fourteen years ago in Russia and Circassia, talked with him and saw him in Egypt and India; and I met him in London in 1870, and he seemed able to converse in any language with equal ease. I have talked with him in English, French, German, Spanish and Latin, and have heard others do the same in Greek, Russian, Italian, Georgian (Caucasus) and Turkish; his replies being always pertinent and satisfactory....

"Upon entering Mme de B.'s rooms this evening, I found several ladies and gentlemen waiting to be introduced to me, and they were amusing themselves with some 'mind-reading' tests given by a boy medium named De Witt C. Hough.... The next day at 2.30 p.m. I had a seance at my own rooms. A cabinet was improvised out of a short square passage between the sitting- and bed-room.... Those present upon this occasion were Mme de Blavatsky, Hon. Robert Dale Owen, Dr. Felliger, Mr. Betanelly, the medium Mrs. Holmes, and myself. The rear door of the passage was sealed by Mr. Owen with strips of thin paper after Mrs. Holmes was sealed up in a bag. Mr. Owen also locked the bedroom door leading into the passage, and put the key in his pocket. We then darkened the room.

"In half a minute hands were shown, and immediately almost, John King's face appeared and was thrust quite through the aperture. He was perfectly materialized, and came as near being a handsome man as he ever did, I presume, and that is quite near. A voice, supposed to be Katie King's,* spoke to us; and calling up Mr. Owen and myself, she, or at all events a female hand, patted our hands.... John King allowed Mr. Owen to feel his hand and beard, and altogether the manifestations were quite as satisfactory, if not more so, than any I had thus far seen at Mrs. Holmes' house....

"The public seance was held at 825, N. 10th Street, at 8 p.m. A gentleman present suggested that I should tie Mrs. Holmes' hands together

* Alleged daughter of John King.

before putting her into the bag, and I did so. John King appeared as usual and allowed six or seven persons to approach and converse with him or shake hands.... I handed John my signet-ring and asked him to hold it for a moment, so that I might hereafter have it as a souvenir of the evening's parley. One of the ladies handed him her ring also, for the same purpose. He soon returned the second ring, but said he should keep mine, which I must say I did not fancy, as it was an expensive intaglio and I was not in the mood of making presents to detached heads and hands.... A surprise was in store for me that night, for when I was about to retire I turned down the pillow to put my watch beneath it, and *there lay my ring* uninjured.

"We held a test stance at 4 o'clock that day [the 21st].... At my last interview with John King at Mme de B.'s rooms, I requested him to give me a private sign when I should next see him at Holmes', and he consented. He came to the aperture at this afternoon seance, and looking at me, *gave the sign* by turning his head from left to right and back again twice in succession. He also gave to Mme de B. a certain sign, known only to themselves.

"On the 25th my last seance was held and it was a very notable one.... It was here that Mme de B. brought her wonderful power to the test. Summoning John King, she intimated her will that Katie King should step out of the cabinet that evening, and he wrote her with his own hand a message to the effect that her orders would 'be obeyed.'... Phenomenal disturbances soon began; raps were heard all over the cabinet, various voices addressed us from within its recesses.... But the crowning test was to come.

"We heard the bolt drawn inside, and in breathless silence watched the cabinet door swing open slowly. I plainly saw a short, thin, girlish figure, clad in white from crown to sole. She stood there motionless for an instant, and then slowly stepped forward a pace or two. By the obscure light we could see that she was shorter and much more delicately built than the medium.... Who she was or what she was, I do not know, but one thing I do know — she was not Jennie Holmes or any puppet or confederate of hers. And I know further, that Mme de B., who sat next to me, uttered one word in a strange tongue, and the spectre immediately withdrew as noiselessly as she had entered. When the meeting broke up, we found Mrs. Holmes in her bag, with its unbroken seals, and in so deep a catalepsy as to alarm Dr. Fellger at first. It was some minutes before she had either respiration or pulse."[5]

On January 30th an article of H.P.B.'s appeared in the *Banner of Light*, Boston, entitled "The Philadelphia Fiasco — or Who is Who?"* and at the end of the cutting she has written: "The Philadelphia Child-Holmes Storm. Mr. and Mrs. Holmes, mediums, are found out cheating. I told so to Olcott before, but he would not believe. The Holmes are frauds. H.P.B. versus Dr. H.T. Child. Child was a confederate. He took money from the Holmes seances. He is a rascal."

Writing to Alexander Aksakoff in February, she says: "I have written an article published in the *Banner of Light* against Dr. Child... General Lippitt, Olcott, Roberts the lawyer, and I have set to work to carry out an enquiry."[6] One of those who communicated with Mme Blavatsky in regard to this article was Professor Corson, of Cornell University. He wrote the very day after its appearance, and said: "It is a deep satisfaction to me, to find therein my own feelings in regard to the Holmes muddle, so mirrored as they are... especially in regard to Dr. Child."[7]

February 9th she replied to Professor Corson: "I have received many letters of thanks for my article, many undeserved compliments, and very little practical help in the way of published statements supporting my theory.... My dear sir, would it be impossible for you to publish a few words stating your opinion, as to the matter.... The editors will print nothing more from me, for they say 'there is no knowing where my literary Russian bombs may explode.' The only good result that has been brought about by my article was the immediate resignation of Dr. Child from his office of the President of Spiritual Association of Philadelphia.... I came to this country only on account of Truth in Spiritualism, but I am afraid I will have to give it up."[8]

February 16th, she wrote to him: "I am here in this country sent by my Lodge on behalf of Truth in modern Spiritualism, and it is my sacred duty to unveil what is, and expose what is not. Perhaps did I arrive here one hundred years too soon. May be, and I am afraid it is so, in this present state of mental confusion... for people seem to care every day less for truth and every hour more for gold — my feeble protest and endeavours will be of no avail; nevertheless, I am ever ready for the grand battle, and perfectly prepared to bear any consequences that may fall to my lot. I pray you, do not take me to be a 'blind fanatic.'... When I became a Spiritualist it was not through the agency of ever-lying, cheating mediums, miserable instruments of the

* Called "The Holmes Controversy" in *A Modern Panarion*.

undeveloped Spirits of the lower Sphere, the ancient Hades.... I found at last, and many years ago, the cravings of my mind satisfied by this theosophy taught by the Angels.*... In my eyes Allan Kardec and Flammarion, Andrew Jackson Davis and Judge Edmonds, are but schoolboys just trying to spell their ABC and sorely blundering sometimes."[9]

March 6th she wrote: "Your article has appeared, and I am glad of it; I knew Colby [editor of the *Banner of Light* would never dare refuse you. My article was sent ten days ago, and will never appear, I am afraid; and so I take the liberty of sending it to you for perusal when you have a moment to spare for it."[10]

Still later she wrote: "I have secured the help of Colonel Olcott, General Lippitt, of Dr. Taylor in the West, Aksakoff in Petersburg, and a dozen others. Spiritualism as it is must be stopped in its progress and given another direction. The delusions and insane theories of some Spiritualists are shameful in our century.... What I ask you is simply to contribute a few times a year some article like the one you sent to the *Banner*."[11]

Another correspondent after the committee's enquiry was one member of it, General Lippitt, of Boston. On March 9th, she wrote to him: "Did I discover any fraud in the materialization of the Holmes?... Fraud is their nature. They are mediums, no mistake about it, but neither will ever offer you a genuine materialization... unless they are in a *genuine* deep trance, one or the other of them... I believe *my eyes, my senses and John*, and know for a certainty that Katie was materialized through them, when Nelson Holmes was in the cabinet in deep trance.... The balance of those Katies was Mrs. White, Child's confederate. I have said."[12]

March 16th she entered in her scrap-book a cutting of her article, "Who Fabricates?—Some Light on the Katie King Mystery,"† which was published in the *Spiritual Scientist*, and added the comment: "Ordered to expose Dr. Child. I did so. The Doctor is a hypocrite, a liar and a fraud. H.P.B."

To her cutting of "The Philadelphia Fiasco," she has attached a fly-leaf on which she has written:

---

* Evidently a substitution for "Masters," of whom she was not yet at liberty to speak to him.
† Called "The Holmes Controversy; Continued" in *A Modern Panarion*.

"IMPORTANT NOTICE"

"Yes. I am sorry to say that I *had* to identify myself during that shameful exposure of the mediums Holmes with the Spiritualists. I had to save the situation, for I was sent from Paris on purpose to America to *prove* the phenomena and their reality and — show the fallacy of the Spiritualistic theories of 'Spirits.' But how could I do it best? I did not want people at large to know that I could *produce the same thing at will*. I had received orders to the contrary, and yet, I had to keep alive the reality, the genuineness and possibility of such phenomena in the hearts of those who from *Materialists* had turned *Spiritualists*; and now, owing to the exposure of several mediums, fell back again, returned to their scepticism. That is why, selecting a few of the faithful, I went to the Holmeses and helped M∴ and *his powers* brought out the face of John King and Katie King in the astral light, produced the phenomena of materialization and — allowed the Spiritualists at large to believe it was done thro' the mediumship of Mrs. Holmes. She was terribly frightened herself, for she knew that *this once* the apparition was real. Did I do wrong? The world is not prepared to understand the philosophy of Occult Sciences — let them assure themselves first of all that there are beings in an invisible world, whether 'Spirits' of the dead or Elementals; and that there are hidden powers in man, which are capable of making a *God* of him on earth.

"When I am dead and gone people will, perhaps, appreciate my disinterested motives. I have pledged my word to help people on to *Truth* while living and — will keep my word. Let them abuse and revile me. Let some call me a Medium and a Spiritualist, and others an *impostor*. The day will come when posterity will learn to know me better.

"Oh poor, foolish, credulous, wicked world!

"M∴ brings orders to form a Society — a secret Society like the Rosicrucian Lodge. He promises help.

H.P.B."[13]

July 22nd there appeared an article (not H.P.B.'s) in the *Spiritual Scientist*, called "Mrs. Holmes Caught Cheating" on which H.P.B. comments in her scrap-book: "She swore to me in Philadelphia that if I only saved her that once she would never resort to cheating and trickery again. I *saved* her but upon receiving her solemn oath. And now she went out of greed for money to produce her bogus manifestations again! M∴ forbids me to help her. Let her receive her *fate*, the vile, fraudulent liar. H.P.B."

Fortunately we have H.P.B.'s explanation of "John King" in her two "Replies to Mr. Arthur Lillie" in *Light* of 1884. In the first she says: "It is stated by Mr. Lillie that I had conversed with this 'spirit' for fourteen years 'constantly in India and elsewhere.'* To begin with, I here assert that I had never heard the name of 'John King' before 1873. True it is, I had told Colonel Olcott and many others that the form of a man, with a dark pale face, black beard, and white flowing garments and *fettah*, that some had met about the house and my rooms, was that of a 'John King' I had given him that name for reasons that will be fully explained hereafter, and I laughed heartily at the easy way the astral body of a living man would be mistaken for, and accepted as, a spirit. And I had told them that I had known that 'John' since 1860; for it was the form of an Eastern Adept, who has since gone for his final initiation, passing through and visiting us in his living body on his way, at Bombay... I have known and conversed with many a 'John King' in my life — a generic name for more than one spook — but thank heaven, I was never yet 'controlled' by one! My medium-ship has been crushed out of me a quarter of a century or more; and I defy loudly all the 'spirits' of the Kama-loka to approach — let alone to control me now"[14]

Mr. Lillie misunderstood the above to refer to Mahatma Koot Hoomi, and in her second "Reply" H.P.B. set him right about that. "'She tells us' says my critic, 'that he (Mahatma Koot Hoomi) comes to her constantly with a black beard and long, white, flowing garments.' When have I told any such thing? I deny, *point blank*, having ever said or written it.... Does he rely upon what I said in my previous letter? In it I speak of an 'Eastern Adept who had gone up for his final initiation, who had passed *en route* from Egypt to Thibet through Bombay, and visited us in his physical body.' Why should this 'Adept' be the Mahatma in question? Are there no other Adepts than Mahatma Koot Hoomi? Every Theosophist at Headquarters knows that I meant a Greek gentleman whom I had known since 1860,† whereas I had never seen Mr. Sinnett's correspondent‡ before 1868."[15]

It is a fact relevant to this appearance of the astral body of the then Arhat

---

* See Colonel Olcott's statement on pp. 207. 208.
† Hilarion Smerdis, of Cyprus.
‡ Master K.H.

Hilarion in her house, that he was at that time in the United States in his physical body. On May 27th, in the *Spiritual Scientist*, the following notice was published: "It is rumoured that one or more Oriental Spiritualists of high rank have just arrived in this country. They are said to possess a profound knowledge of the mysteries of illumination, and it is not impossible that they will establish relations with those whom we are accustomed to regard as the leaders in Spiritualistic affairs. If the report be true, their coming may be regarded as a great blessing; for, after a quarter of a century of phenomena, we are almost without a philosophy to account for them or to control their occurrence. Welcome to the Wise Men of the East, if they have really come to worship at the cradle of our new Truth (!!)" H.P.B. has commented upon this: "At*... and Ill†... passed thro' New York and Boston; thence thro' California and Japan, back. M∴ appearing in Kama Rupa daily."¹⁶

It will be remembered that Colonel Olcott came to the conclusion that there were three "John Kings": one this "messenger of the living adepts," another a mere elemental "worked by H.P.B. as marionette and used as a help toward my education"; and thirdly, "the earth-haunting soul of Sir Henry Morgan, the famous buccaneer." Some light may be thrown on the latter, possibly on the first also, in H.P.B.'s correspondence with General Lippitt.

Writing in April, 1875, she said: "I am not so sure as that of John.... He is vicious enough never to do what he is asked, unless he proposes it himself. Don't you remember how independent he is? I cannot consent, without he tells me to do so.... I send you a strange and weird circular.‡ Read it and tell me how it sounds to you. Ask the Brotherhood to help you. John dares not disobey their orders... I wish I *could* help you for your patent-but, believe me, on my word of *honour*, I am but a slave, an obedient instrument in the hands of *my Masters*. I cannot even write good English, unless they dictate me every word."¹⁷

It may well be that the "viciousness" of John "unless he proposes it himself" is her blind to cover the fact she mentions just afterward, that she is but an obedient instrument in the hands of the Masters; that she herself

---

* Atrya.

† Illarion.

‡ The Circular of the "Committee of Seven of the Brotherhood of Luxor." (See pp. 224, 225.)

cannot initiate a policy (in this case help General Lippitt with his "tipping machine" for spirit communication), but can only carry out the orders given her by this "John" who is a "messenger of the living adepts" or possibly an Adept himself.

But the "John" she describes, in a letter to General Lippitt of June 12th, seems to be the buccaneer: "Now to John King — that *king* of mischievous reprobates. What he did about the house while I was sick in bed, on the point of dying, three volumes could not express! Ask only Mr. Dana and Mrs. Magnon, who are visiting me and live in my house now. When they brought the letters to-day, he had opened every one of them before the postman had time to hand them. My servant maid came running in my bedroom half crying and so scared that she looked quite pale telling me that 'that big fellow spirit with the black beard had torn open the envelopes right in her hand,' and so I read your letter.

"Now let me tell you something, a good advice; unless you know *thoroughly* well *John*, don't trust him more than needed. He is kind-hearted, obliging, ready to do anything for you — if he takes a fancy to you.... *I love him dearly*... but he has vices, and considerably vicious vices too. He is spiteful, and revengeful sometimes; *lies* occasionally... and delights in *humbugging* people. Now I won't undertake to say and testify in a court of justice that *my John* is the John of the London seances, John of the 'phosphorous lamp,' though I am pretty sure he is, and he says so. But the mysteries of the spirit world are so mixed up, they present such a wonderful inextricable labyrinth that — who can tell?

"Look at me. I know John for 14 years. Not a day but he is with me; he made acquaintance with all Petersburgh and half Russia under the name of *Janka*, or 'Johnny'; he travelled with me all over the world. Saved my life *three* times, at Mentana, in a shipwreck, and the last time near Spezzia when our steamer was blown in the air, to atoms, and out of 400 passengers remained but 16 in 1871, 21 of June." Surely this "John" is not the buccaneer, but a fellow-initiate or a Master; yet the following must again refer to the buccaneer:

"He loves me, I know it, and would do for no one more than for myself; [yet] see what tricks he plays with me at the *contrariety*: the least thing I won't do as he would like me to, he begins playing the old Harry, making mischief, and what mischief; he abuses dreadfully, calls me the most wonderful, 'never heard before' names, goes to mediums and *tale tells* them about me, telling them that I hurt his feelings, that I am a vicious liar, an ungrateful so and so; he becomes so powerful that he actually writes letters himself without any medium's help, he corresponds with Olcott, with Adams, with three or four ladies that I do not even know.... I can name you ten persons he corresponds with.* He steals everything in the house, brought Dana $10 the other day, when I was sick.... Dana knows him for 29 years.... He forges people's handwritings, and makes mischief in families.... He plays me the most unexpected tricks — *dangerous* tricks sometimes; quarrels me with people, and then comes laughing and tells me all that he has done, boasting of it and teasing me.

"A few days ago he wanted me to do something *I did not wish to do*, for I was sick and did not think it right. He threw at me a caustic that was under lock in a casket in the drawers, and burned my right eyebrow and cheek; and when on the following morning my eyebrow had become black as jet, he laughed and said I looked like '*a, fine Spanish wench*' I will now be marked for a month at least. I know he loves me, *I know it*,... and he abuses me most shamefully, the wicked wretch....

"Your ideas about the spirit world and mine are two different things. My lord! you will think perhaps, 'John is a Diakka, John is a bad spirit';... not a bit of it. He is as good as any of us any day, but why I tell you and warn you is because I want you to know him, before you keep company with him. Now, for instance, nature has endowed me pretty generously with the *second sight*, or clairvoyant gifts, and I generally *can* see what I am anxious to see; but I can never *present* his tricks, or know of them, unless he comes and tells me himself.†

"Now, last night I had three persons come visiting me, and Dana and Mme Magnon were in my room. John began rapping and talking; I felt very sick and didn't feel like talking, but John insisted. By the way, I have arranged a *dark cabinet* in my spirit room near my bedroom, and Dana of the 'Miracle Club' sits there every night. John made his appearance. 'I say, Ellie.' 'Well, what are you up to again, you villain?' 'I wrote a letter, my lass,' says he, 'a love letter.' 'For God's sake, to whom?' exclaimed I, for I

---

* General Lippit, in a letter of June 16, told H. P. B. that Gerry Brown had received by telegram *direct* a sum of money from "Sir Henry de Morgan." For Colonel Olcott's account, see *Old Diary Leaves*, I, 441.

† Because this "John" is her superior in occult power, or at least her equal.

know him well, and feared some new mischief.

"'You did not receive a letter to-day from Gerry Brown, Ellie, did you?' 'No, I did not. What about Mr. Brown?' 'Well,' answers John, 'he won't write to you no more, he is *mad* with you, for I described you and drew out your portrait first rate to him.' 'What did you tell him, John, you mischievous devil. I want to know.' 'Why,' answers John coolly, 'I didn't tell him much; I only gave him a friendly hint or two, told him about you being such a sweet-tempered She-cat, explained how you *swear* at me in different languages, and assured him that you abused him fearfully to everyone who comes to visit you; furthermore, I told him you looked like a *fancy she-dumpling* sitting up in your bed, as solemn as a Cathedral and as cross as a *butcher's bulldog*. He is disgusted with you, and is going to shut you out from his *Scientist* altogether.'...

"Now, fancy, people listening to that, and I not knowing what to do — to laugh, or feel mad with this mischief-making goblin! I do not know if he invented the story just to tease me, or if he *really* has written to Mr. Brown.... Please, dear Mr. Lippitt, go to Mr. Brown and ask him to tell you if he [John] has *really* written to Mr. Brown. Read him this letter;"[18] to which General Lippitt replied on June 23rd, that he *did* show her letter to Mr. Brown, also Mr. Betanelly's.

Early in March, H. P. B. had mentioned to General Lippitt that John was painting his picture on white satin for the General. "He has finished it at one sitting, but he ordered me to paint some nice flowers round it like a frame, and I work very slow when he does not help me or do it himself."[19] April 3rd, she sent him a post card from Boston saying: "Picture ready and sent by Adams Express Co. Johnny wants you to *try** to understand all the symbols and Masonic signs [on it]. He begs you will never part with this picture and must not let too many persons touch it, nor even approach it too closely. I will explain why I changed house. Sansom St. 3420, West Philadelphia." Some time later, she wrote: "I am glad you like Johnny's picture.... In London *only*, he appears as he is; but bearing still on his dear countenance some likeness to his respective mediums, for it is hard to change completely the particles drawn by him from various vital powers."[20]

Writing to General Lippitt June 30, 1875, she said: "All the

---

* The word *Try* and the gift of the picture of "John" would seem to indicate that General Lippitt was placed in touch with the Brotherhood.

seemingly-signifying-nothing letters, dictated to you by spirits through your stand, are but so many instructions to your Spiritualists in America, written out in cyphered alphabet (the Kabalistic employed by the Rosicrucians and other Brotherhoods of the occult sciences). I am not at liberty to read them out to you *until allowed*. Do not take these words for a dodge. I give you my word of honour it is so. John knows to write that way of course, for he belonged as you know to one of the Orders. Preserve all you may receive in such way *carefully*. Who knows what may yet be in store for blind America ?... John has done all he could do towards helping you with your stand.... He is not even permitted to manifest himself any more, except by letters he writes or words he spells — unless I am perfectly *alone* with him. The time is close when Spiritualism *must* be cleansed of its erroneous misinterpretations, superstitions and ignorant notions.... It must be shown as a Science, a law of Nature... [not] a frolic of blind Force and Matter." [21]

It was of the buccaneer, Sir Henry de Morgan, that Colonel Olcott wrote to General Lippitt in February, 1877 : 'This is the last you or any one will get from him, as the genuine spirit of that appellation has passed into another sphere and lost all attraction for the Earth.' [22]

But it was of John King, the Initiate or Adept, that H. P. B. wrote to Mr. Aksakoff, April 12, 1875 : "The spirit of John King is very fond of me, and I am fonder of him than of anything on earth. He is my only friend ; and if I am indebted to any one for the radical change in my ideas of life, my efforts, and so on, it is to him alone. He has transformed me, and I shall be indebted to him when I 'go to the upper story' for not having to dwell for centuries, it may be, in darkness and gloom. John and I are acquainted from old times, long before he began to materialise in London, and take walks in the medium's house with a lamp in his hands...." [23]*

---

* See Chapter XXXIII, p. 246.

CHAPTER XXXI

The "Spiritual Scientist"

One of the people who wrote appreciatively to H. P. B. concerning her letter in the *Banner of Light*, November, 1874, to Dr. Beard in defence of William Eddy, was Elbridge Gerry Brown, editor of the *Spiritual Scientist*. He sent her a copy of his paper, and invited her to call at his office whenever she might be visiting Boston. Nothing came of this immediately; for Colonel Olcott says: "It was in the first quarter of the year 1875 that we became interested in the *Spiritual Scientist*, a small but bright and independent journal.... The crying need of the hour was a paper which, while recognised as an organ of Spiritualism, could be induced to help in bringing Spiritualists to scrutinise more closely the behaviour and pretended psychical gifts of their mediums, and to patiently listen to theories of spirit being and intercourse with the living.... Our relations with him were brought about by a letter to him (*Spiritual Scientist*, March 8, 1875) and within the next month he had been taken under the favour of the powers behind H. P. B."[1]

Mr. C. Jinarajadasa, when publishing some of the documents of H. P. B.'s scrap-books in his series, "The Early History of the T. S." in *The Theosophist* of 1922 to 1924, remarks: "The Masters who were behind H. P. B. looked not only to her and Colonel Olcott to be the pivot of the movement, but also to a third person, E. Gerry Brown, the young editor of the *Spiritual Scientist* of Boston. Instructions were sent in several letters by the Master Serapis Bey that Mr. Brown was to be helped both financially and by articles for his paper. H. P. B. and Colonel Olcott therefore wrote for the paper, and procured subscribers for it."[2]

This brings us to the subject of Colonel Olcott's probation by the Masters;

whereas he succeeded in meeting the requirements, Gerry Brown failed. The Colonel received a letter from the Brotherhood of Luxor, through H. P. B., with a covering letter of hers from Philadelphia, in which she says: "I had a right and dared withhold for a few hours the letter sent you by Tuitit Bey, for I alone am answerable for the effects and results of my Chief's orders. I am one of those who know *when* and *how*, and that for long years.... The message was ordered at Luxor a little after midnight between Monday and Tuesday. Written out [at] Ellora in the dawn by one of the secretaries neophytes and written very badly. I wanted to ascertain from T. B. if it was still his wish to have it sent in such a state of human scribbling, as it was intended for one who received such a thing for the first time. My suggestion was to let you have one of our parchments on which the contents appear *whenever you cast your eyes on it to read it*, and disappear every time as soon as you have done; for, as I respectfully inferred, you had been just puzzled by John's tricks, and that perhaps your mind, notwithstanding your sincere belief, would need strengthening by some more substantial proof. To this T. B. answered me, *entre autre*, thus:... 'A mind that seeks the proofs of Wisdom and Knowledge in outward appearance as material proofs is unworthy of being let in unto the grand secrets of the "Book of Holy Sophia." One who denies the Spirit and questions him on the ground of material clothing *a priori* will never be able to try.' So you see there a rebuke again....

"I am an *initiated* wretch, and I know what a curse the word '*Try*' has proved to me in my life, and how often I trembled and feared to misunderstand their orders, and bring on myself punishment for carrying them *too far* or not far enough. You seem to take the whole concern for a child's play. Beware, Henry, before you pitch headlong into it.... There is time yet, and you can decline the connection as yet. But if you keep the letter I send you and *agree* to the word *Neophyte*, you are cooked, my boy, and there is no return from it. Trials and temptations to your faith will shower on you first of all. (Remember *my* seven years preliminary initiation, trials, dangers and fighting with all the incarnated Evils and legions of Devils, and think before you accept.) There are mysterious dreadful invocations in the letter sent you, *human* and *made up* as it may appear to you perhaps. On the other hand if you are *decided*, remember my advice if you want to come out victorious of the affray. *Patience, faith, no questioning*, thorough *obedience* and *Silence*."[3]

"*From the BROTHERHOOD OF LUXOR, Section the Vth, to Henry S. Olcott.*

"Brother Neophyte,

"We greet thee. He who seeks Us finds Us. Try. Rest thy mind — banish all f———* doubt. We keep watch over our faithful soldiers. Sister Helene is a valiant, trustworthy servant. Open thy spirit to conviction, have faith and she will lead thee to the Golden Gate of truth. She neither fears sword nor fire, but her soul is sensitive to dishonour and she hath reason to mistrust the future.

Our good brother 'John' hath verily acted rashly, but he meant well. Son of the World, if thou dost hear them both, then try.

"It is our wish to effect an approbrious punishment on the man Child and through thy means, brother. Try. David is honest and his heart is pure and innocent as the mind of a babe, but he is not ready physically. Thou hast many good mediums round thee. Don't give up thy club. Try. Brother 'John' hath brought three of our Masters to look at thee after the stances, thy noble exertions on behalf of our cause now give us the right of letting thee know who they were:

Serapis Bey (Ellora Section)
Polydorus Isurenus (Section of Solomon)
Robert More (Section of Zoroaster)

"Sister Helene will explain thee the meaning of the Star and colours.
"Activity and Silence as to the present.
By Order of the Grand ∴

Tuitit Bey.

"Observatory of Luxor,
*Tuesday Morning,
Day of Mars.*"⁴

Colonel Olcott says in *Old Diary Leaves*: "Little by little H. P. B. let me know of the existence of Eastern adepts and their powers, and gave me by a multitude of phenomena the proofs of her own control over the occult forces of nature. At first, she ascribed them to 'John King,' and it was

---
* A crease in the paper makes this word illegible.

AN APOCALYPTIC VISION

through his alleged friendliness that I first came into personal correspondence with the Masters. Many of their letters I have preserved, with my own endorsement of the dates of their reception.*

"For years, and until shortly before I left New York for India, I was connected in pupilage with the African Section of the Occult Brotherhood; but later, when a certain wonderful psycho-physiological change happened to H.P.B. that I am not at liberty to speak about, and that nobody up to the present suspected, although enjoying her intimacy and full confidence, as they fancy, I was transferred to the Indian Section and a different group of Masters.... The sceptic denies the existence of these adepts.... But their being has been known to thousands of self-illuminate mystics and philanthropists in succeeding generations....

"I was introduced to them by H.P.B. through the agency that my previous experiences would make most comprehensible, a pretended medium-overshadowing 'spirit.' John King brought four of the Masters to my attention: one of whom was a Copt, one a representative of the Neo-Platonic School, one — a very high one, a Master of Masters, so to say — a Venetian, and one an English philosopher, gone from men's sight, yet not dead. The first of these became my first Guru, and a stern disciplinarian he was, indeed, a man of splendid masculinity of character"[5]

To return to the *Spiritual Scientist* and its editor, H.P.B. says in a letter to Professor Corson: "The same morning [as his letter] brought me back my article from Colby, which without further comment he respectfully declined on a bit of a dirty printed slip of paper. Very well; so I began thinking and plotting and scheming, and took the *Spiritual Scientist*, to which little paper I had never paid much attention before... I took up some back numbers and read them through attentively and the more I read the less I found of such trash as I found in the *Religio*, and even in the great and sublime *Banner*.... Then came a gentleman from Boston to visit me, and I learned from him that the editor of the *Scientist* was a very well-educated young man, well-connected enough but poor as poverty itself. To become a Spiritualist and an editor of a Spiritual paper he had quarrelled with all his family, and the consequences were that he had quite ruined himself. The opposition on the part of the *Banner* was untiring... Their persecution of this poor Jerry Brown, who took from the first a contrary course, was

---

* They are in the archives of the Theosophical Society.

merciless.... Of course, I felt fired up like a dry match immediately, got several subscribers for him the same day, and sent him my article.... Then I received a letter from Olcott talking with me at length about the immediate necessity of having in this country a respectable Spiritualistic paper, and that I must try and work for it if I have the cause at heart.... Would you not think if we tried to help that poor Jerry Brown, something might come of it?... If you could only write something serious for his paper... and then, you might find him a few subscribers in Ithaca."[6]

And so the *Spiritual Scientist* became the organ of H.P.B.'s attempt to reform Spiritualism in America, by awakening it to the need of a philosophy. April 17th, there appeared in it a notice, of which Mr. Brown says in an Editorial headed "A Message from Luxor": "The readers of the *Scientist* will be no more surprised to read the circular which appears on our front page than we were to receive the same by post.... Who may be our unknown friends of the 'Committee of Seven,' we do not know, nor who the 'Brotherhood of Luxor'; but we do know that we are most thankful for this proof of their interest, and shall try to deserve its continuance. Can anyone tell us of such a fraternity as the above? And what Luxor is meant?... It is time that some 'Power,' terrestrial or supernal, came to our aid, for after twenty-seven years of spiritual manifestations, we know nothing about the laws of their occurrence.... We cannot help regarding this as an evil of magnitude, and if we could only be satisfied that the appearance of this mysterious circular is an indication that the Eastern Spiritualistic Fraternity is about to lift the veil that has so long hid the Temple from our view, we in common with all other friends of the cause, would hail the event with joy. It will be a blessed day for us when the order shall be, sit lux."[7]

Colonel Olcott says of the circular: "I wrote every word of it myself, alone corrected the printer's proofs, and paid for the printing; that is to say, nobody dictated a word that I should say... nor controlled my action in any visible way. I wrote it to carry out the expressed wishes of the Masters that we — H.P.B. and I — should help the editor of the *Scientist* at what was to him, a difficult crisis, and used my best judgment as to the language most suitable for the purpose. When the circular was in type at the printer's... I enquired of H.P.B. (by letter) if she thought I had better issue it anonymously or append my name. She replied that it was the wish of the Masters that it should be signed thus: 'For the Committee of Seven, brotherhood of luxor.' And so it was signed and published.

"She subsequently explained that our work, and much more of the same kind, was being supervised by a Committee of seven Adepts belonging to the Egyptian group of the Universal Mystic Brotherhood.* Up to this time she had not even seen the circular, but now I took one to her myself and she began to read it attentively. Presently she laughed, and told me to read the acrostic made by the initials of the six paragraphs. To my amazement, I found that they spelt the name under which I knew the adept (Egyptian) under whose orders I was then studying and working. Later, I received a certificate, written in gold ink on thick green paper, to the effect that I was attached to this 'Observatory' and that three (named) masters had me under scrutiny.[8] Here is the circular somewhat abbreviated:

IMPORTANT TO SPIRITUALISTS

The spiritual movement resembles every other in this respect: that its growth is the work of time, and its refinement and solidification the result of causes of working from within.... The twenty-seven years which have elapsed since the rappings were first heard in Western New York have not merely created a vast body of Spiritualists, but moreover stimulated a large and constantly increasing number of superior minds into a desire and ability to grasp the laws which lie back of the phenomena.

"Until the present time these advanced thinkers have had no special organ for the interchange of opinions.... In England the London *Spiritualist*, and in France the *Revue Spirite*, present us examples of the kind of paper that should have been established in this country long ago....

"It is the standing reproach of American Spiritualism that it teaches so few things worthy of a thoughtful man's attention; that so few of its phenomena occur under conditions satisfactory to men of scientific training....

"The best thoughts of our best minds have heretofore been confined to volumes whose price has, in most instances, placed them beyond the reach of the masses. To remedy this evil... a few earnest Spiritualists have now united....

"Instead of undertaking the doubtful and costly experiment of starting a

---

* Compare this with the statement of Master Morya, in 1882: "The sun of Theosophy must shine for all, not for a part. There is more of this movement than you have yet had an inkling of, and the work of the T. S. is linked with similar work that is secretly going on in all parts of the world." — *The Mahatma Letters*, 271.

new paper, they have selected the *Spiritual Scientist* of Boston, as the organ of this new movement....

"The price of the *Spiritual Scientist* is $2.50 per annum.... Subscriptions may be made through any respectable agency, or by direct communication with the editor, E. Gerry Brown, No. 18, Exchange Street, Boston, Mass.

For the Committee of Seven,
BROTHERHOOD OF LUXOR.⁹

The Luxor circular drew forth, among other commentators, a Mr. Mendenhall. In her reply to him, H. P. B. writes: "Some time since a Mr. Mendenhall devoted several columns in *The Religio-Philosophical Journal* [Chicago], to questioning, cross-examining and criticising the mysterious Brotherhood of Luxor.... The Brotherhood of Luxor is one of the sections of the Grand Lodge of which *I am a member*. If this gentleman entertains any doubt as to my statement — which I have no doubt he will — he can, if he chooses, write to *Lahore* for information. If, perchance, the seven of the *committee* were so rude as not to give him the desired information, I can then offer him a little business transaction.

"Mr. Mendenhall, as far as I remember, has two wives in the spirit world. Both of these ladies materialize at Mr. Mott's, and often hold very long conversations with their husband, as the latter has told us.... Let one of the departed ladies tell Mr. Mendenhall the name of that section of the Grand Lodge I belong to. For *real, genuine, disembodied* spirits, if both are what they claim to be, the matter is more than easy; they have but to enquire of other spirits, look into my thoughts, and so on; for a disembodied entity, an immortal spirit, it is the easiest thing in the world to do. Then, if the gentleman tells me the true name of the section — which name three gentlemen in New York, who are accepted neophytes of our Lodge, know well — I pledge myself to give Mr. Mendenhall the true statement concerning the Brotherhood, which is not composed of spirits as he may think but of *living mortals*, and I will moreover put him in communication with the Lodge, as I have done for others."[10]

On the copy of the Luxor circular pasted in her scrap-book, H. P. B. has written the comment: "Sent to E. Gerry Brown by the order of S. and T. B. of Lukshor. (Published and issued by Colonel Olcott by order of

M∴"[11] To this the Colonel has added: "but unconscious of any exterior agency. H. S. O."

Master Serapis at various times wrote about E. G. Brown to Colonel Olcott, who visited Boston twice in 1875: in March and July. "Try to see him alone, and devote most of your time to him; on him depends the success of the spiritual movement, and the happiness as the welfare of all of you." " try to win the Bostonian youth's confidence. Try to make him open his heart and his hopes to you, and forward his letters to the Lodge through Brother John [John King]."[12]

It will be remembered that H. P. B. once wrote to General Lippitt that John King "actually writes letters himself without any medium's help, he corresponds with Olcott, with Adams, with three or four ladies that I do not even know; I can name you ten persons he corresponds with"; and Mr. Betanelly wrote to General Lippitt: "John's desk, his own private table, with his papers and correspondence, nobody in the house dares touch it, or he will play tricks."[13] This is, of course, a Master masquerading under the personality of "John King."

The Master Serapis writes further to Colonel Olcott: "We have your reports, Brother mine; they have been read and filed. Our younger brother is shy and secretive, as you say, but I have advised you of the same beforehand.... He struggles, hesitates and mistakes the whisperings of fear for the prophetic warning of his Conscience — his Atma's voice. Brother mine, it is a hard task to you; but your devotion and unselfish zeal for the Cause of Truth should support and strengthen you. This cause in your country — depends entirely on the closest unity between you three — our Lodge's chosen Triad — you, verily so, you three so utterly dissimilar and yet so closely connected, to be brought together and linked in *one* by the never-erring Wisdom of the Brotherhood. Keep courageous and patient, Brother, and — forward!"[14] The fact that the Triad failed through Gerry Brown may well be one of the reasons why the Cause (then transformed into the Theosophical Society) was transferred from America to India.

May 24th, H. P. B. writes to Mr. Aksakoff: "Disaster has come upon us.... In order to keep up the sinking *Spiritual Scientist*.... I have spent my last two hundred dollars"[15] At the bottom of the Luxor circular she has written: "Several hundred dollars out of our pockets were spent on behalf of the Editor, and he was made to pass through a minor *diksha** This proving of no avail, the Theosophical Society was established.... The man might have become a Power, but preferred to remain an Ass. *De gustibus non disputandum est.*"[16] Later in the scrap-book she has written: "The Editor and Medium, which are Brown, has thanked us for our help. Between Colonel Olcott and myself, we have spent over a 1,000 dollars given him to pay his debts and support his paper. Six months later he became our mortal enemy because only we declared our unbelief in *Spirits*. Oh grateful mankind! H. P. B."[17]

Mr. Jinarajadasa furnishes the conclusion of the *Spiritual Scientist* effort when he says: "Gerry Brown went bankrupt in September, 1878, owing money to both H. P. B. and Colonel Olcott. H. P. B. writes in the scrap-book of the year: 'A constant shower of abuse and sneering in *his* paper against us, and in other papers too, and bankruptcy to end the whole, without a single line of acknowledgment, excuse or regret. Such is Gerry Elbridge Brown the Spiritualist!' So Gerry Brown lost the opportunity offered him by the Masters of becoming one of the noble triad whom future Theosophists would ever hold in reverent gratitude."[18]

* Initiation

CHAPTER XXXII

Marriage And The Shadow Of Death

Colonel Olcott's account of Mme Blavatsky's appearance at the Eddy stances when published elicited the following letter:

"HENRY S. OLCOTT,
"Chittenden, Vt., Eddy's Homestead.

"DEAR SIR,
"Though I have not the pleasure of your personal acquaintance, I take the liberty of addressing to you a few words, knowing your name from the *Daily Graphic* correspondence on Eddy's manifestations, which I read with great interest.

"I learn from to-day's *Sun* that at Eddy's, in presence of Mme Blowtskey, Russian lady, a spirit of Michalko Guegidse (very familiar name to me) has materialized in Georgian dress, has spoken Georgian language, danced Lezguinka, and sung Georgian National Air.

"Being myself a native of Georgia, Caucasus, I read these news with greatest astonishment and surprise, and being not a believer in Spiritualism, I do not know what to think of these manifestations.

"I address to-day a letter to Mrs. Blowtskey, asking some questions about materialized Georgian, and if she left Eddy's, please forward it to her, if you know her address.

"I also earnestly request your corroboration of this astonishing fact, materialized Georgian — if he really came out of the cabinet in Georgian dress and in your presence. If that occurred in fact, and if anybody will regard it as usually trickery and humbug then I will state to you this: There are in U.S. no other Georgians but three, of whom I am one and came first to this country three years ago. Two others I know came over last year. I know they are not in Vermont now and never been before; and I know they do not speak English at all. Besides us three, no other man speaks Georgian language in this country, and when I say this I mean it to be true fact. Hoping you will answer this letter, I remain,

"Yours respectfully,
" M. C. Betanelly."

Later Mr. Betanelly wrote: " I knew Michalko *when alive* in Kutais, and think I could recollect his face at Eddy's if I was there at that night. He was late serf of Alex. Guegidse, a Georgian nobleman, and employed servant in Colonel A. F. Witte's family. Mr. Witte still lives at Kutais, and occupies a position of an engineer under Russian Government."[1]

We have seen that Mr. Betanelly was present at Colonel Olcott's first private seance at Philadelphia. He had become an enthusiastic convert to Spiritualism. Colonel Olcott being the only direct actor in the strange marriage, contracted by H. P. B. and Mr. Betanelly, who has left an account of it, it will be well to quote his record:

" One of my Chittenden letters in the *Daily Graphic* aroused the interest of this Mr. B——, a Russian subject — and led him to write to me from Philadelphia, expressing his strong desire to meet my colleague and talk over Spiritualism. No objections being made by her, he came over to New York towards the end of 1874* and they met. It turned out that he fell at once into a state of profound admiration, which he expressed verbally, and later by letter, to her and to me. She persistently rebuffed him, when she saw that he was matrimonially inclined, and grew very angry at his persistence. The only effect was to deepen his devotion, and he finally threatened to take his life unless she would accept his hand.'[2]

This statement is corroborated by General Doubleday in a letter in the *Religio-Philosophical Journal*, of Chicago, April 28, 1878,[3] in which he states that the above letter from Mr. Betanelly led to the marriage; that he threatened suicide and she married him to prevent it, having been the cause of two suicides in the first flush of her youth and beauty,† Here is one motive

---

* In *Old Diary Leaves* this is misprinted, 1875.

† Her Master once wrote to Mr. Sinnett: " Tell her [Mme Fadeef, H. P. B.'s aunt] I — the Khosyayin (her niece's Khosyayin she called me as I went to see her thrice) gossiped the thing to you, advising you to write to her, furnishing her thus with your autograph — also send back through H. P. B. her portraits as soon as shown to your lady, for she at Odessa [the aunt] is very anxious to have them back, especially

for explanation of this strange marriage.

Of course, Mme Blavatsky supposed she was a widow; she still thought so for many years to come. V. S. Solovyoff quotes from a letter of hers of 1885: "I was naturalised nearly eight years ago as a citizen of the United States, which led to my losing every right to my pension of 5000 roubles yearly as the widow of a high official in Russia." On this he remarks: "What will the modest and honourable N. V. Blavatsky (who though old is still alive) say, when he hears that he is a 'high official in Russia' and that his widow was to receive during his lifetime a pension of 5000 roubles a year?* What an irony of fate!"[4]

Mme Jelihovsky, H. P. B.'s sister, replying to Solovyoff, says:

"Helena Petrovna Blavatsky did not 'give herself out' as a widow, but was recognised as one by the authorities of Tiflis, who in 1884 sent her a testimonial in which she was described as 'widow of Councillor of State N. V. Blavatsky.' As she held no relations with him for more than twenty-five years, she had completely lost sight of him, and did not know, any more than we, whether he was alive or dead. The fault lies with the police of Tiflis, not with her."[5]

H. P. B. herself was horrified when Solovyoff's assertion reached her. She wrote to Mr. Sinnett: "Solovioff threatens me moreover, that Mr. Blavatsky is *not dead* but is a 'charming centenarian' who had found fit to conceal himself for years on his brother's property — hence the false news of his death. Fancy the result if you publish the *Memoirs* and if he is indeed alive and I — no *widow*! I Tableau, and you will lose your reputation along with me. Please *put the book by* — at least its publication." She adds in a postscript: "May be what Solovioff tells me of old Blavatsky 'whom you (I) have prematurely buried' — is a wicked fib of his, thinking the news would overwhelm me, and perhaps it is not. I never had an official notification of his death, only what I learned through my Aunt at New York and again here. 'His country seat ruined, he himself had left years ago' and news had come 'he was dead.' I never bothered my brains about the old man: he never was anything to me, not even a *legitimate*, though hated *husband*. Yet if it turned out to be truth — (his father died when 108 and my own grandmother at nearly 112) and we talking all the while of him as though

the young face.... That's her, as I knew her first, 'the lovely maiden'." — *The Mahatma Letters*, 254.

* Note that she did not say she lost the pension, but any right to it.

he were in Devachan or Avichi — it would bring no end of trouble."⁶

To return to Colonel Olcott's account of the marriage: "He [Betanelly] declared that he would ask nothing but the privilege of watching over her, that his feeling was one of unselfish adoration for her intellectual grandeur, and that he would make no claim to any of the privileges of wedded life. He so besieged her that — in what seemed to me a freak of madness — she finally consented to take him at his word and be nominally his wife; but with the stipulation that she should retain her own name, and be as free and independent of all disciplinary restraint as she then was. So they were lawfully married by a most respectable Unitarian clergyman of Philadelphia, and set up their *lares* and *penates* in a small house in Sansom Street where they entertained me as guest on my second visit to that city — after my book was finished and brought out. The ceremony took place, in fact, while I was stopping in the house, although I was not present as a witness. But I saw them when they returned from the clergyman's residence after the celebration of the rite."

The marriage took place between March 11th and 22nd; for the Colonel's book, *People from the Other World*, was published March 11th, and Mr. Betanelly mentions the move to Sansom Street in a letter to General Lippitt of March 22nd, saying: "This evening I forgot to deliver a letter to Mme I brought from Post Office, and when we were sitting at the dinner table, John went on rapping and telling, and abusing my bad memory, how and why I did not give the letter to her, etc., etc. Since we came to this house, John took away his own picture from the frame twice, kept it several days and brought back — and all this as quick as lightning. There is no end to these wonders. Although a Spiritualist of only five months' standing, I have seen and witnessed more spirit manifestations, and see it more every day, than a great many others have seen in their long lives. John is making most mysterious and remarkable manifestations with us almost every day."⁷

Colonel Olcott tells some interesting incidents that took place during his visit: "The days and evenings of my Philadelphia visit were symposia of occult reading, teaching, and phenomena.... I remember, among others, that one afternoon H. P. B. caused a photograph on the wall to suddenly disappear from the frame, and give place to a sketch portrait of John King, while a person present was actually looking at it.... One day, bethinking me that a sufficiency of towels was but too evidently lacking in her house,

I bought some and brought them home with me in a parcel. We cut them apart, and she was for putting them into immediate use without hemming; but, as I protested against such bad housekeeping, she good-naturedly set to plying her needle. She had hardly commenced when she gave an angry kick beneath the work-table at which she sat, and said, 'Get out, you fool!' 'What is the matter?' I asked. 'Oh,' she replied, 'It is only a little beast of an elemental that pulled my dress and wants something to do.' 'Capital!' I said; 'here is just the thing; make it hem these towels. Why should you bother about them, and you such an atrocious needle-woman as that very hem proves you to be?'

"She laughed, and abused me for my uncomplimentary speech, but at first would not gratify the poor little bond-slave under the table that was ready to play the kindly leprechaun if given the chance. I, however, persuaded her at last; she told me to lock up the towels, with needle and thread, in a bookcase with glass doors lined with thick green silk, that stood at the farther side of the room. I did so and resumed my seat near her, and we fell to talking on the inexhaustible and unique theme that occupied our thoughts — occult science. After perhaps a quarter of an hour or twenty minutes, I heard a little squeaky sound, like a mouse's pipe, beneath the table, whereupon H. P. B. told me that 'that nuisance' had finished the towels. So I unlocked the bookcase door, and found the dozen towels were actually hemmed, though after a clumsy fashion that would disgrace the youngest child in an infant-school sewing-class.

Hemmed they were, beyond the possibility of a doubt, and inside a locked bookcase which H. P. B. had never approached while the thing was going on. The time was about 4 p.m. and, of course, it was broad daylight."[8] This was the little elemental which H. P. B. called "Pou Dhi."

"Her house in Philadelphia was built on the usual local plan, with a front building and a wing at the back which contained the dining-room below and sitting or bedrooms above. H. P. B.'s bedroom was the front one on the first floor (the second, it is called in America) of the main building; at the turn of the staircase was the sitting-room where the towels were hemmed, and from its open door one could look straight into H. P. B.'s room, if her door also stood open.

"She had been sitting in the former apartment with me but left to get something from her bedroom. I saw her mount the few steps to her floor, enter her room and leave the door open. Time passed, but she did not return. I waited and waited until, fearing that she might have fainted, I called her name. There was no reply, so now being a little anxious and knowing she could not be engaged privately since the door had not been closed, I went there, called again, and looked in; she was not visible, though I even opened the closet and looked under the bed. She had vanished, without the chance of having walked out in the normal way, for save the door giving upon the landing, there was no other means of exit; the room was a *cul de sac*.

"I was a cool one about phenomena after my long course of experiences, but this puzzled and worried me. I went back to the sitting-room, lit a pipe, and tried to puzzle out the mystery.... It occurred to me that I was the subject of a neat experiment in mental suggestion, and that H. P. B. had simply inhibited my organs of sight from perceiving her presence, perhaps within two paces of me in the room.

"After a while she calmly came out of her room into the passage, and returned to the sitting-room to me. When I asked where she had been, she laughed and said she had had some occult business to attend to, and had made herself invisible. But how, she would not explain. She played me and others the same trick at other times, before and after our going to India."[9]

As to the marriage, Colonel Olcott writes: "When I privately expressed my amazement at what I conceived to be her act of folly in marrying a man younger than herself, and inexpressibly her inferior in mental capacity; one, moreover, who would never be even an agreeable companion to her, and with very little means — his mercantile business not yet being established — she said it was a misfortune she could not escape. Her fate and his were temporarily linked together by an inexorable Karma, and the union was to her in the nature of a punishment for her awful pride and combativeness, which impeded her spiritual evolution, while no lasting harm would result to the young man." Here we have a second explanation of the marriage.

A third, and rather astounding one, is advanced by V. S. Solovyoff, which must be taken with reservation, as his motive is to place himself in a favourable light before the public and H. P. B. in an unfavourable one. He states that she once wrote to him: "I will tell you what happened to me some years ago in America. I was almost as old and ugly as I am now; but, you see, there are different kinds of ugliness in the world, and so a handsome young Armenian fell in love with me there. He suddenly appears in my house and begins to treat me as only a husband would treat a wife. I order him off, but he does not go, declares I am his wife, and that he has just been legally married to me, married before witnesses, Olcott among them. I turn to Olcott; imagine my horror when he confirms it. He was a witness at the wedding, and signed the register!"[10] This does not agree with Colonel Olcott's statement above that he was not a witness of the marriage.

Mr. C. Jinarajadasa published an article called "H. P. B. and H. P. Blavatsky" in *The Theosophist* of May, 1923, in which he asserts that "had Colonel Olcott remembered what the Master Serapis had told him about this marriage of hers to M. C. B., he would have written quite differently." Before taking up these letters of the Master Serapis, it will be necessary to consider an illness that befell H. P. B. soon after the marriage.

The *Spiritual Scientist* of June 18th states: "Last winter [January] she fell with great force on one of her knees on the sidewalk, and the result was an inflammation of the periosteum, which has progressed so far that it is now uncertain if the limb will mortify and be amputated or become paralysed."[11] It seems that was not all, for on February 13th she had written to General Lippitt: "I nearly broke my leg by falling down under a heavy bedstead I was trying to move and that fell on me."

In April she wrote to General Lippitt: "Received yours this afternoon. Politeness required an answer, but I felt so cross and so sick... that I blew up Olcott, tried to set on a pillary B. [etanelly], had a fight with John, threw the cook into a fit and the canary bird into regular convulsions, and having made myself agreeable in such a general way — went to bed and — dreamt of old Blavatsky; this last occurrence, I took positively for a premeditated insult on the part of Providence, and so, preferring anything to such a nightmare as that one, here I am at 3 a.m., swallowing Brown's lozenges, which make me sneeze, if they *do* prevent me from coughing, and trying to write something in the way of a reasonable sober answer.... I am sadly afraid I will not be able to go to Washington with you. My leg is worse than ever. John had completely cured it, and ordered me to *rest* for three days. I neglected it and from that day I feel it getting worse and worse. It's under regular treatment now. Then my lawsuit* comes off at Riverhead on

---

* As to the lawsuit, on July 1, 1874, she had entered into a partnership in a farm on Long Island.

the 11th of May, I think. I shall have to attend it."[12]

May 21st H.P.B. wrote to Colonel Olcott: "The paralysis has set in. I had the surgeon Pancoast and Mrs. Michener the Clairvoyant. The former says it's too late, the latter promises recovery if I do as *she* tells me. I have taken her again.... I'm too tired to write more."[13]

June 12th she wrote to General Lippitt: "You must thank 'John King' if your last is answered at all, for Mr. B. [etanelly] is West. I sent him away about the 26th of May, when I was taken so sick and the Doctors began thinking of depriving me of my *best* leg, for I thought at that time that I was going 'upstairs' *pour de bon*; and as I hate seeing long faces, *whiners* and *weepers* and such like things when I am sick, I made him clear out. I have in many things cat-like propensities, and one of them is to be ever on the lookout and try '*to die*' alone if I can do it. So I told him to be ready to come back when I write him that I am better, or when somebody else writes him that I am gone *home*, or 'kicked the bucket' as John King very kindly learnt me to say. Well, I did not quite die *yet*, for again like the cats I have *nine* lives in me it appears, and because I am not wanted yet in the bosom of Abraham I suppose; but as I am still in bed very weak, cross, and generally feel *mad* from 12 a.m to 12 p.m., so I keep the chap away yet, for his own benefit and my comfort.

"My leg was going to be chopped off clean but I said 'mortification or sugar plums I *won't* have it!' and I kept my word good. Fancy my father's daughter — on a wooden leg; fancy my leg going to the spirit land before me *pour le coup*! George Wash. Childs would have a nice chance to compose *un quatrain* pretty obituary 'poekry' as Mr. Artemus Ward used to say, closing the verses with the usual refrain of his immortal *Philadelphia Ledger*, 'Gone to meet her leg!' Indeed! So I summoned my best *will power* (my Sunday one) and begged of the doctors and surgeons to go and look for my leg on the Centennial Grounds.

For H.P.B.'s account of the law-suit see "The Early History of the T.S." in *The Theosophist* of May, 1923.

"After they had vanished like so many unclean goblins or *Kako-demons*, I called in *Mrs. Michener clairvoyante*, and had a talk with her. In short, I

Colonel Olcott says: "What anybody might have expected happened: H. P. B. went to live on the farm; got no profits, had a row, acquired debts and a neat little lawsuit which friends helped her to settle long afterward." — *Old Diary Leaves*, I, 31.

had prepared myself to die — didn't care — but decided to die with both legs. The mortification had gone all round the knee, but two days of cold water *poultices*, and a white *pup*, a dog by night laid across the leg, cured all in no time. Nerves and muscles weak, can't walk but all danger is far. I had two or three other *maladies* showing an ambitious design to ornament themselves with *Latin names*, but I stopped it all short. A bit of will power, a nice crisis — tried hard the latter to have the best of me — a healthy tug with the 'pug-nosed messenger,' and there I am. B.... is a soft *ninny*; he would never have described you my *sufferings* so poetically as I did. Would he, *mon Général*?"[14]

June 18th Mr. Betanelly wrote to General Lippitt: "As no doctor could tell how the illness could result of Mme Blavatsky I postponed till to-night my answer to you. All these days Madame was always the same; three or four times a day losing power, and laying as one dead for two or three hours at a time, pulse and heart stopped, cold and pale as dead. John King told truth.... She was in such trance morning Monday and afternoon from three till six; we thought her dead. People say her spirit travels at that time but I don't know nothing of it, and I simply thought several times, all was finished. It's very strange. Those that watch her say, that in nights she gets up and goes right away in spirit room and that she goes strong on her leg though in day she cannot move it or walk at all.... Friday morning she felt better and took directly to write in bed for *Scientist* from Aksakoff.* She expected letters from Boston, but had none, got mad and felt worse, and now she must lay dead one month before she is real dead. Spirits play tricks with her. Why Doctor says three times she was dead, she is very exhausted though."[15]

By June 30th the crisis was over, for she wrote to General Lippitt: "my health is progressing very poorly, but I do not care a sugar plum.... I have to go away, lame as I am, on business which I cannot properly postpone. My way is to Boston and its vicinities, in a radius of about fifty miles around.... Olcott is gone to Boston for a few days, he is sent there on business."[16]

Colonel Olcott, continuing his account of the marriage, writes: "The husband forgot his vows of unselfishness, and, to her ineffable disgust, became an importunate lover. She fell dangerously ill... as soon as she got better...

---

* She evidently wrote the "Notice to Mediums"; for it appeared in the Spiritual Scientist in Boston on June 22nd. See Chapter XXXIV.

she left him and would not go back. When, after many months of separation, he saw her determination unchangeable... he engaged counsel and sued for a divorce on the ground of desertion. The summonses were served upon her in New York, Mr. Judge acted as her counsel, and on the 25th May, 1878, the divorce was granted "[17]

In the letters of the Master Serapis to Colonel Olcott, published by Mr. C. Jinarajadasa, will be found quite another motive for H. P. B.'s marriage to Mr. Betanelly, whom Mr. Jinarajadasa describes as " a peasant," " little better than a workman," a man who " had built up a small business as an importer and exporter." [18] This motive was an intense desire to forward the Masters' cause in America. Having no funds, and being assured by young Mr. Betanelly that he would devote himself and his all to the work of aiding Spiritualism (the then phase of the Cause), H. P. B. took him at his word, and sacrificed her inclinations and sensibilities to the need of the hour.

Master Serapis, in a communication written sometime after March 9th, the date of Master Tuitit Bey's letter to Colonel Olcott as Neophyte, refers to that letter : " Our brother should have received the forwarded messages long before they reached him, were it not for the feverish curiosity that got hold of our sister, to know the contents therein enclosed, by which wrong act she delayed the swiftness of the messages.... We forgive her, for she suffers intensely.... Our sister has just mailed a letter to her Brother Henry in which he will find enclosed an obligation signed by her to the sum of $500... her donation [to the *Spiritual Scientist* ?] in case of death. The possible emergency of such a case is no idle talk of our noble Sister. The Dweller* is watching closely, and will never lose an opportunity, if our Sister's courage fails. This is to be one of her hardest trials... an *Ellorian*† — eternal and immortal is her Augoeides.... Our brother's mission cannot be completed or accomplished during his first stay in the Boston city. Let him plan the ground and prepare it for the reception of our Sister... *if she survives the trial. For on good will to her and on the intensity of magnetic thought concentrated on our Sister much of her safety will depend in the perilous descent to the* ——.‡

* Mr. Jinarajadasa's Note on the Dweller will be of interest : " Throughout these letters about H. P. B. there are several references to the ' Dweller on the Threshold.' This mysterious phrase occurs in *Zanoni* [by Bulwer Lytton], It is evident that challenging the Dweller, and risking one's very existence in the process, is one of the trials of the Initiate. There is no clue in the letters showing what type were the dangers which confronted H. P. B., so that her very life was at stake." (p. 21.)

† A member of the Ellora Section (Indian) of the Great Brotherhood.

‡ Word undecipherable.

Thou knowest not yet, O Brother mine, of all the mysteries and powers of thought, yea, of human thought.... How dangerous for her will be the achievement of her duty and how likely to expect for both of you to lose a sister and a — Providence on earth. Serapis." [19]

In May the Master wrote to Colonel Olcott: " She must encounter once more and face to face the dreaded one she thought she would behold no more. She must either conquer — or die herself his victim.... How solitary, unprotected, but still *dauntless*, she will have to face all the great perils and unknown mysterious dangers she *must* encounter.... Brother mine, I can do naught for our poor Sister. She has placed herself under the stern law of the Lodge and these laws can be softened for none. As an Ellorian she must win her right.... The final result of the dreaded ordeal depends on her and her alone, and on the amount of sympathy for her from her two brothers, Henry and Elbridge, on the strength and power of their *will* sent out by both to her wherever she may be. Know, O Brother, that such will-power strengthened by sincere affection will surround her with an impenetrable shield, a strong protecting shield, formed of the combined pure good wishes of two immortal souls — and powerful in proportion to the intensity of their desires to see her triumphant... if she returns triumphant and alive.... Pray, both of you, for our Sister, she deserves it. Serapis." [20]

June 22nd the Master Serapis wrote : " She feels unhappy and in her bitter hours of mental agony and sorrow, looks to thee for friendly advice and soothing words of comfort. Devoted to the Great Cause of Truth, she sacrificed to it her very heart's blood ; believing that she might help it if she took a husband whose love for her would open his hand and make him give freely, she hesitated not, but tied herself to him she hated. The same law of compensation that brought her to accept this crafty youth....

"Her cup of bitterness is full, O Brother. The dark, mysterious influence is overshadowing all.... Tighter and tighter is drawn round them the pitiless circle ; be friendly and merciful to her, brother... and leaving otherwise the weak and silly wretch, whom fate has given her for husband, to his desert... pity *him* — also him who, by giving himself up entirely to the power of the Dweller, has merited his fate. His love for her is gone, the sacred flame has died for want of fuel, he heeded not her warning voice ; he hates John and worships the Dweller who holds with him communication. At *his* suggestion, finding himself on the brink of bankruptcy, his secret design is to sail for Europe, and leave her unprovided and alone. Unless we help him for the sake of her, our Sister, her life is doomed and for her future will be poverty and sickness.

"The laws which govern our Lodge will not allow us to interfere in her fate, by means that might seem supernal. She can get no money but through him she wedded; her pride must be humbled even before him she hates. Still, there are means left at our disposal to provide for her, and through her benefit yourself and the Cause. Brother John has cleverly worked for her sake in her native place.

The chiefs of the government have sent him orders; if he fulfills them there are millions in the future in store for him.* He has no money and his brains are weak. Will my brother *try* to find him a partner?... I am a poor hand at business and all of the above is suggested by Brother John. I have said. The holy Blessing be with you.   S."[21]

June 25th Colonel Olcott received another letter: "People must respect her purity and virtue, for she deserves it. Brother Henry must have the Wisdom of the Serpent and gentleness of a lamb, for he who hopes to solve in time the great problems of the Macro-cosmal World and conquer face to face the Dweller, taking thus by violence the threshold on which lie buried nature's most mysterious secrets, must *Try* first the energy of his Will power, the indomitable resolution to succeed, and bringing out to light all the hidden mental faculties of his Atma and highest intelligence, get at the problems of Man's Nature and solve first the mysteries of his heart.... Write to our suffering Sister daily. Comfort her aching heart, and forgive the childish shortcomings of one whose true and faithful heart takes no share with the defects of an early spoilt childhood. You must address your reports and daily notes while in Boston to the Lodge through Brother John, not omitting the cabalistic signs of Solomon on envelope. Serapis."[22]

While H. P. B. and Colonel Olcott were in Boston (second visit), in July, 1875, he received the following: "The three of you† have to work out your future yourselves. Our sister's present is dark, but her future may be bright yet. All depends on *yourself* and herself. Let your Atma work out your

---

* In a letter to General Lippitt of March 22, Mr. Betanelly says that he expects to open a big trade between Russia and United States. His letterhead reads: " Betanelly & Co., Importers of Insect Flowers, Raw Silk, Wool, Goat Skins, Persian Carpets, Turkish Tobacco, Oil of Roses, etc. 430 Walnut Street, Perm Buildings, Philadelphia."

† H. P. B., Colonel Olcott, and Elleridge Gerry Brown.

intuitions.... You must not part with Elena if you desire your initiation. But through her you may be enabled to conquer the trials of initiation. They are hard, and you may despair more than once, but do not I *pray thee*. Remember some men have toiled for years, for the knowledge you have obtained in a few months.... Remain firmly linked together and try to inhabit the same places where her fate, guided by the wisdom of the Brotherhood, may lead her to. *Try* to secure for yourself a good situation. *You will succeed*. Try to help the poor broken-hearted woman and success will crown your noble efforts....

"*Try* to help her find the money needed... for the 3rd of next month.... Her money is certain to return into her hands — it will be easy for you to find that loan for her on such security*... poor, poor Sister! Chaste and pure soul — pearl shut inside an outwardly coarse nature. Help her to throw off that appearance of assumed roughness, and any one might well be dazzled by the divine Light concealed under such a bark. My brotherly advice to you, remain in Boston. Do not forsake her cause, your own happiness, the salvation of your younger brother. *Try*. Seek and ye will find. Ask and it will be given unto you.... Watch over her, Brother mine — forgive her outburstings of passion, be *patient, merciful*, and charity bestowed on another will return to thee a hundredfold nobly. Serapis."[23]

A later July letter says: "Thy task in Boston, Brother, is finished for the near present.†... Depart from hence in peace, and *Try* to utilise thy time. John King will see to the Philadelphia problem;‡ she must not be allowed to suffer through the impurity and disillusion of character of the miserable wretch. She *may*, in her despair and straightened circumstances, be tempted to return to Philadelphia and her spouse. *Do not* allow her to do this, Brother mine. Tell her you are both going to Philadelphia, and instead of that take tickets to New York, not further. Once arrived in that port, find for her a suitable apartment, and do not let one day pass without seeing her. Induce her by reasoning to remain therein, for if she finds herself once for a few hours with that polluted mortal, her powers will greatly suffer, for they are at present in a state of transition, and the magnetism must be pure

---

* She recovered $5000 from the Long Island farm, by means of the lawsuit.

† The Colonel and H. P. B. had been guests of Mr. and Mrs. Houghton of Boston, and had carried on the investigation of the clairvoyant powers of Mrs. Thayer. See Chapter XXXIV.

‡ The separation from Mr. Betanelly.

round her. Your own progress might be impeded by any such interference.

"She will want to go to Philadelphia, allow her not, use your friendship and exertions. As I told you before, you will not suffer, Brother mine, any material loss through it.... If you succeed to bring her out before the world in her true light, not of an adept but of an intellectual writer, and devote yourself both to work together the articles dictated to her, your fortune will be made. Make her work, install her, lead her in practical life as she must lead you in spiritual. Your boys,* Brother mine, will be provided for, fear naught for them, devote yourself to your main object. Clear out the paths of both of you for the present which seem dark, and let the future take care of itself. Use your intuition, your innate powers, *try*, you will succeed. Watch over her and let her not come to harm, our dear Sister who is so careless and thoughtless for herself.

"She must have the best intellects of the country introduced to her. You must work both on your intuitions and enlighten them as to the Truths. Your distant future is at Boston,† your present at New York. Lose not a day, *try* to settle her and begin your new fruitful lives together. Keep your room, you may feel me there some time, for I will be with you every time your thought will be upon me and when you need me. Work hand in hand, fear not the immoral man who claims her, his hands will be tied. She must be honoured and respected and sought by many whom she can instruct. *Try* to dissipate in her gloom, her apprehensions for the future, for they interfere sadly with her spiritual perceptions. The germs will grow, Brother mine, and you will be astonished. Patience, Faith, Perseverance. Follow my instructions — let her regain her serenity through you. She will make you acquire knowledge and fame through herself. Do not let her despond one moment, the dreaded —— she‡ passed will bring their reward.... Serapis."[24]

The last letter of interest here was evidently written after they had settled in New York: "Upon returning from the office, know the Brotherhood will be assembled in her room, and seven pairs of ears will listen to your reports and judge the progress your Atma does in relation to intuitional perceptions. Heed her not when she will tell you that your words do not interest her; go on, and know that you are talking in the presence of your

---

* Colonel Olcott had two young sons.
† As Gerry Brown failed them, they went to India instead of returning to Boston.
‡ Word undecipherable.

Brethren. When needed, they will answer you through her. God's blessing upon thee, Brother mine.   Serapis."[25]

CHAPTER XXXIII

The Great Psycho-Physiological Change

he reader will recall Colonel Olcott's enigmatical remark:*
"I was connected in pupilage with the African Section of the
Occult Brotherhood; but later when a certain wonderful psycho-physiological change happened to H.P.B. that I am not
at liberty to speak about, and that nobody has up to the present suspected, although enjoying her intimacy and full confidence, as they
fancy, I was transferred to the Indian Section and a different group of
Masters"[1]

What was this change, and when did it take place or culminate? It is easy to answer the second query: during her illness of May and June, 1875, at Philadelphia. What the change was can be explained only by H.P.B. herself. She tried to give her aunt, Mme Fadeef, and her sister, Mme Jelihovsky, some inkling of it. At this point we shall draw upon an invaluable source of information secured by Mr. Wm. Q. Judge, as editor of *The Path*. He prevailed upon Mrs. Charles Johnston, neice of H.P.B., daughter (Vera) of Mme Vera Jelihovsky, to translate from Russian H.P.B.'s letters to her family, and published them in *The Path* from December, 1894 to December, 1895. Mrs. Johnston writes of the Philadelphia illness:

"At one time H.P.B. was exceedingly ill with advanced rheumatism in her leg. Doctors told her it was gangrened, and considered her case hopeless; but she was successfully treated by a negro who was sent to her by the 'Sahib'† She writes to Mme Jelihovsky: 'He has cured me entirely. And just about this time I have begun to feel a very strange duality. Several times a day I feel that beside me there is someone else, quite separable from me,

---

* Chapter XXXI.
† Colonel Olcott says: "She got better in one night, by one of her quasi-miraculous cures."

present in my body. I never lose the consciousness of my personality; what I feel is as if I were keeping silent and the other one — the lodger who is in me — were speaking with my tongue.

"'For instance, I know that I have never been in the places which are described by my "other me," but this other one — the second me — does not lie when he tells about places and things unknown to me, because he has actually seen them and known them well. I have given it up; let my fate conduct me at its own sweet will; and besides, what am I to do? It would be perfectly ridiculous if I were to deny the possession of knowledge avowed by my No. 2, giving occasion to the people around me to imagine that I kept them in the dark for modesty's sake.

"'In the night, when I am alone in my bed, the whole life of my No. 2 passes before my eyes, and I do not see myself at all, but quite a different person — different in race and different in feelings. But what's the use of talking about it? It is enough to drive one mad. I try to throw myself into the part, and to forget the strangeness of my situation. This is no mediumship, and by no means an impure power; for that, it has too strong an ascendancy over us all, leading us into better ways. No devil would act like that. "Spirits," maybe? But if it comes to that, my ancient "spooks" dare not approach me any more. It's enough for me to enter the room where a stance is being held, to stop all kinds of phenomena at once, especially materializations. Ah no, this is altogether of a higher order! But phenomena of another sort take place more and more frequently under the direction of my No. 2. One of these days I will send you an article about them. It is interesting.'"[2]

Colonel Olcott speaks of this or a similar article when he says: "You will find in an old number of the *New York World* a long account of a reporter's experiences at our headquarters in 47th Street. Among the marvels witnessed, by the eight or ten persons present, was the apparition of a Brother who passed the window and returned. The room was on the second storey of the house, and there was no balcony to walk on."[3] Mrs. Johnston continues:

"The newspapers gave accounts of certain of these phenomena, and described the appearance of astral visitors, amongst others a Hindu. In sending the extracts, H. P. B. comments: 'I see this Hindu every day, just as I might see any other living person, with the only difference that he looks to me more ethereal and more transparent. Formerly I kept silent about these appearances, thinking that they were hallucinations. But now they have become visible to other people as well. He (the Hindu) appears and advises us as to our conduct and our writing. He evidently knows *everything* that is going on, even to the thoughts of other people, and makes me express his knowledge. Sometimes it seems to me that he overshadows the whole of me, simply entering me like a kind of volatile essence penetrating all my pores and dissolving in me. Then we two are able to speak to other people, and then I begin to understand and remember sciences and languages — everything he instructs me in, even when he is not with me any more."[4]

"In the earlier letters of H. P. B. to Mme Jelihovsky, the intelligence which has been referred to as 'enveloping her body' and using her brain, is spoken of as 'the Voice' or 'Sahib.' Only later did she name this, or another 'Voice' a 'Master.' For instance, she writes to Mme Jelihovsky: 'I never tell anyone here about my experience with the Voice. When I try to assure them that I have never been in Mongolia, that I do not know either Sanskrit or Hebrew or Ancient European languages, they do not believe me. "How is this" they say, "you have never been there, and yet you describe it all so accurately? You do not know the languages, and yet you translate straight from the originals!" And so they refuse to believe me. They think that I have some mysterious reasons for secrecy; and besides, it is an awkward thing for me to deny when everyone has heard me discussing various Indian dialects with a lecturer who has spent twenty years in India. Well, all I can say is, either they are mad or I am a changeling!'

"She wrote (about 1875 to 1876) to her aunt, Mme Fadeef, with whom she had been brought up and educated: 'Tell me, dear one, do you take any interest in the physiologico-psychological mysteries? Here is one for you which is well qualified to astonish any physiologist. In our Society there are a few exceedingly learned members — for instance, Professor Wilder, one of the first archaeologists and orientalists in the United States, and all these people come to me to be taught, and swear that I know all kinds of Eastern languages and sciences, positive as well as abstract, much better than themselves. That's a fact! and it's as bad to run up against a fact as against a pitchfork.

"'So then tell me — how could it have happened that I, whose learning was so awfully lame up to the age of forty, have suddenly become a phenomenon of learning in the eyes of people who are really learned? This fact is an impenetrable mystery of Nature. I — a psychological problem, and an enigma for future generations, a Sphinx! Just fancy that I who never had the slightest idea about physics or chemistry or zoology, or anything else — have now suddenly become able to write whole dissertations about them. I enter into discussions with men of science, into disputes out of which I often emerge triumphant.

"'It's not a joke, I am perfectly serious — I am really frightened, because I do not understand how it all happens. It is true that for nearly three years past I have been studying night and day, reading and thinking. But whatever I happen to read, it all seems familiar to me — I find mistakes in the most learned articles by Tyndall, Herbert Spencer, Huxley and others. If some archaeologist happens to call on me, on taking leave he is certain to assure me that I have made clear to him the meaning of various monuments, and pointed out things to him of which he had never dreamed. All the symbols of antiquity and their secret meaning come into my hand, and stand there before my eyes as soon as the conversation touches on them.'

"To Mme Jelihovsky she wrote: 'Do not be afraid that I am off my head. All I can say is that someone positively inspires me — more than this, someone enters me. It is not I who talk and write; it is something within me, my higher and luminous Self, that thinks and writes for me. Do not ask me, my friend, what I experience, because I could not explain it to you clearly. I do not know myself! The one thing I know is, that now, when I am about to reach old age, I have become a sort of storehouse for somebody else's knowledge.... *Someone* comes and envelops me as a misty cloud and all at once pushes me out of myself, and then I am not "I" any more — Helena Petrovna Blavatsky — but someone else. Someone strong and powerful, born in a totally different region of the world; and as to myself, it is almost as if I were asleep, or lying by not quite conscious — not in my own body, but close by, held only by a thread which ties me to it.

"'However, at times I see and hear everything quite clearly; I am perfectly conscious of what my body is saying and doing — or at least its new possessor. I even understand and remember it all so well that afterwards I can repeat it and even write down *his* words.... At such a time I see awe and fear on the faces of Olcott and others, and follow with interest the way in which *he* half-pityingly regards them out of my own eyes and teaches them with my physical tongue. Yet not with my mind but with his own, which enwraps my brain like a cloud — Ah, but really I cannot explain everything.'"⁵

As regards her own Higher Self, which she mentioned above, the following is of special interest: "About this time H. P. B. appears to have been greatly troubled; for though some members of the nascent Theosophical Society were able to get 'visions of pure Planetary Spirits,' she could only see 'earthly exhalations, elementary spirits,' of the same category which she said played the chief part in materialising stances. She writes:

"'In our Society everyone must be a vegetarian, eating no flesh and drinking no wine. This is one of our first rules.* It is well known what an evil influence the evaporations of blood and alcohol have on the spiritual side of human nature, blowing the animal passions into a raging fire; and so one of these days I resolved to fast more severely than hitherto. I ate only salad and did not even smoke for whole nine days, and slept on the floor, and this is what happened:

"'I have suddenly caught a glimpse of one of the most disgusting scenes of my own life, and I felt as if I was out of my body, looking at it with repulsion whilst it was walking, talking, getting puffed up with fat, and sinning. Pheugh! how I hated myself! Next night, when I again lay down on the hard floor I was so tired out that I soon fell asleep and then got surrounded with a heavy impenetrable darkness. Then I saw a star appearing; it lit up high, high above me, and then fell dropping straight upon me. It fell straight on my forehead and got transformed into a hand.

"'Whilst this hand was resting on my forehead, I was all ablaze to know whose hand it was — I was concentrated into a single prayer, into an impulse of the will, to learn who it was, to whom did this luminous hand belong — and I have learned it: there stood over it I myself. Suddenly this second me spoke to my body. "Look at me!" My body looked at it, and saw that the half of the second me was as black as jet, the other half whitish grey and only the top of the head perfectly white, brilliant and luminous. And again I myself spoke to my body: "When you become as bright as this small part of your head, you will be able to see what is seen by others, by the

---

* "This was a proposed rule. H. P. B. accepted a thing proposed as a thing done, and so spoke of it here. But she did not carry out that rule then proposed, and never then suggested its enforcement to me. W. Q. J."

purified who have washed themselves clean — and meanwhile make yourself clean, make yourself clean, make yourself clean." And here I awoke.'[6]

"H. P. B. wrote to Mme Jelihovsky (date unknown) that she was learning to get out of her body, and offering to pay her a visit in Tiflis 'in the flash of an eye.' This both frightened and amused Mme Jelihovsky, who replied that she would not trouble her so unnecessarily. H. P. B. answered:

"'What is there to be afraid of? As if you had never heard about apparitions of doubles! I, that is to say, my body, will be quietly asleep in my bed, and it would not even matter if it were to await my return in a waking condition — it would be in the state of a harmless idiot. And no wonder: God's light would be absent from it, flying to you; and then it would fly back and once more the temple would get illuminated by the presence of the Deity. But this, needless to say, only in case the thread between the two were not broken. If you shriek like mad, it may get torn; then Amen to my existence! I should die instantly....

"'I have written to you that one day we had a visit from the double of Professor [Stainton] Moses. Seven people saw him. As to the Master, he is quite commonly seen by perfect strangers. Sometimes he looks just as if he were a living man, as merry as possible. He is continually chaffing me, and I am perfectly used to him now.* He will soon take us all to India, and there we shall see him in his body just like an ordinary person'"[7]

In *The Path* of January, 1895, Mrs. Johnston writes: "'Directly *Isis Unveiled* was published, H. P. B. wrote to Mme Jelihovsky:

'It seems strange to you that some Hindu Sahib is so free and easy in his dealings with me. I can quite understand you; a person not used to that kind of phenomenon — which, though not quite unprecedented, is yet perfectly ignored — is sure to be incredulous. For the very simple reason that such a person is not in the habit of going deeply into such matters.

"'For instance, you ask whether he is likely to indulge in wanderings inside other people as well as me. I am sure I don't know; but here is something of which I am perfectly certain: Admit that man's soul — his real living soul — is a thing perfectly separate from the rest of the organism; that this peri-sprit is not stuck with paste to the physical "innerds"; and that this soul which exists in everything living, beginning with infusoria and ending with an elephant, is different from its physical double only

---

* Was he "John King"?

inasmuch as, being more or less overshadowed by the immortal spirit, it is capable of acting freely and independently. In the case of the uninitiated profane, it acts during their sleep; in the case of an initiated adept it acts at any moment he chooses, according to his will. Just try to assimilate this, and then many things will become clear to you.

"'This fact was known and believed in, in far distant epochs. St. Paul, who alone among all the apostles was an initiated adept in the Greek Mysteries, clearly alludes to it when narrating how he was "caught up to the third heaven, whether in the body or out of the body, I cannot tell: God knoweth." Also Rhoda says about Peter, "It is not Peter but his angel" — that is to say, his double or his soul. And in the Acts of the Apostles, ch. viii, v. 39, when the spirit of God lifted up Philip and transported him, it was not his body that was transported, not his coarse flesh, but his ego, his spirit and his soul. Read Apuleius, Plutarch, Jamblichus, and other learned men — they all allude to this kind of phenomenon, though the oaths they had to take at the time of their initiation did not allow them to speak openly. What mediums accomplish unconsciously, under the influence of outside powers which take possession of them, can be accomplished by Adepts at their own volition....

"'As to the Sahib, I have known him a long time. Twenty-five years ago he came to London with the Prince of Nepaul; three years ago he sent me a letter by an Indian who came here to lecture about Buddhism. In this letter he reminded me of many things, foretold by him at the time, and asked me whether I would consent to obey him, to avoid complete destruction.* After this, he appeared repeatedly, not only to me but also to other people, and to Olcott whom he ordered to be President of the Society, teaching him how to start it. I always recognise and know the Master, and often talk to him without seeing him. How is it that he hears me from everywhere, and that I also hear his voice across seas and oceans twenty times a day? I do not know, but it is so. Whether it is he personally that enters me, I really cannot say with confidence; if it is not he, it is his power, his influence. Through him alone, I am strong; without him, I am a mere nothing.'

"Soon after the appearance of *Isis Unveiled*, H. P. B. received invitations to write in all sorts of newspapers. This greatly amused her, and she wrote to Mme Jelihovsky: 'It's lucky for me that I am not vain, and besides as

* See Chapter XXX, p. 214.

a matter of fact I have hardly any time to write much in other people's publications for money.... Our work is growing. I must work, must write and write, provided that I can find publishers for my writings. Would you believe that so long as I write, I am all the time under the impression that I write rubbish and nonsense, which no one will ever be able to understand? Then it is printed and the acclamations begin. People reprint it, are in ecstasies! Well, if I could write in Russian and be praised by my own people, then perhaps I should believe that I am a credit to my ancestors, Counts Hahn Hahn von der Rothenhahn, of blissful memory.'

"H.P.B. often told her relatives that she took no author's pride in the writing of *Isis Unveiled*; that she did not know in the least what she was writing about; that she was ordered to sit down and write, and that her only merit lay in obeying the order. Her only fear was that she would be unable to describe properly what was shown her in beautiful pictures. She wrote to her sister:

"'You do not believe that I tell you God's truth about my Masters. You consider them to be mythical; but is it not clear to you that I, without their help, could not have written about "Byron and grave matters," as Uncle Roster* says? What do we know, you and I, about metaphysics, ancient philosophies and religions, psychology and various other puzzles? Did we not learn together, with the only difference that you did your lessons better? And now look at what I am writing about; and people, such people too — professors, scientists — read and praise. Open *Isis* wherever you like, and decide for yourself. As to myself, I speak the truth: Master narrates and shows all this to me. Before me pass pictures, ancient manuscripts, dates — all I have to do is to copy, and I write so easily that it is no labour at all, but the greatest pleasure.'"

---

* General Rostislav Fadeef.

CHAPTER XXXIV

The Miracle Club

he Master Serapis, in his first letter to Colonel Olcott, in March, had said: "Don't give up thy club, try." At that time the Colonel's book was "producing an enormous furore," according to H.P.B. By May, however, she writes to Alexander Aksakoff: "Disaster has come upon us... Olcott is sitting on heaps of his *People from the Other World*, like Marius on the ruins of Carthage, thinking bitter things.... Failure succeeds failure, there is a terrible panic; those who have got money hide it, and those who have not are dying of hunger. Still Olcott does not lose heart. With the thoroughbred sense of a Yankee, he has invented a 'Miracle Club'; we shall see what will come of that. I can answer for myself: so long as my soul remains in my body, I shall stand and fight for the truth."[1]

At that time, H.P.B. was living in Philadelphia and Colonel Olcott in New York. In *Old Diary Leaves* he writes: "In May, 1875, I was engaged in trying to organise at New York with her concurrence a private investigating committee, under the title of the 'Miracle Club.'... The plan was to keep closed doors to all save the members of the Club, who were forbidden to divulge even the place of meeting. 'All the manifestations, including materialisations, to occur in the light, and without a cabinet.'"[2]

The Miracle Club would seem to have been patterned after the model of "The Club" of London, which Master K.H. describes thus in 1882: "The greatest as well as the most promising of such schools in Europe, the last attempt in this direction — failed most signally some twenty years ago in London. It was the secret school for the practical teaching of magick, founded under the name of a club, by a dozen of enthusiasts under leadership of Lord Lytton's father. He had collected together for the purpose, the most ardent and enterprising as well as some of the most advanced scholars in mesmerism and 'ceremonial magick,' such as Eliphas Levi, Regazzoni, and the Kopt Zergvan-Bey. And yet in the pestilent London atmosphere the 'Club' came to an untimely end. I visited it about half a dozen times, and perceived from the first that there was and could be nothing in it.... It has become next to impossible even in India, unless you are prepared to climb to a height of 18,000 to 20,000 [feet] amidst the glaciers of the Himalayas"³ May 27th the following notice appeared in the *Spiritual Scientist*:

A BUDGET OF GOOD NEWS

"The organisation of Colonel Olcott's Miracle Club is progressing satisfactorily. Applications are daily received from those wishing to join, but few selections have been positively made; as it is desired that the Club should be composed of men of such standing, and scientific and other attainments, as shall afford to the public a perfect guarantee of the trustworthiness of any conclusions they may reach. The medium who is to sit with the investigators, being actively interested in certain business operations, has been temporarily called from New York..."⁴

Unfortunately for the Club, the medium's "business operations" were not all that might be desired. A few pages later in his Diary, the Colonel reports: "The intended medium belonged to a most respectable family, and talked so honestly that we thought we had secured a prize. He proved to be penniless, and as H. P. B. in his hour of greatest need had no money to spare, she pawned her long gold chain* and gave him the proceeds: That wetch not only utterly failed as a medium, but was also reported to us as having spread calumnies against the one who had done him kindness."⁵

H. P. B. has pasted a cutting of the "Budget of Good News" in her scrapbook, and commented upon it: "An attempt in consequence of *orders* received from T. B.... through P... personating G. K. ▽ Ordered to begin telling the *truth* about the phenomena and their mediums. And *now* my martyrdom will begin! I will have all the Spiritualists against me in addition to the Christians and the Sceptics. Thy will, O, M! be done! H. P. B."⁶ On this Colonel Olcott comments: "Taking H. P. B.'s remark above as written, it looks as though there would have been no Theosophical Society — it

---

* Probably the long gold chain by which she used to lead her Newfoundland dog on her travels.

looks so, I say — if her intending medium for the Miracle Club had not failed utterly and so precluded my completing the organisation."[7]

H. P. B. was poverty-stricken. In April she wrote to Mr. Aksakoff in Russia: "Since I have been in America I have entirely devoted myself to Spiritualism. Not to the phenomenal, material side of it, but to spiritual Spiritualism, and the propaganda of its sacred truths. All my efforts tend to one thing, to purify the new religion from all filthy weeds." A month later she wrote: "This year I earned as much as 6,000 dollars by my articles and other work, and all, *all* has gone for Spiritualism. And now, in the present humour of infidelity, doubt and blindness, after the Katie King business, it seems to be all over. Once when I had written a sensational article, I used to reprint it in the form of a pamphlet, and sell several thousands at ten cents (a copy), but what can one reprint now? One cannot even get into a quarrel with anyone.... The *Banner of Light* has fallen from 25,000 subscribers to 12,000" In July she says to him desperately: "I am ready to sell my soul for Spiritualism, but nobody will buy it, and I am living from hand to mouth, and working for ten or fifteen dollars when necessity comes"[8]

Colonel Olcott throws light on this intense literary activity of hers when he writes: "The publication of my book led to important results; among others to interminable discussions in the American and English organs of Spiritualism and in the secular press, in which both H. P. B. and I engaged, and to the formation of lasting friendships with several most excellent correspondents, with whom we threshed out the whole subject of Eastern and Western occultism. Almost immediately we found ourselves addressed by enquirers in both hemispheres, and attacked or defended by opponents and sympathisers....

"Mr. C. C. Massey, of London, came over to America expressly to verify, by personal observations on the spot, the accuracy of my account of the Eddy phenomena. We saw much of each other... a close friendship sprang up between us. I had already been brought into the most sympathetic relations with the late Hon. Robert Dale Owen and Mr. Epes Sargent, of Boston. The latter had been the channel for my gaining both a precious correspondent and the dearest of friends in the late Mr. Stainton Moses [Moseyn], M.A., Oxon, teacher of Classics and English in University College, London, and the most honoured and brilliant writer among British Spiritualists"[9]

"His rooted idea was that his teachers — 'Imperator,' 'Kabilla,' 'Mentor,' 'Magus,' *et al*, were all discarnate human spirits; some very ancient, some less so, but all wise and beneficent... Imperator's admonitions... substantially accord with the Eastern rules.... It is now clear to me that one directing Intelligence, pursuing a wide-reaching plan covering all nations and peoples, and acting through many agents besides ourselves, had in hand his development and mine....

"Who 'Imperator,' its agent was, I know not — I do not even know who H. P. B. really was — but I have been inclined to believe that he was either S. M.'s own Higher Self or an Adept; and that 'Magus' and others of S. M.'s *band* were Adepts likewise.... As regards 'Magus,' I have some very interesting data, and have come to a much clearer opinion than I have as to 'Imperator.'

I am almost cerain that he is a living Adept; not only that, but one that had to do with us. In March, 1876, I sent S. M. a bit of cotton wool or muslin impregnated with a liquid perfume which H. P. B. could cause to exude from the palm of her hand at will, asking him if he recognised it. On the 23rd he replied: 'The sandalwood scent is so familiar to me.... The scent we always called "The Spirit Scent" was this;* and we always had it under the best conditions. This for the past two years.... The house where we used to meet would be redolent of it for days.... What a marvellous power it is that these Brothers wield.'"[10]

H. P. B. once wrote to Mr. Sinnett: "K. H. and M. and the Chohan say that the Imperator of his (S. M.'s) early mediumship *is* a Brother, and I will assert it over and over again; but assuredly the Imperator of then is not the Imperator of to-day."[11] Master K. H., writing to Mr. Sinnet at the end of 1883, said: "For the first time in my life I paid serious attention to the utterances of poetical media... M. knew all about them."[12] In another letter of that year he said: "Suffice for me to say that 'Ski' [the guide of Mrs. Hollis-Billing] has more than once served as a carrier and even a mouthpiece for several of us."[13]

The series of weird stories which H. P. B. wrote for the American newspapers, under the *nom de plume* of "Hadji Mora," appeared a little later: the first, "Can the Double Murder?" in the *New York Sun* of December 27, 1875; the second on January 2, 1876. This is entitled "The Luminous

---

* Colonel Olcott called it "the Lodge scent."

Circle" and is to be found in her *Nightmare Tales* as "The Luminous Shield." The third of the series, "The Cave of the Echoes," was refused by the *Sun*, "killed on account of being too horrible!!" she has noted on the cutting in her scrap-book, which is from the *Banner of Light*, instead of the *Sun*. Another of her stories was published in the *Spiritual Scientist* in 1875, "An Unsolved Mystery," which she has annotated: "Written November 27. From the I... Narrative," the Illarion Narrative, as she and Hilarion collaborated in the writing of stories. It is to be found in *A Modern Panarion*, and has recently been reprinted in *Two Stories* by H.P.B.*

In the *Spiritual Scientist* of June 22nd, there appeared a

NOTICE TO MEDIUMS

In compliance with the request of the Honourable Alexander Aksakoff, Counsellor of State in the Imperial Chancery at St. Petersburg, the undersigned hereby give notice that they are prepared to receive applications from physical mediums who may be willing to go to Russia, for examination before a committee of the Imperial University.

To avoid disappointment, it may be well to state that the undersigned will recommend no mediums whose personal good character is not satisfactorily shown; nor any who will not submit themselves to a thorough scientific test of their mediumistic power, in the city of New York, prior to sailing; nor any who cannot exhibit most of their phenomena in a lighted room, to be designated by the undersigned, and with such ordinary furniture as may be found therein.

Approved applications will be immediately forwarded to St. Petersburg, and upon receipt of orders thereon from the scientific commission or its representative, M. Aksakoff, proper certificates will be given to accepted applicants, and arrangements made for defraying expenses.

Address the undersigned, in care of E. Gerry Brown, Editor of the *Spiritual Scientist*, 18, Exchange Street, Boston, Mass., who is hereby authorized to receive personal applications from mediums in the New England States.

HENRY S. OLCOTT.
HELENE P. BLAVATSKY.[14]

Colonel Olcott says: "Naturally enough this letter drew out a good many

---

* See page 55 of the latter for facsimile of another of her comments on it.

applications, and we personally tested the mediumship of several of the parties, seeing some extremely surprising phenomena, and some really beautiful.... In the summer of 1875, a woman named Mrs. Youngs was practising mediumship for a livelihood at New York.... Her chief phenomenon was the causing of the spirits to raise a full-sized heavy piano and making it tilt forward and backward in time to her playing of airs upon it. I heard of her and thought I would *get* H. P. B. to go with me and see what she could do. She consented, so I put into my pocket three things to be used as tests of her mediumship, a raw egg and two English walnuts.... The *Sun* of September 4, 1875, reports the stance:

"'The Colonel here asked to be permitted to make a single test.... Mrs. Youngs consenting, he produced a hen's egg, and asked her to hold it in her hand against the under side of the piano, and then request the spirits to raise it. The medium said that, in the course of her mediumship, such a test had never been suggested, and that she could not say that it would be successful, but she would try. She took the egg and held it as desired, and then rapping upon the case with her other hand, asked the spirits to see what they could do. Instantly the piano rose as before, and was held for a moment suspended in the air. The novel and striking experiment was a complete success.... Colonel now produced a couple of walnuts, and asked the spirits to crack the shells under the piano legs, without crushing the kernels. The spirits were willing, but as the piano legs rested upon rolling casters the test was abandoned.'

"A very much prettier and more poetical stage of mediumship was that of Mrs. Mary Baker Thayer of Boston, Mass., to the examination of whose phenomena I devoted some five weeks of the same summer season. She was a 'flower medium,' *viz.*, a psychic in whose presence rain showers of flowers, growing bushes, vines and grasses, leaves and branches freshly torn from trees.... A long summarised report of my Thayer investigations — in part of which H. P. B. assisted — appeared in the *New York Sun* of August 18, 1875....

"Our kind hostess, Mrs. Charles Houghton, drove into town with me one evening to attend Mrs. Thayer's public stance. H. P. B. declined to go, so we left her talking with Mr. Houghton in the drawing-room. The carriage had been ordered to come for us at a certain hour, but the stance had proved a short one.... As we had nothing better to occupy ourselves with, I asked

Mrs. Thayer to give us three a private stance.... Presently we heard the carriage drive up to the door, and at the same moment I felt a cool, moist flower lightly dropped upon the back of my hand.... It was a lovely, half-opened double moss-rose bud, glistening with drops of dew. The medium, starting as though someone had addressed her from behind, said: 'The spirits say, Colonel, that this is a present for Mme Blavatsky.'

"I thereupon handed it to Mrs. Houghton, and she gave it over to H. P. B. on reaching home, where we found her smoking cigarettes and still talking with our host.... H. P. B. was holding the rose in her hand, smelling its fragrance, and with a peculiar far-away look in her face that her intimates always associated with the doing of her phenomena. Her reverie was interrupted by Mr. Houghton's saying: 'What an exquisite flower, Madame; will you kindly let me see it?' She handed it to him with the same dreamy look and as if mechanically. He sniffed its odour, but suddenly exclaimed: 'How heavy it is! I never saw a flower like this. See, its weight actually makes it bend over towards the stalk!'...

"I took it from him and lo! it weighed certainly very heavy. 'Take care; don't break it!' exclaimed H. P. B. Tenderly I lifted the bud with thumb and finger, and looked at it. Nothing visible to the eye accounted for the phenomenal weight. But presently there sparkled a pin-point of yellow light in its very heart; and before I could take a second look, a heavy plain gold ring leaped out, as though impelled by an interior spring and fell on the floor between my feet. The rose instantly resumed its natural erect position....

"Well, certainly there is an explanation possible in occult science: the matter in the gold ring and that in the rose petals could have been raised from the third to the fourth dimension, and restored back to the third at the instant when the ring leaped out of the flower.... It was not a creation out of nothing, only an *apport*; it belonged to H. P. B., I think, and it is 'hall-marked' or otherwise stamped to indicate its quality.

"It was a great ring for phenomena, certainly, to judge from what happened to it a year and a half later.... H. P. B. and I were living in two apartment suites in the same house [New York]. One evening my married sister, Mrs. W. H. Mitchell, came with her husband to visit H. P. B. and myself, and in the course of conversation asked me to see the ring and bade me tell its history. She looked at it and put it on her finger while I was talking, after which she held it towards H. P. B. in the palm of her hand. But H. P. B., leaving it lying as it was without touching it, closed my sister's fingers on it, held the hand for a moment, then let go, and told my sister to look at it. It was no longer a plain gold ring, for we found three small diamonds embedded in the metal, 'gypsy' fashion, and set so as to form a triangle. How was it done?...

"To return to Mrs. Thayer, we were so pleased with her phase of mediumship that we offered her the chance to go to Russia; but, like Mrs. Youngs, she declined. Similar offers were made to Mrs. Huntoon, sister of the Eddys, and to Mrs. Andrews and Dr. Slade, but all declined. So the affair dragged on until the winter of 1875, by which time the Theosophical Society had come into existence....

"Our search for mediums resulted in out selection of Dr. Henry Slade [May, 1876]. M. Aksakoff sent me $1,000 in gold for his expenses, and in due course he departed on his mission. But... he stopped in London, gave stances, created a great public excitement, and was arrested on the complaint of Professor Lankester and Dr. Donkin on the pretence of trickery. C. C. Massey was his counsel and saved him on a technical point, on appeal. Slade subsequently gave at Leipzig the famous tests by which Professor Zollnor proved his theory of the Fourth Dimension, and visited the Hague and other places before going to St. Petersburg."[15]

CHAPTER XXXV

The Founding Of The Theosophical Society

"I was sent to America on purpose, and sent to the Eddys.* There I found Olcott in love with spirits, as he became in love with the Masters later on. I was ordered to let him know that spiritual phenomena without the philosophy of occultism were dangerous and misleading. I proved to him that all that mediums could do through spirits, others could do at will without any spirits at all; that bells and thought-reading, raps and physical phenomena, could be achieved by anyone who had a faculty of acting in his physical body through the organs of his astral body; and I had the faculty ever since I was four years old, as all my family know. I could make furniture move and objects fly apparently, and my astral arms that supported them remained invisible; all this before I knew even of Masters.

"Well, I told him the whole truth. I said to him that I had known Adepts, the 'Brothers,' not only in India and beyond Ladakh, but in Egypt and Syria — for there are 'Brothers' there to this day. The names of the 'Mahatmas' were not even known at that time, since they are called so only in India. That, whether They were called Rosicrucians, Kabalists, or Yogis, Adepts are everywhere Adepts, silent, secret, retiring, and who would never divulge themselves entirely to anyone unless one did as I did — passed seven and ten years' probation, and gave proofs of absolute devotion, and that he, or she, would keep silent even before a prospect and a threat of death. I fulfilled the requirements, and am what I am.... All I was allowed to say was — the truth. There is beyond the Himalayas a nucleus of Adepts of various nationalities; and the Teschu Lama knows Them, and They act together, and some of Them are with Him and yet remain unknown in Their true character to the average lamas, who are ignorant fools mostly. My Master and K. H. and several others I know personally are there, and They are all in communication with Adepts in Egypt and Syria, and even in Europe."[1]

"I was the first in the United States to bring the existence of our Masters into publicity; and exposed the holy names of two Members of a

* Letter to Dr. Hartmann, April 13, 1886.

Brotherhood hitherto unknown to Europe and America (save to a few Mystics and Initiates of every age), yet sacred and revered throughout the East, and especially in India."[2]

"Master sent me to the United States to see what could be done to stop necromancy and the unconscious black magic exercised by Spiritualists. I was made to meet you and to change your ideas, which I have.* The Society was formed, then gradually made to merge into and evolve hints of the teachings from the Secret Doctrine of *the oldest school of Occult Philosophy in the whole world* — a school to reform which, finally, the Lord Gautama was made to appear. These teachings could not be given abruptly. They *had* to be instilled gradually."[3]

It would seem as if a campaign of preparation was made in the United States, a ploughing of the soil for the coming movement. In her first scrapbook H. P. B. has noted an article called "Proselyters from India," which states that two missionaries were sent to the United States in 1870 — Muljee Thakersey and Tulsidas Jadarjee. They duly reported need of reform. Others had gone to Europe and Australia. These missionaries took back newspapers to show the state of Christian society — murder, rape, theft, poisoning, forgery, drunkenness, suicides, adulteries, infanticides, etc. On this article H. P. B. has commented: "By H. S. Monachesi, F. T. S., October 4, 1875. Our original programme is here clearly defined by Herbert Monachesi, one of the founders. The Christians and scientists must be made to respect their Indian betters. The wisdom of India, her philosophy and achievements, *must* be made known in Europe and America, and the English be made to respect the natives of India and Tibet more than they do. H. P. B."[4] Articles along this line of awakening the West to the spiritual value of the East continued to appear in the newspapers of the United States; for example, "Wong Ching Foo's Mission," "Catechising a Buddhist," "Ye Unspeakable Heathen," "Buddha's Band."

In his *Old Diary Leaves*, I, Colonel Olcott writes: "We may now take up the formation of the Theosophical Society.... The way had been prepared for the organization of such a society by the active discussion, first of Spiritualism and afterwards of some portions of Eastern spiritualistic ideas, since my *New York Sun* reports on the Eddys appeared in August, 1874, and especially since H. P. B. and I met at Chittenden, and used the

---

* Letter to Colonel Olcott, December 6, 1887.

press for the exposition of our heterodox views. Her piquant published letters, the stories that were afloat about her magical powers, and our several affirmations of the existence of non-human races of spiritual beings, drew into our acquaintanceship numbers of bright, clever people of occult leanings. Among these were scientific men, philologists, authors, antiquarians, broad-minded clergymen, lawyers and doctors, some very well-known Spiritualists, and one or two gentlemen journalists attached to metropolitan papers, only too eager to make good 'copy' out of the business.

"It was an audacious thing, certainly, to stand defiant of public prejudice and assert the scientific legitimacy of ancient Magic in this age of scientific scepticism. Its very boldness compelled public attention, and the inevitable result was that, in time, those whom the discussion had drawn together in sympathy should group themselves together as a society for occult research.

"The attempt of May, 1875, to form a nucleus in a 'Miracle Club' having failed, the next opportunity presented itself when Mr. Felt lectured privately to a few friends of ours, in H. P. B.'s rooms at 46, Irving Place, New York, on the 7th of September of the same year. This time there was no failure; the tiny seed of what was to be a world-covering banyan tree was planted in fertile soil and germinated.... [That evening] Mr. Felt gave his lecture on 'The Lost Canon of Proportion of the Egyptians.'... Of course we passed a hearty informal vote of thanks for his highly interesting lecture, and an animated discussion followed.

"In the course of this, the idea occurred to me that it would be a good thing to form a society to pursue and promote such occult research, and after turning it over in my mind, I wrote on a scrap of paper the following : 'Would it not be a good thing to form a Society for this kind of study ?' and gave it to Mr. Judge... to pass over to H. P. B. She read it and nodded assent. Thereupon I rose and, with some prefatory remarks, broached the subject. It pleased the company.... Upon motion of Mr. Judge, I was elected Chairman.... The hour being late, an adjournment was had to the following evening, when formal action should be taken. Those present were requested to bring sympathisers who would like to join the proposed society.... I have an official report of the meeting of September 8th ;... which I will quote :... 'In consequence of a proposal of Colonel Henry S. Olcott that a Society be formed for the study and elucidation of Occultism, the

Cabbala, etc., the ladies and gentlemen then and there present* resolved themselves into a meeting, and upon motion it was *Resolved* that Colonel H. S. Olcott take the chair.... That Mr. W. Q. Judge act as secretary.... Upon motion of Herbert H. D. Monachesi it was *Resolved* that a committee of three be appointed by the Chair to draft a constitution and by-laws, and to report the same at the next meeting.... [The meeting was adjourned until September 13th.]'

... "At the adjourned meeting of the 18th [the '13th' above is evidently a misprint], Mr. Felt continued... the interesting description of his discoveries.... The Committee on Preamble and By-laws reported progress.... Upon motion it was resolved that the name of the Society be 'The Theosophical Society.' The chair appointed the Rev. Mr. Wiggin and Mr. Sotheran to select suitable meeting rooms; and then several new members were nominated and... added to the list of founders....

"The choice of a name for the Society was, of course, a question of grave discussion in Committee. Several were suggested, among them, if I recollect aright, the Egyptological, the Hermetic, the Rosicrucian, etc., but none seemed just the thing. At last, in turning over the leaves of the Dictionary, one of us came across the word 'Theosophy,' whereupon after discussion we unanimously agreed that that was the best of all; since it both expressed the esoteric truth we wished to reach and covered the ground of Felt's methods of occult scientific research."[5]

It would seem that the choice of a name for the Society was not quite so accidental as it appeared to the Colonel. H. P. B., writing to Professor Corson on February 15, 1875 (the Society was not organised till September), remarked: "I found at last, and many years ago, the cravings of my mind satisfied by this Theosophy." In July she had written a marginal note in her scrap-book as follows: "Orders received from India direct to establish a philosophico-religious society and choose a name for it — also to choose Olcott. July, 1875." Elsewhere in the scrap-book, she says: "M. brings orders to form a Society — a secret Society like the Rosicrucian Lodge. He promises help. H. P. B."

Says Colonel Olcott: "The next preliminary meeting was held... on October 30th. The Committee on rooms having reported, Mott Memorial Hall, 64 Madison Avenue,... was selected as the Society's meeting-place. The

---

* There were seventeen.

By-laws were... adopted. Voting for officers was next proceeded with;... the result was announced... as follows:

President:	Henry S. Olcott;
Vice-Pres.:	Dr. S. Pancreast and G. H. Felt;
Cor. Sec.:	Mme H. P. Blavatsky;
Rec. Sec.:	John Storer Cobb;
Treasurer:	Henry J. Newton;
Librarian:	Charles Sotheran;
Councillors:	Rev. J. H. Wiggin, Rev. R. B. Westbrook, Mrs. Emma Hardinge Britten, C. E. Simmons, M.D., Herbert D. Monachesi;
Counsel to the Society:	William Q. Judge.

"The meeting then adjourned over to the 17th November, when the perfected Preamble would be reported, the President deliver his inaugural Address, and the Society be thus fully constituted."[6]

Of the By-laws the first three may be noted:

I. The title of the Society is 'The Theosophical Society.'

II. The objects of the society are, to collect and diffuse a knowledge of the laws which govern the universe.

III. The society shall consist of active, honorary and corresponding members.[7]

The Preamble states that: " In view of the existing state of things, it will be seen that the Theosophical Society has been organized in the interest of religions, science and good morals; to aid each according to its need. The founders being baffled in every attempt to get the desired knowledge in other quarters, turn their faces toward the Orient, whence are derived all systems of religion and philosophy"[8]

Colonel Olcott continues: " On the evening designated, the Society met in its own hired room; the minutes of the previous meeting were read and approved; the President's Inaugural Address was delivered and ordered printed; upon Mr. Newton's motion, thanks were voted to the President; and the Society, now constitutionally organized, adjourned over to the 15th December....

"Though my Inaugural Address* was applauded by my audience and

* For full text of it, see *The Theosophist* of August, 1932.

Mr. Newton, the orthodox Spiritualist, joined with Mr. Thomas, Freethinker, and the Rev. Mr. Westbrook, to get a vote that it be printed and stereotyped — a good proof that they did not think its views and tone unreasonable — yet it reads a bit foolish after seventeen years of hard experience. A good deal of its forecast of results has been verified, much of it falsified."[9]

The Theosophical Society "was to be a body for the collection and diffusion of knowledge; for occult research, and the study and dissemination of ancient philosophical and theosophical ideas: one of the first steps was to collect a library. The idea of Universal Brotherhood was not there, because the proposal for the Society sprang spontaneously out of the present topic."[10]

Writing eleven years later, H.P.B. says of "The Original Programme of the Theosophical Society:" In order to leave no room for equivocation, the members of the T.S. have to be reminded of the origin of the Society in 1875. Sent to the U.S. of America in 1873 for the purpose of organising a group of workers on a psychic plane, two years later the writer received orders from her Master and Teacher to form the nucleus of a regular Society whose objects were broadly stated as follows:

1. Universal Brotherhood;
2. No distinctions to be made by the members between races, creeds, or social positions, but every member had to be judged and dealt by on his personal merits;
3. To study the philosophies of the East — those of India chiefly, presenting them gradually to the public in various works that would interpret exoteric religions in the light of esoteric teachings;
4. To oppose materialism and theological dogmatism in every possible way, by demonstrating the existence of occult forces unknown to science, in nature, and the presence of psychic and spiritual powers in man; trying at the same time to enlarge the views of the Spiritualists by showing them that there are other, many other agencies at work in the production of phenomena besides 'Spirits' of the dead. Superstition had to be exposed and avoided; and occult forces, *beneficent and maleficent* — ever surrounding us and manifesting their presence in various ways — demonstrated to the best of our ability."[11]

Colonel Olcott writes in 1892: "As regards the Theosophical Society, every circumstance tends to show that it has been a gradual evolution, controlled by circumstances, and the resultant of opposing forces, now running into smooth, now into rough grooves, and prosperous or checked proportionately with the wisdom or unwisdom of its management. The general direction has always been kept, its guiding motive ever identical, but its programme has been variously modified, enlarged and improved as our knowledge increased and experience from time to time suggested. All things show me that the movement as such was planned out beforehand by the watching Sages, but all details were left for us to conquer as best we might. If we had failed, others would have had the chance that fell to our Karma, as I fell heir to the wasted chances of her Cairo group in 1871."[12]

In these days when the emphasis has shifted so strongly to the First Object, it is as well to remember that at the founding of the Society that Object did not exist. It was not until 1878, when the Founders merged the Theosophical Society and the Arya Samaj, and decided to go to India, that a "Brotherhood of Humanity" appeared in the declared Objects of the Society. The Circular of 1878 says: "The objects of the Society are various. It influences its fellows to acquire an intimate knowledge of natural law, especially its occult manifestations.... As the highest development on earth of the creative cause man.,. should study to develop his latent powers, and inform himself respecting the laws of magnetism, electricity and all other forms of force, whether of the seen or unseen universes.... The Society teaches and expects its fellows to personally exemplify the highest morality and religious aspirations; to oppose the materialism of science and every form of dogmatic theology; to make known among Western nations the long-suppressed *facts* about Oriental religious philosophies...; finally and chiefly, to aid in the institution of a Brotherhood of Humanity, wherein all good and pure men of every race shall recognise each other as the equal effects (upon this planet) of one Uncreate, Universal, Infinite and Everlasting Cause."[13]

Now that Mr. Trevor Barker had published *The Mahatma Letters*, we are able to read what the Masters Themselves have said in this matter. In February, 1882, Master Morya wrote to Mr. Sinnett, about the founding of the Theosophical Society: "One or two of us hoped that the world had so far advanced intellectually, if not intuitionally, that the Occult doctrine might gain an intellectual acceptance, and the impulse given for a new cycle of occult research. Others — wiser as it would now seem — held differently, but consent was given for the trial. It was stipulated, however, that the experiment should be made independently of our personal management j that there should be no abnormal interference by ourselves.

"So casting about we found in America the man to stand as leader — a man of great moral courage, unselfish, and having other good qualities. He was far from being the best, but (as Mr. Hume speaks in H. P. B.'s case) — he was the best available. With him we associated a woman of most exceptional and wonderful endowments. Combined with them she had strong personal defects, but just as she was, there was no second to her living, fit for this work.

"We sent her to America, brought them together — and the trial began. From the first both she and he were given clearly to understand that the issue lay entirely with themselves. And both offered themselves for the trial for certain remuneration in the far distant future as — as K. H. would say — soldiers volunteer for a Forlorn Hope."[14]

Master Root Hoomi writes in 1880: "The Chiefs want a 'Brotherhood of Humanity,' a real Universal Fraternity started; an institution which would make itself known throughout the world and arrest the attention of the highest minds."[15] And again in 1881: "The present tidal wave of phenomena, with its varied effects upon human thought and feeling, made the revival of theosophical enquiry an indispensable necessity. The only problem to solve is the practical one, of how best to promote the necessary study, and give to the spiritualistic movement a needed upward impulse.... What I meant by the 'Forlorn Hope' was that, when one regards the magnitude of the task to be undertaken by our theosophical volunteers, and especially the multitudinous agencies arrayed, and to be arrayed, in opposition, we may well compare it to one of those desperate efforts against overwhelming odds that the true soldier glories to attempt."[16]

CHAPTER XXXVI
"Isis Unveiled"

Here is Colonel Olcott's account of the writing of *Isis Unveiled*: " One day in the summer of 1875, H. P. B. showed me some sheets of manuscript she had written and said : ' I wrote this last night by order, but what the deuce it is to be I don't know. Perhaps it is for a newspaper article, perhaps for a book, perhaps for nothing : anyway, I did as I was ordered.' And she put it away in a drawer, and nothing more was said about it for some time. But in the month of September she went on a visit to her new friends, Professor and Mrs. Corson, of Cornell University, and the work went on. She wrote me that it was to be a book on the history and philosophy of the Eastern Schools and their relation with those of our own times. She said she was writing about things she had never studied and making quotations from books she had never read in her life ; that, to test her accuracy, Professor Corson had compared her quotations with classical works in the University Library, and had found her to be right. Upon her return to town she was not very industrious in this affair, but wrote only spasmodically....

" A month or two after the formation of the Theosophical Society, she and I took two suites of rooms at 433 West 34th Street, she on the first and I on the second floor, and thenceforward the writing of *Isis* went on without break or interruption until its completion in 1877. In her whole life she had not done a tithe of such literary labour, yet I never knew even a managing daily journalist who could be compared with her for dogged endurance or tireless working capacity. From morning to night she would be at her desk, and it was seldom that either of us got to bed before 2 o'clock a.m. During the daytime I had my professional duties to attend to, but always after an early dinner, we would settle down together to our big writing-table and work for dear life, until bodily fatigue would compel us to stop. What an experience ! The education of an ordinary life-time of reading and thinking was, for me, crowded and compressed into this period of less than two years....

" She worked on no fixed plan, but ideas came streaming through her mind like a perennial spring which is ever overflowing its brim.... Higgledy-piggledy it came, in a ceaseless rivulet, each paragraph complete in itself and capable of being excised without harm to its predecessor or successor. Even as it stands now, after all its numerous re-castings, an examination of the wondrous book will show this to be the case. If she had no plan, despite all her knowledge, does not that go to prove that the work was not of her own conception; that she was but the channel through which this tide of fresh, vital essence was being poured into the stagnant pool of modern spiritual thought?...

"Her manuscript was often a sight to behold: cut and patched, re-cut and re-pasted, until if one held a page of it to the light, it would seem to consist of six, eight or ten slips cut from other pages, pasted together, and the text joined by interlined words or sentences. She became so dexterous in this work that she used often to humorously vaunt her skill to friends who might be present. Our books of reference sometimes suffered in the process, for her pasting was frequently done on their open pages...." [1]

"I corrected every page of her manuscript several times, and every page of the proofs; wrote many paragraphs for her, often merely embodying her ideas that she could not then (some fifteen years before her death and anterior to almost her whole career as a writer of English literature) frame to her liking in English;* helped her to find out quotations, and did other purely auxiliary work. The book is hers alone, so far as personalities on this plane of manifestation are concerned, and she must take all the praise and the blame that it deserves. She made the epoch with her book, and in making it, made me — her pupil and auxiliary — as fit as I may be found to do Theosophical work these past twenty years....

"To watch her at her work was a rare and never-to-be-forgotten experience. We sat at opposite sides of one big table usually, and I could see her every movement. Her pen would be flying over the page, when she would suddenly stop, look out into space with the vacant eye of the clairvoyant seer, shorten her vision as though to look at something held invisibly in the air before her, and begin copying on her paper what she saw. The quotation finished, her eyes would resume their natural expression, and she would go on writing until again stopped by a similar interruption.

"I remember well two instances when I, also, was able to see and even

---

* See Chapter XXII.

handle books from whose astral duplicates she had copied quotations into her manuscript, and which she was obliged to 'materialise' for me to refer to when reading the proofs, as I refused to pass the pages for the 'strike-off' unless my doubts as to the accuracy of her copy were satisfied. One of these was a French work on physiology and psychology; the other, also by a French author, upon some branch of neurology. The first was in two volumes, the other in a pamphlet wrapper.

"It was when we were living at 302 West 47th Street — the once famous 'Lamasery,' and the executive headquarters of the Theosophical Society. I said: 'I cannot pass this quotation, for I am sure it cannot read as you have it.' She said, 'Oh don't bother; it's right; let it pass.' I refused, until finally she said: 'Well, keep still a minute and I'll try to get it.' The far-away look came into her eyes, and presently she pointed to a far corner of the room, to an *étagere* on which were kept some curios, and in a hollow voice said: 'There!' and then came to herself again. 'There, there; go and look for it over there!' I went, and found the two volumes wanted, which to my knowledge had not been in the house until that very moment.

"I compared the text with H. P. B.'s quotation, showed her that I was right in my suspicions as to the error, made the proof correction, and then, at her request, returned the two volumes to the place from which I had taken them. I resumed my seat and work, and when after a while I looked again in that direction, the books had disappeared! After my telling this (absolutely true) story, ignorant sceptics are free to doubt my sanity; I hope it may do them good. The same thing happened in the case of the *apport* of the other book, but this one remained, and is in our possession at the present time." [2]

"We had laboured at the book for several months and had turned out 870 odd pages of manuscript, when one evening she put me the question whether, to oblige —— (our *Paramaguru*) I would consent to begin all over again! I well remember the shock it gave me to think that all those weeks of hard labour, of psychical thunderstorms and head-splitting archaeological conundrums, were to count — as I, in my blind-puppy ignorance, imagined — for nothing. However, as my love and reverence and gratitude to this Master, and all the Masters, for giving me the privilege of sharing in their work was without limits, I consented, and at it we went again." [3]

"H. P. B. was, all the world knows, an inveterate smoker. She consumed an immense number of cigarettes daily, for the rolling of which she possessed the greatest deftness. She could even roll them with her left hand while she was writing 'copy' with her right.... While she was writing *Isis Unveiled*, she would not leave her apartment for six months at a stretch. From early morning until very late at night, she would sit at her table working. It was not an uncommon thing for her to be seventeen hours out of the twenty-four at her writing. Her only exercise was to go to the dining-room or bath-room and back again to her table."[4]

Mr. W. Q. Judge, an almost daily visitor at 'The Lamasery,' wrote: "After she had comfortably settled herself in 47th Street, where as usual she was from morning till night surrounded by all sorts of visitors; mysterious events, extraordinary sight and sounds, continued to occur, I have sat there many an evening and seen in broad gaslight large luminous balls creeping over the furniture or playfully jumping from point to point, while the most beautiful liquid bell-sounds now and again burst out from the air of the room. These sounds often imitated either the piano or a gamut of sounds whistled by either myself or some other person. While all this was going on, H. P. Blavatsky sat unconcernedly reading or writing at *Isis Unveiled*"[5]

A reporter of the *New York Times*, in an article of January 2, 1885, indulged in some reminiscences of the two years during which he visited Mme Blavatsky's *salon*: "Talking by hours together when the right listener was present, and speaking always 'as one having authority,' it is small wonder that Mme Blavatsky made her modest apartments a common meeting-ground for as strange a group of original thinkers as New York ever held. Not all who visited agreed with her. Indeed, there were only a few who followed her teachings with implicit faith. Many of her friends, and many who joined the Theosophical Society which she formed, were individuals who affirmed little and denied nothing. The marvels which were discussed and manifested in her rooms were to the most of them merely food for thought. If the bell-tones of the invisible 'attendant sprite' Pou Dhi were heard, as they were heard by scores of different persons, this phenomenon... was as likely to be chaffed good-naturedly by an obstinate sceptic as it was to be wondered at by a believer.... Sensitive as Mme Blavatsky was to personal ridicule and to slander, she was truly liberal in matters of opinion, and allowed us as great latitude in the discussion of her beliefs as she took in discussing the beliefs of others."[6]

Mr. Judge continues: "On the table at which *Isis Unveiled* was written

DRAWING-ROOM AND DINING-ROOM OF "THE LAMASERY"

stood a little Chinese cabinet with many small drawers. A few of the drawers contained some trifles, but there were several that were always kept empty. The cabinet was an ordinary one of its class, and repeated examination showed that there were no devices or mechanical arrangements in it, or connected with it; but many a time has one of those empty drawers become the vanishing point of various articles, and as often, on the other hand, was the birthplace of some object which had not before been seen in the rooms.

"I have often seen her put small coins or a ring or an amulet, and have put things there myself, closed the drawer, almost instantly reopening it, and nothing was visible. It had disappeared from sight.... The cabinet stood on four small legs, elevated about two inches above the desk, which was quite clear and unbroken underneath. Several times I have seen her put a ring into one of the drawers and then leave the room. I then looked into the drawer, saw the ring in it, and closed it again. She returned, and without coming near the cabinet showed me the ring on her finger. I then looked again in the drawer before she again came near it, and the ring was gone....

"One evening, a little while after the music, Madame opened one of the drawers of the Chinese cabinet, and took from it an Oriental necklace of curious beads. This she gave to a lady present.* One of the gentlemen allowed to escape him an expression of regret that he had not received such a testimonial. Thereupon H. P. B. reached over and grasped one of the beads, and the bead came off at once in Madame's hand. She then passed it to the gentleman, who exclaimed that it was not merely a bead but was now a breast-pin, as there was a gold pin fastened securely in it. The necklace meanwhile remained intact, and its recipient was examining it in wonder that one of its beads could have been thus pulled off without breaking it."[7]

Mr. William Q. Judge wrote the above account, but the ultimate fate of this necklace is to be found in the article in the *New York Times* of January 2, 1885, quoted above. "A lady whose brother† was an enthusiastic believer in the wonderful Russian, but who was herself a devout Methodist and thoroughly antagonistic to Theosophy, was induced to make Mme Blavatsky's acquaintance. They became friends, though they continued widely opposed in belief.

---

* Colonel Olcott's sister, Mrs. Mitchell.
† Colonel Olcott.

"One day Mme Blavatsky gave the lady a necklace of beautifully carved beads of some strange substance that looked like, but was not, hard wood. 'Wear them yourself,' she said. 'If you let anyone else have them, they will disappear.' The lady wore them constantly for over a year. Meantime she moved out of the city.

"One day her little child, who was sick and fretful, cried for the beads. She gave them to him, half laughing at herself for hesitating. The child put them around his neck and seemed pleased with his new toy, while the mother turned away to attend to some domestic duty. In a few minutes the child began crying, and the mother found him trying to take the beads off. She removed them herself, and found that they were nearly one-third melted away and were hot, while the child's neck showed marks of being burned. She tells the story herself, and in the same breath denies that she believes in 'any such things.'"[8]

"Whence did H. P. B. draw the materials which compose *Isis*, and which cannot be traced to accessible literary sources of quotation? From the Astral Light, and by her soul-senses, from her Teachers — the 'Brothers,' 'Adepts,' Sages,' 'Masters,' as they have been variously called. How do I know it? By working two years with her on *Isis* and many more years on other literary work." says Colonel Olcott.[9]

"The glaring contrasts between the jumbled and the almost perfect portions of her MS. quite clearly prove that the same intelligence was not at work throughout; and the variations in handwriting, in mental method, in literary facility, and in personal idiosyncracies, bear out this idea.[10]... Each change in writing was accompanied by a marked alteration in the manner, motions, expression and literary capacity of H. P. B. When she was left to her own devices it was often not difficult to know it, for then the untrained literary apprentice became manifest, and the cutting and pasting began; then the copy that was turned over to me for revision was terribly faulty."[11]

"The needless substitution of new for old 'copy' and transportations from one chapter or volume to another, in *Isis Unveiled*, were confined to such portions of the work as, I should say, were done in her normal condition — if any such there was — and suggested the painful struggles of a 'green hand' over a gigantic literary task. Unfamiliar with grammatical English and literary methods, and with her mind absolutely untrained for such sustained desk-work, yet endowed with a courage without bounds and a power of continuous mental concentration that has scarcely been equalled, she floundered on through weeks and months towards her goal, the fulfilment of her Master's orders. This literary feat of hers surpasses all her phenomena."[12]

"Bouton, [her publisher] spent $600 for the corrections and alterations that she made in galley, page and electroplate proofs.... When the publisher peremptorily refused to put any more capital into the venture, we had prepared almost enough additional MS. to make a third volume, and this was ruthlessly destroyed before we left America; H. P. B. not dreaming that she would ever want to utilise it in India, and the *Theosophist*, *Secret Doctrine*, and her other subsequent literary productions, not even thought of. How often she and I mingled our regrets that all that valuable material had been so thoughtlessly wasted!"[13]

From Ithaca, September 20, 1875, H. P. B. wrote to Alexander Aksakofi: "I am now writing a big book, which I call, by John's advice, *Skeleton Keys to Mysterious Gates*. I will say nice things there about your European and American men of science, Papists, Jesuits, and that race of the half-learned, *les châtrés de la science*, who destroy everything without creating anything."[14] Years later, by modifying it into *The Key to Theosophy*, she used this name for one of her books. She next proposed to call the book *The Veil of Isis*, and the first volume bears that title at the top of each page. However, May 8, 1877, her publisher, Mr. J. W. Bouton, wrote to her that their mutual friend, Mr. Sotheran, had informed him that a book bearing this title had recently been published in England. So, at that late date, the name was altered to *Isis Unveiled*.

About September 17, 1875, H. P. B. went to visit Professor and Mrs. Corson, at Ithaca, New York, and stayed with them till about the middle of October. Dr. Eugene Rollin Corson, their son, sketches an interesting portrait of her in his book, *Some Unpublished Letters of Helena Petrovna Blavatsky*:

"At the time when H. P. B. visited Ithaca, the weather is usually fine. In October there is the Indian Summer; the trees have put on their autumn tints, the mornings and nights are crisp and frosty, with a pleasant warmth in the middle of the day, with the distant hills and lake bathed in the late summer haze. The general outlook is very beautiful. Ithaca proper is in the valley at the foot of Cayuga Lake, and is built upon the east, west and south hills, with the outskirts heavily wooded. My father's home was on the east hill. On this hill the University [Cornell] stands, an imposing array of noble buildings....

"One evening a frost was predicted, and my mother was anxious to get in her potted plants from the porch, when H. P. B. told her not to worry, and she would get 'John' to bring them in. So they went to bed without any concern, and in the morning all the plants were found inside, (p. 35-36)

"In her dress she wore mostly a loose wrapper with a sort of embroidered jacket, as my mother described it to me, with the cigarette papers in one pocket and the tobacco in the other. My father who was a great smoker himself and a judge of tobacco, thought her brand a cheap kind; perhaps her lack of money accounted for it. The cigarettes were countless, and the flowerpots were full of the stubs. She had an elaborate robe, which shows well in the photograph taken by Beardsley.* (p. 27)

"She spent her time at her desk, writing, writing, writing most of the day and way into the night, carrying on a huge correspondence by long letters. Here she started *Isis Unveiled*, writing about twenty-five closely written foolscap pages a day. She had no books to consult, my father's extensive library was almost wholly on English literature... and she rarely consulted him about anything."[15]

Mr. W. Q. Judge bears witness to this same fact in the *New York Sun*, of September. 26, 1892. He says: "*Isis Unveiled* attracted wide attention and all the New York papers reviewed it, each saying that it exhibited immense research. The strange part of this is as I and many others can testify as eye-witnesses to the production of the book, that the writer had no library in which to make researches, and possessed no notes of investigations or reading previously done. All was written straight out of hand. And yet it is full of references to books in the British Museum and other great libraries, and every reference is correct. Either then we have, as to that book, a woman who was capable of storing in her memory a mass of facts, dates, number, titles and subjects, such as no other human being was capable of, or her claim to help from unseen beings is just."

Dr. Corson relates the following amusing incident of her stay: "One day my father said to her: 'It is a pity, Madame, for you not to see the beauties round you. I want to give you a carriage drive, that you may see the

---

* See *The Theosophist*, October, 1929; and Golden Book, 52.

University buildings and the lovely country.' She finally consented to go, but my father begged her not to smoke in the carriage because the people were not used to it, and it would give them a bad impression and might cause comment, especially with a staid university professor. To this she reluctantly consented.

"But before the drive was over, Madame said she would have to smoke a cigarette, she could not stand it a moment longer, and begged that she might get out of the carriage and sit on a stone at the side of the road and smoke in comfort. If the country people took her for a gypsy, why not, what harm would it do? So there sat the author of *Isis Unveiled* and the *Secret Doctrine*, satisfied with her own thoughts and oblivious of everything around her, even the waiting horses and coachman and the carriage with its occupants. Perhaps it was less the tobacco she wanted than the desire to be alone with herself and her own thoughts. When the cigarettes were finished she returned to the carriage and they continued on their drive.

"My father dwelt especially on this incident, as showing the woman's preoccupation. As he repeatedly said to me: 'Never have I seen such an intense creature, intense in her purpose, intense in her endeavour; nothing round her mattered; though the heavens fall she would keep on her way.'"[16]

H. P. B. had given her friends at Ithaca fair warning of this "national sin" of hers — smoking. Replying to their invitation to visit them, she had said: "Alas! my dear Sir, I am really very vicious in my own way, and unpardonably so in the eyes of every true American.... You invite me so kindly to the Cascade; but what will you say when you see your guest stealing away from the room every fifteen minutes to go and hide behind the doors and in the yards and basements to smoke a cigarette? I am obliged to confess that I, like all the women of Russia, smoke in my drawing-room as in the drawing-room of every respectable lady from an aristocratic princess down to the wife of an employee; they smoke according to our national custom in the carriage as well as the foyer of the theatres. I am actually obliged to hide myself like a thief; for the Americans have insulted me and stared me out of countenance, and published about me in the papers, ornamenting my poor self with the most wonderful names, and inventing about me stories, and so forth, till, unable to give up an innocent habit of more than twenty years' standing, I was finally driven to what I consider to be a mean act of cowardice; doing what I am ashamed here in America to proclaim in the face of the world. But if you can forgive me my national sins, then, of course, I will be most happy to avail myself of your kind invitation.... Tell her (Mrs. Corson) I promise never to smoke in her drawing-room."[17]

CHAPTER XXXVII
Who Wrote "Isis Unveiled"?

"The 'copy' turned off by H.P.B. presented the most marked dissemblances at different times. While the handwriting bore one peculiar character throughout, so that one familiar with her writing would always be able to detect any given page as H.P.B.'s, yet when examined carefully one discovered at least three or four variations of the one style, and each of these persistent for pages together, when it would give place to some other of the calligraphic variants.... One of these H.P.B. handwritings was very small but plain; one bold and free; another plain, of medium size and very legible; and one scratchy and hard to read, with its queer foreign-shaped a's and x's and e's. There was also the greatest possible difference in the English of these various styles. Sometimes I would have to make several corrections in each line, while at others I could pass many pages with scarcely a fault of idiom or spelling to correct. Most perfect of all were the manuscripts which were written for her while she was sleeping. The beginning of the chapter on the civilisation of ancient Egypt is an illustration. We had stopped at about 2 a.m. as usual, both too tired to wait for our usual smoke and chat before parting. The next morning when I came to breakfast, she showed me a pile of at least thirty or forty pages of beautifully written H.P.B. manuscript, which, she said, she had had written for her by — well, a Master whose name has never been degraded like some others. It was perfect in every respect, and went to the printers without revision.

"Now it is a curious fact that each change in the H.P.B. manuscript would be preceded, either by her leaving the room for a moment or two, or by her going off into a trance or abstracted state, when her lifeless eyes would be looking beyond me into space, as it were, and returning to the normal waking state almost immediately. And there would be also a distinct change of personality, or rather personal peculiarities, in gait, vocal expression, vivacity of manner, and above all in temper.... She would leave the room one person, and return to it another. Not another as to visible change of physical body, but another as to tricks of motion, speech and manners;

with different mental brightness, different views of things, different command of English orthography, idiom and different, very, *very* different, command over her temper.... Mr. Sinnett says : ' How she could, at the same time, be philosopher enough to give up the world for the sake of spiritual advancement, and yet be capable of going into frenzies of passion about trivial annoyances, was a profound mystery to us for a long while.' Yet, upon the theory that when her body was occupied by a sage, it would be forced to act with a sage's tranquility ; and when not, not, the puzzle is solved."[1]

"In the matter of occupancy (*Avesa*) of H. P. B.'s body, there was one collateral proof continually thrusting itself upon one's notice, if one but paid attention to it. Let us say that the Master A. or B. had been 'on guard' an hour or more, had been working on *Isis*, alone or jointly with me, and was at a given moment saying something to me, or if third parties were present to one of them. Suddenly she (he ?) stops speaking, rises and leaves the room, excusing herself for a moment on some pretext to strangers. She presently returns, looks around as any new arrival would upon entering a room where there was company, makes herself a fresh cigarette, and says something which has not the least reference to what had been talked about when she left the room. Someone present, wishing to keep her to the point, asks her kindly to explain. She shows embarrassment and inability to pick up the thread ; perhaps expresses an opinion flatly contradicting what she had just affirmed, and when taken to task, becomes vexed and says strong things ; or when told that she had said so-and-so, appears to take an introspective glance and says : ' Oh, yes, excuse me,' and goes on with her subject. She was sometimes as quick as lightning in these changes ; and I myself, forgetting her multiplex personality, have often been very irritated for her seeming inability to keep to the same opinion, and her bold denial that she had not said what she certainly said plainly enough the moment before.

"In due time it was explained to me that it takes time, after entering another's living body, to link one's own consciousness with the brain memory of the preceding occupier ; and that if one tries to continue a conversation before this adjustment is complete, just such mistakes as the above may occur.... Sometimes when we were alone has either the departing Somebody said : ' I must put this into the brain, so that my successor may find it there,' or the incoming Somebody after greeting me with a friendly word, asked me what was the subject of discussion before the ' change.' [2]...

It did not need, after we 'twins' had been working together long enough for me to become familiar with her every peculiarity of speech, moods and impulses, [that I should be told in so many words.] The change was as plain as day; and by and by after she had been out of the room and returned, a brief study of her features and actions enabled me to say to myself: 'This is —— or —— or ——' and presently my suspicion was confirmed by what happened".[3]

"When they knew that I could distinguish between them, so as to even have invented a name for each, by which H.P.B. and I might designate them in our conversation in their absence, they would frequently give me a grave bow or a friendly farewell nod when about to leave the room and give place to the next relief-guard. And they would sometimes talk to me of each other as friends do about absent third parties, by which means I came to know bits of their several personal histories."[4]

"By an interesting coincidence, I had just read this passage when a certain circumstance flashed into my memory; and I turned over my old New York files of letters and memoranda until I had found the following. It occurs in some notes I made at the time, of a conversation between myself and one of the Mahatmas, a Hungarian by birth, who on that evening occupied H.P.B.'s body: 'He shades his eyes and turns down the gas in the standing burner on the table. Ask him why. Says that light is a physical force, and entering the eye of an unoccupied body encounters — strikes against, the astral soul of the temporary occupant, gives it a shock and such a push that the occupant might be pushed out. Paralysis of the occupied body is even possible. Extreme caution must be used in entering a body, and one cannot thoroughly fit oneself to it throughout until the automatic movements of the circulation, breathing, etc., adjust themselves to the automatism of the occupier's own body — with which, however far distant, his projected astral body is most intimately related. I then lit a burner of the chandelier overhead, but the occupier at once held a newspaper so as to shade the crown of the head from the light. Surprised, I asked for an explanation, and was told that it was even more dangerous to have a strong top light strike upon the crown of the head than to have light shine into the eyes.'"[5]

"What I noticed was this, that at times when the physical H.P.B. was in a state of extreme irascibility, the body was rarely occupied save by the Master whose own pupil and spiritual ward she was, and whose iron will was even stronger than her own, the gentler philosophers keeping aloof."⁶

"One of these *Alter Egos* of hers, one whom I have since personally met, wears a full beard and long moustache that are twisted Rajput fashion, into his side-whiskers. He has the habit of constantly pulling at his moustache when deeply pondering; he does it mechanically and unconsciously. Well, there were times when H. P. B.'s personality had melted away and she was 'Somebody else' when I would sit and watch her hand as if pulling at and twisting a moustache that certainly was not growing visibly on H. P. B.'s upper lip, and the far-away look would be in the eyes, until presently resuming attention of passing things, the moustached Somebody would look up, catch me watching him, hastily remove the hand from the face, and go on with the work of writing.

"Then there was another Somebody who disliked English so much that he never willingly talked with me in anything but French; he had a fine artistic talent and a passionate fondness for mechanical invention. Another one would now and then sit there, scrawling something with a pencil and reeling off for me dozens of poetical stanzas which embodied, now sublime, now humorous, ideas. So each of the several Somebodies had his peculiarities, as recognisable as those of any of our ordinary acquaintances or friends. One was jovial, fond of good stories, and witty to a degree; another, all dignity, reserve and erudition. One would be calm, patient and benevolently helpful; another testy and sometimes exasperating. One Somebody would always be willing to emphasise his philosophical or scientific explanation of the subjects I was to write upon, by doing phenomena for my edification; while to another Somebody I dared not even mention them"⁷

"Now when either of these Somebodies was 'on guard,' as I used to term it, the H. P. B. manuscript would present the identical peculiarities that it had on the last occasion when he had taken his turn at the literary work. He would by preference write about the class of subjects that were to his taste; and instead of H. P. B. playing the part of amanuensis, she would then have become for the time being that other person. If you had given me in those days any page of *Isis* manuscript, I could almost certainly have told you by which Somebody it had been written"⁸

"We worked in collaboration with at least one disincarnate entity — the pure soul of one of the wisest philosophers of modern times…. He was a great Platonist; and I was told that, so absorbed was he in his life-study that he had become earth-bound, i.e., he could not snap the ties which held him to the earth, but sat in an astral library of his own mental creation, plunged in his philosophical reflections.... There he was, willing and eager to work with H. P. B. on this epoch-making book, towards the philosophical portions of which he contributed much. He did not materialize and sit with us, nor obsess H. P. B. medium-fashion; he would simply talk with her psychically by the hour together, dictating copy, telling her what references to hunt up, answering my questions about details, instructing me as to principles, and playing the part of a third person in our literary symposium.... (p. 243)

"H. P. B. served the Platonist in the most matter-of-fact way as amanuensis, their relation differing in nothing from that of any private secretary with his employer, save that the latter was invisible to me but visible to her.... He seemed not quite a 'Brother' — as we used to call the Adepts then — yet more that than anything else.... He never dropped a word to indicate that he thought himself aught but a living man, and in fact I was told that he did not realise that he had died out of the body. Of the lapse of time he seemed to have so little perception that I remember H. P. B. and I laughed, one morning at 2.30 a.m. when, after an unusually hard night's work, while we were taking a parting smoke, he quietly asked H. P. B.: 'Are you ready to begin?' And I also recollect how she said: 'For heaven's sake, don't laugh deep in your thought, else the old gentleman will surely hear you and feel hurt!'"[9]

"Then again I had ocular proof that at least some of those who worked with us were living men, from having seen them later in the flesh in India, after having seen them in the astral body in America and Europe; from having touched and talked with them."[10]

"One evening at New York, after bidding H. P. B. good-night, I sat in my bedroom, finishing a cigar and thinking. Suddenly there stood my Chohan beside me. The door had made no noise in opening, if it *had* opened, but at any rate there he was. He sat down and conversed with me in subdued tones for some time, and as he seemed in an excellent humour towards me, I asked him a favour. I said I wanted some tangible proof that he had actually been there, and that I had not been seeing a mere illusion or *maya* conjured up by H. P. B. He laughed, unwound the embroidered Indian cotton *fehta* he wore on his head, flung it to me, and — was gone. That cloth I still possess, and it bears in one corner the initial… M∴* of my Chohan in thread-work."[11]

"She and I were in our literary work-room in New York one summer day after dinner. It was early twilight, and the gas had not been lighted. She sat over by the south front window, I stood on the rug before the mantelpiece, thinking. I heard her say: 'Look and learn'; and glancing that way, saw a mist rising from her head and shoulders. Presently it defined itself into the likeness of one of the Mahatmas, the one who later gave me the historical turban, but the astral double of which he now wore on his mist-born head. Absorbed in watching the phenomenon, I stood silent and motionless. The shadowy shape only formed for itself the upper half of the torso, and then faded away and was gone; whether re-absorbed into H.P.B.'s body or not, I do not know. She sat statue-like for two or three minutes, after which she sighed, came to herself, and asked if I had seen anything. When I asked her to explain the phenomenon, she refused, saying that it was for me to develop my intuition so as to understand the phenomena of the world I lived in. All she could do was to help in showing me things, and let me make what I could out of them."[12]

"Can anyone understand my feelings upon discovering on a certain evening that I had unsuspiciously greeted a staid philosopher with a hilarious levity that quite upset his usual calm? Fancying that I was addressing only my 'chum' H.P.B., I said: 'Well, Old Horse, let us get to work!' The next minute I was blushing for shame, for the blended expression of surprise and startled dignity that came into the face showed me with whom I had to deal…. This was the one for whom I had the most filial reverence. It was not alone for his profound learning, lofty character and dignified demeanour, but also for his really paternal kindness and patience. It seemed as if he alone had read to the bottom of my heart, and wished to bring out every little spiritual germ that lay there as a latent potentiality. He was, I was told, a South Indian personage of long spiritual experience, a Teacher of Teachers; still living among men ostensibly as a landed proprietor, yet known for what he was by nobody round him. Oh, the evenings of high thinking I passed with him; how shall I ever compare them with any other experience of my life!…

"It was this Master who dictated the 'Replies to an English F. T. S.' on questions suggested by a reading of *Esoteric Buddhism*, which was published

---

* Facsimile in *The Theosophist*, August, 1932, and *Old Diary Leaves*, I, 434.

in *The Theosophist* for September, October, November, 1883. It was at Ootacamund at the house of Major-General Morgan, when shivering with the cold and her lower limbs swaddled in rugs, she sat writing them.* One morning I was in her room reading a book, when she turned her head and said : 'I'll be hanged if I ever heard of the Iaphygians. Did you ever read of such a tribe, Olcott?' I said I had not; why did she ask? 'Well', she replied, 'the old gentleman tells me to write it down, but I'm afraid there is some mistake; what do you say?' I answered that if the Master in question gave her the name, she should write it without fear, as he was always right. And she did. This is an example of the multitudinous cases where she wrote from dictation things quite outside her personal knowledge."[13]

"I got an awful rebuke one evening. I had brought home a while before two nice, soft pencils, just the thing for our desk work, and had given one to H. P. B. and kept one myself. She had the very bad habit of borrowing penknives, pencils, rubber and other articles of stationery and forgetting to return them; once put into her drawer or writing-desk, there they would stay, no matter how much of a protest you might make over it. On this particular evening, the artistic Somebody was sketching a navvy's face on a sheet of common paper and chatting with me about something, when he asked me to lend him another pencil. The thought flashed into my mind, 'If I once lend this nice pencil, it will go into her drawer and I shall have none for my own use.' I did not say this, I only thought it; but the Somebody gave me a sarcastic look, reached out to the pen-tray between us, laid his pencil in it, handled it with his fingers of that hand for a moment, and lo ! a dozen pencils of the identical make and quality ! He said not a word, did not even give me a look, but the blood rushed to my temples, and I felt more humble than I ever did in my life. All the same, I scarcely think I deserved the rebuke, considering what a stationery-annexer H. P. B. was!"[14]

"I have spoken of the part of *his* that was done by H. P. B. in *propria persona* which was inferior to that done for her by the Somebodies. This is perfectly comprehensible, for how could H. P. B., who had no previous knowledge of this sort, write correctly about the multifarious subjects treated in her book ? In her (seemingly) normal state, she would read a book, mark the portions that struck her, write about them, make mistakes, correct them,

---

* This Master is called the Regent of India. See my " Brothers " of Mme Blavatsky for an account of these " Replies " in Chapter IV, " Master Morya and the Regent of India."

discuss them with me, set me to writing, help my intuitions, get friends to supply materials, and go on thus as best she might, so long as there were none of the teachers within call of her psychic appeals. And they were not with us always, by any means.

"She did a vast deal of splendid writing, for she was endowed with a marvellous natural literary capacity; she was never dull or uninteresting; and she was equally brilliant in three languages, when the full power was upon her. She writes to her Aunt that when her Master was busy elsewhere, he left his substitute with her, and then it was her 'Luminous Self,' her Augoeides, which thought and wrote for her. About this I cannot venture an opinion, for I never observed her in this state: I only knew her in three capacities, viz., her proper H.P.B. self; with her body possessed or overshadowed by the Masters; and as an amanuensis taking down from dictation. It may be that her Augoeides, taking possession of her physical brain, gave me the impression that it was one of the Masters that was at work: I cannot say. But what she omits telling her Aunt is, that there were many, many times when she was neither possessed, controlled, nor dictated to by any superior intelligence, but was simply and palpably H.P.B., our familiar and beloved friend,* latterly our teacher; who was trying as well as she could to carry out the object of her literary mission.

"Despite the mixed agencies at work in producing *Isis*, there is an expression of individuality running throughout it and her other work — something peculiar to herself.[15]... Then how are we to regard the authorship of *Isis*, and how H.P.B.? As to the former it is unquestionably a collaborated work, the production of several distinct writers and not that of H.P.B. alone.... The question is highly complex, and the exact truth will never be known as to the share which each of the participants had in it. The personality of H.P.B. was the mould in which all the matter was cast, and which therefore controlled its form, colouring and expression, so to say, by its own idiosyncracies, mental as well as physical. For, just as the successive occupiers of the H.P.B. body only modified its habitual handwriting but did not write their own; so in using the H.P.B. brain, they were forced to allow it to colour their thoughts and arrange their words after a fixed fashion peculiar

---

* Says the Colonel: "The jocund side of H. P. B.'s character was one of her greatest charms. She liked to say witty things and to hear others say them. Her salon was never dull, save to those who had no knowledge of Eastern literature and understood nothing of Eastern philosophy." — *Old Diary Leaves*, I, 456.

to it. Like as the daylight passing through cathedral windows becomes coloured to the tints of the stained glass, so the thoughts transmitted by them through H.P.B.'s brain would have to be modified into the literary style and habits of expression to which it had been by her developed."[16]

H.P.B. wrote to her family: "When I wrote *Isis*, I wrote it so easily that it was actually no labour, but a real pleasure. Why should I be praised for it? Whenever I am *told* to write, I sit down and obey, and then I can write easily upon almost anything — metaphysics, psychology, philosophy, ancient religions, zoology, natural sciences, or what not. I never put myself the question: 'Can I write on this subject?' or 'Am I equal to the task?' but I simply sit down and *write*. Why? Because *somebody who knows all* dictates to me.... My Master and occasionally others whom I knew in my travels years ago.... Please do not imagine that I have lost my senses. I have hinted to you before now about *Them*, and I tell you candidly, that whenever I write upon a subject I know little or nothing of, I address myself to *Them*, and one of Them inspires me, i.e., He allows me to simply copy what I write from manuscripts, and even printed matter that passes before my eyes in the air, during which process I have never been *unconscious* one single instant.... It is that knowledge of His protection and faith in His power, that have enabled me to become mentally and spiritually so strong... and even He (the Master) is not always required; for, during His absence on some other occupation, He awakens in me His substitute in knowledge.... At such times it is no more *I* who write, but my *inner Ego*, my 'luminous self,' who thinks and writes for me."[17]

In another letter she says to her sister: "Well, Vera, whether you believe me or not, something miraculous is happening to me. You cannot imagine in what a charmed world of pictures and visions I live. I am writing *Isis*, not writing, rather copying out and drawing what she personally shows to me. Upon my word, sometimes it seems to me that the ancient Goddess of Beauty in person leads me through all the countries of past centuries which I have to describe. I sit with my eyes open, and to all appearances see and hear everything real and actual around me, and yet at the same time I see and hear that which I write. I feel short of breath; I am afraid to make the slightest movement, for fear the spell might be broken. Slowly, century after century, image after image, float out of the distance and pass before me, as if in magic panorama; and meanwhile I put them together in my mind, fitting in epochs and dates, and know *for sure* that there can be *no mistake*. Races and nations, countries and cities, which have for long disappeared in the darkness of the prehistoric past, emerge and then vanish, giving place to others, and then I am told the consecutive dates.

"Hoary antiquity makes way for historical periods; myths are explained to me with events and people who have really existed; and every event which is at all remarkable, every newly turned page of this many-coloured book of life, impresses itself on my brain with photographic exactitude. My own reckonings and calculations appear to me later on as separate coloured pieces of different shapes in the game which is called *casse-tête* (puzzles). I gather them together and try to match them one after the other, and assuredly it is not I who do it all, but my ego, the highest principle which lives in me. And even this with the help of my Guru and Teacher who helps me in everything. If I happen to forget something, I have just to address him, or another of the same kind in my thought, and what I have forgotten rises once more before my eyes — sometimes whole tables of numbers passing before me, long inventories of events. They remember everything. They know everything. Without Them, from whence could I gather my knowledge?" [18]

Master Koot Hoomi, wrote to Mr. Sinnett in 1882: "It was H. P. B. who, acting under the orders of Atrya (one whom you do not know), was the first to explain in the *Spiritualist* the difference between *psyche* and *nous, nefesh* and *ruach*, Soul and Spirit. She had to bring the whole arsenal of proofs with her, quotations from Paul and Plato, from Plutarch and James, etc., before the Spiritualists admitted that the Theosophists were right. It was then that she was ordered to write *Isis* — just a year after the Society had been founded. And as there happened such a war over it, endless polemics and objections to the effect that *there could not be in man two souls*, we thought it premature to give the public more than they could possibly assimilate, and before they had digested the 'two Souls'; and thus the further subdivision of the trinity into seven principles was left unmentioned in *Isis*.... She obeyed our orders, and wrote purposely veiling some of her facts." [19]

Colonel Olcott says: "Upon its appearance, *Isis* made such a sensation that the first edition was exhausted within ten days. The critics on the whole dealt kindly with it.... The truest thing said about it was the expression of an American author that it is 'a book with a revolution in it.'" [20]

As to her command of English at that time, H.P.B. wrote to Colonel Olcott January 6, 1886: "When I arrived in America, I could hardly speak English and could not write it at all-it is a fact, as you know. *Isis* is the first work, with the exception of a few articles corrected by you and others, that I ever wrote in English in my life; and it was mostly dictated by K. H., as you know (Kashmiri). I learnt to write English with him, so to say. I took up all his peculiarities, even to writing sceptic with a k —— which I dropped in India, and he preserved the habit. What wonder then that similarity is found between the style of *Isis* and letters to Sinnett?* I told you and you know, that I spoke English ten times as badly as I do now, yet forty, fifty pages at a time would be written of *Isis* MSS. without one mistake. Please remember that — that I hardly spoke and could not write English at all. I had not spoken since my childhood almost, as I told you. The first time when I spoke nothing but English for months was, when I was with the Masters — with Mahatma K. H. and of course I got his style."[21]

---

* The Mahatma K. H.'s letters to Sinnett.

CHAPTER XXXVIII

H. P. B. — *American Citizen And Russian Patriot*

1878 was an important year in H. P. B.'s life: she barely escaped cremation, she became an American citizen, and then left the United States forever. The first contingency Mme Jelihovsky describes as follows:

"In the spring of 1878 a strange thing happened to Mme Blavatsky. Having got up and set to work one morning as usual, she suddenly lost consciousness and never regained it until five days later. So deep was her state of lethargy that she would have been buried had not a telegram been received by Colonel Olcott and his sister, who were with her at the time, emanating from him she called her Master. The message ran, 'Fear nothing, she is neither dead nor ill, but she has need of repose; she has overworked herself.... She will recover.' As a matter of fact she recovered and found herself so well that she would not believe she had slept for five days. Soon after this sleep, H. P. Blavatsky formed the project of going to India."[1]

H. P. B.'s own account of it, in a letter to Mme Jelihovsky, is this: 'I have not written to you for a month, my well-beloved friend, and could you guess the cause of it? One beautiful Tuesday morning in April I got up as usual and as usual sat down at my writing-table, to write to my Californian correspondents. Suddenly, hardly a second later, as it seemed to me, I realized that for some mysterious reason I was in my bedroom and lying on my bed, it being evening and not morning any more. Around me I saw some of our Theosophists and doctors looking at me with the most puzzled faces, and Olcott and his sister Mrs. Mitchell — the best friend I have here, both of them pale, sour, wrinkled as if they had just been boiled in a saucepan.

"'What's the matter? What's gone and happened?' I asked them. Instead of answering, they heaped questions upon me: what was the matter with me? And how could I tell — nothing was the matter with me. I did not remember anything, but it certainly was strange that only the other moment it was Tuesday morning, and now they said it was Saturday evening; and as to me, these four days of unconsciousness seemed only the twinkling of an eye. There's a pretty pair of shoes! Just fancy, they all thought I was dead, and were about to burn this dismantled temple of mine. But at this, Master telegraphed from Bombay to Olcott: 'Don't be afraid. She is not ill but resting, but now she will be well.' Master was right. He knows everything, and in fact I was perfectly healthy. The only thing was, I did not remember anything. I got up, stretched myself, sent them all out of the room, and sat down to write the same evening. But it is simply awful to think about the work that has accumulated. I could not give a thought to letters."[2]

"H. P. B. was compelled for various reasons to become an American citizen.* This troubled her considerably, as, like all Russians, she was passionately devoted to her country," says Mrs. Johnston, her niece, in *The Path*. H. P. B. wrote to her aunt, Mme Fadeef:

"My dearest, I write to you because otherwise I would burst with a strange feeling which is positively suffocating me. It is the 8th of July to-day, an ominous day for me, but God only knows whether the omen is good or bad. To-day it is exactly five years and one day since I came to America, and this moment I have just returned from the Supreme Court, where I gave my oath of allegiance to the American Republic and Constitution. Now for a whole hour I have been a citizen with equal rights to the President himself. So far so good: the workings of my original destiny have forced me into this naturalization; but to my utter astonishment and disgust I was compelled to repeat publicly after the judge, like a mere parrot, the following tirade: that I would renounce forever and even to my death every kind of submission and obedience to the emperor of Russia; that I would renounce all obedience to the powers established by him and the government of Russia; and that I would accept the duty to defend, love and serve the Constitution of the United States alone. So help me God in whom I believe! I was awfully scared when pronouncing this blackguardly recantation of Russia and the emperor. And so I am not only an apostate to our beloved Russian Church, but a political renegade. A nice scrape to get into, but how am I to manage to no longer love Russia or respect the emperor? It is easier to say a thing than to act accordingly."[3]

Interviewed for the *New York Star* of June 28, 1878, on this approaching event (she was the first Russian woman ever naturalised in the United States), she is reported as saying: "The American people are better than my own because they are more polite to women."

* See Chapter XXVII.

"Are you in favour of female suffrage?"

"I don't desire to vote myself, but I don't see why I shouldn't be allowed to. All women should have the privilege. My papers say that I am a citizen, and are not all free and independent in this country? Women vote in Russia, and it is not a privilege either; they are obliged to do it. I am astonished to see that it isn't the same here. But I can't see how it makes much difference who votes and who doesn't. Married? No, I am a widow, a blessed widow, and I thank God! I wouldn't be a slave to God Himself, let alone man."[4]

On her arrival in India in 1879 (which might not have been possible at all had she remained a Russian subject) she was for some time shadowed as a possible Russian spy. The question of her citizenship came up before the public through the Press, and we find her replying in a letter to the editor of the *Bombay Gazette*, of May 13, 1879:

"On the very day of my return from a month's travel, I am shown by the American Consul two paragraphs, viz. one in your paper of the 10th inst., which mentions me as the 'Russian Baroness,' and one in the *Times of India* of the 8th, whose author had tried hard to be witty but only succeeded in being impertinent and calumnious. In this last paragraph I am referred to as a woman who calls herself a 'Russian princess.'...

H. P. B.'s COAT OF ARMS (COUNTESS)

"My present business is to take the *Gazette* to task for thrusting upon my unwilling republican head the Baronial coronet. Know please, once for all, that I am neither 'Countess,' 'Princess,' nor even a modest 'Baroness,' whatever I may have been before last July. At that time I became a plain citizen of the U. S. of America — a title I value far more than any that could be conferred on me by King or Emperor. Being this I could be nothing else, if I wished; for, as everyone knows, had I been even a princess of the royal blood before, once that my oath of allegiance was pronounced, I forfeited every claim to titles of nobility.

"Apart from this notorious fact, my experience of things in general, and peacocks' feathers in particular, has led me to acquire a positive contempt for titles, since it appears that outside the boundaries of their own Fatherlands, Russian princes, Polish counts, Italian marquises, and German barons are far more plentiful *inside* than *outside* the police precincts. Permit me further to state — if only for the edification of the *Times of India* and a brood of snarling little papers, searching around after the garbage of journalism — that I have never styled myself aught but what I can prove myself to be — namely, an *honest* woman, now a citizen of America, my adopted country, and the only land of *true* freedom in the world."[5]

The Founders of the Theosophical Society had left America December 19, 1878, and arrived in Bombay February 16, 1879. Their departure created a great stir in the New York Press, of which the following article from the *New York Herald* is a sample:

AUCTION SALE OF CURIOS

"Mme Blavatsky, the author of *Isis Unveiled*, has been a resident of New York for over five years. Her life has been passed mostly in Eastern countries, and she is one of the few Europeans of liberal education who have become thoroughly Oriental, not only in tastes but also in religion.

"Her house for the past two years has been the centre of a movement in modern thought which has attracted attention all over the world. To the investigators of Spiritualism she became as one who, accepting the phenomena as genuine, explained them by a still more surprising philosophy than the Spiritualists themselves.

"Under her leadership a Society was formed embracing people who actually believed in magic, and some of whom professed to have learned its principles. The story of the Rosicrucians was told over again in New York. The Society was a secret one, but enough of its beliefs and objects was made public to excite bitter opposition in many different classes and ridicule in others.

"Taking a French flat at 8th Avenue and 47th Street, Mme Blavatsky furnished it in the most curious manner, and crowded every room with strange trophies of travel. Oddities of all kinds, from Siamese idols to Parisian toys, filled her parlour; while stuffed beasts and tropical leaves and grasses adorned the corners. The house was always open to her friends and their friends, and it was Liberty Hall. A freedom that never became licence marked the talk, and religious and philosophical controversy was always in order. To this parlour came strangers from all parts of the world, and some of the best known citizens of New York were frequent visitors.

"*Isis Unveiled*, published a year ago, became well known as an attack on dogmatic religion and modern science, and was the means of attracting great numbers of scholars to 'The Lamasery.' Dr. J. A. Weisse, the philologist, and Professor Alexander Wilder are among her warmest friends, and the Princess Rackovitz (now the wife of a New York journalist) and the Countess Paschkoff have been among her honoured guests. General Doubleday of the U.S. Army, John L. O'sullivan, ex-Minister to Portugal, and his wife met there with Methodist bishops, Catholic priests, artists, actors, infidel writers, journalists, Spiritualists, physicians, Freemasons and other notable people.

"Colonel Chaille Long, the African explorer, is a friend of Mme Blavatsky's uncle, General Fadeyef, the Russian soldier and diplomatist, and favourite of the Grand Duke Alexander of Russia ; and has been a frequent visitor at 'The Lamasery.' Masons of the highest degree were there often ; for the lady, together with her other attainments, numbers a knowledge of Masonry not excelled by many Grand Masters, and she possesses a diploma from England, sent by John Yarker, of the highest degree of the Rite of Memphis.

"The social nature of the evenings in the little parlour was a great element of the success of the movement. The Society itself has attained a world-wide notoriety. English, French, German, Turkish, Hindu and Russian papers abound in allusions to it ; and while branch societies all over the world have been established, a coalition has been formed between the Theosophical Society and the Arya Samaj of India, which is a great reform Vedic Society. Mme Blavatsky avows her connection with secret societies in the East ; and has said for a long time that, as soon as she should have done what she came to America to do, she would return to India. This time, she now says, has arrived; and she is making preparations to depart at no distant day. Therefore it was that yesterday the auctioneer's flag waved at her door, and the curios not already disposed of were sold to the highest bidder."[6]

In spite of her American citizenship, Mme Blavatsky remained ever a true Russian patriot. Her sister, Mme Jelihovsky, writes: "During the war between Russia and Turkey, Héléna Petrovna had not a moment's peace. All her letters written during 1876-1877 are full of alarms for her compatriots, of fears for the safety of those members of her family who were actively engaged in it.* She forgot her anti-materialist and anti-spiritualist articles in order to breathe forth fire and flame against the enemies of the Russian nation....

"When she heard of the famous discourse of Pius IX, in which he taught the faithful that 'the hand of God could direct the scimitar of the Bashibazouk toward the uprooting of schism,' in which he gave his blessing to Mohammedan arms, as used against the infidel Orthodox Greek Church, she fell ill. Then she exploded in a series of satires so envenomed and so clever that the whole American press called attention to them, and the Papal Nuncio at New York, the Scotch Cardinal MacKloskey, thought it advisable to send a priest to parley with her. He gained little from that, however, for Mme Blavatsky made a point of relating the occurrence in her next article, saying that she had begged the prelate to be so good as to talk to her through the press, and she would then most certainly reply to him....

"All that she made in the way of money during the war, from her articles in the Russian newspapers, together with the first payments she received from her publisher [for *Isis Unveiled*], were sent to Odessa and Tiflis for the benefit of the wounded soldiers or their families, or to the Red Cross Society.

"In October, 1876, she gave fresh proof of her powers of clairvoyance. She had a vision of what was happening in the Caucasus, on the frontier of Turkey, where her cousin, Alexander Witte, Major of the Nijni-Novgorod Dragoons, narrowly escaped death. She mentioned the fact in one of her letters to her relations. As often before she had described to us apparitions of persons who warned her of their death weeks before the news could be received by ordinary means, we were not greatly astonished."[7]

---

* Her uncle, Rostislav Andreevich Fadeef, her cousin, Alexander Julievich Witte, and her sister Vera's son, Rostislav Nicolaevich Yahontoff.

"On hearing of the Emperor's death (Tsar Alexander II), she wrote to Mme Jelihovsky: 'Good heavens! what is this new horror? Has the last day fallen upon Russia? Or has Satan entered the offspring of our Russian land? Have they all gone mad, the wretched Russian people? What will be the end of it all, what are we to expect from the future? Oh, God! people may say if they choose, that I am an Atheist, a Buddhist, a renegade, a citizen of a Republic; but the bitterness I feel! How sorry I am for the Imperial family, for the Tsar martyr, for the whole of Russia! I abhor, despise, and utterly repudiate these sneaking monsters — Terrorists. Let everyone laugh at me if they choose, but the martyr-like death of our Sovereign Tsar makes me feel — though I am an American citizen — such compassion, such anguish, and such shame that, in the very heart of Russia, people could not feel this anger and sorrow more strongly.'

"H. P. B. was very pleased that the *Pioneer* [of Allahabad] printed her article on the death of the Tsar and wrote to her sister about it: 'I have put into it all I could possibly remember, and just fancy, they have not cut out a single word, and some other newspapers reprinted it! But all the same, the first time they saw me in mourning, many of them asked me, "What do you mean by this? Aren't you an American?" I got so cross that I have sent a kind of general reply to the *Bombay Gazette*: not as a Russian subject am I clothed in mourning (I have written to them), but as a Russian by birth, as one of the many millions whose benefactor has been this kindly, compassionate man now lamented by the whole of my country. By this act I desire to show respect, love, and sincere sorrow at the death of the sovereign of my mother and my father, of my sisters and brothers in Russia. Writing in this way silenced them, but before this two or three newspapers thought it a good opportunity to chaff the office of the *Theosophist* and the *Theosophist** itself for going into mourning. Well, now they know the reason and can go to the devil.'

"On being sent a portrait of the dead Emperor in his coffin, H. P. B. wrote to Mme Fadeef on the 10th of May, 1881: 'Would you believe it, the moment I glanced at it something went wrong in my head; something uncontrolled vibrated in me, impelling me to cross myself with the big Russian cross, dropping my head on his dead head. So sudden it all was that I felt stupefied with astonishment. Is it really I who during eight years,

---

* *The Theosophist* came out in a mourning cover.

since the death of father, never thought of crossing myself, and then suddenly giving way to such sentimentality? It is a real calamity: fancy that even now I cannot read Russian newspapers with any sort of composure! I have become a regular and perpetual fountain of tears; my nerves have become worse than useless!'"[8]

In a letter in *The Path* of March, 1895 (a letter of 1879), H.P.B. writes: "From Simla I wrote an article for the *Novoe Vremya*, 'The Truth about the Nephew of Nana Sahib.' I have gathered the most elaborate information about this scamp. Golos constantly prints letters written by this liar, as if to incite England to make war on Russia. And *Novoe Vremya* disdained to print my note. For what reason? Besides being true, it is written as a free contribution. One would think they might have believed in the good intention of a country-woman of theirs, a Russian who is at the very source of the information about this self-proclaimed and false ally of Russia.... And yet our papers won't print my articles!"

Mme Pissareff emphasises this fact also when she says: "Out of all her literary work, which revealed to Western Europe the occult teachings of the ancient East, only one book, *The Voice of the Silence*, has been translated into Russian up to last year [written for *The Theosophist* of January, 1913]; and her literary name [Radha Bai] is known only by the Indian Sketches, which under the title *From the Caves and Jungles of Hindustan* were published in the Russian *Messenger* (*Vyestnik*) in the beginning of the eighties."

Mrs. Johnston goes on to say: "In spite of the lack of courtesy on the part of the Russian newspapers in regard to herself, H.P.B. always subscribed to many Russian magazines and papers; and having no time to read these during the day, she robbed herself of sleep during the short five or six hours of her nightly rest, in order to know what was going on in her own country. The arrival of one of these newspapers gave rise to the following psychometric experience in the autumn of 1880. Writing to Mme Fadeef, H.P.B. expressed her gratitude for a parcel of newspapers she had sent her:

"'And what an interesting thing happened to me not long since! I received your bundle of *Novoe Vremya*, and went to bed a little after ten (you know I get up at five). Having taken up one of the newspapers, without choosing, just the nearest one, I stretched myself and went deep into thought about a certain Sanskrit book which I thought would help me to make good fun of Max Müller in my magazine. So you see it was by no means about you

I was thinking. And the newspaper lay all the time about my head on the pillow, partly covering my forehead.

"'All at once I found myself transported into some strange and yet familiar house. The room I saw was new to me, but the table in the middle of it an old acquaintance. And there, sitting at the table, I saw you, my darling comrade, sitting smoking your cigarette and deeply thinking. The supper was laid on the table, but there was no one else in the room. Only it seemed to me that I caught a glimpse of Aunt* going away through the door. Then you raised your hand and, taking a newspaper from the table, put it aside. I had just time to read its heading, *Herald of Odessa*, after which everything disappeared.

"'To all seeming, there was nothing strange in this occurrence but here is something strange. I was perfectly sure that it was a number of the *Novoe Vremya* that I had taken up, and having noticed in my vision some slices of black bread beside you, I was suddenly seized with such a desire to taste some of it — even a wee crumb-that I felt its taste in my mouth. I thought to myself: What does it all mean? What can be the cause of such a fancy? And in order to get rid of a desire that could not be gratified, I unfolded the newspaper and began to read. When lo! it actually was the *Herald of Odessa*, and not at all the *Novoe Vremya* in my hands. And, moreover, crumbs of my longed-for rye-bread were sticking to it!

"'And so these fragments on touching my forehead transmitted to my consciousness the whole scene as it probably happened at the precise moment of their sticking to the newspaper. In this case, crumbs of rye-bread have taken the place of a photographic apparatus. These dry pieces of bread gave me such intense delight, having transported me for a brief moment to you. I was quite filled with the atmosphere of home, and in my joy licked up the biggest crumb, and as to the small ones — here they are. I have cut them out as they stuck to the paper, and send them back to you. Let them return home with some of my own soul. This may be rather a silly proceeding, but perfectly sincere.'"9

Finally she writes to her sister Vera: "People call me, and I must admit I also call myself, a heathen. I simply can't listen to people talking about the wretched Hindus or Buddhists being converted to Anglican Phariseeism or the Pope's Christianity; it simply gives me the shivers. But when I read

* Mme Witte.

about the spread of Russian Orthodoxy in Japan, my heart rejoices. Explain it if you can. I am nauseated by the mere sight of any foreign clerical, but as to the familiar figure of a Russian pope, I can swallow it without an effort... I do not believe in any dogmas, I dislike every ritual, but my feelings towards our own church-service are quite different. I am driven to think that my brains lack their seventh stopper.* Probably it is in my blood... I certainly will always say: a thousand times rather Buddhism, a pure moral teaching, in perfect harmony with the teachings of Christ, than modern Catholicism or Protestantism. But with the faith of the Russian Church I will not even compare Buddhism. I can't help it. Such is my silly, inconsistent nature."[10]

It may be "silly" and "inconsistent"; but it certainly is a conclusive bit of proof that Helena Petrovna Blavatsky still occupied her body — at least sometimes.

---

* The Russian for "a bee in his bonnet."

CHAPTER XXXIX

Who Was H. P. B.

Colonel Olcott says that one of the motives which prompted him to write *Old Diary Leaves* was, that he " might leave behind for the use of the future historian as accurate a sketch as possible of that great personality-puzzle, Helena Petrovna Blavatsky, co-founder of the Theosophical Society....

" I knew her as companion, friend, co-worker, equal — on the plane of personality; all her other colleagues stood with her in the relation of pupil to teacher, or as casual friends, or passing acquaintances, or mere correspondents. None knew her so intimately as I, for none save me saw her in all her many changings of mood, mind and personal characteristics. The human Helena Petrovna, with her unchanged Russian nature, fresh from Bohemian circles in Paris; and the 'Madame Laura,' the bays and bouquets of whose concert tours of 1872-3 as a pianist in Italy, Russia and elsewhere, were not long wilted when she came to New York through Paris, were as well known to me as, later on, became the 'H. P. B.' of Theosophy....

"Just because I did know her so much better than most others, she was a greater mystery to me than to them.... How much of her waking life was that of a responsible personality, how much that of a body worked by an overshadowing entity? I do not know. On the hypothesis that she was a medium for the Great Teachers, only that and nothing more, then the riddle is easy to read; for then one can account for the alterations in mind, character, tastes and predilections which have been touched upon; then the H. P. B. of the latter days fits on to the Helena Petrovna of New York, Paris, Italy and all other countries and epochs.

" And what does the following passage (written in my Diary by her hand on the page for the 6th December, 1878) mean, if not that? It says: '*We* got cold again, I think. Oh, unfortunate, empty, rotten old body!' Was this 'empty' body empty of its proper tenant? If not, why should the phrase have been written with her hand in a variant of her proper handwriting? We shall never get at the truth. If I recur again and again to the problem, it is because the deeper I go into these incidents of the past, the more exciting and baffling grows the mystery"[1]

"One Mahatma, writing me about some occult business, speaks of it — the H.P.B. body — as 'the old appearance'; again in 1876 he writes about 'it and the Brother inside it'; another Master asks me — *à propos* of a terrific fit of anger to which I had (unintentionally) provoked H.P.B. 'Do you want to kill the body?'; and the same one, in a note of 1875, speaks of 'those who represent us in the shell' — the underscoring of the word being his."[2]

"There were intervals when her body was not occupied by the writing Mahatmas; at least I assume it to be so, although I have sometimes been even tempted to suspect that none of us, her colleagues, ever knew the normal H.P.B. at all, but that we just dealt with an artificially animated body, a sort of perpetual psychic mystery, from which the proper *jiva* was killed out at the battle of Mentana, when she received those five wounds and was picked out of a ditch for dead. There is nothing intrinsically impossible in this theory."[3]

"I have noted above how various Mahatmas, in writing to me about H.P.B. and her body, spoke of the latter as a shell occupied by one of themselves. In my Diary of 1878, I find entered under date of October 12, and in the H.P.B. manuscript of Mahatma 'M,' the following: 'H.P.B. talked with W. alone until 2 after midnight. He confessed he saw three DISTINCT individualities in her. He knows it. Does not wish to say so to Olcott for fear H.S.O. will make fun of him!!!' The underscorings and points of exclamation are copied literally. The 'W.' mentioned was Mr, Wimbridge, who was then our guest.

"To account for an entry made by another person in my Diary, I must explain that when I left New York on professional business.., the daily record was written up by 'H.P.B.,' the noun of multitude. In the entry of October 13 the same hand, after specifying the seven visitors who called that evening, writes of one of them: 'Dr. Pike, looking at H.P.B. several times, started and said that no one in the world impressed him so much. Once he sees in H.P.B. a girl of 16, at another an old woman of 100, and again a man with a beard!'

"On October 22, the same hand writes: 'H.P.B. left them (our visitors of that evening) in the dining-room and retired with H.S.O. to the library to write letters. N—— (a certain Mahatma) left watch and in came S—— (another adept), the latter with orders from ∴ to complete all by the first day of December' (for our departure for India).

"On November 9, in another modified H.P.B. script, is written: 'Body sick and no hot water to bathe it. Nice caboose.' November 12, in the 'M' script: 'H.P.B. played a trick on me by suddenly *fainting*, to the great dismay of Bates and Wim. Used the greatest will-power to put up the body on its legs.'

"November 14, in the same handwriting: 'N—— decamped and M. walked in (from and into the H.P.B. body is meant). Came with definite orders from ∴ *Have to go* at the latest from 15 to 20 Dec.' (to India). November 29, another Mahatma writes that he had 'answered the Russian Aunt.' ... Finally, not to dwell upon one subject too long, on November 30, a third Mahatma writes: 'Belle Mitchell came at 12 and took away the S—— (Mahatma M.) for a walk and drive. Went to Macy's. Had to materialise rupees. H.P.B. came home at 4.'

"I have also various letters from the Mahatmas alluding to H.P.B. in her own individual capacity, sometimes speaking very frankly about her peculiarities, good and bad."[4] "They would also speak about the absent H.P.B., distinguishing her from the physical body they had borrowed from her."[5] "As I understood it, she herself had loaned her body as one might loan one's typewriter, and had gone off on other occult business that she could transact in her astral body, a certain group of Adepts occupying and maneuvering the body by turns."[6] In fact, H.P.B. said as much when she and Colonel Olcott were in London *en route* to India, in January, 1879:

"The next evening, after dinner H.P.B. explained to ourselves and two visitors the duality of her personality and the law which it illustrated. She admitted without qualification that it was a fact that she was one person at one moment and another the next. She gave us an astounding bit of proof in support of her assertion. As we sat chatting in the gloaming, she silent near the window with her two hands resting on her knees, she presently called us and looked down at her hands. One of them was as white, as sculpturesque as usual; but the other was the longer hand of a man, covered with the brown skin of the Hindu; and on looking wonderingly into her face, we saw that her hair and eyebrows had also changed colour, and from fair brown had become jetty black! Say it was a hypnotic *maya*, yet what a fine one it was; produced without the utterance of a word by way of suggestion! It may have been a *maya*; for I recollect that the next morning her hair was still much darker than naturally, and her eyebrows quite black. She noticed this herself on looking into the mirror in the drawing-room, and remarking to me that she had forgotten to remove all traces of the change, she turned away, passed her hands over her face and hair two or three times, and, facing me again, was her natural self once more."[7]

"I have used the word 'obsession,' but am well aware of its wretched insufficiency in this case. Both 'obsession' and 'possession' have been made to signify the troubling of a living person by evil spirits or demons.... Yet what other term is available in English? Why did not the Early Fathers invent a more decent word to signify the possession, control, occupancy or overshadowing of a person by good spirits, than that of 'filling'? 'And they were filled with the Holy Ghost, and began to speak with other tongues, as the spirit gave them utterance.'[8]... The word 'epistasis' will not do for us; for that means 'inspection, superintendence, command, management,' which does not cover the case. Epiphany is not much better, *epiphaneia* being a shining upon, manifestation, etc. We have no word; yet one is greatly needed at this stage of our psychical research, and for it we must go to the East.

"This occupancy by living persons of another living person's body, though so outside our Western experience that we have no word for it is, like all else in psychological science, known and defined in India. *Avesa* (pronounced Ahveysha) is the act of possessing, i.e., entering and controlling, a human body belonging to a human being (*jiva*).

"It is of two kinds: when the Adept's own *amsa*, or astral body is withdrawn from his physical body and introduced into the other person's body, it is then called *Svarupavesa*; but when by his mere *sankalpa* (will-power) he influences, broods over, or controls that other person's body to do that which would otherwise be beyond its power, e.g., to speak an unlearnt foreign tongue, to understand unfamiliar branches of knowledge, to instantly disappear from the sight of bystanders, to transform itself into a terrifying shape, as of a serpent or a ferocious animal, then the thing is called *Sahty avesa*.

"This gives us all we need; and so, as we took 'Epiphany' from the Greek, why should we not agree to adopt the easy word *Avesa* from the Sanskrit, since it is ready to our hand, and means the very thing that we toddling babes in the nursery of adeptship, must have to get on with in our studies?

It applies only to the physical commerce between two living persons, or to the overshadowing and inspiration of a living person by a superior spiritual entity; and must not be degraded to signify the occupancy of a medium's body or its control for the production of phenomena, by a dead man's soul. That is called *grahana*, and the elementary (dead man's soul) gr&ham (pronounced grah-hum), the same word being used for the occupancy of a living body by an elemental, or Nature-spirit."⁹

Colonel Olcott proceeds to discuss *Avesa* and various forms of occupancy of bodies by others than the original owner, which those who care to may read in Chapter XVI of *Old Diary Leaves*, Vol. I. It will be of interest here to quote from "A Hindu Chela's Diary," which Mr. W. Q. Judge published in *The Path* of 1886, and which was reprinted in *The Theosophist* of June, 1928.

"X. came to see us. He never speaks of himself, but as 'this body.' He told me that he had first been in the body of a fakir who, upon having his hand disabled by a shot received while passing the fortress Bhurtpore, had to change his body and choose another, the one he was now in. A child of about seven years was dying at that time, and so before the complete physical death, this fakir had entered the body and afterward used it as his own. He is, therefore, doubly not what he seems to be. As a fakir he had studied Yoga science for 65 years; but that study having been arrested at the time he was disabled, leaving him unequal to the task he had to perform, he had to choose this other one. In his present body he is 53 years old, and consequently the inner X. is 118 years old.... In the night I heard him talking with Kunala, and found that each had the same Guru, who himself is a very great Adept, whose age is 300 years, although in appearance he seems to be only 40!...

"After I had finished my work and was preparing to return here, a wandering fakir met me and asked if he could learn from me the proper road to Karli. I directed him, and he then put to me some questions that looked as if he knew what had been my business, and several of his questions were apparently directed to getting me to tell him a few things Kunala had told me just before leaving Benares, with an injunction of secrecy. He left me saying: 'You do not know me, but we may see each other.' I got back last night and saw only X., to whom I related the incident with the fakir, and he said that it was none other than Kunala himself using the fakir's body who said those things, and if I were to see that fakir again he would not remember me and would not be able to repeat his questions, as he was for the time being taken possession of for the purpose by Kunala, who often performs such things. I asked him if Kunala really entered the fakir's body, and X. replied that, if I meant to ask if he had really and in fact entered the fakir's person, the answer was no; but if I meant to ask if Kunala had overcome the fakir's senses, substituting his own, the answer was yes, leaving me to make my own conclusions. [A case of *Saktyavesa*.]

"I was fortunate enough yesterday to be shown the process pursued in either entering an empty body or in using one which has its own occupant. I found that in both cases it was the same.... By any person but Kunala I would not have allowed my own body to have been made use of for the experiment. But I felt perfectly safe, that he would not only let me in again, but also that he would not permit any stranger, man or *gandharva*, to come in after him.

We went to —— and he.... The feeling was that I had suddenly stepped out into freedom. He was beside me, and at first I thought that he had but begun. But he directed me to look, and there on the mat I saw my body, apparently unconscious. As I looked, the body of myself opened its eyes and arose. It was then superior to me, for Kunala's informing power moved and directed it. It seemed even to speak to me. Around it, attracted by those magnetic influences, wavered and moved astral shapes, that vainly tried to whisper in the ear or to enter by the same road. In vain I They seemed to be pressed away by the air or surroundings of Kunala. Turning to look at him, and expecting to see him in a state of *samadhi*, he was smiling as if nothing, or at the very most but a part of his power, had been taken away.... Another instant and I was myself again, the mat felt cool to my touch, the *bhuts* were gone, and Kunala bade me rise." [A case of *Svarupavesa*.]

A contemporary of H. P. B. to whom Avesa occurred, at least for a time, was Babu Mohini M. Chatterji. H. P. B. wrote to Mr. Sinnett, late in 1883, that "Olcott will probably sail for England on various business, and Mahatma K. H. sends his *chela*, under the guise of Mohini Mohun Chatterji, to explain to the London Theosophists of the Secret Section every or *nearly every* mooted point.... Do not make the mistake of taking *the Mohini you knew* for the Mohini who will come. There is more than one *Maya* in this world, of which neither you nor your friends... is cognisant. The ambassador will be invested with an *inner* as well as with an *outer* clothing.* *Dixit*." [10]

In *The Path* of August, 1892, is published a letter of hers, in which she says: "These things were done because I alone was responsible for the issues, I alone had to bear the karma in case of failure, and no reward in case of success... I saw the T. S. would be smashed, or that I had to offer myself as the scapegoat for atonement. It is the latter I did. The T. S. lives — I am *killed*, killed in my honour, fame, name, in everything H. P. B. held near and dear, for the body is mine, and I feel acutely through it.... False? No one of us was false.... I may err in my powers as H. P. B. I have not worked and toiled for forty years, playing parts, risking my future rewards, and taking karma upon this unfortunate appearance, to serve them, without being permitted to have some voice in the matter. H. P. B. is not infallible. H. P. B. is an old, rotten, sick, worn-out body, but it is the best I can have in this cycle. Hence follow *the path I show* — the Masters that are behind, and do not follow me or my Path. When I am dead and gone in this body, then you will know the whole truth. Then will you know that I have *never*, never, been false to anyone, nor have I deceived anyone; but had many a time to allow them to deceive themselves." [12]

If there could still exist any doubt as to the fact that Helena Petrovna Blavatsky remained in touch with the H. P. B. body, surely it would be dispelled by the vehement Russian patriotism and the adherence to the Greek Orthodox Church which H. P. B. avowed to the end of her life, as seen in the previous chapter. However, it was the Augoeides, not the personality, of Helena Petrovna Blavatsky, which kept the contact, a state of affairs depicted in her statement to Mr. Sinnett in 1882: "I hope Mrs. Gordon will not dishonour by *evoking* me with some medium. Let her rest assured that it will never be my spirit nor anything of me — not even my shell, since this is gone long ago." [13]

One wonders *when* that shell disappeared. If a guess might be hazarded, it would be that Mme Blavatsky personally held on to the body, more or less fully, after its "death" at the battle of Mentana, 1867, until the great "psycho-physiological change" at Philadelphia in 1875. It will be remembered that Master Serapis wrote to Colonel Olcott at that time: "Her powers are at present in a state of transition," and added that the Colonel should try

---

* See also the story, "if it be a story," says the author, which appeared in *The London Forum* of November, 1934, entitled "Migdoi Carnot."

to "bring her out before the world in her true light not of an Adept but an intellectual writer." Henceforward Mme Blavatsky was no longer the real occupant of the body, but only one of a number of occupants who utilised it. One of her statements in a letter to Colonel Olcott of February 24, 1888, seems to bear out this theory. She says: "Babaji gave up his personality when sent to Simla to Sinnett, as I used to do in America and earlier."[14] And it is to be noted that Babaji also met the Dweller on the Threshold.*

When, in India, Messrs. A. P. Sinnett and A. O. Hume came into close relation with H.P.B. and asked for communications from the Adepts through her agency, misunderstandings and trouble soon arose. After a specially unpleasant incident at Simla the Master Koot Hoomi wrote to Mr. Sinnett, in the autumn of 1881:

"I am painfully aware of the fact that the habitual incoherence of her statements — especially when excited — and her strange ways make her in your opinion a very undesirable transmitter of our messages. Nevertheless, kind brothers, once that you have learned the truth, once told that this unbalanced mind, the seeming incongruity of her speeches and ideas, her nervous excitement, all that in short is so calculated to upset the feelings of sober-minded people, whose notions of reserve and manners are shocked by such strange outbursts of what they regard as her temper, and which so revolt you — once that you know that nothing of it is due to any fault of hers, you may perchance be led to regard her in quite a different light.

"Notwithstanding the fact that the time is not yet ripe to let you entirely into the secret; and that you are hardly yet prepared to understand the great Mystery, even if told of it; owing to the great injustice and wrong done, I am empowered to allow you a glimpse behind the veil.

"This state of hers is intimately connected with her occult training in Tibet, and due to her being sent out alone into the world to gradually prepare the way for others. After nearly a century of fruitless search, our chiefs had to avail themselves of the only opportunity to send out a European *body* upon European soil, to serve as a connecting link between that country and our own. You do not understand? Of course not.

"Please, then, remember what she tried to explain, and what you gathered tolerably well from her, namely the fact of the *seven* principles in the *complete* human being. Now, no man or woman unless he be an initiate of the

---

* H. P. B. speaks of this in Letters of H. P. Blavatsky to A, P. Sinnett, p. 187.

'fifth circle,' can leave the precincts of Bod-Las [Tibet] and return back into the world in his integral whole — if I may use the expression. *One*, at least, of his seven satellites has to remain behind for two reasons: the first, to form the necessary connecting link, the wire for transmission — the second, as the safest warranter that certain things will never be divulged. She is no exception to the rule, and you have seen another exemplar — a highly intellectual man — who had to leave one of his skins behind; hence, is considered highly eccentric. The bearing and status of the remaining *six* depend upon the inherent qualities, the psycho-physiological peculiarities of the person, especially upon the idiosyncrasies transmitted by what modern science calls 'atavism.'

"Acting in accordance with my wishes, my Brother M. made to you through her a certain offer, if you remember. You had but to accept it, and at any time you liked you would have had for an hour or more the real *bai-tchooly* to converse with, instead of the psychological cripple you generally have to deal with now."[15]

H. P. B. herself wrote to Mr. Sinnett, March 17, 1882: "Now, do you really think that you know me, Mr. Sinnett? Do you believe that, because you have fathomed — as you think — my physical crust and brain; that, shrewd analyst of *human* nature though you may be, you have ever penetrated even beneath the first cuticles of my *Real Self*? You would gravely err, if you did. I am held by all of you as *untruthful*, because hitherto I have shown the world only the true *exterior* Madame Blavatsky. It is just as if you complained of the *falseness* of a moss and weed covered, and *mud*-covered, stony and rugged rock, for writing outside '*I* am *not* moss covered and mud plastered; Your eyes deceive you, for you are unable to see beneath the crust,' etc. You must understand the allegory. It is not *boasting*, for I do not say whether *inside* that unprepossessing rock there is a palatial residence or a humble hut. What I say is this: you *do not know* me; for whatever there is inside it, it is *not what you think* it is; and to judge of me, therefore, as of one *untruthful* is the greatest mistake in the world, besides being a flagrant injustice. I (the inner real 'I') am in prison and cannot show myself as I am, with all the desire I may have to. Why, then, should I be held responsible for the *outward* jail-door and *its* appearance, when I have neither built nor yet decorated it?... No; you *do not hate* me; you only feel a friendly, indulgent, a kind of *benevolent contempt* for H. P. B. You are right there, so far *as you knew her*, the one who is ready to fall to pieces. Perchance you may find out yet your mistake concerning the other — the well hidden party."[16]

This explanation seems to add a few more veils to the mystery. And so we must leave the question, "Who was H. P. B.?" — with one last utterance of the Sphinx, written in her author's copy of *The Voice of the Silence*:

H. P. B. to H. P. Blavatsky with my kind regards.

Appendix

Chronological Table

1831
Born at Ekaterinoslaw, August 12 (Russian, July 30-31).

1834
Sister Vera born.

1842
Brother Leonide born.
Mother died, went to live at grandfather's.

1844-45
Visited London with father.
Also France and Germany.

1848
Married at Djellallogly, July 7.
Fled in October.
Travelled with Countess Kisselev.
Egypt — the Copt, Paulos Metamon.

1849
Paris. Mesmerist wanted her, fled.

1850
Constantinople.
Found Metrovitch wounded.
Father married second time.
Toured Europe with Countess Bagration.
Visited Germany.

1851
New Year at Paris. London, lived on Cecil Street, Strand, and at Mivart's Hotel.
August 12, met Master in Hyde Park.
Canada to New Orleans.
Through Texas to Mexico.
Received legacy.

1952
Reached Bombay at end of year, with Englishman and Hindu.

1853
First attempt on Tibet.
Prevented by British Resident at Nepal.
South India.
Java.

SECOND TABLE

Dates on "a scrap of paper" found at Adyar by Annie Besant "in writing I do not recognise, and unsigned. I give them for what they are worth. — A. B."

Athens.
Smyrna.
Asia Minor.
First attempt on Tibet failed.

Met her Master in London.
South America.

Through Pacific Islands to India.
Second attempt on Tibet failed.

Returned to England, via China, Japan, America.

Singapore.	
England, left owing to Crimean War.	
America at end of year.	

1854

New York to Chicago.	United States.
Over the Rockies with caravan.	
San Francisco.	

1855

America to India, via Japan and the Straits.	Central America.
Reached Calcutta.	

1856

Lahore met Kulwein and friends.	To India via Egypt.
Through Kashmir to Lehin Ladakh.	
Second attempt on Tibet.	
Over border with Tartar Shaman.	

1857

Master told her to leave India, because of coming trouble.	Third attempt on Tibet, just before Sepoy Rebellion.
Madras to Java in Dutch ship.	Failed.

1858

London.	Returned to Russia.
France.	
Germany.	
Russia, Pskoff, end of year.	

1859

Pskoff.	
St. Petersburg.	
Rougodevo.	

1860

Wound reopened, very ill.	
Spring left for Tiflis.	
Three weeks' journey by coach from Moscow to Tiflis. First met Illarion.	

1861

Resided at Tiflis.	In Tiflis from 1861-1863.
Metrovitch and wife there.	

1862

Roamed about Georgia, Imeretia, and Mingrelia.	
Had Passport, dated August 23, "to proceed to Provinces of Tauris, Cherson and Pskoff."	
Bought house at Ozoorgetty.	

1863

Very ill at Ozoorgetty, sent to Tiflis.	Egypt.
	Persia.

Spent 3 1/2 days with General Blavatsky there. (She says a year in letter to Biliere-French.)

1864

Kiev Servia.
Karpat Mts.
Italy, Greece, Egypt, Tibet.

Crossed Central Asia to Tibet.
Successful.

1865

In Tibet with Master

1866

In Tibet with Master

Flying visit to Italy.
Back to India and the north.
To the Kuenlun Mts., Lake Palti, and Tibet.

1867

Italy.
Took child to Bologna.
To Russia, child died.
Returned to Italy on same Passport.
Wounded at Battle of Mentana, November 2.
Florence, about Christmas.

1868

Florence to Antemari.
Toward Belgrad, where in mts. had to wait.
Constantinople, passing through Serbia and Karpat Mts. ("Double Murder.")
Back to Tibet.
First met Mahatma K. H.

1869

In Tibet with Master.
Signora Teresina Metrovitch died (probably) April 7, 1870

1870

Metrovitch sent to Egypt by aunt, Mme Fadeef, to look for H. P. B.
November 11, aunt received K. H.'s letter.
December H. P. B. crossed from India, in one of first steamers through Suez Canal.

1871

Cyprus, saw Illarion, who foretold death of Metrovitch.
Returning ship Eunumia blown up, June 21.
Alexandria.
Cairo — Miss Emma Cutting (Coulomb).
Societe Spirite.
The Copt-Paulos Metamon.

1872	1872
Metrovitch died April 19.	Returned to Russia via Egypt and Greece.
Cairo till April.	
Syria, Palestine, Palmyra.	
Odessa, Russia — May, 18 moons after letter.	
To Bukharest to visit Mme Popesco.	

1873	
March.	Odessa to Paris.
June.	Paris to New York, ordered.
July 7.	Arrival in New York.
July 15.	Father died.
Oct. 29.	Cable from sister Elise, re inheritance.

1874	
June 22.	Articles of Partnership in a farm on Long Island, N.Y.
July 1.	Partnership begins, H.P.B. goes to farm to live.
Sept. 17.	Colonel Olcott goes to Chittenden, Vt., to Eddy home.
Oct. 14.	H.P.B. goes there. Returned to 124 E. 16th Street, N.Y.
Nov.	She wrote to Colonel, asking him to get her journalistic work. He called on her in New York, at 236 Irving Place.
Dec.	They are both in Hartford, Conn., conferring about his book People from the Other World, with his publisher there.

1875	
Jan.	Colonel's address in New York, 7 Beekman Street. H.P.B. fell on the sidewalk in New York and injured her knee.
Jan. 4	Colonel arrived at Philadelphia, where H.P.B. was already, and joined her at Mrs. Martin's, in Girard Street. They investigated the Holmes mediums and Dr. Child. Later a Committee of Investigation formed.
Jan. 25	Colonel held his last stance in Philadelphia.
Jan. 29	Colonel at Havanna, New York, to investigate medium, Mrs. Compton.
Feb.	"John King" begins his own portrait for General Lippitt.
Feb. 13	H.P.B. writes General L. that a bedstead fell on her leg as she was trying to move it.
Feb. 22	She writes General L. leg is no better.
March 1	Colonel is in Hartford; his book will come out in ten days. Colonel goes to Boston also.
March 9.	H.P.B. writes General L. she is very sick and miserable; doesn't know why (leg). Wishes she were "home upstairs."
March 9.	Colonel taken as Neophyte. Letter sent to him by Tuitit Bey.
March 16.	H.P.B. is ordered to expose Dr. Child.
March 22.	M.C. Betanelly writes General L. they are living at 3420 Sansom Street; (therefore are married) that he hopes to open a big trade with Russia; that wonderful manifestations take place in the house daily.
March 24.	H.P.B. writes General L. that Colby of the Banner has refused her article, and asks him to call upon Mr. E.G. Brown, editor of the Spiritual Scientist in Boston, to whom she has sent it, and urge him to publish it. Olcott's book is creating a furore.

April 2.	H. P. B. in Boston; sent General L. John King's picture from there.
April 12.	She is in Philadelphia; also Colonel, from 4-22 at least.
Before 17.	She writes General L. leg is worse; John had cured it and ordered three days' rest. She did not rest it, result worse. She enclosed Luxor circular.
April 17.	Luxor circular, "Important to Spiritualists," appears in the Spiritual Scientist.
April 17.	She writes General L. that she must go to Riverhead, April 26, as her lawsuit is coming on then; so can't go to Boston.
May 1.	H. P. B. writes General L. from New York that she has won her lawsuit and saved $5000 of what she has lost. But further complications. Returning at once to Philadelphia.
May 21.	Paralysis of leg has set in. She has been entrusted with task of instructing him (H. S. O.) but wishes More had been instead. Lodge will send article this week, more to follow.
May 24.	She writes Aksakoff that disaster has come upon them; panic in country; Olcott's book not selling.
May 26.	She sends Betanelly away. Amputation of leg threatened.
May 27.	Notice in Sp. Sc. that two or more great "Oriental Spiritualists" have passed through New York and Boston to California and Japan. H. P. B. says they are Hilarion and Atrya, and that M. is appearing daily in Kama Rupa.
May 27.	"Budget of Good News" also appears in Sp. Sc.t stating that Colonel Olcott's "Miracle Club" is progressing favourably. H. P. B. comments upon it, that she is ordered to tell the truth about phenomena, and now her martydrom will begin. Master Serapis writes to Colonel that she is in great danger, must descend into —— and conquer or die; is facing the "dreaded one." "At(rya) and Ill(arion) passed through New York and Boston, thence to California and Japan, back."
June 18.	Betanelly writes General —— she is very ill; trances last hours; doctors have thrice declared her dead; but she is reported as going to the "spirit room" at night.
June 19.	She writes General L. she is "tired of all this dying business. Wishes she could die once for all."
June 22.	Master Serapis writes to Colonel that "her cup of bitterness is full" and asks Colonel to comfort her.
June 22.	"Notice to Mediums," re going to Russia appears in Sp. Sc.
June 25.	Master Serapis asks Colonel to write to her daily.
June 30.	She writes to General L. that her health is still very poor, but danger is over, and she must go to Boston, though lame. Colonel Olcott is in Boston.
July 7.	She writes General L. she is leaving on a mission to set right damage done to R. D. Owen by Dr. Child. Will see him in Boston.
July 15.	"My first occult shot " — A Few Questions to 'Hiraf' — written in Boston. She and Colonel are guests of Mr. and Mrs. Houghton. They investigate Mrs. Thayer's phenomena. Master Serapis writes to Colonel : —"The three of you (Brown) must work out your future together. Try to help the poor broken-hearted woman. Master Serapis writes to Colonel : —"Task in Boston is finished. Do not let her return to Philadelphia, but take her to New York with you."

Aug.	H.P.B. had rooms in New York, first at 23, then 46 Irving Place. She and Colonel investigating Mrs. Young's phenomena.
Sept. 7.	Meeting in her rooms, at which the formation of a Society was broached.
Sept. 10.	She writes Aksakoff that there are terrible attacks on them from all sides.
Sept. 18.	Second meeting on formation of a Society: Committee on Preamble and By-Laws reported; Resolution to call it the Theosophical Society.
Sept. 20.	She is at the Corson's, in Ithaca. Remains for about a month.
Sept. 23.	"An Open Letter Such as Few Can Write — Mme Blavatsky to Her Correspondents." In Sp. Sc.
Nov. 17.	Inaugural Address of Colonel Olcott as President T. S., Mott Memorial Hall, New York.

1877
	Isis Unveiled published, September or October, at New York.

1878
May 25.	Divorced from M. C. Betanelly.
July 8.	Became an American citizen by taking the Oath of Allegiance to U.S.A. Dec. 18. H.P.B. and Colonel sail from New York, for India.

1879
Feb. 16.	Arrive at Bombay, having stayed a fortnight in England en route.
April.	They visit Carli Caves and Rajputana.
Oct.	The Theosophist is founded.
Dec. 4-30.	They visit Mr. and Mrs. A. P. Sinnett, at Allahabad.

1880
May 7.	They sailed from Bombay for Ceylon with a party of six F. T. S.
May 25.	They took Panchasila (Buddhist Five Vows) at Galle, Ceylon.
July 14.	They sail from Galle, to return to India.
Sept. 8-Oct. 21.	At Simla, visiting the Sinnetts. A. O. Hume sends the first letter to Master K. H. through H.P.B. and receives a reply from Mahatma K. H., the beginning of The Mahatma Letters.
Dec. 1.	They go to Allahabad to visit the Sinnetts. H.P.B.'s Caves and Jungles of Hindustan published in Russian.

1881
Feb. 19.	Arhat Illarion visited Founders at Bombay, en route to Tibet.
March.	Mr. and Mrs. Sinnett go to England.
June.	Mr. Sinnett returns.
Sept. 30-Dec. 1.	Master Morya visits the Founders, in his physical body, at their house in Bombay.
Oct.	H.P.B. visits Simla, Umballa, Dehra Dun.
Nov.	H.P.B. is at Allahabad for a few days. Sinnett's Occult World is published in England.

1882
Jan.	Mrs. Sinnett returns to India; both visit the Founders at Bombay.
March.	H.P.B. visits the Sinnetts at Allahabad for a few days.
April 6.	H.P.B. joins Colonel at Calcutta.

April 19.	They sail for Madras.
April 23.	Arrive at Madras.
May 3.	They go down Buckingham Canal by boat, found Nellore Lodge.
May 31.	They visit Huddlestone Gardens at Adyar, to inspect it. Decision is made to buy it as the future Headquarters of the T. S.
June 8.	They are back in Bombay.
June 16-24.	They visit Baroda.
Sept.	H. P. B. is in Sikkim with the Masters.
Nov.	She is at Darjeeling with the Masters.
Dec. 17.	The Founders leave Bombay to take up residence at Adyar, Madras.
Dec. 19.	Arrive at Adyar. Theosophical Books published: Dr. Anna Kingsford's The Perfect Way, Hints on Esoteric Theosophy, by A. O. Hume.

1883

Feb.	The Sinnetts spend a few days at Adyar, en route to England.
July 17-Sept. 16.	H. P. B. is at Ootacamund, at General Morgan's home. Sinnett's Esoteric Buddhism is published in England.

1884

Feb. 7.	H. P. B. left for Wadhwan, Varel, etc., en route to Bombay.
Feb. 20.	H. P. B. and Colonel sail for Europe from Bombay, with Mohini M. Chatterji and Padshah, on S.S. Chandemagore.
March.	Nice, Paris.
April.	London at the Sinnett's.
May.	The Coulombs expelled from Adyar, by the Board of Control in charge there.
June, July.	H. Schmiechen painted portraits of the two Masters, in London.
July 24.	H. P. B. and her party arrived at Elberfeld, the Gebhard's home.
July 26.	V. S. Solovyoff arrived there.
July 31.	F. W. H. Myers and his brother arrived.
Sept. 10.	Damodar wrote of a Missionary Plot at Madras, with the Coulombs.
Sept. 15.	H. Schmiechen arrived to paint H. P. B.'s portrait.
Sept. 15.	Cable from Madras re Coulomb attack.
Sept. 28.	Mme N. A. Fadeef left, having visited H. P. B.
Oct. 2.	The Sinnetts arrived to take part in a Council re Coulomb attack.
Oct. 20.	Colonel Olcott sailed for Madras.
Oct. 31.	H. P. B. sailed from Liverpool to Egypt, with Mr. and Mrs. Cooper-Oakley, on the S.S. Clan MacCarthy. C. W. L. joined them in Egypt.
Dec. 17.	They arrive at Colombo.
Dec. 21.	They arrive at Madras. The Preliminary Report of the Society for Psychical Research is published. H. P. B.'s Mysterious Tribes of the Nilgiris is published in Russian; The Idyl of the White Lotus, by Mabel Collins; Man: Fragments of Forgotten History, by Two Chelas (M. M. Chatterji and Mrs. Holloway).

1885

Jan.	Hodgson is at Adyar, investigating for The Society for Psychical Research.
Jan. 14.	Colonel and C. W. L. sail for Burma.

Jan. 28.	Cable sent to Colonel to recall him, owing to H.P.B.'s illness.
Feb. 5.	H.P.B. on the point of death.
March 19.	Colonel returns to Adyar.
March 29.	H.P.B. resigns as Recording Secretary of the T.S.
March 31.	She sails for Europe, in the S.S. Tiber with Babaji, Dr. Franz Hartmann and Mary Flynn.
April-July.	Naples.
July.	Switzerland, en route to WUrzburg.
Aug.	Würzburg, Germany, where the Sinnetts visit her, also Miss Arundale.
Dec. 31.	The Report of the Society for Psychical Research is published and received by H.P.B. through Sellin. H.P.B.'s Voice of the Silence is published; Sinnett's novel, Karma; Mabel Collins's Light on the Path.

1886

May 8.	H.P.B. leaves Würzburg.
May-June.	She is at Elberfeld with the Gebhards.
June 24.	She arrives at Ostend, Belgium. Sinnett's Incidents in the Life of Mme Blavatsky is published, also his novel United.

1887

May 1.	H.P.B. left Ostend for London.
May 14.	She founds Blavatsky Lodge, London.
Sept.	She founds the magazine Lucifer.

1888

H.P.B. established the Esoteric School of Theosophy. She was awarded the Subba Row Medal for 1888, as having contributed the best Theosophical essay of the year —"The Esoteric Character of the Gospels," published in Lucifer. The Secret Doctrine was published; also Mabel Collins's novel, The Blossom and the Fruit.

1889

H.P.B.'s Key to Theosophy was published. Colonel Olcott visited Europe, arriving in London, September 24.

1891

May 8. H.P.B. died in London.

"A Modern Priestess Of Isis"

his book was published in Russian by V. S. Solovyoff, after the death of H. P. B.; therefore her sister, Mme Vera Jelihovsky, took up the cudgels on her behalf and replied in a pamphlet called *H. P. Blavatsky and a Modern Priest of Truth*. She included in this pamphlet Solovyoff's letters to H. P. B., which letters show him to be, not a "cool-headed critic engaged on scientific enquiry," but an ardent seeker and disciple, eager for instruction and aid. Solovyoff's book was later translated into English by Walter Leaf, with a Prefatory Note by Henry Sidgwick, on behalf of the Society for Psychical Research in England. The following quotation from the Translator's Preface demonstrates the spirit of the translator, and speaks for itself:

"The evidence offered by Mr. Solovyoff falls into two distinct classes, which require separate consideration. There is, firstly, that which rests upon his own narrative; secondly, that which consists of documentary evidence, chiefly in the shape of letters written by Mme Blavatsky herself.... (These letters form part of his narrative.)

"When we come to Mr. Solovyoff's own narrative, the documentary evidence, important though it is, takes second place; though it may either confirm or contradict the narrative, it is not such as to form by itself a proof positive of Mme Blavatsky's fraudulence. The vital question is, does Mr. Solovyoff tell the truth....? If he does, then, of course, there is an end of theosophy as a system of doctrine based upon communication from hidden Masters, of whom Mme Blavatsky was the prophet.... So far, then, as Mme Jelihovsky's own testimony goes, we shall not allow it to weigh against Mr. Solovyoff's high position in Russian society and literature. (!)

"The only question for us is whether any of his letters, quoted by Mme Jelihovsky, are so inconsistent with his narrative as to lead us to refuse him credence. It is clear that these letters and Mr. Solovyoff's own narrative present two very different pictures of his mental attitude during 1884 and 1885. The narrative represents Mr. Solovyoff, with the exception of short phases when he was carried away in spite of himself, as a cool-headed critic engaged on a scientific enquiry. The letters show that he was more than coquetting with belief during the greater part of the period. Readers have the materials for a judgment before them, and must decide for themselves as to the bearing of this on Mr. Solovyoff's credibility.... Letter marked (B) does, so far as I can judge, imply a real inconsistency with Mr. Solovyoff's narrative; it implies that he has not correctly represented the mental attitude in which he found himself after the Würzburg conversations. I confess that I am not satisfied with his own explanation that the whole letter is merely bantering. In fact, under the circumstances the 'bantering tone' itself requires explanation. It seems to me the letter of a man who is 'hedging.'... (However, Mr. Leaf then proceeds to explain this away.)

"Thus, though Mr. Solovyoff's letters give us a decidedly different picture of his mental attitude from that drawn by the narrative, I cannot see that either they or Mme Jelihovsky's statements can cast any material doubt on the truth of the facts which he states....(!)

"To the vast majority of sensible people, the question of Mme Blavatsky's honesty has already been so convincingly disposed of, as to remove any *a priori* doubts concerning the veracity of any person who declares her an impostor. For them the simple assertion of a gentleman in Mr. Solovyoff's position is sufficient; as he cannot add to the force of evidence already unanswered and unanswerable; so there can be no presumption against him when he adds to its variety. (!)

"The correspondence with Mr. Aksakoff proves beyond the possibility of refutation, (1) that at one time, in spite of her subsequent vehement denials of the fact, Mme Blavatsky was a professed spiritualist in the ordinary sense of the word. She therefore adopted the 'theosophical' attitude of hostility to spiritualism only after 1874, and had recourse to deliberate falsehood to conceal the fact. (2) At this period she is entirely silent as to the Mahatmas who guided her action; her guardian and teacher is the 'pure spirit' John King, well known at the séances of Williams and other professional mediums in both hemispheres; he is her 'only friend' and thus occupies the place later taken by Morya and Koot Hoomi. With these two facts the whole legend, according to which she had, before her stay in America in

1874, received initiation and instruction from her Mahatmas in Thibet, and ever since stood in continuous relations with them, is shown to be a later fabrication. The foundation of her whole theosophical teaching is a mere lie" (Both these points have been cleared up in these *Personal Memoirs*.)

Out of 366 pages of the English edition of Solovyoff's book, 284 are taken up by his narrative. Appendix A consists of an *Abstract of Pamphlet* Entitled " *H.P. Blavatsky and a Modern Priest of Truth*, [11] *Reply of Madame Y. to Mr. V. S. Solovyoff*, by Mme Vera Jelihovsky. (Mme Jelihovsky was called Mme Y. by Solovyoff in his narrative.)

Her argument is that "Mr. Solovyoff has no right to write about Mme Blavatsky at all, for he knew very little of her. His whole acquaintance with her covered only six weeks in Paris, as much at Würzburg, and a few days at Elberfeld. Further, his ignorance of English made him incapable of studying her theosophical writings, the whole of which were, with the exception of *Isis Unveiled*, at that time untranslated....

"Mr. Solovyoff's statement that the 'phenomena are indissolubly bound up with theosophy' is untrue. I myself never laid any weight on these phenomena, though I have always admitted my sister's high gifts in the way of psychical powers.... Indeed, most of those who are now the chief supporters of theosophy — Mrs. Besant, Professor Bockh, Fullerton, Eyton, etc., have never seen any phenomena. Hartmann's *Talking Image of Urrur*, which Mme Blavatsky reprinted in *Lucifer*, is a satire on those who think that phenomena are of the essence of theosophy."

Mme Jelihovsky publishes in her pamphlet letters of V. S. Solovyoff to herself and to Mme Blavatsky, written in 1884 and 1885; and these letters present a very different picture of his mental state and opinions from that which he gives in his narrative afterwards, when he wished to dissociate himself from Mme Blavatsky in the minds of his orthodox Russian friends and circle of readers, because of the attack made on her by the Coloumbs and the Society for Psychical Research.

Appendix B is made up of a *Reply to Mme Jelihovsky's Pamphlet*, by Solovyoff. Appendix C, called *The Sources of Mme Blavatsky's Writings*, is by Wm. Emmette Coleman.

The book is introduced by a *Prefatory Note* by Henry Sidgwick, who says: "I am authorised by the Council of the Society for Psychical Research to state formally on their behalf that the present translation of Mr. Solovyoff's

Modern Priestess of Isis has been made and published with their approval.... When the contents of Mr. Solovyoff's book became known to the Council, it seemed clear that certain portions of it (the 'Confession' of Mme Blavatsky and her letters to Aksakoff) constituted an important supplement to the statement of the results of the inquiry into 'Theosophical phenomena' carried out by the Committee of the Society in 1884-5. Our original idea was to publish a translation of these portions in the supplement of our *Proceedings*; but on further consideration it seemed to us clearly desirable, if possible, that the greater part of Mr. Solovyoff's entertaining narrative should be made accessible to English readers.

"For such English readers as were likely to be interested in learning anything more about Mme Blavatsky would not so much desire additional proof that she was a charlatan — a question already judged and decided (how hastily!) — but rather some explanation of the remarkable success of her imposture.... Whether the Theosophical Society is likely to last much longer, I am not in a position to say; but even if it were to expire next year, its twenty years' existence would be a phenomenon of some interest for the historian of European society in the nineteenth century; and it is not likely that any book will be written throwing more light on its origin than *A Modern Priestess of Isis*." (!)

What a short-sighted judgment of the Theosophical Society and its Founder! Solovyoff's book is out-of-print and forgotten, while Mme Blavatsky's works are constantly more and more widely read and under stood. For instance, her "Confession," which Mr. Sidgwick considers" an important supplement " to the *Report* of the Society for Psychical Research that pronounced Mme Blavatsky a charlatan, moves Dr. Eugene Rollin Corson to say in his book, *Some Unpublished Letters of Helena Petrovna Blavatsky** "To the admirers of H. P. B. this document did not detract from their admiration for her or their devotion to her, but they certainly lamented the fact that she had made the confession to this insufferable cad " (Solovyoff). Dr. Corson devotes pages to the analysis of the " Confession" and declares: "The first part is real genius, and shows the literary artist at her best.... I know nothing like it in literature.... It is a glorious outburst against injustice with the hunted animal at bay. It is no 'confession,' but an heroic attack on her enemies. There is no admission of guilt of any kind; she has harmed no

* Pages 80-83.

one ; if left alone she is harmless ; but if attacked she will kill and die herself in the struggle, for death means nothing to her. If her enemies see the charlatan and the impostor in this, they have neither insight nor intuition."

Bibliography

H. P. B.'s Scrapbooks.	(Scrap.)
Isis Unveiled. London, 1910.	(Isis.)
Secret Doctrine. London, 1893.	(S. D.)
Caves and Jungles of Hindustan.	(Caves.)
Mysterious Tribes of the Nilgiris.	(Mys. Tribes)
A Modern Panarion.	(Mod. Pan.)
Archives of the Theosophical Society.	(Archives.)
H. S. Olcott's *Old Diary Leaves.*	(O. D. L.)
People from the Other World.	(P. O. W.)
The Mahatma Letters to *A. P. Sinnett.* Ed. by A. Trevor Barker.	(Mah. Let.)
Letters of H. P. Blavatsky to A. P. Sinnett. Ed. by A. Trevor Barker.	(Let. H.P.B.)
Some Unpublished Letters of Helena Petrovna Blavatsky. E. R. Corson.	(Cor. Let.)
Incidents in the Life of Madame Blavatsky. A. P. Sinnett. (Inc.)	(1913 ed.)
Reminiscences of H. P. Blavatsky. Countess Wachtmeister	(Rem.)
Hints on Esoteric Theosophy. A. O. Hume.	(Hints.)
A Modern Priestess of Isis. V, S. Solovyofif.	(M. P. I.)
The Golden Book of the Theosophical Society. C. Jinarajadasa.	(G. B.)
Early Teachings of the Masters of the Wisdom.	(E. T.)
Letters from the Masters of the Wisdom. I and II.	(Let. M. W.)
The Tibetan Book of the Dead. W. Y. Evans-Wentz.	(Tib. Book.)

Magazines

The Theosophist.	(Theos.)
The Path. "Letters of H. P. Blavatsky." By Mrs. C. Johnston.	(Path.)
Lucifer. "Helena Petrovna Blavatsky." By Mme Jelihovsky.	(Luc.)
The Canadian Theosophist.	(Can. Theos.)

References

Chapter I
[1] Let. H. P. B. — 149
[2] Inc. — 17
[3] Let. H. P. B. — 150
[4] Scrap. XX (Lillie) — 190
[5] Theos. (Pissareff) — Jan., 1913, 503
[6] Let. H. P. B. — 150
[7] Inc. — 38
[8] Let. H. P. B. — 150
[9] Ibid. — 160
[10] Ibid. — 159
[11] Luc. — Nov., 1894

Chapter II
[1] Theos. — April, 1884
[2] Hints — 120

Chapter III
[1] Inc. — 20, 21
[2] Ibid. — 19–20
[3] O. D. L., III (2nd Ed.) — 9
[4] Inc. — 21–30

Chapter IV
[1] Theos (Pissareff) — Jan., 1913
[2] M. P. I. — 229
[3] Scrap. XXII — 32
[4] Theos. (Pissareff) — Jan., 1913
[5] Inc. — 39
[6] Let. H. P. B. — 214
[7] Ibid. — 217
[8] Ibid. — 157
[9] Luc. — Nov., 1894
[10] Inc. — 41
[11] Ibid. — 40
[12] Ibid. — 41–45
[13] P. O. W. — 320
[14] Inc. — 42, 44
[15] Theos. — May, 1923
[16] Cor. Let. — 85
M. P. I. — 177

Chapter V
[1] Inc. — 42
[2] Theos. — July, 1913
[3] Theos. — Feb., 1909

Chapter VI
[1] Inc. — 44
[2] O. D. L., I — 432
[3] Isis, I — 382
[4] Theos. — April, 1884
[5] Scrap., I — 48
[6] P. O. W. — 328–332
[7] Isis, I. — 474

Chapter VII
[1] Isis, I — 546–548
[2] Ibid. — 595–599

Chapter VIII
[1] Let. H. P. B. — 150
[2] Ibid. — 150
[3] Rem. — 56–58

Chapter IX
[1] Inc. — 45–48
[2] Let. H. P. B. — 151
[3] Inc. — 48
[4] O. D. L., I — 459
[5] Inc. — 48, 49
[6] Theos. — April, 1893
[7] Inc. — 49, 50
[8] Let. H. P. B. — 151

Chapter X
[1] Isis, II — 598–602
[2] Ibid. — 626–628

Chapter XI
[1] Inc. — 55, 84
[2] Let. H. P. B. — 151
[3] O. D. L., II — Chapter IV
[4] Caves — Chap. II, III
[5] Let. H. P. B. — 153
[6] M. P. I. — 14
[7] Caves — 126, 127
[8] Ibid. — 121, 122
[9] Ibid. — 103, 104

Chapter XII
[1] Caves — 207

Chapter XIII
[1] Caves — 256–280

Chapter XIV
[1] Caves — Last Chapter

Chapter XV
[1] Isis, I — xi
[2] Ibid. — 42, 43
[3] Ibid. — 368, 369
[4] Ibid. — 141, 142
[5] Ibid. — 445, 446
[6] Ibid. — 463, 464

7 Isis, I	467–471	4 Isis, II	607–608
8 Ibid.	383	5 Ibid.	609, 610
9 Isis, II	622	6 Ibid.	615–617
10 Ibid.	606–607	7 Ibid.	618
11 Ibid.	621	8 Ibid.	617
12 Ibid.	611, 612	9 Theos.	March, 1887
13 Isis, I	561–567	10 Path	Jan., 1896
14 Mys. Tribes, Theos.	July, 1910		

Chapter XVI

1 Luc.	Nov., 1894
2 Inc.	63–65
3 Ibid.	67–70

Chapter XVII

1 Luc.	Nov., 1894
2 Inc.	70–75
3 Ibid.	100
4 Ibid.	102
5 Ibid.	99
6 Ibid.	105

Chapter XVIII

1 Luc.	Nov., 1894
2 Inc.	110–112
3 Ibid.	112
4 Ibid.	112–114
5 Let. H. P. B.	156
6 Luc.	Dec., 1894
7 Scrap. I	48
8 Inc.	115, 116
9 Theos.	May, 1887
Review of Sinnett's *United*.	
10 Inc.	117–119

Chapter XIX

1 Inc.	59
2 Ibid.	60
3 Ibid.	61
4 Ibid.	66, 67
5 Ibid.	81–84
6 Ibid.	72, 73
7 Ibid.	100, 101
8 Ibid.	114, 115
9 Ibid.	118
10 Ibid.	119
11 Ibid.	120

Chapter XX

1 Let. H. P. B.	151
2 Luc.	Dec., 1894
3 Let. H. P. B.	154, 155
4 Isis, II	308–315
5 Scrap. VII	30a
6 Isis, II	571, 572
7 Ibid.	629–633

Chapter XXI

1 Scrap. XIX (Lillie)	292
2 Scrap. XX (Lillie)	190
3 Tibetan Book of the Dead	7

Chapter XXII

1 Theos.	March, 1922
2 O. D. L., I	257–259
3 Ibid.	263
4 Ibid.	259
5 Mah. Let.	478–480
6 Theos.	June, 1883
Editorial Note on "Zoroastrianism"	
7 S. D., I	25, 26
8 Theos., "Reply VII"	Oct., 1883
9 S. D., I	38
10 O. D. L., I	262
11 O. D. L., II	59
12 Let. H. P. B.	76
13 Ibid.	32
14 Mah. Let.	480
15 Ibid.	22
16 Theos.	Feb., 1908
17 Mah. Let.	296
18 Inc.	115
19 Mah. Let.	422, 423
20 Early Teachings	ix, x, xi
21 Path	March, 1893
Theos.	Dec., 1907
22 Inc.	84

Chapter XXIII

1 Let. H. P. B.	144
2 Scrap. XIX (Lillie)	292
3 O. D. L., I	9, 263, 264
4 Let. H. P. B.	151–153
5 Let. M. W., I	59
6 Let. H. P. B.	151–153
7 Can. Theos.	June, 1927

Chapter XXIV

1 Scrap. XIX	292
2 Let. M. W., II (facsimile)	5
3 Let. H. P. B.	153
4 Ibid.	215
5 Ibid.	153
6 Inc.	124
7 Archives	
8 Inc.	125
9 Archives	
10 Inc.	129, 130
11 Ibid.	126, 127
12 Archives	
13 O. D. L., I	23
14 Inc.	129
15 Cor. Let.	33
16 O. D. L., I	458, 459
17 Let. H. P. B.	153, 154

18 O. D. L., I	28	5 P. O. W.	452
19 Luc.	Dec., 1894	6 Mod. P. I.	240
20 O. D. L., I	20	7 Archives	
21 Rem.	147	8 Cor. Let.	123
		9 Ibid.	127
		10 Ibid.	130
		11 Ibid.	165

Chapter XXV

1 Let. H. P. B.	148	12 Theos.	Feb., 1924
2 Ibid.	188, 189	13 G. B.	8
3 Ibid.	99	14 Scrap. XIX (Lillie)	292
4 Ibid.	147	15 Scrap. XX (Lillie)	190
5 Ibid.	143	16 Theos.	Oct., 1922
6 Inc.	55, 56	17 G. B.	12
7 Scrap. VII	30a	18 Theos.	May, 1924
8 Let. H. P. B.	154	19 Theos.	Feb., 1924
9 Mod. P. I.	178	20 Theos.	March, 1924
Cor. Let.	85–86	21 Theos.	April, 1924
10 Let. H. P. B.	143–146	22 Archives	
11 Ibid.	189–191	23 Mod. P. I.	246
12 Mod. P. I.	177		
Cor. Let.	85		

Chapter XXXI

1 O. D. L., I	72
2 Theos.	July, 1922
3 Theos.	March, 1922
4 Theos.	April, 1922
5 G. B. (facsimile)	13, 14
O. D. L., I	17
6 Cor. Let.	156
7 Archives	
8 O. D. L., I	74–76
9 G. B. (facsimile)	18
10 Mod. Pan.	61
11 G. B.	18
12 Let. M. W., II	16
13 Theos.	April, 1924, and March, 1923
14 Let. M. W., II	16, 17
15 Mod. P. I.	251
16 G. B. (facsimile)	18
17 Let. M. W., II	14, 15
18 Ibid.	15

Chapter XXVI

1 Archives

Chapter XXVII

1 Mod. P. I.	141
2 Cor. Let.	85
Mod. P. I.	178
3 Let. H. P. B.	151
4 Ibid.	154
5 Ibid.	144
6 Path, Vol. V	187
7 Path, Vol. VII	248
8 Archives	

Chapter XXVIII

1 O. D. L., I	24
2 Ibid.	20–22
3 Theos.	Dec., 1931
4 O. D. L., I	29

Chapter XXIX

1 P. O. W.	293, 294
2 O. D. L., I	1–5
3 Ibid.	70
4 Scrap. XX (Lillie)	190
5 Inc.	103, 104
6 Path	Feb., 1895
7 Inc.	137–139
8 P. O. W.	355
9 Mod. P. I.	234
10 Ibid.	266
11 Ibid.	267, 268
12 Inc.	166

Chapter XXXII

1 P. O. W.	305
2 O. D. L., I	55
3 Archives	
4 Mod. P. I.	115, 116
5 Ibid.	303
6 Let. H. P. B.	179, 180
7 Theos.	Feb., 1924
8 O. D. L., I	43
9 Ibid.	43–47
10 Mod. P. I.	165
11 Archives	
12 Theos.	May, 1924
13 Theos.	April, 1923
14 Theos.	Aug., 1923
15 Theos.	April, 1924
16 Ibid.	
17 O. D. L., I	57
18 Let. M. W., II	21
19 Ibid.	33
20 Ibid.	35

Chapter XXX

1 O. D. L., I	10
2 Theos.	Oct., 1907
3 O. D. L., I	31, 68
4 Ibid.	10–12

21 Let. M. W., II	24	9 O. D. L., I	208
22 Ibid.	38	10 Ibid.	225
23 Ibid.	27	11 Ibid.	243
24 Ibid.	30	12 Ibid.	224
25 Ibid.	37	13 Ibid.	216
		14 Mod. P. I.	257
		15 Cor. Let.	25–36
		16 Ibid.	26, 27
		17 Ibid.	132, 133

Chapter XXXIII

1 O. D. L., I	17
2 Path	Dec., 1894
3 Hints	112
4 Path	Jan., 1894
5 Path	Dec., 1894
6 Path	Dec., 1894
7 Path	Jan., 1894

Chapter XXXVII

1 O. D. L., I	210
2 Ibid.	289–291
3 Ibid.	243
4 Ibid.	246
5 Ibid.	275
6 Ibid.	257
7 Ibid.	244
8 Ibid.	246
9 Ibid.	238–243
10 Ibid.	236
11 Hints	110
12 O. D. L., I	266
13 Ibid.	247–249
14 Ibid.	245
15 Ibid.	251, 252
16 Ibid.	255, 256
17 Inc.	157
18 Path	Jan., 1895
19 Mah. Let.	289
20 O. D. L., I	294, 297
21 Archives	

Chapter XXXIV

1 Mod. P. I	250
2 O. D. L., I	25
3 Mah. Let.	209
4 Theos.	June, 1922
5 G. B. (facsimile)	15
O. D. L., I	34
6 G. B. (facsimile)	15, 16
7 O. D. L., I	26
8 Mod. P. I.	246, 250, 253
9 O. D. L., I	58
10 Ibid.	310–325
11 Let. H. P. B.	22
12 Mah. Let.	426
13 Ibid.	417
14 Mod. Pan.	35
15 O. D. L., I	81–101

Chapter XXXVIII

1 Luc.	Jan., 1895
2 Path	March, 1895
3 Path	Feb., 1895
4 Archives	
5 Theos.	Aug., 1931
6 Archives	
7 Luc.	Jan., 1895
8 Path	April, 1895
9 Ibid.	March, 1895
10 Ibid.	Nov., 1895

Chapter XXXV

1 Theos.	Oct., 1907
2 Ibid.	
3 Ibid.	
4 G. B. (facsimile)	28
5 O. D. L., I	113–132
6 Ibid.	134, 135
7 G. B. (Complete By-Laws)	23
8 Archives	
9 O. D. L., I	135–138
10 Ibid.	120
11 Theos.	Aug. 1931
12 O. D. L., I	24
13 Ibid.	400
14 G. B.	26
Mah. Let.	263
15 Ibid.	24
16 Ibid.	35

Chapter XXXIX

1 O. D. L., II	vi
2 O. D. L., I	247
3 Ibid.	263
4 Ibid.	291
5 Ibid.	247
6 Ibid.	246
7 O. D. L., II	7
8 O. D. L., I	266
9 Ibid.	266
10 Let H. P. B.	65
11 Theos.	Nov., 1907
12 Let H. P. B.	38
13 Archives	
14 Mah. Let.	203
15 Ibid.	465, 466

Chapter XXXVI

1 O. D. L., I	202, 205
2 Ibid.	208–210
3 Ibid.	217
4 Ibid.	452
5 Inc.	147
6 Ibid.	167
7 Ibid.	151–153
8 Ibid.	164

www.ingramcontent.com/pod-product-compliance
Lightning Source LLC
Chambersburg PA
CBHW021957160426
43197CB00007B/155